Critical Masses

Critical Masses

Opposition to Nuclear Power in California, 1958–1978

Thomas Raymond Wellock

THE UNIVERSITY OF WISCONSIN PRESS

HD
9698
.U53
W45
1998

The University of Wisconsin Press
2537 Daniels Street
Madison, Wisconsin 53718

3 Henrietta Street
London WC2E 8LU, England

5 4 3 2 1

Printed in the United States of America

Earlier versions of three chapters have appeared previously, and acknowledgment is made
to the publishers. Chapter 1 appeared in *California History*, Summer 1992; chapter 4 appeared in *The Atomic West*, edited by Bruce Hevly and John Findlay (Univ. of Washington
Press, 1998); and chapter 6 appeared as "'Stick It in L.A.!' Community Control and Nuclear
Power in California's Central Valley," in the *Journal of American History*, 84(3)(December
1997).

Library of Congress Cataloging-in-Publication Data
Wellock, Thomas Raymond.
    Critical masses: opposition to nuclear power in California, 1958–1978 / Thomas
Raymond Wellock.
    346 pp.   cm.
    Includes bibliographical references and index.
    ISBN 0-299-15850-0 (cloth: alk. paper).
    ISBN 0-299-15854-3 (pbk.: alk. paper)
    1. Antinuclear movement—California—History.   2. Nuclear energy—Government
policy—California—History.   3. Political participation—California—History.
I. Title.
    HD9698.U53C38   1998
    333.792'4'09794—dc21   97-37754

For my wife, Pamela,
my father, Raymond,
and to the memory of my mother, Edith

Contents

Illustrations

Acknowledgments

Completing this study of opposition to nuclear power in California was as much a result of kindness as of my own efforts. I begin my list of thanks at the beginning. Robert Cohen, my thesis advisor at the University of Toledo, proved a valuable mentor and more than anyone influenced my move to Berkeley. James Gregory supervised my first foray into this subject and provided advice on a number of chapters. I owe a great debt to my dissertation chair, Richard Abrams, for encouragement and always recognizing when I had overreached. Carolyn Merchant provided wonderful editorial and substantive comments on my chapters. The late Aaron Wildavsky influenced my thinking about how ideology affects public perception of risk. I am saddened at his untimely death. Bruce Cain provided input in his stead. James Kettner has been a generous and valuable departmental advisor. I am indebted to the advice of Brian Balogh, who refereed my manuscript and provided invaluable advice on how to revise it. Nuclear Regulatory Commission historian J. Samuel Walker also read the manuscript with a fine eye for detail and provided me with primary material used in his own research. The University of Wisconsin Press has been a pleasure to work with.

This study could not have been completed without the contributions of activists I sought out for interviews and sources. I thank them all. I would especially like to acknowledge those who provided me with personal material, including Diane Hyde, Ron Doctor, Richard Sextro, David Pesonen, Joseph Fontaine, Jim Neufeld, George Nickel, Joel Hedgpeth, James Burch, Hazel Mitchell, James Payne, and Huey Johnson. Gene Tackett agreed to an interview and saved me from nights in the Bakersfield Motel 6 by putting me up in his home. Without having met me before, Cindy Clark and Mary DeMarle graciously accommodated me in their home during my research trips to Los Angeles. Karl and Jean Kortum were the most generous hosts I have ever met. They unearthed their files, showed me diaries, and fed me lunch on many occasions. Karl's recent death has deprived this world of an extraordinary mind and writer. I will miss him.

Many friends and peers cheerfully endured the task of reading and editing chapter drafts. Most of all, I benefited from the friendship and advice of Jill Schlessinger, who made me a better writer in her review of most of the dissertation. The University of California, Berkeley's Western history dissertation group including Karen Bradley, Brad Hunt, Edith Kaneshiro, Cecelia O'Leary, and Lorena Oropeza read most of the chapters and provided a friendly setting to discuss my ideas. My thanks also goes to the history department's dissertation reading group for commenting on chapters 4 and 5. The talented pen of Ann Fidler spruced up my introduction, and Linda Song wrestled gamely with chapter 2 and the introduction.

A journey as long and, at times, isolating as pursuing a Ph.D. should not be undertaken alone. I could not wish for a better companion on life's uncertain trips than my wife, Pamela. With support and patience, she listened to my intellectual struggles during our ritual nightly dog walks of Bob. Pam read and edited my work, shared my successes and anxiety attacks (even at 3 A.M.), and believed in me more than I did. Her capacity for love and sacrifice humbles me.

Critical Masses

Introduction

On a typical summer day in Toledo, Ohio, in 1989, Terry Lodge leaned back in his law office chair musing about bugs. They seemed like an apt metaphor for the antinuclear movement. Lodge had been a leading antinuclear activist in the Midwest and on the losing side in far more contests than he cared to remember. Many nuclear proponents blamed the movement for nuclear power's demise, but Lodge dismissed this as "naive." Nuclear power, he argued, "collapsed under its own weight. . . . We were gnats flying around the giant's head. Whether we got slapped didn't matter because the giant was going to do what ever it was going to do."[1] In the face of an impenetrable federal regulatory system, the antinuclear movement did not accomplish much.

Lodge's thesis has been a flawed but typical view of the antinuclear movement among activists, scholars, and the press.[2] According to this analysis, the images that dominated the evening news of long-haired protesters clinging to the gates of nuclear facilities and their utopian visions captured the public imagination, but the impact, like the images, was fleeting. Huge protest movements sprang up around projects at Seabrook, New Hampshire, and Diablo Canyon, California, only to collapse as these plants went on line. Protesters contended that the centralized and undemocratic nature of nuclear regulation, born as it was in the Cold War, prevented them from influencing the Atomic Energy Commission (AEC) or its successor, the Nuclear Regulatory Commission (NRC). State and local governments were similarly impotent as they either promoted nuclear power or found their efforts at regulation preempted by the federal government. Nuclear power, it seemed, was the epitome of democracy's failure in recent history. As consumer advocate and antinuclear spokesman Ralph Nader contended, "formidable barriers" erected by nuclear experts in government and industry had cut the people out of the process and "concentrated political and economic power in a few hands." With "highly centralized institutions," the federal government could use "the heavy exercise of police power" to control dissent.[3]

This study goes beyond the popular conceptions of the antinuclear movement and looks at the local activists, politicians, and scientists who transformed nuclear energy regulation. Far from being pesky but harmless gnats, the antinuclear movement halted nuclear construction by modifying the underlying values of state energy regulation. By generating state and local resistance to federal atomic promotion, this conflict encouraged one of the most significant trends of the seventies: the resurgence of local politics and populist revolts against reputedly undemocratic federal programs. After decades in which America's society and institutions had become more centralized, the sixties marked the beginning of a countertrend of decentralization, and a less negotiated style of politics emerged among particular issues.

The drift toward decentralization in the sixties and seventies contradicted the prevailing organizational tendencies in America's culture and institutions. As historians of the organizational synthesis have documented, professions, businesses, and government developed along increasingly interdependent paths as America modernized. This alliance undermined the local, democratic politics of the nineteenth century and encouraged the rise of an administered state of bureaucrats, experts, and industrial leaders. The dramatic success of the union between the federal government, industry, and scientific expertise during World War II produced a consensus supporting federal control over a host of policy areas. So close and exclusive was this relationship that critics and political scientists called it an "iron triangle."[4] There were few democratic avenues open in policy for citizen input.

Nor did citizens clamor for such influence. Wary of partisan politics, the public was happy to accept federal and expert guidance. Weakened challenges from communism and socialism in the fifties held out the hope that policy decisions would be based not on ideology, but on expert management. Politically, there was an extreme right and a center occupied by liberals like John Kennedy, journalist I. F. Stone noted, but "there is no longer a left." Kennedy agreed. America's remaining problems "are technical problems, are administrative problems," he argued. "They [involve] sophisticated judgments which do not lend themselves to the great sort of 'passionate movements' which have stirred this country so often in the past."[5] Recruiting the "best and the brightest," including Nobel Prize winner Glenn Seaborg to chair the Atomic Energy Commission, the rise of a technical elite to federal administrative posts was completed by the early sixties.

Regulation of atomic energy was the epitome of Kennedy's dispassionate, administrative approach that gave the technical elites a free hand. Few objected as the 1946 and 1954 Atomic Energy Acts gave exclusive control over nuclear power to the executive branch and the atom's congressional oversight branch, the Joint Committee on Atomic Energy.[6] These acts left regulation and licensing of civilian nuclear power plants firmly in the hands of the Atomic Energy Commission. State governments made desultory demands for greater input, but atomic regulators successfully resisted burdening the fledgling industry with state roadblocks. Amendments in 1959 delegated to the states only minimal powers to administer atomic issues of health and safety, their traditional role.[7] The AEC also constrained the public's influence. Congress required the commission, despite its objections, to hold hearings on every construction permit. But the AEC limited the scope of the hearings to narrow, technical questions of nuclear safety that allowed little room for uninitiated citizens to raise broader objections to a power plant.[8] Frustrated opponents dismissed the hearings as pro forma affairs that were little more than, in the words of one activist, a "fraud, a kangaroo court."[9] The AEC, it seemed, was a typical federal agency "captured" by the industry it regulated and committed to speeding atomic development and isolating citizens and the states from a significant role.

But America's regulatory system proved far less centralized and insulated than its critics imagined. By the seventies, the federal dominance of the postwar period was beginning to look more like a brief interlude than a persistent trend. They would retain a great deal of power, but the sciences, government, and industry found their authority undermined by a broad public disenchantment with the nation's leadership. By the seventies, iron triangles had given way to a "new social regulation." Particularly in areas of social welfare, consumer and occupational protection, and environmental regulation, iron triangles dissolved into ideologically driven networks that spread beyond bureaucrats, scientists, and industry to include public interest groups, citizen activists, journalists, and sympathetic politicians. As competing interests neutralized one another's influence, regulators tended to be arbiters rather than captured agencies of industry interests. The new social regulation demonstrated that America's regulatory system could accommodate groups who endeavored to incorporate new values in decision making.[10]

On the surface, atomic regulation appeared to have escaped the decentralizing forces and the New Social Regulation with only minor changes. The replacement of the boosterist Atomic Energy Commission with the more impartial Nuclear Regulatory Commission in 1974 did not alter regulatory procedures or make them more democratic. Critics maintained that the NRC retained the AEC's heavy bias toward promoting nuclear power.[11] And despite some well-known exceptions such as Seabrook, Diablo Canyon, and Shoreham, the hearings process rarely caused much of a delay or a plant cancellation.

But such a conclusion focuses its attention on federal regulatory stasis and misses the flourishing regulatory activity among the states. In California, Minnesota, and New York, activists in league with sympathetic regulators and politicians outflanked the federal government's authority over nuclear power construction. In the wake of the accident at Three Mile Island and Supreme Court rulings, many states followed suit and assumed de facto authority to prohibit nuclear plants, even encroaching on the federal government's previously supreme dominion over nuclear safety issues.[12] Long after the movement against nuclear power declined, a coalition of state politicians and citizen activists, along with massive public antipathy, provided a powerful base of resistance to nuclear projects and federally proffered solutions to the nation's radioactive waste disposal problem. The loss of federal power was evident in policy over new energy projects. Consensus building between citizens and state officials, known as "open planning," on all forms of energy choices has been an important trend in the eighties and nineties.[13]

Nowhere was regulatory decentralization more evident than in California. The Golden State is littered with those now infamous monuments to the atom wars: abandoned nuclear sites. On the coast, utilities proposed then scrapped sites at Point Arena, Bodega Bay, Davenport, Nipomo Dunes, Point Conception, Malibu, and Sunset Beach. Ocean sites were best for water-thirsty nuclear plants, but in an effort to appease critics, utilities turned inland and tried to build on several arid sites no engineer would recommend as practical. These projects too came to nothing. However, unlike canceled projects elsewhere, none of these plants failed owing to slumping electricity demand, construction costs, or federal regulatory delays. In fact, federal regulators were almost completely absent in many of the controversies in California because state regulators had expanded their power over nuclear construction. To understand this decentralization of power, a closer inspection of the influence of the antinuclear movement's values and actions is in order.

To date, there has been little effort by scholars to thoroughly incorporate the antinuclear movement into their accounts of nuclear power's demise. They relegate to the periphery of their analysis manifestations of changing social patterns such as the antinuclear movement in favor of structural factors in regulation, the internal dynamics of the Atomic Energy Commission, and the peaceful atom's poor economics.

To those interested in economic and technical factors, the nuclear industry's collapse was simply one of the largest economic and managerial debacles in United States history. No other modern technology began its life with such widespread public support, yet suffered such a complete reversal. Technological enthusiasm, terrible utility management, slumping demand, and the failure to standardize reactor designs were the significant factors in the spiraling costs of reactors. The antinuclear movement may have indirectly increased costs by forcing regulators to demand expensive safety measures, but they were not the root of the industry's problems.[14]

Sociologists and political scientists with interests in state institutions have sought to augment this economic interpretation and "bring the state back in" to the analysis of movement behavior and political processes. A number of comparative studies between the United States and European nations such as France and Germany that had very different experiences with the peaceful atom are particularly helpful in this area. In this battle between the people and the experts, success for nuclear power depended on national policy makers' protection of the industry from opponents. The French government, with an even more highly centralized and undemocratic regulatory process than that of the United States, completely defeated a large antinuclear movement. Tight regulation in France, moreover, allowed it to achieve substantial savings by demanding standardization of reactor design and construction. None of this was possible in an open system of governance. The United States' laissez-faire attitude toward reactor design allowed engineering firms to drive up costs with a plethora of reactor designs. In the United States and Germany, nuclear elites could not prevent the antinuclear barbarians from storming the many regulatory gates open to them. Regulation proved particularly porous at the policy implementation phase when activists could appeal to the courts to block construction. This slowed construction time and prevented policies that might have saved the economics of nuclear power.[15] But although the antinuclear movement is accorded a more prominent role in institutional histories, they share with economic studies a tendency to view the antinuclear movement as a secondary actor. In some studies, institutions are such a strong causal force that they are responsible even for origins of the antinuclear movement itself.[16]

In keeping with this structural bent, historians have also attempted to "reorganize the organizational synthesis" to explain decentralization and nuclear power's decline. In Brian Balogh's important work *Chain Reaction*, the loss of authority among federal bureaucrats and scientists was rooted in the contradictions of their World War II alliance. The enemy was the scientists and administrators themselves. Once in administrative positions where they promoted various programs, scientists tended to oversell the promise of the peaceful atom to win public opinion. But the incessant increase in the number and variety of scientists in the postwar years created interdisciplinary conflict and pushed technical debates into public view. When they were unhappy with a policy decision, dissenting scientists severely weakened the authority of their peers by allying with environmental movements of the seventies.[17]

The preceding scholarship delved extensively into the economic and institutional causes of the peaceful atom's fall from grace, but there are few serious studies of the antinuclear movement's influence on society at large. Using a top-down approach, analysts have agreed that the antinuclear movement was a derivative of industry problems, ineffective, and a latecomer that "made little dent in the policy making arena."[18] However, scholars have not conducted much local research to substantiate their claim. Antinuclear activism was isolated and scattered, and much of the action took place in state forums. The role of decentralization becomes more apparent only when one examines the movement at the local level. While retaining some of their insights, this study will correct the existing imbalance in the scholarship by focusing on the antinuclear movement's influence and roots.

This book contends that to understand the origins of the antinuclear movement and the changes it inspired, it is essential to recognize the fundamental political importance of values. New social values as much as any other factor brought the antinuclear movement to life. Values reached into the scientific community, changed views, and remade the terms of debate. Values, too, transformed the regulatory system in California in an environmentally friendly and democratic fashion. And it was values that federalized nuclear regulation, pushing control to the state level. As the authority of public officials declined in the seventies, the antinuclear movement's message spread out beyond its environmental moorings to appeal to populist elements. These groups had been mounting their own critque of the liberal state and were drawn to the movement's anti-authoritarian, antifederal rhetoric. This success across the ideological spectrum remade the antinuclear movement into a broad-based public ethos rather than a coherent movement.

The wellspring of these new values lay in national social patterns after World War II that marked America's transition to a different society.[19] As historian Samuel Hays demonstrated in his study of the modern environmental movement, suburban expansion, greater disposable wealth, education, and the rise of service industries encouraged particular elements of society to value physical and spiritual amenities whose monetary value was unclear.[20] These "nonmaterialist values" included greater personal freedom and health, a protected ecosystem, and an

environment that was scenic and free from pollution. Such nonmaterialist values were especially popular among young, well-educated white
Americans who valued amenities more than economic growth or technological progress.[21] Nonmaterialists argued for a return to simpler
lifestyles, amenities, and community power as solutions to the harmful
effects of modern society such as pollution. The shift in values indicated
that even as the traditional left declined in the fifties, a new conflict was
brewing. This one would be predicated on a confrontation between nonmaterialism and the growth-oriented priorities that had informed socio-
economic policy in the country throughout its history.

Nonmaterialist values first emerged in changing patterns of consumption and a desire for greater aesthetic amenities. Outdoor recreation, for example, mushroomed in popularity and increased the
demand for parks. But Americans soon moved beyond a simple preoc-
cupation with preserving nature. Recognizing a link between threats to
nature and threats to humans, citizens demanded an environment free
from industrial pollution, pesticides, and radioactive fallout. Aesthetics
fused with these newer health concerns to form the basis for a new environmental movement that questioned the given wisdom of scientific
experts. Opposition to nuclear power emerged from this new environmental consciousness.

Nuclear opposition expanded beyond its environmental origins to include other groups favoring a nonmaterialist worldview. As a young,
better educated generation reached maturity by the early seventies, nuclear opposition included a broad coalition opposed to the political authority behind the peaceful atom.[22] The progressive wing of the
Democratic Party focused on demands for participatory democracy
and personal empowerment more than jobs and economic growth, issues that had historically concern liberal politicians.[23] Progressives expanded the objections to nuclear power from the aesthetics and safety
issues favored by moderate environmentalists to a fundamental critique
of government, industry, and scientific authority. The public, they believed, had been seduced into giving up their rights by a "small elite
corps of nuclear experts" and persuaded to an "abject worship of technology" through the seductive language of progress.[24] Unwilling to accept personal risks imposed on them by scientific elites, peace groups
and former New Leftists joined the nuclear opposition to challenge the
corporate and federal power structure.[25] For these groups, nuclear
power served as a symbol of the moral and political failure of the modern American state.

The influence of nonmaterialist values eventually reached far beyond public attitudes and citizen activists to pervade state structures,

politics, and scientific research. Operating like an advance guard, non-materialist values prepared the way for the antinuclear movement by winning over key politicians and scientists. Current scholarship, whether stressing values or state-centered theories, universally accepts the idea that nuclear controversies pitted the people against experts. Hays claimed that activists derived their attitudes from "daily life" while experts drew their views from the perspective of their professions. This "detachment" from the public by scientists led to the intractable conflict that followed. Antinuclear and other nonmaterial values appeared as outsiders trying to crack through the iron triangles. When experts, politicians, and citizens did work together, it was an accident of shared interest rather than shared beliefs.[26] While such a dichotomy in perspectives existed, the insider/outsider distinction is at best fuzzy. Decisions by key politicians and studies by scientists were driven far more by nonmaterialist values than has been previously acknowledged.[27] When activists needed sympathetic scientists or influential politicians, the converts were already waiting for them.

Confronted with what they perceived was an exclusive federal establishment, this network of activists shifted the nuclear debate to state and local forums. In California, the antinuclear movement had considerable advantages in the state's unique population base and institutions, even when compared with other antinuclear hot spots such as Massachusetts or Minnesota. The state's history of conservation dates back to 1892 with the founding of the politically aggressive Sierra Club. Strengthening this conservation tradition were postindustrial patterns in the Bay Area and Los Angeles that enlarged middle-class constituencies interested in environmental issues. Along with the Northeast, California became the region most devoted to nonmaterial values. As one of the key centers of sixties activism, the Golden State attracted politically active citizens who later played a central role in the antinuclear movement.[28]

While nonmaterialist values provided the starting point for the assault on America's iron triangles, they alone could not inaugurate the broad regulatory changes that followed. Nations such as France experienced similar cultural shifts, but their regulators easily defeated the antinuclear movement. In part, it was the United States' federal system that allowed multiple points of access and influence for activists. But federalism alone does not explain why some states challenged federal atomic control and lost where California succeeded. The Golden State's history indicated that success depended on institutional activism, resources, and access to expertise. California, with a well-funded and aggressive state government, demanded its own role in the energy debate.

The Golden State was not an empty vessel for either side to fill, but a dynamic actor in its own right. Why this was so can best be explained through the perspective of state-centered theory. Drawing from the framework laid out by Theda Skocpol in her study of the origins of United States social policy, this study will analyze several processes: (1) the way state institutions affected the goals, behavior, and accomplishments of activist organizations; (2) the changing nature of state government as politicians pursued policy objectives; and (3) the ways that previous policies and state resources influenced current politics.[29]

The latter two processes were evident in California's activist resource management institutions, ideal vehicles to lead an insurgency against federal power. Where other states ritually deferred to the initiative of industry, the Golden State's Progressive heritage and expansive state government made its officials more engaged in the formulation of energy policy. Having already wrestled with related problems of coastal management, state resource officials eagerly incorporated nuclear plant siting into their responsibilities.[30] Officials and politicians expanded state power by creating a huge new bureaucracy to analyze energy problems. Such state capacity allowed its regulators to act independently to formulate solutions that turned the tide against nuclear power in California.

A reciprocal relationship between antinuclear activists and state government institutions shaped their respective behaviors and altered the fundamental nature of energy policy in the state. With the notable exception of Diablo Canyon, where ineffective opponents resorted to direct-action protests, antinuclear activists succeeded in California by seeking political reform. A powerful coalition of nonmaterialist politicians, regulators, and scientists, and an accommodating political and regulatory system, allowed antinuclear activists to rack up a number of legal and regulatory victories. Lobbying and voter initiatives, moreover, proved remarkably effective in reshaping energy regulation.[31] These victories influenced the behavior of the state by incorporating nonmaterialist values into regulation and science. Scientists brought nonmaterial values to scientific inquiry with studies that undermined industry conclusions about energy consumption. In 1974, with the force of these studies behind it, the environmental lobby prodded state legislators into creating the California Energy Commission whose mission and philosophy embraced some aspects of the nonmaterialist viewpoint. As a result, the energy commission defeated nuclear projects and challenged the federal government's radioactive waste disposal program.

As the antinuclear movement undermined the authority of science and the federal government, its message spread out beyond its nonmaterialist moorings to appeal to populist elements who were mounting their own critique of the liberal state. In particular, antinuclear activists connected with the public as they campaigned for participatory democracy and citizen control of technology through the state voter initiative system. They hoped citizen activism would hasten the dawn of new communities based on economic democracy, tolerance, and personal fulfillment. Ultimately, the public was too conservative to accept their communal ambitions, but even conservatives embraced the movement's populist efforts toward greater state and community control over the nuclear industry.

A populist vision of community, antinuclear activists learned, was very malleable, and often quite conservative. The renewal of community power in the seventies surprised those who predicted its demise in the wake of a trend toward mass politics and culture.[32] The concept of community gained importance as the economic strain of the 1973 energy crisis and national disgraces such as Vietnam and Watergate sent Americans in search of a less grandiose focus for their loyalties than national identity. Right-wing populists reconfigured the ideal of community into a haven for middle-class capitalists free from the taint of cosmopolitan culture and the meddlesome dictates of federal programs such as forced busing.[33] Determined to preserve their hard-won lifestyles, populists could be convinced to oppose nuclear power if the issue was cast in antigovernment, anti-elite terms and if their veneration of self-governing communities could be appealed to.

The populist appeal of the antinuclear movement's message was first evident in the Central Valley where farmers used populist rhetoric against proposed nuclear power plants. They portrayed their bucolic lifeways as pawns in a game of power and greed played by competing urban interests. Variations on the theme of agrarian myth were trotted out as the farmers called on their neighbors to reject the alleged needs of the state in favor of local interests. Idealizing the Central Valley as an agrarian paradise, the rhetoric of localism invested the concept of community with new power and enhanced identity. Community became a means of protecting existing social bonds and preserving local interests and culture.

It was this broad retreat from a national identity, strengthening of state and local power, and decline in respect for authority that made the unthinkable notion of opposing the peaceful atom politically possible. By 1978, California governor Jerry Brown became the first politician of national stature to take an unequivocal stand against nuclear power and not suffer for it. Under his administration, state authorities successfully prevented the state utilities from building new nuclear plants and launched an inquiry into federal waste disposal management. That a state successfully assaulted the federal government's once inviolable control over the peaceful atom demonstrated the extent of the nuclear establishment's disintegration. Californians had established the basis for a state and local revolt a year before the shock of the Three Mile Island accident forced a similar change nationally.

There remains the question of whether the California antinuclear movement was a leading case or simply a "great exception" that cannot explain the experience of other states. This study finds that California was a leading case in spirit, but largely exceptional in its institutional response. In spirit, the nonmaterialist values that were so strong in California and the Northeast now permeate nearly every region of the country, even particularly hostile regions like the mountain states.[34]

Accordingly, "ecopopulist" resistance to nuclear programs has popped up in some of the most unlikely states such as Texas and Mississippi. Other states have copied the Golden State's antinuclear laws and emphasis on promoting conservation. Taking the issue to the people through the initiative and referendum system remains a popular tactic of opposition. State governments, too, have embraced the anti-Washington theme and often lead opposition to nuclear power and waste disposal projects.[35]

Yet, California led other states into antinuclear opposition precisely because of unique capabilities that few states could, or cared to, match. Institutionally, the state's resource management structure dwarfed that of any other state. Many states created electric energy agencies or committees in the seventies, but California alone created a massive energy bureaucracy. A five-hundred-person commission was a small burden to the nation's largest state. Few other states had the resources to develop innovative government programs in opposition to nuclear power. California and its utilities remain pioneers in alternative energy sources, conservation, and utility regulation.

The voices of the Central Valley farmers, progressive activists, and members of legislative committees and agencies tell the tale of community, culture, and identity in this study of the antinuclear movement in California from 1958 to 1980. This study is divided into two periods: the formation of opposition, 1958–1973; and broadening the movement, 1973–1978. The first three chapters examine early conflicts over nuclear power from 1958 to the coalescing of state and environmental opposition as the result of the energy crisis of 1973. These early battles established the constituency and issues that would dominate the more visible movement of the seventies. In the beginning, local citizens, state agencies, and environmentalists often entered the fray by objecting to no more than a power plant's ugly features. As the debate over nuclear power continued, these groups emerged committed to protecting communities, state authority, and environment from the depredations of modern technology. The issues surrounding nuclear power transformed values embedded in state regulation and altered the fundamental nature of the environmental movement. California energy regulators entered the conflicts of the mid-seventies committed to reducing state dependence on nuclear power and expanding the role of citizen involvement in the regulatory process. The environmental movement entered the same era determined to reduce energy consumption by destroying the promise of the peaceful atom.

The last three chapters discuss the broadening of the antinuclear activism beyond its environmental base after 1973 and the ways in which citizens eventually succeeded in working through state and local institutions to defeat nuclear power projects. Critical to the growing numbers of nuclear power opponents was the decline of Vietnam War activism and the economic shocks of the energy crisis, which encouraged former New Leftist, religious, and antiwar activists to impress their desire for pure democracy, moral fervor, and anticorporatism on the antinuclear movement. As the movement undermined the authority of the nuclear establishment, opposition spread to ideologically diverse groups. A conservative populist culture in California, resentful of government intrusion in local control, tenaciously fought a government-led program to build nuclear plants in the Central Valley. Several political and institutional factors aided antinuclear success: the state voter initiative system; a progressive political climate in Sacramento, numerous locally controlled resource management institutions, and the passage of environmental laws that allowed citizens to open up a nuclear project to public review.

The decline of the nuclear establishment's power and authority in the public mind was root not simply in economic and institutional factors as scholars suggest, but in the postwar patterns that transformed the values of American society. Penetrating the walls around America's iron triangles, nonmaterial values filtered into the public consciousness, the legislature, the scientific community, and ultimately the attitudes toward nuclear safety and energy regulation that had given federal regulators a free hand. Even as the atom's supporters retained control of federal regulation, they could not block antinuclear activists in California where new public values were particularly strong and government was accessible, well funded and aggressive. With access to resources and expertise, activists, politicians, and scientists effectively formulated new ideas regarding energy use that challenged the nuclear establishment. Undermining scientific and government authority allowed citizens across the ideological spectrum to join what amounted to a populist rejection of the peaceful atom.

California's nuclear opposition stimulated a cultural and political decentralization that has yet to run its course. The antinuclear movement vanished in the early eighties. But its legacy was an extensive antinuclear ethos in the body politic with the political weapons to prevent any further projects. The nuclear controversy and the decline of the industry represent not the failure of democracy and our federal system, but its reinvigoration.

1

The Battle for Bodega Bay, 1958–1964

"No other location offered so many scenic values and at the same time met the needs of [the movie *The Birds*]," director Alfred Hitchcock wrote of his choice of Bodega Bay, California, as the spot for shooting his 1963 suspense film. "The ocean to the west, the broad expanse of bay to the east and south, the dramatic green hills rising from the water's edge, and the picturesque little bay community nestled against the shore made Bodega Head a vantage point I should like to revisit again and again in the years to come. I wish every Californian might have the opportunity to see its beauty in person as I have seen it."[1]

After watching Hitchcock's story of avian Armageddon, vacationers probably skipped Bodega rather than risk a confrontation with the thousands of seabirds that plied its peninsula and harbor mudflats hunting for food. But they were missing out on a sublime spot. This fishing village fifty miles north of San Francisco so impressed Hitchcock in a 1942 visit while shooting *Shadow of a Doubt* in nearby Santa Rosa that twenty years later he instantly chose the location for his new movie.[2] Bodega Bay was an ideal contrast for the themes of *The Birds*. Its remoteness, bucolic fishing industry and dairy farming, and exceptional beauty provided a dramatic backdrop for a story of a seemingly docile nature seeking irrational revenge on isolated, helpless victims. Schoolchildren, lonely men and women, unsuspecting citizens, the birds attacked them all, and there was little anyone or, the movie hinted, even the military could do.

17

It was no wonder that some critics and the public believed the birds who descend from the heavens in their attacks to be a metaphor of nature taking revenge for society's abuse of it.[3] Recent scholars contend that its message focuses on the fragility of human relationships, and that it was not a story of nature's wrath. But it was Hitchcock himself who encouraged the vengeful-nature interpretation in the trailer for the film. In interviews, Hitchcock promoted the idea that the movie was a comment on "the complacency of people who refuse to recognize that there are problems in the world."[4]

Public reaction to *The Birds* indicated that it held more meaning than the typical thriller. Alfred Hitchcock had capitalized on postwar America's love of natural beauty and its fear of nature's violent potential when pushed too far. Love and fear. These are powerful emotions that can make for a successful suspense film. But these emotions also had a strong motivating force off the screen as the basis for a political movement. As it had for *The Birds*, Bodega would provide the dramatic backdrop for the birth of the antinuclear movement.[5] The battle for Bodega Bay was a seminal event that helped meld the public's love of the natural environment and its fear of human abuse of nature into a larger critique of modern society.

Alfred Hitchcock was not alone in his interest in Bodega Bay's beauty; the Sierra Club and California's Division of Beaches and Parks recognized that the Bodega Head peninsula was a potential aesthetic resource for the state. In response to the public's intensifying use of state parks, the club supported Beaches and Parks' plans to acquire the Bodega headlands. Also vying for the land was the University of California for a marine research facility in the new park to study its unique ecology. But in the spring of 1958, physician Edgar Wayburn, chairman of the Sierra Club's conservation committee, received a confidential letter. The sender wished to remain anonymous because he did not "know how far the long arm of PG&E [Pacific Gas and Electric Co.] reaches in this matter." Knowing that the Sierra Club was the leader of a growing conservation movement, the writer hoped the club would lead opposition to what he had learned of PG&E's plans. According to the letter, the nation's largest utility had approached Rose Gaffney, the owner of a large tract of land on the Bodega Head Peninsula, inquiring into its purchase. This news disturbed Wayburn. PG&E, he knew, was not interested in Bodega's scenery.[6]

When the utility representatives looked at Bodega, they saw a place to make the electricity and they moved quickly to get it. PG&E representatives told Gaffney that Beaches and Parks had withdrawn its interest,

Independent and lively, Rose Gaffney fought PG&E's takeover of her land. She had lived on the Bodega peninsula nearly her entire life. After the utility abandoned its plans to build on her land, it was turned over to the State Department of Parks and Beaches for use as a state park. Courtesy Joel Hedgpeth.

and she would have to sell her land to the utility. Gaffney was a widowed curmudgeon whose family roots on the Head dated back to nineteenth-century Mexican land grants. A large woman with a bellowing voice and a face as weathered and cracked as the Head itself, Gaffney often protected her property by chasing intruders away with a baseball bat. Defiantly, she retorted that she had no desire to sell to PG&E. But the aging woman was impotent to stop them.[7] Gaffney later recalled, "[PG&E] told me that they had condemnatory powers greater than those of the State of California."[8] States, in fact, had delegated their power of eminent domain to electric utilities, since power plants were considered to be in the public interest. On 23 May 1958, Norman Sutherland, the utility's president, announced that land acquisition was under way.

In launching its bid to construct the nation's first commercially viable nuclear power plant, PG&E, like the Sierra Club, was responding to postwar patterns spurred by America's economic affluence. As Americans stuffed their homes with the latest electrical appliances and gadgets, PG&E looked about ambitiously for new power sources and sites. The ruggedness of the area, its isolation from large population centers, and its geology made Bodega an attractive location for a nuclear plant. Like much of the gorgeous California coast, Bodega was the result of some of the most violent forces on the planet—tectonic movement and pressure. Bodega Head, a crooked arm jutting out into the Pacific, sits astraddle the San Andreas fault and forms the natural breakwater for the bay. At the tip sits a huge knot of granite pushed northward along the fault from a distant southern location. The granite Head, PG&E thought, would make for a solid reactor foundation. The harbor would protect the power plant from inclement weather and allow heavy equipment to be brought in by barge. Hoping to muscle past other interests, PG&E acquired the site. This action would embroil PG&E in what *Time* called "the bitterest controversy in its 111-year history" and one of the most embarrassing defeats by a utility company.[9] The utility found itself ill prepared to deal with the new kind of value conflicts that would dominate in the decades to come.

The traditional public-versus-private power wars that utilities were used to engaging in, while not unimportant, took a back seat to the central conflict between America's traditional economic growth priorities and nonmaterial values. A nonmaterial coalition composed of local citizens and sympathetic politicians, conservationists, and scientists, first objected to PG&E's violation of the aesthetic values of the area. But soon they expanded their critique to questions of reactor safety that directly challenged the authority of the nuclear establishment. Sitting literally atop the major earthquake fault in America, Bodega embodied the public's desire to preserve scenic beauty, its wish for public participation, and its fear that perhaps society could not control the destructive force unleashed by technology. At some point, deference to authority and greater economic growth were not worth the cost to the environment and quality of life.

The Bodega conflict was palpable evidence that nonmaterialism's new popularity would have profound implications for the political system as America shifted to a postindustrial society.[10] Public demand for outdoor amenities had resulted in a policy of park expansion that had led to the showdown at Bodega. Similarly, more affluent Americans feared threats to their health from industrial sources of pollution.[11] These quality-of-life concerns challenged the primacy of policies aimed at economic and industrial growth.[12] The new values were at odds with an older worldview that favored economic development. Progrowth politicians, businessmen, and experts favored using Bodega as a source of jobs and as the birthplace for new technology. Previously the site's economic value would have swept aside all other concerns, but now the routine construction of a power plant faced resistance from many noneconomic interests unwilling to allow experts to dictate society's development.

Nonmaterialist values found political expression generally in the ideology of the left wing of the Democratic Party and proved to be an important base of support for antinuclear activists. White progressives were the most committed supporters of lifestyle politics, pluralist political coalitions, and environmentalism. As questions over the plant extended beyond aesthetics to include nuclear safety, weapons proliferation, and demands for participatory democracy, opposition would reach beyond its conservationist roots to progressive elements. Unwilling to accept involuntary risks imposed on them by scientific elites, the progressive community such as peace groups and nascent New Leftists joined the nuclear opposition.[13]

Nuclear power was particularly susceptible to attack because the technology appeared to be elitist at a time when political progressives viewed authority with skepticism. Well educated and idealistic, progressives maintained that all issues carried political implications and elitism only served the entrenched political order. They were attracted to the Jeffersonian ideal of active citizen politicians making decisions that affected their lives.[14] More radical elements saw in nuclear power opposition a catalyst for more fundamental change. Contemptuous of society's "abject worship of technology" and fearful of the sinister forces they saw in the nuclear establishment, radicals favored more militant tactics of confrontation.[15] The Bodega experience indicated that the same intellectual milieu that would spawn the New Left also influenced the antinuclear movement in the early sixties.[16] The salient issue of earthquake hazards that antiplant activists used to attack the nuclear plant has led researchers to overlook the broader political aspirations of the antinuclear forces.[17] Activists employed safety questions in public debate, but a desire for participatory democracy and decentralized decision making also motivated them. This is not to say that activists identified with the New Left, but rather that they shared their critique of centralized authority.

But in the early sixties the public did not share such far-ranging criticisms of the political order, and opponents would have to rely on sympathetic scientists to challenge scientific authority. While the atomic testing fallout controversy of the fifties had tarnished the image of nuclear experts, the public was not inclined to challenge without reason the new priesthood of engineers and physicists within the nuclear industry, utilities, and the AEC. Even conservationists, many of whom were themselves physicians, professors, and attorneys, supported the AEC's emphasis on expertise and disdained citizen activism. Thus, scientists who shared the values of the antinuclear movement and who could talk with authority proved crucial in sowing doubt of scientific expertise among the public.

While antinuclear activists tended to come from progressive circles, opposition to nuclear development often crossed ideological boundaries. Nonmaterialism as a set of values had a broad appeal and thus had different ideological manifestations. Conservatives in Southern California, attuned more to protecting the scenic view from their sundeck than to defending public access to aesthetic beauty, would oppose nuclear power when it directly threatened their property. This was the economic calculus of nonmaterialism. Suburban homes along scenic stretches of the California coast were as much an aesthetic resource as any park. But this resource was consumed as a private possession, and, a different constituency would defend it. In the wake of the Bodega controversy, just such a group formed in opposition to a power plant proposed at Malibu beach.[18] This story will be discussed later in the chapter.

The very different motives evidenced by Bay Area activists and Southlanders point to the importance of accounting for regional variation. Without a regional approach, it would be difficult to explain why the San Francisco Bay area was the vortex of so much environmental activism in general and the source of so much of the Bodega opposition. By contrast, metropolitan areas in the Midwest produced relatively little opposition to any project. The Bay Area's demographic and political organizations heightened and exaggerated the liberalizing tendencies evident throughout the nation.

Although such value shifts came sooner and faster to San Francisco, they did not come easy. Traditional values could not be tossed aside. A sharp conflict between old and new values was most evident within the Sierra Club. An organization whose senior members favored its traditional mission of promoting hiking, mountain climbing, and preserving scenic lands, the club became divided as new ideologies filtered into the organization. Bodega marked the beginning of a transition from the traditional conservationist agenda to a new generation's aspiration to limit the influence of economic growth and technology on the environment generally. But divisions within the club were so strong that it was unable to act decisively against PG&E. In moving beyond aesthetic preservation to the more politically charged question of reactor safety, the Bodega Head insurgents had to quit the club. In 1962, they formed a political organization that challenged the nation's consensus on the value of growth and technology.

The exit of the dissenters did not solve the Sierra Club's conflict. Bodega strengthened the resolve of some militant club members to oppose nuclear energy. At the same time, other club members persisted in their faith in nuclear energy as a relatively benign alternative to using fossil fuels and building more hydroelectric dams in wilderness areas. Horrified at the vitriolic attacks launched by antiplant activists on public and utility officials, these conservationists resolved to work quietly with utility officials to smooth the way for nuclear plant construction. Bodega hardened positions that, in the subsequent conflict at Diablo Canyon, proved impossible for the club to reconcile.

The Bodega controversy also changed California's government. It inspired a persistent expansion of the state's undeveloped regulatory capacity to deal with questions of aesthetics and safety issues associated with nuclear power. Founded at a time when economic growth dominated regulatory thinking, county and state agencies proved poor advocates of aesthetic preservation during the Bodega controversy. With no government mechanism to weigh environmental considerations in choosing power plant locations, activists had to bypass traditional regulatory channels with what political mechanisms were available to them. This regulatory failure demonstrated to state officials that they needed to develop a system that considered these new values. Moreover, the democratic impulses so evident among Bodega activists impinged on the secretive nature of local and state government relations with industry. Used to quiet, elite negotiations, county politicians were beset by angry constituents accusing them of betraying public trust in acceding to PG&E demands without public input. No longer satisfied with the liberal consensus on elite decision making, the public would demand a

regulatory system that afforded greater access to technological decisions affecting their community and quality of life.

Science, too, changed as a result of this conflict. The fact that there
were sympathetic scientists who helped antinuclear activists revealed
that there was dissension even among scientists as to reactor safety. Assurances as to the safety of nuclear power had already been attacked as
a result of above-ground weapons testing, which had created the fallout
controversy of the late fifties and early sixties. As rising levels of iso-
topes appeared in everyday food items, public concern over the adequacy of the Atomic Energy Commission's safeguards against radiation
dangers spread. This concern spilled over into the civilian industry as
the risks associated with it were publicized during the Bodega controversy. These scientific revelations, coming as they did in the context of
a value shift in favor of personal health, could only hurt public perceptions of scientific authority.

Declining trust in scientific authority was not the only casualty. Nuclear fears, once planted in the public mind, endured. Even after atmospheric testing had ended and the Bodega plant was scrapped, the
atom never regained the image of purity it once enjoyed.

Business as Usual: Conservationists and Local Government

In 1958, scenic beauty, not science, was the main issue in public concern
over Bodega Bay. After being alerted to PG&E's plans for Bodega Bay,
Edgar Wayburn spent the Labor Day weekend in 1958 camping near the
Head. He met with Rose Gaffney and viewed the Indian artifacts she
had collected from the area. He strolled among the ecological habitats
interspersed among its high granite cliffs and sand dunes. The peninsula contained a vast array of flora and fauna in its grasslands, intertidal
pools, harbor mudflats, and marshes. While these ecosystems of Bodega
Head were of interest to scientists who hoped to establish a marine research center, Wayburn was there for the view. The Sierra Club did not
take much interest in ecology, only aesthetics. Convinced that Bodega
Head's splendor needed to be saved, Wayburn attended the first meeting of the new Redwood chapter of the Sierra Club and encouraged
them to spearhead the opposition to construction of any power plant.[19]
The club's board of directors passed a resolution at their summer 1958
meeting in Yosemite National Park directing that "action be taken for
[Bodega's] immediate acquisition" by the state.[20]

The Sierra Club's quick moves gave the appearance that it was laying
the groundwork to launch a campaign to protect a section of California's
natural beauty. It was the kind of action the public expected of the na-

tion's most active environmental organization. The club had already broken with its sleepy past in the thirties and forties when it was mostly a band of hikers and mountain climbers, most of whom were uninterested in political activity.[21] In response to increased logging of wilderness and dam projects in the Southwest, the club abandoned its limited public role in 1953. The club had taken on a dam proposal at Echo Park, Utah, and won. The board of directors approved the formation of chapters outside California and agreed to take on more vigorous campaigns to protect scenic areas from encroachment. The club's opposition to Bodega, based as it was on aesthetics and wilderness preservationism, fit well with its new philosophy. Thus early power plant opponents such as Dr. Joel Hedgpeth, director of the Marine Biology Station at the University of the Pacific, were confident that the Sierra Club would step in to help Gaffney.[22]

The activist public image of the club hid internal divisions over its mission and style that made it hesitant to act against PG&E. Board members feared alienating PG&E and were not willing to go beyond simply criticizing the plant's threat to a scenic area. The utility had already recruited conservationist support, as Edgar Wayburn discovered, when the Redwood chapter offered little opposition. "They were new people," he recalled, "and some of them were influenced locally by PG&E. . . . PG&E would find out the club leadership would be opposed to something and go to local club members to get their support.[23] Citizens opposing the Bodega plant for more politically adventurous reasons would have to find active support elsewhere.

There were few friends to be found, however, as PG&E struck up easy alliances with local business groups and politicians. County officials had never been enamored with the recommendation of California's Division of Beaches and Parks and the National Parks Service that Bodega Head be added to the state park system. In 1955, the legislature appropriated over $300,000 for Bodega's acquisition as part of a larger program of expanding the state's overused park system.[24] But with tax revenues on their minds, the Sonoma County Planning Commission ignored the state's plans and developed a 1956 master plan for Bodega Bay without reference to a possible park on the Head. The commission preferred to think that the Head would eventually be used for residential subdivision or a resort and opposed the idea of a state park that would remove the land from the tax base.[25] Pacific Gas and Electric's plans for Bodega Head were a godsend to county officials. The location of a power plant on the Head was just the kind of industrial development that county officials were looking for to build up the tax base.

In this respect, Sonoma County politicians were typical of their peers in favoring economic development over all other concerns. Conservationists had long complained that effective land use planning for the California coast was impossible as long as development-friendly county officials controlled land use decisions. In a less pithy version of Calvin Coolidge's maxim "The business of America is business," the chairman of the Sonoma Harbor Commission argued that the job of government "is to create the proper environment to attract private enterprise."[26] Sonoma County behavior in the Bodega story was only an example of this larger development philosophy that conservationists would grapple with in the decade to come.

Even if we take account of this philosophy, Sonoma County acted in a less than admirable fashion when they ruthlessly chased tax dollars, made secret deals, ignored the desires of county residents, and failed to ask the most elementary questions about the power plant's influence on the county. In violation of the Brown Act, which prohibited public officials from holding secret meetings with private interests, the board of supervisors met in 1957 with PG&E and decided in favor of the project. The county then informed Beaches and Parks that it had chosen PG&E over the park proposal.[27] The real decision in favor of the plant came in those private meetings, and not in the official votes held in 1959 and 1960.

With the majority of the board of supervisors already having decided to support the power plant, local residents, most of whom opposed the project, found their appeals summarily dismissed. Instead of holding public hearings, the supervisors promoted the development of scenic areas. Supervisor E. J. "Nin" Guidotti remarked that "it just didn't make sense to him to have 'a beautiful area' [like Bodega] and 'just leave it undeveloped forever.'" With a power plant Bodega would "be developed a lot faster than if the PG&E plant were not located there."[28] County administrator Neal Smith added that the plant's power lines through Doran Park would look "artistic." He derided opposition to the plan as "just a lack of understanding," even though the supervisors themselves did not officially know whether the plant was to be nuclear or fossil fueled.[29] To cultivate their support, PG&E treated the supervisors to junkets at plants near Morro Bay and Hunter's Point.[30] In late 1959 and early 1960 the board ignored 1,300 petition signatures from angry residents and approved two use permits for the Bodega plant by a vote of four to one.[31]

The actions by the county supervisors indicated the inherent weakness of local government and its complete faith in expertise. Citizens had no legal recourse to force a more thorough review of PG&E's proposal. In the period before significant environment legislation had been passed, there was no systematic review process to ensure a full public airing of a particular project. Such a hearing would have provided the public with crucial information that the utility had thus far refused to divulge. PG&E had chosen Bodega specifically to be a nuclear plant site but refused to admit this in public. As late as 1959, its representatives would concede only that "an atomic plant will be built in one of the nine Bay area counties. . . . as soon as it can be done at a reasonable cost."[32] PG&E's deliberate obfuscation of its plans frustrated early opponents who found it impossible to fight an enigma when no public official would support them.[33] With the plant within shouting distance of the San Andreas fault and with its proximity to the region's ecologically sensitive fishing and dairy industries, it would have been logical for the supervisors to demand more information. The supervisors assented to PG&E's plan because it met the overriding objective of fostering continued economic growth of the region. They trusted the technical expertise of PG&E's engineers to design a plant that was safe.

The California state government proved no more willing to confront PG&E than county politicians had been. On behalf of the Sierra Club, Edgar Wayburn appealed to the California Public Utilities Commission's (PUC) president to consider aesthetics and land use issues under its broad regulatory powers. The Sierra Club's hopes were dashed by the president's reply that "the matter of the particular location. . . is, usually, left to the discretion of the [utility] management unless a clear abuse thereof is shown." Typically, state PUC's would intervene on aesthetic questions if utility action would, as one industry publication reported, "shock the conscience of the community as a whole." The burden of proving that a community was shocked rested with the complainant.[34] The PUC's refusal to consider aesthetics meant that no public agency was responsible for the protection of scenic areas. That responsibility lay with the conscience of a private corporation.

As far as opponents could tell, pleas to the Atomic Energy Commission regarding reactor safety issues were destined to fail as well. Professor Joel Hedgpeth, the power plant's most persistent critic, sent letters to the AEC and his congressman, Clem Miller, in hopes of arousing some interest. A noted conservationist, Miller dejectedly reported to Hedgpeth his opinion that the AEC was more interested in accelerating atomic construction than investigating earthquake hazards.[35]

Shut out of government channels, Bodega Bay citizens groped for some effective vehicle to fight PG&E. The majority of villagers took a dim view of construction of the power plant, and cared little for the tax benefits it offered. They agreed with the Sierra Club that the plant and its power lines would be a wart on the landscape. Fishermen feared that the plant's location and thermal discharge would interfere with their livelihood. Others did not want their simple, isolated lifestyle disturbed. In 1959, local activist Hazel Mitchell recalled, residents created the Bodega Bay Chamber of Commerce to exhort area residents to become more politically active and write their representatives. It was a logical if pitifully small step toward local opposition. So small was the group that members would often resort to scouring the local restaurants to constitute a quorum at their meetings. The chamber had little influence on the Bodega issue, and was no match for the promotional campaign launched by PG&E to sell the peaceful atom.[36]

Promoting the Atom

PG&E zealously curried favor among the public and decision makers for Bodega because its entire strategy for the future hinged on public acceptance of nuclear power. PG&E's choice of nuclear energy was preordained for strategic as well as economic reasons. Strategically, PG&E's commitment to the peaceful atom must be understood in the context of its wars with public power advocates and municipally owned utilities in California. Public power colored the way PG&E looked at everything. The utility had fought public power voter initiatives in the twenties and thirties. It had also waged a constant battle to limit the Bureau of Reclamation's development of hydroelectric facilities along the American, Sacramento, and Trinity Rivers.[37] Municipal utilities had waged lobbying efforts in Congress to construct independent transmission facilities in the Central Valley. By the early sixties, PG&E had lost five percent of its capacity to the municipals. The public power movement also began clamoring for access to nonhydroelectric power facilities including nuclear power.[38]

Because of economics and federal legislation, the peaceful atom seemed to be the decisive weapon in PG&E's holy war with the "creeping socialism" of public power. By the mid-fifties, it was clear that "free enterprise" would lead the development of nuclear power and thus enjoy the federal subsidies that accompanied it. The bitter failure of 1956 legislation favored by public power advocates, known as the Gore-Holifield bill, that would have directly involved the federal government in the design and operation of prototype reactors left smaller public utilities far behind in accessing and mastering nuclear plant technology. The high capital costs required to train staff, design, and build a nuclear plant made it attractive only to large utilities such as PG&E. Until 1970, moreover, nuclear plants were considered experimental by the AEC. This was an important designation since it exempted plant projects from antitrust review by the Justice Department[39] And so PG&E was free to build its own plants and squeeze out municipal utilities from access to power facilities. The effective utility campaign against public power quieted public animosity toward private facilities.[40] The wounds sustained by public power advocates, who were accused of being Communists, festered for years. Public power supporters would have to wait for the right opportunity to resume the fight.

Regardless of the antitrust issue, nuclear power was technically and economically attractive to PG&E. The utility had relied on hydroelectric power through World War II. In the face of an explosion of demand brought on by postwar expansion, PG&E had few hydroelectric sources left to develop. Fossil plants had improved in efficiency, but there were problems. Even in the age before pollution was a cardinal sin, coal was not feasible since California was far from sizable coalfields. PG&E resorted to more expensive oil-burning facilities in its service area throughout the fifties.[41]

As a result, PG&E had been eyeing nuclear power since 1951 when it proposed its first nuclear project.[42] In the late fifties, PG&E launched an ambitious project in cooperation with General Electric in developing the Vallecitos prototype reactor near San Jose and a larger version at Humboldt Bay near Eureka. Bodega was to become the first pillar in what PG&E modestly called the "Super System." Designed to satisfy PG&E demand through 1980, the Super System relied exclusively on scores of nuclear power plants. "We will depend on the atom more and more as time passes," president Norman Sutherland announced. All of these power plants were to be built along the Pacific Ocean. Utility officials had fought the water and power wars long enough to know that locating power plants inland would raise the ire of Central Valley agribusiness, which would object to the extensive water requirements of nuclear plants. PG&E planned to have nuclear sites strung along California's beautiful coastline like a "picket fence," as one opponent later surmised.[43] Bodega was to be the first "picket" in this long-range strategy. Grand, bold, and seemingly invincible, the Super System was on a collision course with the growing quality of life values that made the California coast aesthetically alluring.

In the summer of 1961, PG&E removed any remaining doubt regarding what type of plant Bodega would be. In simultaneous announcements the Atomic Energy Commission declared that nuclear fuel costs would be cut 34 percent, and PG&E revealed that Bodega would be a 325 megawatt reactor. Bodega was to be a "groundbreaking" facility. The AEC and PG&E hailed it as the first "economically competitive atomic power plant" in the industry.[44] PG&E later revealed that Bodega would be home to at least four nuclear reactors of progressively larger sizes as part of its Super System.

In promoting the nuclear plant, PG&E officials tried to turn enthusiasm for nature to their advantage. Reaching back into America's past, PG&E offered to build a park that would outflank Sierra Club purists. While conservationists preferred their wilderness devoid of human influence, utility promoters recognized that the public had been just as fascinated with juxtapositions of technology and nature. Nineteenth-century paintings of the American wilderness, for example, usually included a railroad train steaming smartly through the center of a vast expanse. The implication was that soon civilization would arrive to claim this natural beauty for itself.

PG&E provided a modern version of this imagery by implying that America would move beyond its wilderness past while preserving just enough for the sake of novelty. Its illustrations of the plant showed it nestled in the shadow of the massive Head. The plant, painted in white, represented the clean shiny future befitting the "White City" imagery promoted by peaceful atom advocates.[45] PG&E offered to preserve the Head's past by opening an Indian artifacts museum housed in buildings of "rustic" design. "If these plans are developed as we believe possible," a spokesman noted, "the combination of the natural attributes of Bodega Head with the newest in technological developments will provide a most interesting spot for people. . . to see the old and new, for which the State is famous." Its dubbing the site the "Bodega Bay Atomic Park" best exemplifies PG&E's hope that it could reconcile the public's desire for outdoor amenities with their love of technology.[46] While such efforts raised the hackles of purists in the Sierra Club, it seemed a satisfactory compromise between these conflicting materialist and nonmaterialist desires. Utilities elsewhere used the same tactic with dubious success. New York's Consolidated Edison Company used similar drawings for its controversial Storm King station. These drawings were so attractive, one industry publication argued, they were sure "to assuage the feelings of even the most sensitive conservationist."[47] Storm King would fare no better than Bodega, but for the moment the tactic was successful in quieting opposition.

So successful were PG&E's promotional efforts that the opposition had completely collapsed when the PUC held hearings in San Francisco in early 1962. There was little interest in the hearings, and they were sparsely attended. Even the Sierra Club was absent. Joel Hedgpeth, who had placed his faith in the club, denounced its failure to act. In a letter to the PUC he charged that the club had "betrayed the memory of its patron saint, John Muir, who fought Hetch Hetchy on his deathbed."[48]

The Sierra Club: Cracks in the Facade

The Sierra Club had not betrayed Muir; they had reached a philosophical crossroads that left them divided and confused. Bodega helped launch a fractious dispute among the club hierarchy that worsened over the next decade. Debates over Bodega were part of a shift in club priorities from preserving scenic beauty to an environmental perspective that focused on the problems of modern industrial life. In particular, the club's singular reliance on aesthetic arguments was insufficient to deal with new problems like pollution and population growth. By the end of the fifties, some club members feared their generation would be the last to have any chance of saving the wilderness unless economic and population growth came under control. The discredited theories of the nineteenth-century economist Thomas Malthus were taken off the shelf and put back to work. Neo-Malthusian tracts had reappeared in the late forties and early fifties.[49] Their authors' message was that humanity had to restrict its demands on nature to avoid catastrophe. This message was particularly attractive in California, where a burgeoning population generated pollution and threatened wilderness resources. The Sierra Club found itself fighting this Malthusian problem as freeway and development proposals threatened state parks.

Board member Edgar Wayburn and executive director David Brower were key leaders who subscribed to this neo-Malthusian outlook. Wayburn could envision the day when the wilderness would be lost forever "unless we change our way of doing things."[50] Brower was even more aggressive, arguing that to save the wilderness the Sierra Club had to abandon its nonpartisan stance. The executive director argued that boldness, "not objectivity," served environmental purposes best.[51] Brower, a World War II veteran, had a warlike sense of the club's mission. "Dave was militant," one club insider remarked; "he came out of the war believing the greatest general in the world was George Patton." Brower often employed military metaphors to describe conservation campaigns. The club's seventeen thousand members, he noted in his diary, were "about like [the size of] a division" and were ready for action. "Maneuvers are over."[52]

Despite the tough talk, David Brower still occupied a centrist position in the Sierra Club's ideological spectrum. Brower was not averse to compromise as long as all the facts of the deal were known. The executive director was also sensitive to accusations that he opposed progress or technology. Yet he inclined toward the view that the conflict between society and wilderness was a zero-sum game. At the Fifth Wilderness Conference in 1957, he declared that the club's fight against development was one not of "blind opposition to progress, but of opposition to blind progress." Yet there is a note of desperation in his argument that "the wilderness we have now is all that we and all men will ever have."[53] Brower's two statements proved irreconcilable. Some club members would choose the former and try to harmonize growth and nature through planning; those in the latter camp drew a line and stood absolutely for nature, even if that meant radical social and political changes. The fact that both impulses existed within the mind of the same man demonstrated the conflict felt by conservationists.

Conservatives in the Sierra Club were more sanguine about preserving nature and more worried about preserving a system of negotiation and compromise. Leading the conservatives was an anomalous place for attorney Richard Leonard. Leonard and Brower were, literally, the closest of friends. They had spent the better part of their adult years clinging to each other as they scaled the most difficult mountains in the Sierra. Like Brower, Leonard was a fighter. He and Brower had led the push by the "Young Turks" for the club to take a more aggressive position on conservation issues. But the San Franciscan differed from his friend in two key respects. Brower instinctively distrusted government and industry elites. Leonard was above all an elitist whose faith in expertise and leadership was unshakable. "We can accomplish more by dealing with intelligent people at the top [of government] or industry," he remarked in an interview, "who then give orders and gradually make changes in the philosophy of the people under them."[54] Because of this trickle-down philosophy, Leonard thought it essential to preserve good relations with leaders, to the point that he would rather lose a conservation battle than lose a system of elite negotiation. It was this faith in elites that caused Leonard to dissent from the key tenet of Malthusianism. He did not see the conflict between society and nature as a zero-sum game and thus shared none of Brower's urgency over wilderness. He was confident that the best minds could apply "corrective action" to the vexing problem of growth.[55]

Leonard's philosophy was violently at odds with the more radical wing of the Sierra Club—the club staff. Brower personally recruited a cadre of young, idealistic conservationists from institutions such as the University of California at Berkeley. It was through this link that the influence of Berkeley's radical community, with its focus on popular democracy and civil liberties, spilled over onto the conservation movement. Many, such as conservation editor David Pesonen, who joined the Bodega fight, held an open contempt for the Old Guard's elitism and institutional emphasis. Pesonen was tough-minded and opinionated. He had no intention of being the kind of compliant underling Leonard envisioned.

These philosophical differences would be played out in schisms over what were the proper tactics for the Sierra Club to engage in. The directors worried that the aggressive positions advocated by the staff would be seen as overtly political and risk the club's tax-exempt status. Brower had bridled at the "cringe benefits" of IRS exemption that rendered the club's "hands bound. . . and our voice muffled."[56] The Sierra Club board of directors was not unaware of staff contempt and resolved to prevent public exposure of dissenting opinions. The conservatives on the board of directors decided to rein in Brower's activities by passing what was dubbed the "gag rule." The 1959 resolution proscribed club officials from making any statement that impugned the motives or integrity of public officials.[57] Perceiving these restrictions as a deliberate attempt to embarrass the staff, the executive director was bitter.[58]

The Bodega controversy dramatized the Sierra Club's internal conflict when dissent seeped out anyway. In December 1960, Phillip Flint, a member of the club's conservation committee, sent a letter to Berkeley's chancellor, Glenn Seaborg, and Governor Edmund Brown to request their assistance on the Bodega power plant question. Flint hinted that there had been collusion between PG&E and public authorities. He claimed that PG&E has "bypassed much of the public debate which should accompany the solution to such a problem."[59] The club's board of directors was scandalized that the letter escaped club review. It was not that the directors trusted PG&E. In fact, board member Lewis Clark concluded that the letter expressed "a number of beliefs . . . that are shared . . . by a majority of the officers of the Club." But "through faulty internal communication we have succeeded in antagonizing both the PG&E and the county Supervisors, thus jeopardizing the possibilities of persuasion."[60] The board of directors, still controlled by conservatives, reiterated that such uncontrolled communications were unacceptable. For the moment, the club refused to budge. Leadership would have to come from elsewhere.

Coalescing of Opposition

It would be something of an exaggeration to say that one man revived opposition fortunes, but not by much. Karl Kortum, founder and director of San Francisco's Maritime Museum, now a national park, had been watching quietly from the sidelines as the Bodega story unfolded between 1958 and 1962. Kortum was a perfect museum director. He had a fine eye for detail, aesthetics, and an obsession for locating and recording history, both maritime and his own.[61] But Kortum was no stuffy curator. His family roots in California reached back several generations; his great-grandmother, a member of the ill-fated Donner party, had stayed alive on the corpses of her less fortunate companions. In a more civilized style, Kortum grew up the son of a chicken rancher in Petaluma, then the poultry capital of the world.[62]

Kortum was never meant for chicken ranching. In the late twenties, as a boy of eleven, his imagination was sparked by the formidable flotilla of square-rigger ships used in the Alaska salmon-packing trade tied up in Alameda near Oakland. Back in Petaluma Kortum consumed such novels such as *Westward Ho!* and developed a passion for sailing ships in the same way some people love their pets. A hopeless romantic, he went to old ship graveyards and slept on the decks of the derelicts. After proudly sailing the last commercial square-rigger ship through the Golden Gate during World War II, Kortum began his single-minded pursuit of establishing the Maritime Museum.[63]

This protracted struggle to establish a museum had honed Karl Kortum's political skills. Over his lifetime, Kortum and his wife Jean would also successfully fight highway development, commercialization of Fisherman's Wharf, and high-rise projects in the city. Both Kortums were adept amateur politicians and skilled campaigners for any cause they took up. But the struggle to create a museum had also left Kortum with a contempt for bureaucrats and engineers. Kortum was a visionary and a romantic. He did not suffer gladly the utilitarian attitudes of engineers and enjoyed any opportunity to "cut them down to size."[64]

It was with considerable distress that Karl Kortum watched PG&E's nuclear plans for the only significant harbor between San Francisco and Eureka. With the idea of writing a letter to the editor of the *San Francisco Chronicle*, a tactic that served him well in past fights, Kortum took his family north to Bodega. On the way, he interviewed fishermen in Tomales Bay. Reluctant to discuss it at first, they admitted their fear that the power plant might ruin marine life and fishing. Kortum learned that the mariners and Bodega residents had opposed the plant in large numbers at an Army Corps of Engineers hearing but to no avail. The Kortums continued on, talking to Joel Hedgpeth and Rose Gaffney. Gaffney showed the Kortums around the Head and let them inspect her massive collection of Indian relics that she had been gathering for almost fifty years.[65]

Karl Kortum had seen enough. He concluded that the Bodega controversy was a work of arrogance by engineers who had not the slightest care for nature or the local community. Years later, the thought of such engineers could still get his dander up: "What a pack of fools!" He returned to his home that was adorned with deadeyes, lanterns, gears, and countless relics from various sailing ships. Seating himself at a captain's desk from the nineteenth-century square-rigger *Enos Soule*, Kortum wrote a lengthy piece to his good friend and editor of the *Chronicle*, Scott Newhall.[66] Newhall prominently displayed Kortum's letter on the editorial page. In the letter, Kortum accused PG&E of subverting the democratic process. The engineers at PG&E, he claimed, had given Bodega "the triumphant glance of demigods" and seized it for themselves. Most effective was Kortum's recreation of an imagined PG&E official convincing another that the utility should "grab" Bodega.

"Our engineering boys think we ought to grab Bodega Head." "They do? (low whistle) That might be a little rough." "Why? . . . " "Well, it's more scenic. The State park people and the national park people are already on record for public acquisition." "We'll just buy, fast. Get in ahead of them. It's legal. . . ." "What about public protest? This one could get a little noisy." "Keep it at the county level. . . . Every service club in every town has our people in it rubbing shoulders. . . ." "Have you got an angle? I mean apart from the fact that we want it." "Oh sure. We'll get out some releases and speeches on how the county tax base will be improved. We might even try calling it a tourist attraction." "And the county officials?" "They're o.k. We'll set the tone up there and they'll respond to it. Just as elected representatives should. Oh you might get some idealist. . . ."

Why did these things happen, Kortum asked in his letter. "The answer is simple. Our engineering demigods are obsolete." Engineers in their indifference to public sentiment were running afoul of public opposition to projects such as bridges and highways. It was up to the public to stop Bodega, Kortum pleaded. He appealed for concerned citizens to "take five minutes to write a letter" to the Public Utilities Commission.[67]

The public response to Kortum's plea was overwhelming. Letters from 240 individuals and over one thousand petition signatures demanded that the PUC hearings be reopened.[68] The PUC relented and agreed to hold additional hearings. In the meantime, to coordinate opposition, Kortum met with other vocal plant opponents such as *Chronicle* writer Harold Gilliam, Joel Hedgpeth, and Berkeley professor J. B. Neilands who had collected the petition signatures in front of the Berkeley Food Cooperative.[69] They formed an ad hoc group under the unwieldy name of the Northern California Association to Preserve Bodega Head and Harbor. Fortunately, most involved simply used the moniker "the association."

The new hearings brought together other plant opponents as well. Rose Gaffney brought a colorful slide show and her short temper. She tangled with glowering PG&E representatives who maintained that discussions of aesthetics had no value in PUC hearings. Gaffney kept the hearings interesting by rising up from her seat periodically to bellow out attacks on various public officials. In support of Gaffney's displays on Bodega's beauty came, at last, the Sierra Club. David Brower dispatched two young, aggressive staff members, conservation editor David Pesonen and lawyer Phillip Berry. The club had sent the pair to fight the power plant only on preservationist grounds, and the two men did exhort the PUC to abandon their passivity and consider the "highest and best use of the land."[70]

But Pesonen and Berry soon departed from the aesthetic script. They steered into uncharted waters to explore the hidden motives of public officials and the safety of nuclear power. In testimony, club member Phillip Flint accused the utility of "collusion" with county officials and similar involvement with the Beaches and Parks Division and the University of California. Pesonen supported Flint and claimed Bodega was a "sacrifice" for "an experimental feather in the company's economic hat." Phillip Berry followed up by arguing that the University of California appeared to be an accomplice by their "complete reversal in position" in 1960, when they abandoned plans for a marine research station at Bodega that cleared the way for the plant.[71] He asked that university faculty and officials be subpoenaed to, as he later put it, "tell the whole truth of [the university's] failure to oppose PG&E's application."[72] Despite these aggressive tactics, Gaffney's slide show, and extensive news coverage, the PUC approved PG&E's application.

The Sierra Club's representatives were pleased that they had put the Bodega issue prominently before the public and aroused opposition, but their tactics made them prophets without honor among the club leadership. If Berry and Pesonen thought they were going to be congratulated for putting pressure on PG&E, they were rudely shocked to find that the club had no intention of supporting them. Their behavior incensed senior members of the club, such as Bestor Robinson, who demanded that the club staff abide by the gag rule and avoid personal attacks.[73] "The idea of playing hardball with big corporations—Standard Oil or PG&E and who have you—was a jarring thing to [the board's conservatives]," Berry later surmised. "It was not the way things were done at the Pacific Union Club."[74] Pesonen, in particular, bothered club members. He had exhibited an uncomfortable willingness to extend the critique of the power plant to include radiation hazards to marine life, dairy farming, fishing, and the local population. Furious that the conservation editor would criticize expertise, Richard Leonard attacked Pesonen in an executive committee meeting. Leonard later justified his position by arguing that the club had to offer "cooperation" with public officials and criticize them in an "objective and constructive manner."[75]

Pesonen was undaunted. Convinced that the Sierra Club's stand on scenic values could not defeat PG&E, he suggested that the club use the issue of safety to cast doubt on the plant. Pesonen had overstepped himself. Even his most likely ally, David Brower, remained silent. Neither the board nor Brower could countenance a proposal that would challenge government and industry leaders and scientists. Richard Leonard considered Pesonen an "extremist."[76] But years later Brower rejected the radical label for Pesonen: "He may have frightened [the directors] a bit. I think they realized, as PG&E later realized, that they were up against a tough customer. . . . I think that simply he was right and I wavered. That was a time when I could have been tougher; I could have said, "If Pesonen goes, you're going to lose another David too."[77]

Although Pesonen quit the staff to lead the fight against the plant, his departure did not settle the dispute over Bodega or the club's activism. Brower continued to argue that the gag rule made the club a "see-no-evil, hear-no-evil, speak-no-evil organization with negligible effectiveness."[78] Club attorney Phillip Berry hammered out a letter to Leonard attacking his "obsession with the idea of maintaining the Club's favorable tax status," which risked its historic mission.[79]

Richard Leonard did not accept these arguments for practical and philosophical reasons. A believer in tight organizational discipline and elite negotiation, Leonard could not countenance insubordination, fearing it would undermine overall effectiveness. Leonard and others were willing to lose Bodega in order to preserve amicable relations with public officials. As board member Bestor Robinson argued, the Sierra Club had to leave each conflict with its stature enhanced, regardless of "whether we lose the particular issue involved."[80] For this reason, Phillip Berry's accusations at the Bodega plant hearings raised serious ethical questions. Leonard read the 1959 resolution to Berry verbatim and averred that "the 'goal of winning' . . . does not permit one to disregard the 'means.'"[81]

The question of tactics was only a symptom of a larger difference that was growing worse with every conservation battle the Sierra Club faced. The radicals in the club were convinced that modern society represented a catastrophic threat to the environment that had to be fought with militant tactics. To Pesonen, supporters of industrial expansion were not reasonable individuals with whom conservationists might differ, but enemies. Leonard never harbored such fears and assumed that rational planning could reconcile development pressures with the environment. Over the next two years, the majority of the club's directors supported and never wavered from the position to oppose power plants only when located "along ocean and natural lake shorelines of high scenic value."[82] The dissenters lost this round; the club would not take the radical steps necessary to lead the fight against Bodega.

The departure of Pesonen was a disturbing indication that the Sierra Club could not deal effectively with internal dissent and a portent of the future fracturing of the environmental movement. The only way for individuals to pursue paths that the board proscribed was to leave. Pesonen recognized that the club's internal squabbling and lack of focus made an effective campaign almost impossible. Pesonen set out on the pathbreaking trend of creating a single-issue organization that could effectively reach and educate local citizens without the restrictions of a large organization.[83] Such decentralization of authority in the environmental movement would become common in the future.

David Pesonen's departure from the Sierra Club was also an early marker of the future course of conservationism away from aesthetic preservation to the broader antigrowth and democratic reform agenda of the environmental movement of the seventies. Besides protecting the environment, Pesonen's key motivation in conservation issues was a fear that industrialization and economic progress would corrupt existing institutions and the democratic process. Pesonen railed against the suburban development that threatened the proposed Point Reyes National Park and Bodega Head. He ridiculed a government study that argued for modest planning measures to control growth. "It is not growth itself that is the problem," the report insisted, "but the pattern of growth." To the contrary, Pesonen responded, "growth is the problem" that might overwhelm society. "Progress, the flower of the poppy," he warned, "has debauched [the political system] at Bodega Bay."[84]

David Pesonen's critique of society extended beyond an environmental perspective to include elements of the nascent New Left that was popular in the San Francisco Bay area. A self-described "nonviolent anarchist," he held to a philosophy of decentralization, participatory democracy, and a deep distrust of elites controlling technology. Mass society, be believed, had abdicated control of their lives and political power to a "small elite corps of nuclear experts" in an "abject worship of technology" based on the seductive language of progress.[85] He longed for social reform. Just two years before Berkeley's 1964 Free Speech Movement, he complained that "a really socially important idea would be an orphan [at Berkeley]."[86]

Articulate, confident, idealistic, Pesonen was something of a loner and tended to look suspiciously on those who were not as committed as he to a cause. He may have even held a silent grudge against PG&E. His father, a Bureau of Reclamation official, was a strong public power advocate. This left Pesonen, by his own account, without any "particular

Jean Kortum and David Pesonen confer after a hearing on the Bodega project. Kortum's political expertise and Pesonen's organizational skills produced a model grassroots organization. Courtesy David Pesonen.

awe" of PG&E.[87] It may have been this last trait that was most important. It required someone with these qualities to lead a cause most considered hopeless against one of the nation's largest utilities.

Pesonen found kindred spirits in the leadership of the Northern California Association to Preserve Bodega Head and Harbor, who took him on as the organization's executive secretary. With full-time jobs, Karl Kortum and the other co-founders of the association did not have the time or the drive to run a campaign. J. B. Neilands gave Pesonen a job at his lab at the University of California, but the latter spent most of his time investigating the Bodega issue.[88] Pesonen began his campaign by writing an investigative article. He borrowed the massive newspaper clipping file that Joel Hedgpeth maintained on Bodega and in September of 1962 published a series of articles in the *Sebastopol Times*.

The result was an investigative tour de force that laid bare how the political system had been corrupted in the blind pursuit of progress. Pesonen's close analysis of events depicted a local government that slavishly followed PG&E's every wish to ensure that the plant was added to the tax base. "The company had undoubtedly obtained vague commitments from a few key individuals in the county and then pursued them, exploiting promises given." The conspiracy reached every level of government, according to Pesonen. The university and the Beaches and Parks Division had been similarly influenced through "subtle perhaps political pressure" by the AEC, the governor, or PG&E.[89]

It was an educated guess, but Pesonen's conspiracy theory was at least half correct. Supervisor "Nin" Guidotti confessed later that the supervisors had held secret meetings with PG&E as early as 1957. He even admitted that these rendezvous were in violation of the Brown Act, which prohibited such covert dealings. But the supervisors insisted that these meetings were nothing more than fact-finding missions and that no decision was made until 1960. "We did not meet in alleys to fool anyone," Guidotti insisted. "Everything we did was open and above board."[90] Correspondence in the archives of the University of California at Berkeley indicates otherwise. The supervisors had decided in favor of PG&E even before the utility's announced intention to acquire Bodega in 1958. This commitment was firm enough that Beaches and Parks withdrew its interest in Bodega Head[91]

But Pesonen's accusation of complicity by the Beaches and Parks Division and the University of California is probably unwarranted. The supervisors could stymie the park project or the university's research facility since such plans needed county approval. Moreover, PG&E had offered Beaches and Parks and the university its cooperation in working out an agreement to share the land and assiduously obliged their needs. In 1960 for example, Chancellor Seaborg scrapped the university's plans for the marine station when it seemed likely that thermal pollution would damage its usefulness. PG&E quickly offered to alter the plant's design to minimize the danger. There was little incentive to use aggressive tactics against the utility especially when it was doubtful that they would work. Seaborg consulted university counsel as to the possibility of a legal challenge. They advised him that the university would have to demonstrate a need that no other sites did exist. Later that year, when professors requested that the chancellor fight for Bodega, Seaborg knew this avenue was unlikely to succeed.[92] Nevertheless, Pesonen's articles convinced many that a conspiracy existed and encouraged them to join the plant fight.

Pesonen's articles left David Brower chastened and embarrassed that the Sierra Club had not acted. He did what he could to help Pesonen "under the table" by printing the articles as a pamphlet, "A Visit to the Atomic Park."[93] He suggested to the club's board that the pamphlet be a club publication, but Brower found the club board unmoved. The directors balked and agreed only to "distribute" the pamphlet. Brower exploded in a letter to the executive committee protesting that the club was "indulging in massive hesitancy. . . . The only adequate coverage was by Dave [Pesonen], who stood his ground and fought for what the Sierra Club was founded to fight for. . . . I have been on the firing line for ten years, sometimes moving forward above ground, but too often lately crouched in a foxhole because of vague fears not my own."[94]

Club members were genuinely confused as to the best policy toward nuclear power. Former president Harold Bradley donated money to the "young Galahad" Pesonen, but thought the club was contradicting itself by opposing nuclear power when it had been its "strong belief" earlier that the atom could replace hated dams. Brower had made just this atoms-not-dams argument when the club successfully opposed a dam that threatened Dinosaur National Monument. Bradley mused to Brower that "you and I . . . used this argument fervently—and believed it. Now here it is!" Bradley thought raising safety issues now could undermine future, scenic battles. "I suspect we shall be fighting the [Dinosaur] dam again one of these days. How strong will the argument sound if we oppose nuclear reactors today on grounds of danger?"[95]

Pesonen felt none of Bradley's discomfort with ideological inconsistency or Richard Leonard's desire to be objective. When Joel Hedgpeth gave testimony that was honest but damaging to the association's efforts, Pesonen chided: "If you had been as unscrupulous as [the opposition] just this once, it would have strengthened our position immeasurably."[96]

For help he turned to like-minded individuals on the Berkeley campus. Berkeley's faculty had a long history of environmental interest, and their growing alienation from the university administration made them a logical ally. As the Free Speech Movement and Bodega Head controversy attest, students and faculty were willing to use militant tactics and political insurgency.[97] In the fall of 1962, Pesonen, other Sierra Club members, and Berkeley graduate students and professors organized an educational meeting in Sonoma County. The meeting sponsored a number of speakers to discuss topics of safety and the political implications of PG&E's plans.

At the meeting, the sponsors brought together the themes of aesthetics, no-growth, democracy, and safety to convince residents to join the plant fight. Activists claimed that the Bodega plant would radically alter the character of the rural county. They warned the audience of 150 that "preparations for growth are a primary cause of growth." To maintain a community in which they would want to raise their children, they encouraged the audience to avoid participating in the politics of expansion and base their choices not on economics but on social values.[98] Pesonen brought his anti-elitist message to the forum, decrying the "abdication of the citizens' responsibility into the hands of government experts."[99] The speakers exhorted the audience to organize "neighborhood meetings" and letter-writing campaigns.[100] Pesonen's most potent weapon proved to be Alexander Grendon, the state's leading atomic official. In countering the protesters' warning about the plant, Grendon informed the audience that they were wasting their time, since it was up to the industry and AEC to determine the appropriateness of a site. County resident Doris Sloan, who had been only marginally active in the fight thus far, was "outraged" by Grendon's arrogance, as was most of the audience. As she later recalled, it was the political issues that motivated her to assume leadership of the local campaign.[101] Pesonen had gained a valuable ally. Sloan had been active in beautification campaigns against billboards and knew how to organize at the local level. The people left that night with a hope and determination that infected the organizers; in the margin of Pesonen's speech was scribbled: "All is not lost."[102]

Only the kind of no-holds-barred campaign that the Sierra Club refused to engage in could halt the regulatory steamroller that was pushing the Bodega plant along. On the very day of the Sonoma County meeting in late 1962, the state PUC gave its approval to Bodega subject to thermal pollution and radiation studies.[103] Pesonen's association responded to the crisis by devising a strategy that followed three paths— vocal and aggressive citizen protest, legal intervention, and questioning the integrity of public officials.

Protests and legal suits would not halt construction, but they would force the controversy to the front page of the local press. Pesonen and other members filed four appeals to the PUC requesting a new hearing; all were denied. Members accused the university of attempting to silence the faculty and of hiding a correspondence file that would prove its complicity with PG&E. Doris Sloan and others charged the supervisors with "what appears to be a malfunctioning of the democratic process." They repeatedly petitioned the Sonoma board and were twice rejected and eventually restrained from discussing Bodega at supervisor meetings. All this activity, extensively covered by the media, forced government officials to openly stifle their constituents.[104]

The association also launched a drive to destroy the reputation of their opponents. "Nin" Guidotti had built up a substantial pool of ill will in Sonoma, and David Pesonen succeeded in uniting the "Nin haters" to initiate a recall petition drive for violations of the Brown Act. It was a campaign Pesonen considered the "keystone" to their entire effort.[105] Guidotti was a good target since he had a talent for verbally abusing his rivals and making pithy, embarrassing statements that made headlines.[106] The opposition sponsored a "Nin Day" on which they held a parade in his hometown featuring his effigy drawn and quartered.[107] Although the recall effort failed on a close ballot in the fall of 1963, the days when the supervisors could ignore the public were at an end.

The anti-authoritarian attitudes manifest in the campaign against the Bodega plant were appealing to groups other than college-age students. At the same time that activism was stirring at Berkeley, Sonoma County residents were also responding to the message. "It was people wanting participatory democracy," Sloan remembers, "wanting a say in decisions, wanting an end to arbitrary decisions made by elected officials.[108] Whether someone was a student of an allegedly impersonal university, a citizen of a rural community, or a conservative homeowner, an unresponsive government offended shared values. When Pesonen spoke of subversion of the democratic process, it was not necessary to be a college student to know what he meant.

By early 1963, this message of public activism and decentralized decision making espoused by the Association to Preserve Bodega Head had drawn in a broad array of activists. The movement's organizers ranged from far-right libertarians to former members of the Industrial Workers of the World. Through leafleting and door-to-door visits, association activists were able to tap into a general discontent with a local political system so secretive that even boards of education held closed meetings. Sonoma State College students held a sympathy march in

This cartoon, published July 16, 1963, was one of the several by O'Rooney and indicative of the strong support the *Sebastopol Times* provided opponents of the Bodega nuclear plant. Courtesy Sonoma West Publishers, Inc.

May to protest the "travesty" perpetrated by the supervisors. They called for the "spontaneous thinking and the liberal and individualistic freedom of all mankind." The students wanted each citizen to "have the privilege and also the responsibility to voice his own reasoned opinion in any public matter."[109]

BODEGA BAY BENEFIT

SUNDAY, JULY 28, 1963 - 4:00 PM TO MIDNIGHT

EARTHQUAKE McGOON'S
630 CLAY ST., SAN FRANCISCO

TURK MURPHY'S JAZZ BAND
BARBARA DANE
GOODTIME WASHBOARD THREE
MALVINA REYNOLDS
THE FIRING SQUAD

Guest Artist ☞ **LU WATTERS** ☜ *Guest Artist*

Donation $5.00 per Person* 50¢ children under 12
Tickets Available at the Door
**All Proceeds Will Go To The Association To Preserve Bodega Head
And Harbor From P.G.&E.'s Proposed Atomic Power Plant**
Voting Members Of The Association $2.50 Per Person

For Reservations Call YU 6-1433 or GA 1-9405

The Bodega activists raised the money in an eight-hour benefit that featured jazz musician Lu Watters, who came out of retirement, the Turk Murphy Jazz Band, and folk singer Malvina Reynolds. Poster from the author.

The antinuclear activists also attracted supporters through social activities and attention-getting publicity stunts that highlighted fear of fallout. Pesonen maintained interest in the association through picnics and outdoor parties at Doran Park. Communist folk singer Malvina Reynolds wrote antinuclear pieces for the campaign. Jazz musician Lu Watters took a personal interest in the cause and came out of retirement to play for the association at the San Francisco nightclub, Earthquake McGoon's. Watters even made a record called "Blues over Bodega." The association pioneered the idea of holding balloon releases at its parties to demonstrate where reactor plant fallout would travel in case of an accident. Years later, antinuclear activists would regularly use these releases to gain media attention.[110] By 1963, David Pesonen had transformed the Northern California Association to Preserve Bodega Head and Harbor from a disorganized band of a dozen individuals into a force of nearly two thousand members with a budget of ten thousand dollars.[111]

Nuclear Fear

Embedded in all the activists' gaiety, however, was an ominous link between the dangers of military weapons and those of nuclear plants, a link that could potentially undo all of the assurances promoters of the peaceful atom had made to the public about nuclear safety. Could power plants contribute to nuclear weapons proliferation? Antinuclear activists argued they could. With Bodega following closely on the heels of the Cuban missile crisis, peace groups warned that atomic plants would supply plutonium for nuclear weapons production. The Women's International League for Peace and Freedom, an internationally respected peace group, denounced the plant because it feared that the plutonium produced in the plant would be used to make bombs. "We feel that in the light of the above fact, nuclear fueled electric generating plants can hardly pass under the guise of peaceful development of atomic energy."[112]

An even more effective link between warlike and peaceful atoms was the potential fallout that might occur during a nuclear plant accident. Doris Sloan recalled that while people joined the fight for political reasons, reactor safety clearly worried the less activist public: "With the grassroots in Sonoma County, safety was clearly the issue. Most people didn't care [about politics]. . . . If you're trying to get people aroused about what is going on . . . you use the most emotional issue you can find."[113] Fear of radioactive contamination served the Bodega Association's purposes perfectly. In January 1963, it disseminated an analysis using the "food-chain argument" popularized by Rachel Carson's recent *Silent Spring*. It warned that cows near Bodega could ingest radioactive fallout from grass.[114] Dairy farmers and local creameries recognized the threat to their business and agreed to foot some of the association's legal fees.[115]

The fallout issue pointed to a gender difference among the protesters. Whether from bombs or power plants, the threat to milk was one that aroused women to protest more than men. As was the case on most environmental issues, women responded more to practical personal threats than did their male counterparts. Women activists were generally less interested in the muscular political issues. Milk, on the other hand, was an almost sacred food. The potential contamination of cow's or women's breast milk represented a direct physical threat.[116]

By stressing this safety argument, the Bodega activists were on the cutting edge transforming the conservation movement into one that focused on the effects of technology on the environment and human health. The movement prior to the early sixties had concentrated on making scenic and recreational land available to the public. By the middle of the decade, opposition to pollution and pesticides dominated this new environmental movement.[117]

Environmental issues were particularly effective among a populace increasingly concerned with their health. PG&E officials without much luck ridiculed the Bodega Association's "lack of knowledge plus a deliberate program of misinformation" and maintained that the plant could be built safely under San Francisco's Union Square.[118] But these assurances pacified no one in a year when fallout from atmospheric testing had peaked. The balloon release was a direct appeal to such fears. Bodega activists used examples from civilian power to validate the comparison. Radioactive debris from a 1957 reactor accident in Windscale, England, had fallen on the countryside and infected milk supplies.

While nuclear power was not viewed as being as dirty as coal power, the fallout controversy did sully its squeaky clean image. Fallout, whether from bombs or from reactors, took on the image of poison and contamination. Even after the test ban treaty was signed, the atom never quite regained its reputation for purity. How could promoters in good conscience sell the idea of the "White City" powered by "clean" atomic energy when that source came to be associated with pollution and "death dust"? Malvina Reynolds used this image of impurity in her song on Bodega, "Take It Away." "We've got to take over PG&E, it's become a dreadful pest. It's spreading atomic poison stuff over all the Golden West. They're starting a plant at Bodega, a place that was wild and pure; They call it an atomic park, it's an atomic sewer."[119]

Recasting nuclear power as a life-threatening technology also converted the debate from a technical or conservation issue into a moral one. The enormity of nuclear power's threat deeply impressed some activists. There were deeper, more systemic issues at stake than aesthetics, safeguarding democracy, or even milk supplies; any one of these might be solved by rational negotiation or experts. When all these elements came together the Bodega cause became a fight against an invidious and life-threatening technology and the system that created it. This was not something that could be negotiated with. Not, at least, for David Pesonen.

In a moment akin to a religious conversion, David Pesonen had a revelation. "It was a beautiful evening, a touch of fog," Pesonen recalled of a night he drove to an antinuclear meeting in Petaluma. The Sonoma landscape evinced a soft mysteriousness, a living quality that was threatened by industry and nuclear development in a new and sinister form. "I had a feeling of the enormousness of what we were fighting: that it was antilife. I had an insight into the mentality of it, I began to see it as the ultimate brutality, short of nuclear weapons."[120] One did not plan for and accept "antilife," Pesonen concluded, but stood absolutely against it. Pesonen would spend the better part of the next two decades doing just that.

Pesonen had crossed a divide to a moral environmentalism, a passage akin to what many individuals experienced at all points of sixties activism. Such an emotional recognition of the systemic problems American society faced was at the core of the Port Huron statement, women's rights, and ethnic movements, and especially the environmental movement of the seventies. The implications of this new, morally based politics became clear only later with the rise of a contentious and legalistic political process that was less tolerant of compromise. Richard Leonard was right: Pesonen was an extremist. But it would not be long before many in the environmental movement including David Brower joined him.[121]

Pesonen understood that his and the association's move toward a radical critique held risks. It was only 1963, and he had strayed far ahead of public sentiment. The association had drifted so far from the original aesthetic roots of the controversy that some in the group wanted to shed the conservationist label altogether. Pesonen was not unsympathetic, but he realized how much the radicals needed the respectable image of conservationism. The Bodega Association *had* attracted some Communists. Pesonen admitted in private that even the association's lawyer, Benjamin Dreyfus, was "pink" and headed the leftist National Lawyers Guild. Malvina Reynolds was a Communist, and so were some of the local supporters in Sonoma County. This had not gone unnoticed by the West Coast anticommunist media. In 1963, the right-wing press hurled charges of Communism at the Bodega activists. Even supposedly mainstream politicians and groups such as Orange County's Republican congressman, Craig Hosmer, and the Marin County Republican Association attacked the "ultra-liberal fronts" opposing the power plant as in league with Communists.[122] J. Edgar Hoover apparently worried that the association and the Sonoma State student protests were efforts to discredit the government and private enterprise. The FBI opened a file to track association activities.[123] Moreover, correspondence indicates that PG&E investigators offered incriminating information on Bodega activists to Congress's Joint Committee on Atomic Energy (JCAE) apparently in hopes the JCAE would launch an investigation to discredit the Bodega opposition.[124] Thus the limited help that the Sierra Club offered on aesthetic issues provided respectability that protected Pesonen's group from excessive red-baiting.[125]

Enter the Liberals: San Francisco's Democratic Clubs

Antinuclear activists also picked up support and credibility from the Democratic Party, as nonmaterialist values began to reorient the party's priorities. But shifting the party from its traditional emphasis on economic to quality-of-life issues required diligent campaigning. As much as David Pesonen had done to organize local opposition and investigate the shady side of the Bodega story, he was not skilled in nor was his aloof personality suited to party politics. Jean Kortum, Karl Kortum's wife, proved the political mastermind. Her contacts with the San Francisco and California Democratic apparatus proved crucial. Jean Kortum's influence with Democrats was possible because of demographic changes that transformed the postwar political base of San Francisco into the most progressive in the nation.

In the fifties and sixties, "The City" left the working-class moorings that had tied it to class-based politics. San Francisco became a more multicultural city with a large, well-educated service industry and a politics oriented toward single issues. Labor issues declined in importance as federal laws rationalized business-labor relations and as union strength shrank with the rise of more white-collar jobs. As service workers, blacks, and Hispanics replaced Irish and Italian neighborhoods, a new pluralistic population base was there for the taking by any party capable of appealing to the priorities of the new voters. Conforming to national trends, Democrats seized this opportunity to reclaim power in the Bay Area.[126]

Giving voice to these new values was a powerful new party organization. Democrats won considerable advantage over the GOP by the 1953 formation of the California Democratic Council, an extraparty organization composed of amateur political activists. The CDC overcame the state's Progressive Era legacy of weak political parties. Energized in the wake of Adlai Stevenson's presidential candidacy, the council composed of smaller Democratic Clubs organized on behalf of party candidates and campaigned on specific issues.[127] The club movement blossomed in the fifties with thousands of amateur political activists.

Although many citizens in lower economic classes were Democrats, it was the middle classes and well-educated citizens who dominated the club movement. The clubs became centers for a strongly liberal, nonmaterialist ideology favoring civil rights, international arms control, and quality of life issues.[128] In San Francisco these liberalizing tendencies in the clubs were even more pronounced, and dozens formed throughout city neighborhoods.

The clubs succeeded in tipping the balance of power in the state as politicians such as Alan Cranston, Edmund "Pat" Brown, and Clair Engle rose to national and statewide office. The clubs also altered San Francisco's political structure. The clubs recruited the city's new minority populations into the Democratic coalition and in 1964 elected the first Democratic mayor San Francisco had seen in decades and Willie Brown, California's most successful black politician. By the time of the Bodega controversy, the club movement had reached the zenith of its power and influence.[129]

Beholden to new political interests, Democratic politics took on a new hue. Single-issue politics replaced the old labor-business dichotomy that dictated politics in the thirties. Labor was still in the Democratic camp, but unions were just as likely to side with Republicans and business interests on development issues. The clubs' Stevensonian Democrats were more interested in preserving environmental amenities than in jobs and development. The clubs fiercely opposed urban projects such as high-rise construction and freeways.[130]

Jean Kortum was typical of the amateur politicians the club movement produced, whose primary concern focused on quality-of-life issues and personal empowerment. Expected to fill the role of middle-class housewives, women such as Kortum nevertheless pursued outlets for their talents and made up a large portion of the rank-and-file activists. Kortum focused her energies on city beautification and in the process expanded the power of women like herself. "That is the part that attracts me," she told a reporter in 1969, mixing issues of beautification with a desire for personal power, "the humanistic view of the city and the right of the people to demand it."[131] With an English degree and a stint as a reporter in Oakland, Kortum was articulate and politically savvy. A member of the New American Democratic Club, Kortum had worked to elect Adlai Stevenson and was a consistent foot soldier for the emerging political machine of Congressman Phillip Burton. She spent much of her time recruiting black voters in the Western Addition section of the city. It was this broad familiarity with California politics that allowed Kortum to recognize that the California Democratic Council could be a powerful political ally.[132]

Jean Kortum acted silently in orchestrating party support.[133] This was partly a matter of tactics, but it was also typical of the subordinate seen-not-heard role women had to play in political campaigns. The Bodega Association's public leadership was entirely male. Women such as Kortum and Doris Sloan had less visible grassroots positions. Dave Pesonen acted as the public lightning rod for the association, and, as a result, would deservedly receive much of the credit when PG&E canceled construction. But Jean Kortum's activities were just as crucial.

Jean Kortum needed to win as many local endorsements for the Bodega Association as possible to convert better-known politicians.[134] She started by recruiting an antifallout group, Parents and Others for Pure Milk, and the city's Democratic Clubs to picket PG&E's offices carrying signs such as "Iodine & Milk Don't Mix." With a substantial letter-writing and lobbying campaign, she won a 1963 resolution from the California Democratic Council charging PG&E with "arrogant disregard of the public interest" and for being in collusion with Sonoma County officials.[135]

The CDC victory was important because Kortum could now use the CDC and the state party to pressure key politicians in the state and Congress. Converts included Governor Edmund Brown, who declared his opposition but confessed he could do little to reverse the PUC. Lieutenant Governor Glenn Anderson took an even stronger position, urging the AEC to withhold plant approval. Representative Phillip Burton, Jean Kortum's close political ally, introduced legislation asking the Department of the Interior to study the plant site.[136] These were symbolic gestures, but they lent respectability to the antinuclear activists and made the AEC's regulatory responsibilities more difficult by keeping the issue before the public.[137]

Nationalizing Opposition: Politics and Science

It would require both Jean Kortum's and the Bodega Association's influence with a dash of scientific uncertainty to convert their most im-

Jean Kortum organized a picketing demonstration at PG&E's headquarters in San Francisco to stress safety issues including possible milk contamination and danger from earthquakes. Photo by Karl Kortum, copyright © 1997 Jean Kortum.

portant ally, secretary of the interior and the darling of conservationists, Stewart Udall. Udall was in a position to exert considerable influence on the Atomic Energy Commission. Jean Kortum used CDC contacts to lobby the secretary, but Udall was not about to take on the political risk of challenging the AEC unless he had good cause and saw that it was in his department's interest.[138] The association would need personal persuasion, political support, and scientific evidence to do this. Fortunately for them, they had all three.

The Bodega Association's most direct access came about because Stewart Udall wanted to write a book. In 1962 and 1963, Udall was working on *The Quiet Crisis*, a best-selling conservationist tract calling for a new land ethic.[139] In working on the manuscript, Udall had re-

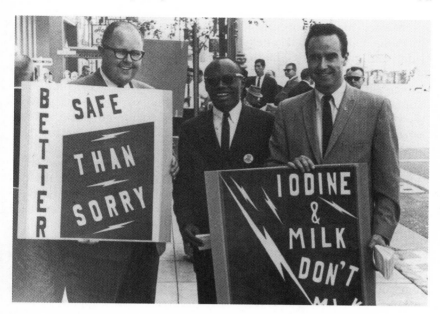

Two rising stars in Philip Burton's political machine, Willie Brown, *center,* and John Burton, *right,* participated in the picketing. Brown and Burton would go on to long careers in Sacramento. Brown, notably, rose to the speakership of the Assembly and later became mayor of San Francisco. Photo by Karl Kortum, copyright © 1997 Jean Kortum.

cruited *Chronicle* writer and co-founder of the Bodega Association Harold Gilliam. Taking a leave of absence from the paper, Gilliam had gone to Washington as a special assistant to Udall. Once ensconced in the capital, Gilliam tried to recruit Interior support to oppose Bodega. Udall, however, was not persuaded by Gilliam's initial attempts. While Interior might object to Bodega based on aesthetics, it was obvious that this was not a sufficient issue to arouse substantive action. Gilliam needed other allies.[140]

Harold Gilliam found his next recruit more helpful. Undersecretary James Carr had been a congressman in Northern California, was a strong public power advocate, and no friend of Pacific Gas and Electric. Carr took to the Bodega issue with an alacrity that startled even Gilliam. Carr became the first federal official to speak out against the Bodega plant in February 1963. Carr expressed his horror at the desecration of California of which Bodega was a symbol. His comments received substantial press coverage and hinted that the Department of the Interior might be moving against the project.[141]

Stewart Udall, apparently at Carr's urging, asserted Interior authority in the heretofore unchallenged domain of the AEC.[142] At this point, Udall had only a suspicion that the Bodega site's proximity to the San Andreas fault might be dangerous, and so he proceeded through quiet contacts. In an unpublicized February 1963 letter to the director of the Bureau of the Budget, Udall asked for a formal arrangement between the AEC and Interior to review AEC projects that related to the "conservation efforts" of the department. Citing the potential seismic hazards with the Bodega plant, Udall indicated that the Interior's Geological Survey should evaluate the site.[143] The AEC had little expertise in seismic safety, and it initiated high-level discussions with the Department of the Interior to develop a memorandum of understanding to conduct the necessary studies.[144] Udall, noting that he had "felt for some time" that Interior's jurisdiction in atomic cases was too limited, initiated a review of the Bodega project.[145]

Pesonen's association continued apace looking for safety problems with the Bodega site, and the help of sympathetic scientists provided the breakthrough. Their coup came in recruiting help evaluating the site's seismic hazards.[146] There were scientists who shared conservationist sentiment and were willing to lend their expertise to fight PG&E. While driving his jeep through the eastern California desert, Pierre St.-Amand, a California seismologist, heard a radio broadcast in which Pesonen and other Bodega activists made their case. As Pesonen later recalled, St.-Amand phoned him and said, "I heard that tape. I want to come up and help."[147] St.-Amand was the first in a string of experts who, inspired by their values, chose to use their knowledge to undermine the iron triangles of the nuclear establishment.

Doris Sloan escorted St.-Amand to the Bodega site in early April 1963, on a weekend when no construction crews were working. As Sloan remembered, that cold rainy day "was one of the high points of my life. . . . I couldn't believe my eyes . . . we came around the corner and the gate was open and there was no PG&E person in the little gatehouse to keep you from walking in." As the two slogged through the mud toward the empty site, St.-Amand exclaimed "'ooh' and . . . 'ah,'" as his eyes came to rest on what he later called a "spectacular" earthquake fault slicing through the excavation. St.-Amand found that the site was not the "island of granite" PG&E called it, but a less sturdy, fractured quartz diorite.[148] St.-Amand later told the press that "a worse foundation condition would be difficult to envision."[149]

The Bodega Association kept St.-Amand's findings under wraps from the public until August 1963, but the preceding April the seismologist quietly sent his findings to Harold Gilliam at the Department of the In-

An aerial view of Bodega Bay looking south provides dramatic evidence of the threat posed by earthquakes. The San Andreas fault zone was just about 1,000 feet from the proposed reactor site. Capable of sudden shifts, Bodega Head, right of the fault zone, had moved twelve feet northward during the 1906 San Francisco earthquake. Courtesy David Pesonen.

terior. Gilliam ensured that St.-Amand's findings received the attention of the Geological Survey's experts.[150] After reviewing St.-Amand's report, the Survey drew disturbing conclusions. Seismologists described the hazard of locating a plant near the San Andreas fault as one of "serious if not grave concern" and argued that it was "unreasonable" to assume the plant could be built safely. The director of the Survey recommended an on-site evaluation.[151]

St.-Amand's science, Harold Gilliam and Jean Kortum's lobbying, and Stewart Udall's conservation ethic together reinforced the reciprocal links between science, political support, and values. Udall's own worldview made him receptive to the appeals of conservationists, but this alone was not sufficient for decisive action. To act against the authority of the AEC, Udall needed public support to weather counterattacks and legitimate scientific facts to discredit PG&E's findings. Nor would scientific facts brought to light by an outsider have had sufficient influence if Interior was not receptive. But the combined effort was decisive. Stewart Udall now had the technical and political support to launch a public challenge to the AEC.

"Grave concern" was the most popular sound bite that the Bay Area's front-page news stories quoted from Stewart Udall's open letter to the AEC outlining his fear for the seismic safety of the Bodega plant.[152] Without mentioning St.-Amand's findings, but knowing what they would find, Udall called for extensive investigation of the Bodega site by the Interior Department's Geological Survey. Udall's grandstanding had the association ecstatic and the AEC privately seething. AEC officials thought that they had worked out an agreement with Udall to do seismic studies, but the secretary had turned Bodega into a public spectacle. There was little the AEC could do about Udall but pledge its support to investigate seismic hazards.[153] PG&E ally Congressman Craig Hosmer attacked Udall for political motives, but the secretary easily survived such attacks as Jean Kortum organized public support through a letter-writing campaign.[154]

As was expected from St.-Amand's report, the Geological Survey inspection revealed a fault through the reactor site. Survey spokesman J. P. Eaton declared the site unsuitable, noting that "acceptance of Bodega Head as a safe reactor site will establish a precedent that will make it exceedingly difficult to reject any proposed future site on the grounds of extreme earthquake risk."[155] What no one understood was that the reverse of Eaton's analysis was true as well. Rejection of Bodega would make it "exceedingly difficult" to accept any future site with seismic problems.

PG&E had no intention of surrendering; however, it soon learned that refuting expert opinion in a field as poorly understood as seismology was nearly impossible. Personally committed to the site, PG&E president Norman Sutherland found it hard to accept defeat. The PG&E staff considered Eaton to be little more than Stewart Udall's "hatchet man" and brought out their own expert, who declared that the fault had not been active for over forty thousand years.[156] PG&E modified its construction design in April 1964 to accommodate any possible shifting. With these changes, PG&E concluded with confidence that "the possibility [of a site-damaging quake] is so remote that for all practical purposes it may be disregarded."[157] Pesonen retaliated, noting that the only experts that were not concerned about the fault's quake potential were on the utility payroll.[158] This argument was exaggerated, but the Bodega Association had succeeded in revealing the uncertainty of expertise on seismic issues. There was an expert for any viewpoint, thus raising the question of what should be done when experts disagree.

The editors of the *Chronicle* spoke for many in demanding certainty on nuclear safety. "It would be unthinkably reckless and irrational to go ahead on a 'who knows?' basis. The sole warrant for going ahead must be on the basis of safety 'beyond a shadow of a doubt.'"[159]

With experts in disarray, the political attacks on the plant mushroomed as practically the entire state Democratic hierarchy went on record in opposition to it. Included were moments of personal tragedy. Clair Engle was dying. A staunch liberal, foe of PG&E, and public power advocate, he had risen to the top of California politics, winning a Senate seat in 1958 only to have his career and life cut short by a brain tumor. Engle's health had degenerated so badly by 1964 that when called on to vote for cloture on the civil rights bill, he had to be wheeled into the Senate chamber, where, unable to speak, he raised his hand to his eyes to vote "aye." But Clair Engle wanted to hold onto his seat. To prove he could still function, he resolved to fight an old foe one last time.[160]

In April 1964, a weak hand gripped the desk and two aides braced him up as Clair Engle rose to introduce a bill asking for a delay in construction of the Bodega plant until all the safety issues had been resolved. Engle's only word was a long "A . . ." gasped forth as the hushed Senate waited for more. Unable to go on, Engle relented and allowed a fellow senator to introduce the resolution. Even as he was assisted from the Senate floor, the bill was referred to the oblivion of the Joint Committee on Atomic Energy. The senator would not live to see the plant canceled. But Engle's poignant performance helped force the AEC to consider the political risks of approving the Bodega plant.[161]

The final AEC decision, in fact, was a mixture of the political and technical. The Bodega controversy was not what the AEC wanted for its fledgling nuclear program. Chairman Glenn Seaborg had declared early in 1963 that the nuclear power program had "gone critical," and the AEC submitted a report to the president that claimed nuclear power was on the threshold of economic competitiveness.[162] But the program was bogging down everywhere. Residents in Malibu fought a plant proposal, in what appeared to be a Bodega-inspired movement. The Ravenswood reactor in Queens, just across the East River from Manhattan, had also run into insurmountable resistance because of its proximity to ten million residents. The AEC was anxious to ally public fears and assure friend and foe alike that safety, not nuclear promotion, was uppermost in its mind. When faced with inconclusive evaluations by geologists and intense public concern, the AEC staff was inclined to let Bodega die.[163]

Ultimately, the Bodega Association's successful effort to divide science halted the project. PG&E suspended construction in October 1963

PG&E construction site at the mouth of Bodega Bay Harbor. The fault that forced
cancellation of the project ran through the foundation for the reactor building—the
circular pit in the foreground. Courtesy David Pesonen.

when the fault controversy erupted. As Pesonen's association celebrated
in October 1964 its first annual "Empty Hole in the Head Day," the
AEC released two contradictory reports. An advisory panel of scientists
within the AEC recommended in favor of PG&E's application, but the
commission proved divided. The full-time AEC staff recommendation
concluded that PG&E's new design was untried and could not provide
reasonable assurance against earthquake hazards.[164] The staff analysis
proved decisive. The utility, noting that it never intended to build on the
site "if any reasonable doubt exists about the [plant's] safety," took
Pesonen's advice to "bow out gracefully" and canceled construction on
30 October 1964.[165] The Sierra Club's president, Will Siri, praised the
utility's "public spirited" decision and called for the establishment of a
state park at the site.[166] A few years later, Bodega would, in fact, become
part of the state park system.

Lessons in Democracy and Conservation

At the heart of the opposition's objection to Bodega was a desire for a
more democratic political system. The end of the project launched a new
period of soul-searching in which the regulatory system tried to reform

Activists Hazel Mitchell and David Pesonen posed for this celebratory photo the day after the plant was canceled by PG&E. Pesonen amended the bumper sticker on his car to reflect the successful outcome of the campaign. Courtesy Hazel Mitchell.

itself. The Bodega victory had made plain representative government's failure to account for the public will. In hearings before the state assembly, Jean Kortum charged that there had been a "uniform gutlessness on the part of elected officials" in challenging PG&E. Taken aback, legislators debated why the system had failed to act decisively in the incident, and state agencies drew up plans to consider how scenic values could be considered in siting controversies.[167]

The victory validated citizen participation in exclusive debates. Some in the media were genuinely surprised to admit that perhaps it was not so wrong for "genuinely concerned people to question . . . [atomic power] even when given assurances that everything is 'perfectly safe.'"[168] Citizens in Sonoma County disgusted with the behavior of the county supervisors decided to take the initiative. They formed the Valley of the Moon, Inc., to "enable the citizens of the valley . . . to participate more actively in its development" and to watch over the activities of the supervisors with a distrustful eye.[169] Although he once speculated that existing institutions could not be reformed, Pesonen's activism had succeeded in making the state government somewhat more responsive to its citizens and citizens more committed to politics.

The organization that stopped the Bodega reactor was a forerunner of the kind of coalition that would form a decade later against many nuclear plants. Structurally, David Pesonen's association would be a model of the single-issue groups that would come to dominate a decentralized environmental movement in the seventies. The left-liberal coalition in the association was also a model. Bodega, perhaps, came along a bit too early to keep this coalition together. More pressing issues surfaced and drew away activists to peace groups and the New Left. There were, after all, wars to stop, civil rights to be won, and revolutions to wage. It would be only after these aspirations for social transformation subsided and public consciousness had changed that the sixties generation could focus on energy issues. Pesonen himself was not quite the radical he appeared. In his late twenties, young enough to be attracted to its message but a few years too old to identify with the social and cultural ferment of the age, Pesonen spent much of the sixties in law school. He would return to the nuclear fight later in the decade more formidable and committed to stopping nuclear power.

For the rest of the decade, the nuclear power fight would be left to those who had been dealing with it from the beginning—the conservation movement. Because of the Bodega controversy, the Sierra Club was destined to be the organization to confront this issue. The club's refusal to take a significant role in the fight had heightened tensions among the board of directors. The Bodega Association's success led to guilt. Director

Jules Eichorn pleaded for a more forceful role. "This is no longer a local affair," he wrote to Edgar Wayburn, "but a national one and we, as the supposed leaders of conservation, are backing down on the very basis for our existence."[170] Some younger men had joined the board in the early sixties and they were as radical as Pesonen. Director Fred Eissler, an English teacher, considering the association's activities to be "one of the model conservation campaigns of our day," hoped to use the nuclear issue in the future.[171] By contrast, conservatives were horrified at the humiliation PG&E received and considered the entire episode a "tragedy."[172]

Board member Fred Eissler and President Will Siri emerged as the principal antagonists in the debate over nuclear policy and safety, and would clash repeatedly on the question in the future. Eissler repeatedly raised questions of safety against nuclear power. But as president, Siri represented the club as favoring nuclear plants located along nonscenic sections of the Pacific coast.[173] As a result, the club could do no more than declare its neutrality on the safety debate.[174]

The sixties were a dangerous time for the Sierra Club to be a house divided. Despite its ambivalent role in the controversy, its power had been increased by Bodega. Because of the Bodega Head fiasco, PG&E had little stomach to face conservation forces a second time and in the mid-sixties sought negotiations with the club on the utility's proposed Diablo Canyon nuclear plant. By then, the cleavages resulting from the Bodega debate had widened dramatically, and the pronuclear settlement at Diablo would tear the club apart (see Chapter 2).[175]

The changes wrought in the sixties were also structural, and here Bodega foreshadowed the decentralization of club authority. While it is fashionable to dismiss the New Left of the sixties and its accomplishments, single-issue activism has come to dominate the political landscape. Some environmental historians consider the environmental movement to be palpable evidence of a resurgent desire for participatory democracy.[176] Bodega was a precursor of this trend.

Malibu: Southern Stepchild of Bodega

Bodega had other implications for nonmaterialist values, scientific authority, and regulation of nuclear power at the federal and state level. These trends became more clear in the wake of a plant controversy in Southern California on the coastline of Malibu.

The scientific uncertainty surrounding the AEC evaluation of the seismic hazards of the Bodega site would become a regulatory Waterloo that no California utility managed to escape completely. This was immediately clear at the Malibu nuclear plant proposed by the Los Angeles Department of Water and Power. Malibu's fate was almost a duplicate of Bodega's. Almost. The Malibu plant similarly failed in the face of large local opposition, nuclear fear, and scientific uncertainty over seismic hazards. The AEC again proved divided regarding seismic questions. but the very different context from which opposition arose reveals a paradox—nonmaterialist values had a very materialist side.

Malibu was no backwater fishing village like Bodega. In the early decades of the century it too had been a ranch owned by a feisty widow who fought off all efforts to develop it.[177] By the sixties, however, there was little trace of its bucolic past. Here no ragtag army of peasants, fishermen, and conservationists greeted the power plant. Malibu's beautiful beaches and panoramic views of the Pacific had attracted a colony of movie stars and other wealthy individuals seeking the aesthetic pleasures the area offered along with easy access to Los Angeles. Others such as the Marblehead Land Company and comedian Bob Hope saw economic profit in the nonmaterialist enjoyments the land offered. In this more conservative setting, opposition to nuclear power emerged Los Angeles-style to protect land values and the lifestyles of wealthy property owners.

This concern for land values was able to unite traditional enemies such as development interests and homeowners. While residents tended to fight further residential development after they moved to the area, they joined developers in vehemently opposing industrial incursions that would lessen the attractiveness of Malibu.[178] Many Malibu residents had fled Los Angeles in the postwar period to find just such a refuge to raise families. To resident and developer alike, outdoor amenities had personal and economic value. And as early as the fifties, Southern California suburbanites had fought development projects of all kinds. As one utility executive quipped, "These people would have complained if someone had only wanted to build a bowling alley." In defending their property, they appropriated the language of conservationists. Protecting suburban development in Southern California was as much a "conservation" value to Malibu residents as saving Bodega Head was to the Sierra Club.[179] The difference was that the latter group fought to preserve amenities for public enjoyment, while the former wanted to develop them for private residences and the Marblehead Land Company's coffers. The name did not exist yet, but Malibu activists were forerunners of the NIMBY (Not In My Backyard) Syndrome.[180]

The Los Angeles Department of Water and Power (LADWP) had not taken account of this potentially hostile attitude when settling on the Malibu site in late 1962, but it had other reasons to avoid suburbanization. With Los Angeles already well advanced into a suburban sprawl, derisively called the "slurb syndrome," it was difficult to find a sparsely populated power plant site close to those who would use the electricity. LADWP tried to outrace developers on this crabgrass frontier and establish a nuclear site before it was overrun with split-level homes. The AEC had expressed some misgivings because Malibu already skirted the limits of population requirements, but LADWP satisfactorily modified its design. With the site nearly forty miles from the San Andreas fault, LADWP expected that engineering for seismic hazards would be a routine affair.[181]

LADWP was less successful winning support from local residents. The utility strained to avoid PG&E's mistakes by sponsoring a public outreach program. Utilities continued to think that opposition was based on a lack of understanding of "facts" and believed that sufficient education was the best method of reducing opposition. But Malibu homeowners formed an opposition group anyway called Malibu Citizens for Conservation, led by architect Terry Waters, who fittingly specialized in the construction of fallout shelters.[182] Not by coincidence this was at the height of agitation against the Bodega plant, and David Pesonen had reportedly gone to Malibu to offer advice. But while some members sympathized with conservationist goals, the group was led by nonconservationists like Waters and the president of Richfield Oil Corporation.[183]

The sentiments of the Malibu opposition paralleled the nuclear fears and aesthetic objections of their Northern California counterparts, but they differed in the political goals and economic interests. What is clear from letters received by the AEC from angry residents is that there was a close linkage between the exclusivity of Malibu, its beauty, safety, and "property values." Over and over residents repeated these concerns, arguing that protection from such industrial development was a right gained by their financial investment. The plant should not be built, one resident argued, since "the present residents choose to bring their families here because of its scenic and healthy surroundings and have invested a great deal of money and energy for that reason."[184] The Marblehead Land Company echoed these sentiments, arguing that the power plant represented such a "blight" that it would "diminish property values."[185]

Residents, homeowner associations, and landowners descended on county officials in an attempt to halt the project by denying it a use permit. At hearings by the Planning Commission, entertainment figures Angela Lansbury and Frankie Laine, and attorneys for Bob Hope, added star quality to the hearings. Lansbury argued that putting a plant in Malibu made her "hair stand on end. . . . The two words 'atomic energy' are the most horror packed words in the English language." Laine supported Lansbury and added that he feared a depreciation in residential property values.[186] The planning commission, however, approved the plant.

The Malibu opponents had better luck when the issue was taken up by the Los Angeles County Supervisors. In April 1964, before a packed house, the supervisors lost their nerve and bowed to the political pressure. They voted 5 to 0 to reverse the planning commission's decision and rejected a construction permit on the basis of the nuclear fears expressed by residents. Without the public pressure, it is likely the supervisors would have approved the power plant. In a personal letter to Congressman Craig Hosmer, supervisor Burton Chace defended the board's reversal since "our office has been swamped with mail for the past several months from hundreds of residents." Hosmer replied that he understood "perfectly the political problems facing the Board." Expressing shock at the decision, LADWP officials vowed to build anyway, citing the dubious legality of county jurisdiction over another government agency.[187]

This left many wondering why LADWP had asked for the permit in the first place. It indicated that LADWP intended the proceedings to be for appearances only. Believing it had only the AEC to answer to, LADWP marched confidently into the AEC construction permit hearings.

By the time the AEC convened its hearings in March 1965, LADWP's position had deteriorated. Public concern had mounted in the wake of the Alaskan earthquake of 1964 and LADWP's Baldwin Hills dam disaster. A burst reservoir in Baldwin Hills had killed five people, raising doubts about the ability of the department's engineers. The opposition had also marshaled substantial scientific and political opposition. The Malibu Citizens for Conservation matched its success with the supervisors by garnering the avid backing of California's new and extremely conservative senator, former song-and-dance man George Murphy.[188]

But in these very technical hearings, the more important factor was expertise. For this reason, the opposition case boiled down to the deep pockets of the Marblehead Land Company and the phalanx of experts, including the ubiquitous Pierre St.-Amand, that it paraded before the licensing panel. The hearings soon became a series of lurid headlines. A meteorologist hired by the opposition made predictions of an "atom cloud" over Los Angeles. A marine biologist predicted the effect on sea life would be enormous.[189]

But the key issue was the discovery of faulting through the reactor site. Malibu was forty miles from the San Andreas fault and considered less dangerous than Bodega. But was it safe enough? As with Bodega, the contest settled down to a maddening debate among seismologists. It became apparent that seismology was as dismal a science as economics. There was simply no way of gaining a consensus on the relative danger of any crack in the earth. Characteristically, the opposition's star expert, California Institute of Technology professor Barclay Kamb, made much of the fissures in the site, while experts for LADWP pooh-poohed the possibility of ground movement. The fate of the plant boiled down again to the Geological Survey, but their conclusions revealed the difficulty of ascertaining earthquake safety from experts.

What seemed like a semantic quibble in a Geological Survey report turned out to be a high-stakes battle over defining acceptable risk, a battle that would cost the nuclear industry much in California. It started before the hearings with a preliminary finding in 1964 by the Geological Survey that concluded that the probability of permanent ground displacement at Malibu was "very low." This sounded good for the utility, but was "very low" acceptable when talking about potential catastrophe? The AEC was disturbed. It noted that similar wording had been used by Bodega by the Geological Survey. Since the Survey believed that Bodega was a higher risk than Malibu, the AEC asked the geologists to use different wording to note the difference. The Survey obliged and switched "very low" to "negligible." But "negligible" connoted that the risk could be neglected—something the Survey argued the AEC could not do. And it later revised the evaluation to "very low" once more.[190] The lawyer for the Malibu opponents, William Norris, revealed this waffling assessment under cross-examination and charged the AEC and the Survey with prevaricating.[191]

Regardless of the validity of this accusation, the assessment of "very low" meant that the reactor design had to allow for ground movement. The AEC staff, wanting to use their position on Bodega as a kind of benchmark, disagreed. The staff argued that power plant designers should disregard faults with a lower risk than those at Bodega. But the AEC proved to be a house divided once more. In July 1966 after massive hearings, the AEC board holding the licensing hearings, and later the AEC commissioners, ruled in favor of LADWP, but with a fatal proviso: LADWP had to come up with a design to accommodate movement. The ruling was at odds with what had just transpired at Bodega, where the AEC staff had refused to allow a novel PG&E design to compensate for fault movement. But the licensing board for the Malibu reactor asked LADWP to come up with something similar. It was, Congressman Craig Hosmer lamented, "the kiss of death."[192]

Redesigning the plant was too costly for the utility. LADWP's chief engineer, Eugene Koffman, privately informed the AEC that the project was a "dead duck." Although LADWP made a stab at fulfilling the AEC redesign order, it abandoned the plant in 1970. Koffman asked the AEC if it understood what this decision would do to nuclear power in California. The AEC replied that it was aware, but with the uncertainty of seismic hazards, there was little the agency could do. AEC commissioners were not willing to take the political risk of overruling their own licensing board when the peaceful atom's future looked so promising. Since the 1964 defeat of Bodega, nuclear orders had poured in across the country in what was called the "great bandwagon market." It is unlikely that the AEC was much concerned with the overall effect Malibu would have on the industry.[193] The NIMBYs had won the day.

Taken together, Bodega and Malibu left an ambiguous legacy for the California utility industry and nuclear opposition. Somehow amid the wave of nuclear orders and giddy excitement of an industry coming of age in the sixties, the image of the atom as a clean shiny new technology of the future was lost. The linking of Bodega and Malibu to nuclear fallout contributed to an image of nuclear power as a dirty, soiled, dangerous force that had to be isolated from the community. After the utopian "White City" images the atomic establishment disseminated in the fifties, the AEC spent most of the sixties trying to minimize nuclear fears.[194] Weapons blasts were kept underground to isolate them from the environment, and nuclear plants needed the same degree of isolation. Never again would plants come close to cities.

Bodega and Malibu laid bare the uncertainty underlying much scientific knowledge. Without clear scientific authority, the future of nuclear power in California was clouded. Any opposition group could count on finding faults in a site chosen for a coastal nuclear plant. The California landscape was not a solid mass with only one big San Andreas crack in it. It was a collection of fractured rocks that would slip, slide, and pulverize themselves over geologic time. Could a nuclear plant sit safely on top of this rolling mass of crushed stone? Perhaps. But there was no clear idea of what constituted an acceptable site. After the Bodega defeat, industry observers were furious at AEC conduct, predicting the effects of this "sorry affair" would last a long time. They were right. But what was the AEC to do? It had to admit it did not have a clear answer since earthquake science was still too young for definitive conclusions.[195] This would raise further doubt about the AEC and its experts' ability to safeguard the public.

The most significant regulatory change, however, would come at the state level rather than at that of the federal government. As conservationists had argued from the beginning, a place as beautiful as Bodega should never have been a potential nuclear site. But the state had been ill prepared to object. "The long battle of Bodega Bay is a symbol that contains within it the whole future of California," Harold Gilliam wrote in 1964. "This lesson of Bodega should be shouted from the housetops: There is no agency in the State of California to protect the people's interest in maintaining open space."[196] California officials had done little more than act as spectators as their citizens did battle with the AEC. This, some state agencies resolved, should not happen again. Bodega and Malibu provided a new opening for state bureaucrats to take a stronger hand in power plant regulation. Resource officials hoped to develop a system that would bring California into the nuclear age while protecting the coastline. As a result, California would end up taking a stronger role in energy issues than any other state in the country (chapter 3).

Bodega and Malibu further showed that nonmaterialism could transcend ideological categories. Certainly individuals on the left with strong progressive motivations would remain the most consistently antinuclear. But conservatives at Malibu demonstrated that nonmaterialism was also a commodity to be consumed by those who could pay for it. When their interests, such as family safety, quality of life, and property values, were threatened, they too would turn against the atom. Malibu and Bodega point to the importance of understanding regional differences in culture and politics in explaining methods or rhetoric of protest.

Over the next several years, however, the trajectory of nuclear opposition followed developments within the emerging environmental movement, and in California that meant the Sierra Club. Even as politicians and bureaucrats struggled to find an effective way of resolving the nuclear dilemma, a revolution in attitudes among conservationists made a regulatory solution nearly impossible. In the sixties, the conservation movement would make its shift to environmentalism and a more aggressive position against nuclear power. But first, conservationists had to determine their philosophy on a host of issues, including energy, pollution, and growth. Would they wage their campaigns with the environmental moralism of a David Pesonen or the pragmatism of a Richard Leonard? Pesonen would prove more prescient, but what lay ahead for the Sierra Club was its most acrimonious fight since John Muir's battle against the Hetch Hetchy Dam. The battle that was not joined at Bodega Bay would instead be fought over the club's support for the Diablo Canyon nuclear power plant.

2

The Rise of Environmental Opposition to Nuclear Power, 1964–1974

"This is to some extent as much a religious organization as an ordinary Club," director Edgar Wayburn said in 1969 of the Sierra Club. "I know the value of the image of a prophet or saint leading the legions of the righteous. There is no question that [David] Brower personifies the burgeoning power of the conservation movement to the public." David Brower had led the club into the modern environmental era Wayburn knew. Wayburn had been one of Brower's key supporters in this endeavor. But to save the Sierra Club, he would have to join the majority in May and accept the prophet's resignation. The words from the devoted as they filed into San Francisco's Sir Francis Drake Hotel to hear Brower's resignation speech confirmed Wayburn's theological assessment: "His supporters believe that the prophet can do no wrong." "The Sierra Club is itself a religious movement." "Conservation is a religious movement. So you get sects . . . Dave Brower has been the prophet leading the faithful." "There is a pre-Eden strain in Dave, no question." "They are crucifying him, and they are self-congratulating bourgeoisie."[1]

The three years of turmoil following the club's endorsement of a nuclear power plant at Diablo Canyon ended in schism. Brower and his followers left the club to form the Friends of the Earth and expound a morally based environmentalism. The club's ejection of Brower suggested that it would take a conservative path. Members decided that Brower's pure principle had threatened the organization's survival and credibility. Despite appearances, the expulsion of Brower had fundamentally changed the club's philosophy from wilderness preservation to an environmental and antinuclear viewpoint.

The club's conflict and transformation provide a valuable example of the forces that turned environmentalists throughout the country from supporters to enemies of nuclear power. Diablo Canyon would be the Sierra Club's "nuclear crucible."[2] Over this slot in the Santa Lucia coastal range, the club would do battle with itself over the issues raised but not confronted at Bodega Bay. The time had not been ripe at Bodega to discuss the problem of industrialization embodied in nuclear power or the new moral environmentalism that David Pesonen espoused. The club still adhered to its preservationist focus of stopping dam construction in wilderness or preventing the logging of redwoods. The club's narrow focus on Bodega's aesthetic problems fit with this traditional perspective.[3] Despite Pesonen's best efforts, the club refused to expand its mission into issues of safety, industrial pollution, or democratic control of technology. Diablo Canyon changed all of that.

Diablo was the bridge the Sierra Club crossed to join the modern environmental movement. Where previously nonmaterialist values and the search for a better quality-of-life centered on scenic and outdoor amenities, after Diablo Canyon protecting the ecosphere and human life from the depredations of modern society was paramount. Nuclear power brought into relief the conflict between the club's wilderness philosophy and environmentalism. Safety requirements mandated that nuclear power be located in isolated locations that often were wilderness areas along the California coast. Through its efforts to accommodate these plants while protecting wilderness, the club came to a deeper realization: nuclear power was merely a portent of an invading army of homes and factories driven by economic and population growth. The Sierra Club had to confront whether a preservationist perspective was sufficient to address the root problem of growth. The battle over Diablo Canyon symbolized the fusing of two distinct traditions—wilderness preservation and public health movements seeking to improve urban industrial life under one broad environmental perspective.[4]

Postwar affluence and rising educational levels created the conditions and the constituency for this new environmental movement. The robust expansion of the nation's industrial complex provided numerous incidents of pollution, health hazards, and incursions into wilderness. Corporations, scientific expertise, and regulatory agencies that supported this industrial expansion appeared as an oppressive authority and, as David Pesonen argued, "antilife." Hostility to industrial boosters in business, science, and government expanded as generational change swelled conservation ranks with the children of the middle class. Baby boomers represented a sizable nonmaterialist cohort who were concerned with pollution and distrusted authority. Well educated and employed in nonindustrial positions, these young activists valued quality of life and personal empowerment more than a continued expansion of the nation's material wealth.[5]

As young activists flooded into conservation organizations, the Sierra Club could not escape the generational conflict that engulfed the nation in the sixties. It was a small outdoor society of middle-age professionals that had won dramatic battles such as stopping dams planned for the Grand Canyon area. But its success caused growing pains and ideological tensions that overwhelmed it. Board of director meetings grew acrimonious, revealing differences between "old-line" conservatives and younger, progressive factions.[6] Whether developing a policy on DDT spraying in national parks or one on off-road vehicle driving, the club would proceed only after exhausting deliberation. Conservatives such as director Richard Leonard called for moderation, organizational credibility, and reasoned negotiation with corporate and government heads. But Leonard's allies eventually retired, and progressives came aboard with an ecological anticorporate philosophy. They refused to compromise with those they considered enemies of nature.

When Sierra Club president Will Siri won an endorsement from the board for a private deal he negotiated with Pacific Gas and Electric to swap a power plant site at the ecologically sensitive Nipomo Dunes for an unknown parcel near Diablo Canyon, he inaugurated a tempest that was not stilled until David Brower's ouster. Conservatives argued that upholding the board's decision was essential to maintain the club's credibility. Predicting ecological catastrophe, the antiplant faction argued that principle must take precedence even if it meant embarrassing the club by revoking its endorsement. The Sierra Club membership rejected that argument and voted for credibility over the demands for pure principle by the charismatic David Brower. The ouster of the progressives led to a new group, Friends of the Earth (FOE), that favored charismatic leadership and transforming personal values more than the substantive policy battles that interested the Sierra Club. The club became a large, democratically run organization that aimed at passing practical environmental legislation.

In defeating the progressive faction, however, the conservatives found they had lost the war over values and policy. In the early seventies, the Sierra Club passed resolutions to curb population and economic/energy growth to limit further wilderness incursions and pollution. Nuclear power, in particular, became the antithesis of the environmental movement's new emphasis on limits. The peaceful atom embodied a limitless energy future and its long-lived radioactive wastes a limitless threat to the biosphere and to future generations.

The Sierra Club and Friends of the Earth (FOE) arrived at their antinuclear positions along slightly different paths. The ouster of David Brower from the club's executive directorate freed him and the other founders of FOE to embrace moral environmentalism. They opposed nuclear power for ethical reasons such as its threat to human genetics, democracy, and future generations. Those who remained with the Sierra Club sympathized with these sentiments but did not condemn nuclear power until 1974. They cited eminently practical reasons of safety and nuclear waste disposal problems for their opposition. But the underlying reason for the club's position was similar to that of FOE's and based largely on the ethics of leaving nuclear waste to future generations. The conversion of organizations as powerful as the Sierra Club and FOE to antinuclear activism helped nationalize the antinuclear movement. With large memberships in California, they exerted considerable influence on the state's antinuclear movement and energy politics.

In the wake of the first Earth Day in 1970, mainline organizations such as the Sierra Club and Friends of the Earth along with elements from the student movement and scientist activists coalesced into the modern environmental movement. The addition of the latter groups to the antinuclear coalition indicated that the movement was no longer strictly environmental. Former sixties activists brought to the antinuclear movement desires for social justice, participatory democracy, and personal empowerment. Even less tolerant of compromise than many environmental activists, militant antinuclear activists advocated confrontation instead of mediation, lawsuits instead of informal agreements among leaders, and local, democratic campaigns instead of a centralized movement.

Antinuclear activism gained strength from an infusion of scientists and engineers eager to use their expertise to further their nonmaterial philosophy. While the new environmentalism criticized scientific authority, the movement needed expertise to support positions they arrived at intuitively. Scientists, conversely, sought to infuse their research with the nonmaterialist values to humanize their disciplines. In the process, dissident scientists shifted the focus of research from military applications to a comprehensive analysis of the problems of an industrial society.

The values of this new movement clashed with growth-oriented priorities that had informed the country's socio-economic policy throughout its history. A coalition of pro-growth politicians, businessmen, and scientists continued to advocate energy expansion as a solution to the nation's woes. Activists engaged the power industry in a debate over America's profligate energy use. And nuclear power became the salient issue on which the two sides clashed. If the environmental movement was to convince the public to accept energy limits, the immediacy of ecological dangers, and democratic control of technology, it had to overturn the cornucopian philosophy of nuclear advocates.

The Cornucopian View

Although the first coming of the peaceful atom just after the dropping of the atomic bomb did not fulfill its initial promise, the second coming in the sixties offered to propel an extraordinary boom in electricity use that advocates claimed would revolutionize society. Despite defeats of nuclear power plants at Bodega Bay, Malibu, and New York City, Americans in the sixties indicated that they had no intention of limiting consumption. With electric power requirements growing at an eight percent annual rate, orders for nuclear plants surged. Jersey Central Power and Light's order of a below-cost plant from General Electric inaugurated the sixties' "great bandwagon market." General Electric's gamble that this initial economic loser would later reap them ample rewards paid off as reactor orders flooded nuclear manufacturers. Utilities placed $650 million in orders in 1965. More startling was when the Tennessee Valley Authority (TVA) dropped what *Fortune* called "An Atomic Bomb in the Land of Coal," negotiating a $250 million contract with GE for a nuclear facility. That nuclear power could best fossil fuels in an area close to coal sources was astounding. "Nuclear power has come of age," a power executive beamed.[7] The early problems with the public and press during fallout scares disappeared. The number of nuclear opponents remained small and the press reported largely on the positive aspects of the nuclear industry.[8]

Critics, such as David Pesonen, condemned their fellow citizens' apparently mindless race to consume energy. "The atom has the power to mesmerize men," Pesonen said, "leading them to preposterous incantations, afflicting them with what Sir Charles Snow has called 'the euphoria of gadgets.'" It was this celebration of technology and power that one antigrowth advocate in the Sierra Club could dismiss as "a general gleeful, thoughtless prostration before the 8% [electric] growth curve."[9]

But it was hubris on the part of critics to deride a resource that had revolutionized the life of common Americans. Electric power had been a central element of the liberal platform to raise America's standard of living since the twenties. Critics scoffed at America's fascination with modern appliances, but there were few things in the New Deal as important as its power programs. No one had to tell Lyndon Johnson about the value of electric power. As a young congressman, he succeeded in securing a loan from the New Deal's Rural Electrification Administration (REA) to bring power to the Pedernales, Texas, hill country. Without power, the hill residents resembled members of some preindustrial society more than citizens of the greatest economic power of the twentieth century. The burden lifted from women, stoop shouldered from carrying water hundreds of yards each day, was so dramatic that the most popular name for a son in those parts became Lyndon. David Lilienthal, as the head of the TVA, had generated similar enthusiasm through grassroots campaigns. If there were any New Deal programs that improved people's perceptions of government and their enthusiasm for technology, they were the REA and the TVA.[10]

There was no other lesson for a politician and society except that abundant energy could lift humankind to a new level of civilization. The limitless power of the atom seemed the final step to this new society. David Lilienthal went on the become the first head of the Atomic Energy Commission, where he attempted to marshal a similar grassroots effort on behalf of nuclear power. Similarly, Lyndon Johnson avidly promoted nuclear power during his administration. It was for want of energy, Johnson effused to an audience, that mankind "sold his brother into slavery, and he enslaved himself to the machine . . . . By learning the secret of the atom, we have given mankind—for the first time in history—all the energy that mankind can possible use." This instrument of destruction, he said, "can become the key to a golden age of mankind."[11] This was not empty rhetoric. Johnson championed new uses for the atom such as water-desalting plants in arid regions.

Another liberal, Atomic Energy Commission chairman Glenn Seaborg, was more explicit in arguing that electricity was the basis of a new American culture. At the Commonwealth Club, Seaborg told San Francisco's elite, "This great social, cultural, industrial complex that has blossomed here on the West Coast is in the real sense of the word a 'High Energy Society.' [It is] a truly modern technological culture whose measure of advancement can almost be equated to its consumption of energy—and particularly energy in its most usable form: electricity." Seaborg warned there were dangers to this civilization if energy ran short. But he reassured his audience that the right energy source had arrived in the form of cheap, clean atomic energy.[12]

The electric industry readily expanded the boundaries of this "High Energy Society" frontier in speeches, articles, and advertisements. In their most garish form, ads celebrated the proliferation of appliances, 166 kinds, such as one showing a happy housewife wearing pumps and a cocktail dress poised to clean her kitchen armed with every conceivable device. The ad announced, "As homemaker Mother's job is the biggest in the world . . . and electricity has made it easier for her." This was a "euphoria of gadgets" perhaps, but they were gadgets with a higher purpose. Unlimited electric power had the potential to create a new kind of society, more civilized and humane. In the coming "Age of Energy Unlimited," one electric power official predicted, farmers would be freed from the "drudgery" of their existence, each factory worker would have an unlimited number of electric-powered "helpers," and mother could make dinner for guests and still have time to "fix herself up" or "spend more time with her family." The abundance of electricity would allow Americans to turn to social welfare work, civil service, and teaching.[13]

Boundless sources of power would save the environment too. Electricity was the power source that would end pollution. This argument was attractive to members of the Sierra Club. David Brower had favored nuclear power instead of dams in the fifties. Director Will Siri, a biophysicist at the University of California, could wax positively eloquent about the benefits of the peaceful atom.

[Nuclear power] is one of the chief long-term hopes for conservation, perhaps next to population control in importance . . . . Cheap energy in unlimited quantities is one of the chief factors in allowing a large rapidly growing population to preserve wildlands, open space, and lands of high scenic value . . . . With energy we can afford the luxury of setting aside lands from productive uses. Even our capacity and leisure to enjoy this luxury is linked to the availability of cheap energy. . . . [The discussion on nuclear power] will not end until some future date when our children look back from the clean comfortable world driven by nuclear energy and wonder what all the fuss was about. The rest of the universe runs on nuclear energy, why not us.[14]

Except for local critics and a few left-wing dissenters like Fred Eissler and Davis Pesonen, people expected to benefit from the peaceful atom. Nuclear-generated electricity represented all the possibilities of American society. It was a chance to cut free from the limits of history; a twentieth-century Turner thesis with an endless energy frontier would eliminate all problems through the safety valve of growth. Anyone rethinking America's commitment to energy growth had to confront the cherished belief that slowing energy growth would cost the country jobs, lead to a degeneration in civil society, and rob the nation of its identity. Conservationists straddled the issue by accommodating growth while protecting wilderness and scenic areas.

PG&E and "Responsible" Conservationists

Despite the embarrassment at Bodega Bay, Pacific Gas and Electric hoped to join the enthusiasm for nuclear power and hop on the "great bandwagon market" with its Super System of coastal nuclear plants. In 1963, after evaluating ten coastal sites, the utility purchased 1,100 acres in San Luis Obispo County's Nipomo Dunes.[15] The county was economically depressed and, unlike Bodega Bay, did not have a large local fishing or dairy industry to be threatened. With the jobs and tax benefits the plant would bring, residents and most local politicians were enthusiastic. Nipomo Dunes was, then, an attractive spot for PG&E.

The problem for PG&E was precisely that the Dunes was an attractive spot, and there were ominous signs that Nipomo could turn into another Bodega. The West Coast did not have any other large area of sand dunes with a unique well-preserved ecosystem. The State Division of Beaches and Parks targeting Nipomo Dunes on its master plan for park acquisition. The Sierra Club passed resolutions in 1963 opposing power plants along "ocean and natural lake shorelines of high recreation and scenic value" and demanded park status for the Nipomo Dunes.[16] The club was certain to fight PG&E on Nipomo early and often.

Still licking its wounds from Bodega, PG&E recoiled at taking on the Sierra Club, whose campaigns to save wilderness had earned it national prominence. Its relatively ample resources to mount a legal challenge made it a force that an industry or government agency disregarded at some peril. President Robert Gerdes, a lawyer, wanted no part of a protracted legal battle. The time when PG&E could act unilaterally in its construction plans was gone; a new system of negotiation was needed. PG&E decided it was time to come courting "responsible" conservationists.[17]

Dialogue with PG&E deepened the club's ideological divisions. Opposed to private negotiations, David Brower rebuffed PG&E's peace feelers, but there were elements of the club willing to engage in insider negotiations to protect scenic areas. PG&E found a less direct and ultimate more controversial route to club leadership through Kathleen Jackson, who as a local Sierra Club leader in the San Luis Obispo chapter. A woman of unbelievable energy and dedication, she adopted the cause of saving Nipomo Dunes with a devotion that exhausted mere mortals. Jackson believed private negotiations avoided embarrassments like

This photo of Nipomo Dunes was taken by *Sunset* travel editor and Sierra Club board member Martin Litton as part of the Sierra Club's campaign to protect the area. Ironically, Litton would join the faction that favored saving Diablo Canyon instead, arguing that it was more ecologically significant and representative of the Californian coast. Courtesy the Sierra Club Pictorial Collections, The Bancroft Library, University of California.

Bodega. She contacted PG&E, who then brought Jackson to the Humboldt reactor the utility was constructing. "I came back from that Humboldt trip," Jackson wrote, "awed by atomic power and impressed with how much I did not know . . . and determined to drop the idea of fighting to keep PG&E out of the Dunes for atomic power reasons, but to fight [for] the principle of preservation of unique scenic and ecological resources of the Dunes."[18]

Through Kathy Jackson, PG&E established a quiet line of communication with Doris Leonard, wife of director Richard Leonard, who would act as an intermediary with Sierra Club leaders. Doris Leonard and former Parks Service official George Collins ran Conservation Associates, a three-person organization that mediated disputes with conservationists, public agencies, and corporations. Richard Leonard recalled the utility's visit with him and his wife: "PG&E representatives started a kind of crying session, pointing out that every time PG&E picked a plant site for one of their nuclear plants, it turned out that it was in a proposed state park site. They had just been ousted from Bodega Head . . . . So here they were again in trouble with the park people."[19] PG&E agreed to enlist Conservation Associates to aid it in negotiating a solution to Nipomo Dunes.

PG&E had found conservationists who were anxious to work with it and hold the line against club members it regarded as extremists. Moved by PG&E's dilemma, Doris Leonard later noted sympathetically that PG&E appeared to be "hurting badly" from its Bodega debacle. She and Richard Leonard did not approve of the way conservationists like David Pesonen had ridiculed PG&E and considered the entire episode a "tragedy."[20] For avowed conservationists, this was an odd comment. What was tragic about the saving of Bodega? The Sierra Club had won considerable bargaining power while doing little more than hold Pesonen's coat as he battled the utility. Neither Conservation Associates nor the club would now be negotiating with PG&E to save Nipomo Dunes had Pesonen not humiliated PG&E. Extremism, at Bodega, had been no vice.

To the Leonards, Bodega was tragic because those involved in saving it placed ends over the means of negotiation and compromise. Challenges to the social structure and lines of authority were not worth the victory.[21] In the context of the sixties, perhaps, it is not surprising that the Leonard faction in the club reacted so strongly to critics of authority. They favored "quiet key negotiating" with leaders of government and industry. Doris Leonard distrusted rebels who "cry out blindly" against nuclear power.[22] For club conservatives, the Diablo negotiations were not simply about saving Nipomo Dunes. They were a chance to prove that negotiation and compromise worked.

For compromise to work when the club staff and some board members opposed it, negotiations would have to be limited to conservatives. In a July 1963 meeting, Doris Leonard arranged a meeting of PG&E executives with club president Edgar Wayburn, and conservation chairman Randall Dickey. As outgoing president, Wayburn, a club moderate, turned over the Nipomo negotiations to Will Siri. Like the Leonards and Jackson, Siri was pronuclear and favored coastal siting of power plants to eliminate the need for dams in wilderness areas. Conservation Associates established itself as the primary mediator, kept Will Siri posted as negotiations progressed, and "fed [Kathy Jackson] information that we thought she should have whenever it was right to do so."[23] Conservation Associates, the Sierra Club, PG&E, and the California Resources Agency set to work evaluating ways either to accommodate a power plant at Nipomo Dunes or find another site such as the attractive Wild Cherry Canyon just west of San Luis Obispo. Restricted to supporters of nuclear power, or at least those who did not question its value, the negotiations bypassed club dissenters.

Whether the move was deliberate or by chance, closed-door negotiations proved to be a mistake. Forgoing any effort to obtain broad input, Siri and Jackson exposed themselves to attack if the deal had flaws. Quiet negotiations, moreover, violated the Sierra Club's tradition of group decisions. Michael McCloskey, a staff member who would eventually become executive director, complained that he "never felt comfortable with the way that [Nipomo] was done behind closed doors. In fact, I cannot think of any other instance in the twenty years I have been employed by the Club where there was a unilateral negotiation of such a conclusive nature."[24] It was not enough that Siri had a majority of the directors who still believed in compromise, not when there were directors like Fred Eissler.

Fred Eissler was an environmental prophet. He often was the first to goad the Sierra Club into looking at issues that interested few people but would later emerge as important themes in environmentalism. He fought for resolutions on population control in the mid-sixties, opposed urban and industrial growth, and encouraged the club to expand beyond its traditional mission of wilderness preservation and to look at pollution problems and questions of nuclear safety. He favored greater citizen activism in club chapters at a time when the board of directors still exerted significant leadership on issues. Above all, Eissler demanded that the club be uncompromising.

Eissler's principles were later vindicated, but the man never. He was an outsider on the board of directors. An English teacher in Santa Barbara, Eissler did not have a background that commanded respect from his fellow members. He was not a San Franciscan when that still counted to many members. Yet Eissler was often the cause of his own problems. He was an emotional, at times eloquent, but more often shrill proponent of his views. "He came across as an intractable, rigid, irritating person," Will Siri recalled.[25] Eissler distrusted and perhaps even hated corporate leaders. He often mistook dissent for conspiracy. He callously accused volunteers who worked endless hours on the Nipomo project of being agents of the utility. "It seems to me you must be working for PG&E," Kathy Jackson recounted him telling her. "Are you?"[26]

Eissler's worldview was a blend of sectarian and apocalyptic ideas that were common among radical conservationists.[27] Eissler feared that a calamitous natural disaster awaited the world if population and economic growth continued. Society had to embrace environmental beliefs or catastrophe would result. In such a predicament opponents were not to be dealt with in a cooperative fashion, but resolutely opposed. There was no time for reasoned negotiation or bargaining away club principles for the sake of compromise. Those who advocated such a course must be conspiring with the enemy.

Eissler's fears manifested themselves in the resolute positions he advocated. In a series of letters to Will Siri, Fred Eissler lobbied for "a hard-line on the Dunes," noting that it was only such forceful positions that had made PG&E "wobble." "The Club has been opposed to a plant in the Dunes, a good clean, clear conservation position that we should hold to." Eissler could not win a resolution opposing nuclear power from the club, but he strove to prevent the club from taking any position favoring the peaceful atom. Supporting alternative sites for Nipomo was "an action which gives tacit approval to the use of nuclear power and compromises the Board's position." "It would be unfortunate and supererogatory for us to endorse the Wild Cherry Canyon site," Eissler told Siri. He advocated that the club take no position on alternatives. Perhaps foreseeing his own independent opposition, he argued that a Sierra Club endorsement of any site would "gratuitously undercut the citizens' organization that would wish to tackle PG&E on what ever valid grounds there are."[28]

Will Siri, more sanguine about the fate of the planet, dismissed Eissler's absolutism. The Sierra Club's president believed endorsing alternatives was a responsible course toward cooperation. Questions of radiation hazards raised by Eissler compromised the club's neutrality on nuclear power. Publicly, Siri held to this position, arguing that the club was not concerned with nuclear safety, only with preserving the Nipomo site. Privately, however, Siri undercut the club's neutral position when he assured state resource officials, "We in the Sierra Club are fully aware of the rapidly growing energy needs of California, and we realize that these needs can best be met with nuclear power plants placed, for the most part, along our coast."[29]

Siri's position was also buffeted by pressures from the right who opposed any consideration of aesthetics when economic opportunity beckoned. This was evident in San Luis Obispo County, where the Sierra Club met open hostility from the public. With much fanfare, Will Siri had gone down with PG&E officials to inspect Nipomo Dunes. While he spoke positively of PG&E's "enlightened view," the local press griped that the club's presence "completely changes the complexion of what had looked like a peaceful negotiation to placing the PG&E plant on a mutually satisfactory location in the Dunes."[30] Kathy Jackson tried to assuage the press that the "Sierra Club agrees that power, atomic power, is needed and we hope that by working together a site can be found along the coast which will be of the highest value."[31] But Jackson met with an unfriendly reception when she tried to increase local appreciation of the Dunes by leading nature walks. One the day of the walk, power plant supporters sponsored a large "progress march" with a thirty-car caravan carrying signs such as "Sierra Club Go Home," "We Can't Eat Wildflowers," "Less Walking, More Working," and "Work, Not Welfare." Community leaders drove to Sacramento to lobby for the plant. Encouraged by the support, one PG&E official blustered, "We bought the Nipomo property and we intend to build a power plant, not sand castles."[32]

Beset by resistance from the left and right, Siri, Doris Leonard, and Jackson pressed on ignoring dissent in hopes that a deal would silence their critics. Siri and Jackson "avoid[ed] working with the opposing forces within the [Sierra Club's local group]," Jackson wrote.[33] After three years of negotiation, this strategy had apparently paid off. The ranch owner of the Wild Cherry Canyon site was not willing to sell his property, but he did offer another section a few miles to the west of Diablo Canyon. Diablo Canyon won the support of PG&E, the State Resources Agency, and Conservation Associates. PG&E flew Siri, Conservation Associates, and Richard Leonard down to Diablo Canyon to join Kathy Jackson for an inspection. They were unimpressed with Diablo's scenic beauty and left ready to endorse the site.

In a presentation to the Sierra Club's board of directors on 7 May, Siri argued passionately for a quick decision on Diablo to save Nipomo Dunes. Kathy Jackson argued that Diablo was a "gash, a slot in a steep coastal hillside . . . a deep canyon bare except for grass . . . with no trees and an intermittent creek."[34] There were only two dissenters. David Brower, the minutes reported, was "disturbed by the speed with which the matter was brought before the Board without adequate study and without more people having had a chance to be aware of the importance of the terrain that the Board was accepting as an alternative." He and Fred Eissler argued for more time for the Los Padres chapter and other board members to inspect the site. "It is not our business . . . to support this alternative site," Eissler argued. The Sierra Club supported Siri, but avoided using a pronuclear resolution drawn up by Richard Leonard. The final resolution took no position on the peaceful atom. This was not enough for Eissler. "Recommendation of the Diablo Canyon site . . .

would be tantamount to approval of nuclear power generation, a process, including waste disposal, still presenting many conservation dangers." To endorse an atomic site, he told Siri, would require a "broader review of the ramifications of the environmental impact from this power source." Eissler stood alone in a 9 to 1 vote with two abstentions on a resolution where, "The Sierra Club . . . considers Diablo Canyon, San Luis Obispo County, a satisfactory alternative site to the Nipomo Dunes for construction of a PG&E generation facility; providing that (1) marine resources will not be adversely affected; (2) high-voltage transmission lines will not pass through Lopez Canyon . . . ; (3) air pollution and radiation will not exceed licensed limits." Fred Eissler did win a resolution that the club would determine a policy on the peaceful atom. "Such a policy is essential before action is taken on siting of power plants and related problems of environmental contamination."[35]

Conservatives could be proud of a deal that had pioneered a formal role for conservationists in power plant siting decisions. "I am confident," Siri wrote to PG&E, "that the present policy of review with conservation organizations [of] the proposed sites for major installations early in the planning stage will go far toward eliminating costly and damaging open conflicts." President Shermer Sibley responded that "men of reason and goodwill" could always reach a suitable compromise and extended a welcome to incoming club president George Marshall.[36] PG&E, Conservation Associates, and the Redwood chapter of the Sierra Club moved to establish similar negotiations for a power plant proposed at Point Arena on the Northern California coast.[37] These advances, however, came at a terrible cost to the club.

The era of good feelings came to an abrupt halt because of the shifting ideology of the Sierra Club and the secrecy surrounding the original negotiations. The ascension of George Marshall to the club presidency symbolized both trends. Marshall had been an active conservationist and an editor of nature journals. Unlike Siri, Marshall was no fan of nuclear power and suspicious of "propagandists of the power industry and the Atomic Energy Commission [who] cover up problems." He refused to allow Conservation Associates to handle negotiations on the Point Arena facility "without, as far as I know, consulting with conservation organizations."[38] Within a few weeks of the 6 May board meeting, Marshall expressed misgivings about the deal. Contrary to the facts presented at the May meeting, the power plant would sit on the visible coastal terrace and not hidden in Diablo Canyon. Marshall was also worried about nuclear safety. "If atomic reactor power plants are perfectly safe," he asked Will Siri, "why is it that PG&E has been considering sites in relatively remote coastal areas?"[39]

With a more open president, Fred Eissler pried open the debate with the help of sympathetic expertise. In response to an inquiry by Eissler, Charles Washburn, a California State University professor, estimated that by the year 2000 California would need eighty new nuclear power plants clustered at twenty to thirty coastal sites. Whether population grew or not, power demand would continued to skyrocket. "Can you name 20 or 30 coastal sites each large enough to hold about five power plants? Washburn wrote to Marshall. "If there is a shortage of suitable sites now, what will the situation be in twenty years? It seems clear to me that then the only undeveloped land along the coast will be park land."[40] This did not bode well for the future of Nipomo Dunes or any other park on the coast. The Sierra Club was dimly becoming aware that it had a much larger problem on its hands.

Marshall responded by upbraiding Siri and the Leonards' failure to treat the siting problem holistically. Marshall wrote to Doris Leonard, "The whole problem of where future power plants, whether atomic or other types, should be placed would seem to me to require much greater consideration than just falling in line with the apparent program of PG&E and some of the other major power companies. It would seem to me highly undesirable if the entire coast becomes dotted with a string of individual power plants." He noted to Siri, "We must consider this overall picture, for if we do not, our standing resolution against the construction of power plants at scenic sites along the coast will be a dead letter."[41] Henceforth, he announced, the club would evaluate power plant sites "in the context of what is happening generally to California's coastline." Instead of cooperating with the utility, he criticized PG&E because it had "proceeded with such speed on [Point Arena]."[42] But Marshall was trying only to revise policy, not to reverse the Diablo endorsement. Despite the misunderstanding on the location of the plant, it would still be visible only to shipping on the Pacific. After some grumbling, the issue appeared resolved.

The return of board member and *Sunset* magazine photographer Martin Litton from a trip to the Middle East would destroy the serenity of the Sierra Club and ignite two years of open warfare. Martin Litton was every bit the bomb thrower that Fred Eissler was. The son of a veterinarian and a pious mother, he learned early to see the divine hand in nature's wonders and to distrust human pride. He grew up in Southern California in the early decades of the century when the California wilderness remained untrammeled. He spent much of his youth camping in the Sierra where it was possible never to see another soul for weeks. As a travel editor for *Sunset*, he decried the destruction of California's natural splendor with a flaming pen.[43]

Martin Litton did not like people. It was not a personal dislike; there were just too many of them trampling wilderness. As a species, he believed, humans were doomed by their arrogance in the presence of nature. "If a man has not become God, he certainly has tried to," he wrote, by determining which species might live or die. But, he warned, "nature imposes its own balance."[44] He denounced any sort of human presence in wilderness. "Martin won't even stop at a filling station out in the middle of the country because he doesn't think it ought to be there," one admiring club staffer noted.[45] Litton favored a drastic reduction in population to halt encroachment on park land. He derided as "ludicrous" Siri's argument that stabilizing population was sufficient. "It must be obvious that stabilizing population at the present level of technological civilization will give us no hope for survival; anyone who has really thought about it knows that we have already run out of Earth and nothing we can do will keep humankind in existence for as long as another two centuries.[46] Litton was so convinced that a major die-off of humankind was necessary that when asked if he worried about nuclear accidents, he replied, "No, in fact, I really didn't care because there are too many people in the world anyway."[47]

It was Martin Litton's refusal to compromise and his aggressive posturing that made him a hero to younger members of the Sierra Club. But his ideological purity came at a price. As was the case with Fred Eissler, Litton's ideology and personality were an explosive mix of apocalypticism, rigidity, suspicion, and contempt for those who disagreed with him. He infuriated his fellow board members by calling these men of considerable accomplishment "boobs" or "stupid."[48] Confident that only radical solutions worked, he accused as conspirators club members who even moderately disagreed with him. As a result, Litton could not tell when he was winning a point. "[Litton] doesn't quite have a sense of where he has exceeded propriety," Will Siri recalled. "You can almost see it—the attitudes [of others] change, and so sometimes in a battle you want him to continue. Let him go; he'll lose his case."[49] The antithesis of Richard Leonard, he valued ends over means: "I think that playing dirty, if you have a noble end, is fine."[50]

When Martin Litton learned of the club's deal with PG&E he went beyond Marshall's action to reverse the endorsement. Litton photographed Diablo Canyon and returned with pictures that he argued proved the area's scenic worth. The canyon was not a treeless slot, but held a large grove with some of the world's largest oaks. PG&E confirmed that the power lines from the plant would destroy the grove. In an angry letter to PG&E he claimed the club's was a "fraudulently obtained vote." Litton also alleged that "the Board, apparently relieved at

Isolated from the development pressures by the Santa Lucia Range, Diablo Canyon, the dark slot in the lower right corner, appeared to be ideally suited for a nuclear power plant. But this isolation, power plant opponents argued, also made it one of the few relatively undisturbed places on the California coast that included the world's largest examples of coast live oak and a well-preserved tidal zone. Courtesy of the Sierra Club Pictorial Collections, The Bancroft Library, University of California.

the opportunity to make peace with PG&E, had acted upon misleading recommendations without taking the time or the trouble to investigate the situation for itself."[51]

Unfortunately for Will Siri and Kathy Jackson, Litton's accusations were largely correct. Neither Jackson nor Siri had entered the canyon on their inspection and could not see the oak grove. Litton's photos convinced Jackson that she had made a mistake. "I, myself, have developed misgivings about Diablo Canyon as a location for an industrial installation," she wrote Siri.[52] At the same time, Fred Eissler won a resolution, which was later revoked, from the Santa Lucia Group requesting that the Sierra Club restudy the Diablo issue.[53]

But while Litton and Eissler had undermined the wisdom of the Diablo decision, Litton's letter to PG&E was a tactical mistake. By exceeding the bounds of propriety, Litton inadvertently allowed the conservatives to shift the debate from the merits of the issue to the need to be credible and respect authority. Photographer Ansel Adams was irate that a director had publicly aired his opposition to board policy. Adams threatened to sue Litton if he did not issue an apology.[54] Litton brushed Adams aside with predictions of apocalypse. "Perhaps it is unfortunate that you do not live downwind from Diablo Canyon; perhaps your feelings about that part of the coast would be different." He asked Adams:

Are we going to go on yielding up the California coast forever? Because that's just the way it will be unless the line is drawn now. The demands for coastal sites for defacing developments are never going to end unless the human race disappears, and we can't count on that . . . . It is not proper for us to advocate annihilation of life and beauty along our shores or in our rivers to assist utilities, private or public, to obtain the federal subsidies that are spurring them in this race to build all the atomic plants they can regardless of actual need for power.[55]

Litton's ranting only made it easier for conservatives to avoid dealing with the merits of the decision. For Leonard and Adams, usually joined by Siri, Diablo became a cause to preserve organizational integrity and "amicable agreements."[56]

Beneath these fulminations, however, Litton and Eissler were successfully pushing a new environmental perspective. Over the next two years, the progressives forced the Sierra Club to deal more and more with Diablo Canyon as an environmental instead of an aesthetic issue. At the next meeting of the board in September 1966, Fred Eissler asked the club to preserve Diablo for its biodiversity. Calling the Diablo coastline a unique "ecological unit," the Santa Barbara teacher asked for a resolution demanding a moratorium on power plant construction including Diablo until the state developed a shoreline master plan. Picking up on Washburn's analysis, Brower returned to the growth issue: "If a doubling of the state's population in the next twenty years is encouraged by providing the power resources for this growth, the state's scenic character will be destroyed. More power plants create more industry, that in turn invites greater population density." Siri argued weakly that it was futile to fight growth. "The consumption of energy has for decades accurately followed projections of need and nothing short of world-wide disaster could alter the growing power needs of the nation." With the board unwilling to backtrack, Siri successfully amended the moratorium motion to exempt Diablo. Eissler, however, picked up the votes of two directors for his motion, with George Marshall abstaining.[57]

Now Brower and his allies were winning. Perhaps sensing that the agreement was in trouble, PG&E flew some of the Sierra Club directors over Diablo Canyon in Frank Sinatra's Lear jet piloted by Danny Kaye. But the trip only convinced some directors that they had made a mistake. Wayburn returned convinced he had been "lied to" by PG&E.[58] Brower argued that the "new evidence" allowed the Sierra Club to oppose Diablo without appearing to be reversing its policy. He noted that the directors had thought the plants were to be in the canyon and not on the coastal terrace. Nor had the club sufficiently studied alternative sites as had been its procedure in opposing a pumped storage facility at Storm King in New York. Five directors favored reversal of the Diablo policy. Other directors were wavering. The board resolved to put the issue to the club membership. This was the first time since the Hetch Hetchy controversy that the membership would vote on a board decision.[59]

In a move indicative of the club's shift away from aesthetic issues, the board resolved to perform an ecological survey and study of economic alternatives to Diablo. Even Will Siri voted for the ecological study, leaving Adams and Leonard isolated.[60] The studies' results heartened the dissenters. The committee reported that alternative sites to Diablo were in fact acceptable and economical. They reported that the site was only "one of two extensive seashore areas in California of unique unmarred quality." "It is the richest marine complex south of Mendocino County." The report also noted that scientists knew little about the effect of radioactive effluents and "heated water discharge" on marine life. The committee argued that Diablo was "remarkably worthy of preservation" for "the combination of values of the undersea, coastal shelf, mountain and canyon ecologies which are distinctively represented in the area."[61] Hugh Nash, a plant opponent, reported later that the directors listening to the reports looked sick as the committees laid out their conclusions.[62] Director Paul Brooks noted that most board members now thought that the Diablo endorsement was a mistake, but there was no majority for a reversal.

In blundering on the Diablo negotiations, Siri had opened the door to those who advocated an environmental agenda rather than narrow wilderness preservationism. A patient strategist for the other side might have realized that in losing the Diablo issue, he had won the larger battle over whether the club would embrace a new environmental agenda. Moreover, new members were joining the board who shared Fred Eissler's progressive vision. Directors had recognized that the quiet negotiations of Diablo were not acceptable and that the club should not compromise without first conducting a broad inquiry into the ecological impact of its decisions. Had Eissler been patient and diplomatic, he might have realized that Siri's support for the ecological studies was a tacit admission that he agreed. But neither Eissler nor Litton was a patient person. As prophets of the apocalypse, they had little patience for a long-term campaign. "This battle was lost not so much because I was clever but because they lost it," Siri argued years later. "Eissler could have won that battle, but Eissler was his own worst enemy. . . . They did not understand that when they treated opponents ruthlessly they were going to alienate a lot of people who were in the middle."[63] Despite their gains, the antiplant faction was about to make a serious error.

Typical of the radicals' impatience was the infamous "half Bulletin." When Ansel Adams and Will Siri did not submit their arguments in favor of the Diablo resolution to the *Bulletin* on time, Brower and the staff decided to go to press anyway, thinking that the blank pages would embarrass Siri and Adams. Instead their ploy outraged many centrist directors and chapter leaders. The *Bulletin* often ran late anyway, so the maneuver looked like dirty play. Richard Leonard excitedly wrote Siri, "Dave is in the open now. . . . [You] switched at least two votes to your side . . . by simply not getting your homework in on time. . . . Though we may lose the battle I now think we may win the war. Can we somehow stage a get-together in which to plan concerted action to force [Brower] further to tip his hand?"[64] Leonard's note, however, indicated that Litton and Eissler were not the only ones who used illicit means to achieve their "noble" end.

The bungling by the Save-Diablo faction helped cement an alliance of conservatives and moderates who objected to Brower's leadership of the Sierra Club for a variety of reasons. Those in the coalition opposed Brower for his notoriously poor financial management, philosophy, and methods. There were hard-line conservative leaders who resented the club's forays into scientific and technical issues. But the conservative philosophy was in the minority, and had the Diablo debate been framed simply as an ecological or technical issue, it is very possible that the conservatives would have lost.[65] But because of the harsh rhetoric and tactics of the Save-Diablo faction, moderates felt comfortable aligning with conservatives to protect the respectability and authority of the club.

The plea for organizational integrity won the day, but it did not resolve the fight. The antiplant forces lost in decisive fashion as the membership supported the Diablo deal by a margin of 69 to 31 percent.[66] But the Save-Diablo faction was unwilling to accept the vote, and the fight degenerated into open warfare. Martin Litton dismissed the defeat by

the "brain-washed membership" and continued to work on overturn-
ing the Diablo resolution.[67] He embraced conspiratorial notions of his
opponents. He warned darkly of the "Siri/PG&E/Leonard combine"
and worked behind the scenes to stage events to "embarrass" the club.[68]
For the antiplant faction, there was silver lining in the vote. The membership had elected progressive directors to the board. With a new antiplant majority, Brower's allies hoped emerging problems with nuclear
power and increasingly popular environmental attitudes could still reverse the club's position.

The Problem of Industrial Growth and Thermal Pollution

By the late sixties, population and economic growth were changing the
way environmentalists looked at the world. David Brower and Fred
Eissler had argued for controlling population growth, but Diablo
Canyon demonstrated that lifestyle and industrialism were as much a
problem as population growth.[69] As Charles Washburn pointed out,
economic growth assured that coastal power plant siting would continue whether population increased or not. The Sierra Club had always
hoped to minimize the impact of growth through a kind of industrial
containment policy that place plants close to urban areas.[70] By breaking
containment and threatening wilderness, Diablo crystallized thinking
within the club that California was reaching the limits of its capacity to
support society and absorb pollution. What started as a site-specific debate on Diablo turned into a discussion about the wisdom of growth in
general. This debate would help unite the club's traditional wilderness
emphasis with public health issues associated with industrialization.

Reflecting its evolving philosophy, the Sierra Club published Stanford biologist Paul Ehrlich's huge best-seller *The Population Bomb*.
Ehrlich's predictions of massive die-offs or even nuclear war if population growth was not halted received most of the headlines. But the Stanford biologist understood that growth problems also stemmed from
uncontrolled use of fossil fuels or nuclear power. Giving society cheap
abundant energy would be like giving a machine gun to an idiot child,
he remarked. In writing the foreword for the book, David Brower predicted that the resources of nature "would not sustain [humankind] in
[its] old habits of growing and reaching without limits."[71] Humankind's
pollution of the biosphere would eventually impose a limit.

Pollution was merely a symptom of the growth problem, and clean
nuclear power, it turned out, was not immune. The thermal pollution
controversy of the late sixties was crucial in upsetting the environmental advantage claimed by the nuclear industry. Water used to cool fossil

and nuclear plants had traditionally been discharged back into the rivers, lakes, and oceans at an increased temperature of about 10 to 20 degrees. Far less efficient than fossil-fueled plants, nuclear power discharged nearly 50 percent more hot water than a conventional plant of the same size. Authorities admitted that they did not know what the subtle changes in the metabolism and breeding habits of animals might be because of the warmer, oxygen-depleted waters. Alarm spread when it was reported that between 1962 and 1967, ten fish kills were caused by thermal pollution from electric plants. Accordingly, thermal pollution concerns mounted as the nuclear industry planned to churn out ever larger power plants in the sixties.[72]

Although environmental and sporting organizations had favored nuclear plants because they were cleaner than conventional plants, they now expressed alarm when the Atomic Energy Commission claimed it did not have jurisdiction to control thermal pollution. They were not soothed by the AEC's effort to cast thermal pollution in a positive light by calling it "thermal enrichment."[73] The AEC's avoidance of the issue did not help its image at a time when its dual function of promoting and regulating nuclear power was coming under fire. This unclear jurisdictional authority was later clarified by federal legislation, but not before nuclear power had lost significant prestige.[74] Until 1968, coverage of nuclear plants in popular magazines was almost devoid of negative stories. That year, the tone of articles shifted permanently to neutral or negative because of thermal pollution.[75]

Thermal pollution posed little danger to a body of water as large as the Pacific Ocean, but some members of the Sierra Club saw the controversy as a way of reversing the club's position on Diablo Canyon. In 1968, David Brower wrote Edgar Wayburn calling for a policy reversal.

A lot of thermal pollution, in prospect, has flowed from prospective power sites since the Board's earlier action [on Diablo], and the threat has been of growing concern among many national conservation organizations. . . . The likelihood of damage to marine resources is of such magnitude that the Diablo development . . . is now in conflict with the Club's existing resolution and we should feel free to bring this opposition into the open.[76]

If the utility spent money on the plant before thermal pollution was adequately studied, Brower warned, "it will be politically impossible to require the utility to correct itself."[77]

Brower used the thermal pollution issue to raise a larger question of whether any economic growth was acceptable to the environment. Brower argued that the club needed to halt companies "rushing to build facilities to generate" or the planet's ecosphere might be destroyed. The

Water Resources Council, in fact, warned that power plants in the year 2020 would be churning out more hot water than the flow of the entire Mississippi River.[78] Brower averred, "Every cause is a lost cause unless we question the addiction to growth."[79] Framing Diablo in terms of pollution and growth, Brower and his allies concluded that no nuclear plant was the best one.

Admitting a "Mistake"

With new attitudes about growth and pollution winning converts, the showdown over Diablo Canyon came in December 1968. The argument focused on the ecological impact of thermal pollution. Critical to the process was director and nuclear engineer Lauerence Moss, who raised enough uncertainty to counter Will Siri's efforts to minimize the problem. Winning the debate, the antiplant faction retracted the Sierra Club endorsement. The board agreed, however, to put the vote again before the membership.[80]

Even as the antiplant faction appeared to have won the battle on Diablo Canyon, the actions of David Brower brought them down. Brower often ignored the board when they limited his authority in spending money, publishing books, and leading campaigns. There were many interpretations of Brower's behavior, including that of writer Wallace Stegner, who believed Brower had been "bitten by the worm of power."[81] But it was more likely that Brower simply believed his own rhetoric that the environmental crisis was so dire that it had to override the club's integrity. He asked, "Isn't the biggest mistake of all the mistake of letting the face of the coast be despoiled to save our own?"[82] As the Diablo conflict worsened, Brower sought the counsel of the true believers, who saw themselves as "Christians in the catacombs" predicting catastrophe and waiting for a religious revolution. They were ready to risk anything, including the survival of the club, to save the planet. Paul Ehrlich, a Brower ally, summed up this view.

Though the oldtime conservationists may understand that there is a crisis, they still want to be gentlemen while the world is dissolving. We know what doesn't work: the quiet, gentle approach. If somebody told me there was a 50-50 chance Brower would destroy the Sierra Club, I'd say go ahead, it's a bargain. The world is going to tumble around its ears if the Sierra Club—or someone—doesn't do the job in the next five years. If the Sierra Club's main worry is the preservation of its own existence, there won't be any environment left for it to exist in.[83]

Driven by the logic of his arguments, Brower took foolish risks when he could not afford to lose allies. The effort to fire Brower by the conservative faction of Adams and Leonard swelled into an open revolt by club chapters. Brower would likely have survived if he had limited his insubordination to Diablo Canyon, but he spent lavishly on questionable campaigns. The final straw came when Brower unilaterally ran a full-page ad in the *New York Times*, an immensely expensive move, calling for an "Earth National Park." Brower allies, such as Phillip Berry, and others who had rejected earlier calls for Brower's head could stand it no longer.

Brower's behavior assured that the 1969 elections would be a referendum not on the merits of Diablo Canyon but on organizational integrity and the wisdom of allowing one individual to run the Sierra Club. The election would implicitly consist of two referendums—one on Brower's handling of club affairs and the other on the Diablo decision. But because of Brower's behavior, both issues would be decided in terms of whether members wanted a fiscally responsible, democratically run club or one with a charismatic leader who answered to no one but principle. It was a rout. None of the Brower candidates won election, and the membership upheld the original Diablo resolution by more than 3 to 1.[84]

No religious war would be complete without a purge, and the Sierra Club would have a dandy.[85] The Sir Francis Drake Hotel near San Francisco's Union Square was packed to the gills with reporters and long-time members, as David Brower entered the Empire Room to tender his resignation. The meeting would go as Leonard had planned. Martin Litton leaped to his feet and declared, "This election has been rife with perjury, calumny, and fraud!" Leonard sat motionless until the tirade was over and business resumed. Brower submitted his resignation with an emotional speech. Embracing environmental themes, he warned the audience to fight against "undisciplined technology" and "addiction to growth." He announced the formation of a group, later named Friends of the Earth, committed to moral environmentalism. The new group would embody the views of Aldo Leopold and Paul Ehrlich and look "at the whole earth there as one ecosphere." The board accepted Brower's resignation 10 to 5.[86]

Although Leonard was a force behind Brower's removal, he did not relish it. Many had thought Brower's motivation was some messianic complex or a massive ego. Leonard knew better. In the hotel lobby moments before the vote, the San Francisco attorney noted, "The basis of his drive is that the earth is going to hell fast and something has to be done about it. Because of this, Dave will spend the resources of any organization he is with in unlimited fashion. 'We're not trying to save money, we're trying to save the world,' he will say, and then he will put thirty thousand dollars or so into another newspaper advertisement, without being authorized to do so by the board. . . . I have no personal animosity toward Dave. We just have to save the Sierra Club, that's all."[87] The organizational imperative had won. Brower, Litton, and Eissler thought that survival of the earth hung in the balance at Diablo and thus believed that anything, even the Sierra Club, was worth sacrificing. The club membership was not ready to admit that the earth's predicament was nearly that dire. They were ready to save the earth, but they insisted it be through an effective, responsibly run organization.[88]

Friends of the Earth and the Sierra Club after Brower

"I became a born-again anti-nuclearist," David Brower confessed of the conversion experience he underwent because of the Diablo Canyon conflict.[89] Brower's conversion was an apt metaphor for the whole environmental movement. With so much of the Sierra Club's controversy shrouded in personality and organizational debate, it was easy to miss how the Diablo debate pushed the club toward an ecological and ethical perspective similar to Brower's.[90] This conversion was in line with much of what was occurring around the country in 1969 as the new environmental movement was about to launch itself from the first Earth Day in 1970. Both the Sierra Club and Friends of the Earth would embrace this new perspective. With Brower gone and the factionalism relieved, the Sierra Club had a much easier time accepting Brower's ideas. Naturally, Brower's antinuclear ideas developed faster in Friends of the Earth.

Brower concluded that the nation's obsession with energy had denied individuals their humanity, and he was determined to give Friends of the Earth (FOE) an ethical perspective that would separate it from the Sierra Club's more pragmatic, scientific approach. In September 1969, Brower's followers gathered in Aspen, Colorado. Unshackled from the Sierra Club, the conference speakers gave full expression to their moral environmentalism and apocalyptic fears. "Everywhere we find expanding population but shrinking resources; new horizons but old miseries; growing technology but dwindling spirit. Our drive for more is giving us less." The conference members designated "approaches to equilibrium," including population control, to halt growth, and developed "an ecological ethic that will influence all human affairs" and "create an economic system not based on growth and not abusive of the earth." FOE would attempt to change public attitudes through "symbolic" antitechnological campaigns that would keep the public focused on issues while educating them on the larger goal of ethical transformation.[91] Personal conversion became a

Early construction at the Diablo Canyon site. PG&E's victory would lay the basis for more unified state and environmental opposition in the future. Photograph by Martin Litton. Courtesy William E. Colby Memorial Library, Sierra Club, San Francisco.

trademark of FOE's approach and distinguished it from the substance-oriented Sierra Club. Energy issues would take center stage in their campaigns, and an early target would be electric power, especially nuclear power plants.

By 1971, Friends of the Earth had taken the lead in opposing nuclear power. An international meeting of FOE called for a moratorium on construction and operation of nuclear plants because of the immorality associated with waste disposal problems and genetic mutation. FOE concluded that nuclear energy was antithetical to "the safety of life on earth" and thus morally objectionable.[92]

Surprisingly, the Sierra Club moved in the same direction as Friends of the Earth. FOE more readily used moral and ethical justifications, while the Sierra Club couched its positions in scientific arguments. But the club was motivated by FOE's ethics. The two organizations moved philosophically closer to each other; so much so that Phil Berry would refer to FOE as the club's "sister" organization.[93] The differences between the two organizations were often semantic. As Berry admitted about the difference between his style and Brower's, "It all amounted to the same thing. you voted the same way whether you're convinced that it [the issue involved] was horrible, or just bad or gravely doubtful."[94] The club would also arrive at its antinuclear positions only after a great deal of input from its chapters. The Sierra Club would be vigorous, but within the limits of a club consensus and economic solvency.

The ascension of Phillip Berry to the presidency represented a melding of Richard Leonard's need for organizational integrity with the purism of David Brower. This surprised those who thought the election signaled a conservative resurgence. The environmental movement was changing, and even the conservatives knew this shift was inevitable. What they wanted was a solvent Sierra Club. Within these fiscal and democratic restraints, Berry implemented a David Brower program. "The old guard felt they could trust us to be financially responsible and not run off on some tangent," Berry said after his elevation to the presidency.[95] At the club's first annual meeting in the post-Brower era, Berry announced a "bold and constructive program of publicly responsible conservation. . . . So there will be no retreat and no further pause. There must be dynamic movement ahead—without compromise of principle—as far and fast as possible toward our finest conservation goals." The comment about compromise was a rebuke to supporters of the Diablo decision. The club's guiding principle would be that it "never be a party to a convention that lessens wilderness."[96] The club rejected quiet negotiation in favor of confrontational legal tactics that had caused so much argument in the Bodega conflict. Abandoning compromise was not a pragmatic decision, but one of principle. Because of Diablo Canyon, a club official admitted, "[the club] finally realized . . . that [compromise] was not justified in terms of our own ideals and our own convictions and our own purposes."[97]

Phil Berry brought with him a younger generation's militancy and environmental perspective. At thirty-two, he was the youngest president in Sierra Club history, and it showed in substance and style. When providing a photo to accompany his oral interview for the club's oral history series, he did not choose a typical studio portrait or a shot of himself hanging off some ledge in the Sierra as elder leaders had done. Instead he selected a photo that showed him picketing the San Francisco headquarters of Standard Oil. On those steps, Berry issued the opening salvo of the club's militant campaign: "Companies had better learn soon that it's going to be an all-out war."[98]

The rhetoric of the Sierra Club under Berry was audacious and ominous. Berry presented a "Plan for Survival" and even adopted Brower's military metaphors when discussing environmental campaigns. The new president could talk about "lining up our guns on the enemy" with a casualness that would have been repugnant to conservatives such as Dick Leonard.[99] Club publications also sported a military motif. The club issued a "Battlebook" series intended to acquaint community activists with its key arguments on issues such as energy and pollution. As executive director Michael McCloskey declared to the readers of *Fortune*, "Our strategy is going to be to sue and sue and sue. Eventually the utilities are going to have to take us seriously." McCloskey was hardly exaggerating: by early 1970 the club was involved in fifty-five legal actions around the country.[100] The club's philosophy moved beyond its traditional wilderness perspective to include critics of modern technology and industrialization such as scientists René Dubos and Barry Commoner. It aimed to create a program "essential to global survival." The Survival Committee became a center where club members took ideas developed by environmental philosophers and turned them into a practical platform.

The most troubling issue was growth—population, economic, and energy, especially energy. Berry recalled, "It became obvious to us there was one big central block of issues attached to energy." "Energy itself slowly came to be recognized as one of the chief disrupters of the environment," Will Siri agreed. "Almost everywhere that environmental problems arose there were energy aspects to them." The club determined to develop an electric power policy.[101] The focus on electric energy to the exclusion of other energy problems stemmed from the Diablo controversy, rapid power plant construction, and incursions on the coastline in California.

The shifting focus of the Sierra Club and Friends of the Earth was symptomatic of the changing values of American society that allowed the environmental movement to transcend traditional wilderness advocates and organizations. Despite the Sierra Club's increased power, it found it had to share the spotlight instead of lead battles. The new movement was made up of countless progressive organizations and individuals such as consumer advocacy groups, legal foundations, scientific researchers, and sixties activists attempting to revolutionize American society. As a result, nuclear opposition became more diffuse. It became a conglomeration of organizations with similar nonmaterialist sympathies but different emphases and strengths. After Earth Day in 1970, the movement came to resemble a large ant colony where there is no discernible leader but the work still gets done. Earth Day provided the movement with new activists to do the work.

Expanding the Movement: Earth Day

The Sierra Club and Friends of the Earth had embraced the broad problems of the new environmental movement just in time to reap the outpouring of environmental sentiment on the nation's first Earth Day. Militant anticorporate campaigns were just what a new generation of environmental activists were demanding. On the heels of such well-publicized environmental disasters as the "death" of Lake Erie and the 1969 oil spill near Santa Barbara, public awareness of pollution peaked. A concomitant decline in antiwar activism just before the South Vietnamese and United States invasion of Cambodia provided an opening for new issues to engage the ideals of college-age activists. The first few months of 1970 witnessed campus demonstrations and "teach-ins" on the environment patterned on those held during the height of antiwar activity. At first, a fear of a radical influx of New Leftists into Earth Day activities led the Sierra Club to an uninspired embrace of these demonstrations. Phil Berry warned the board that some of those who joined the festivities were either corporations trying to burnish their environmental image or "anarchists" looking to overthrow government institutions.[102] He should not have been so worried. Earth Day proved to be the kind of event moderate students hungered for.

"We want to stop the war, end pollution—and beat Stanford!" a Berkeley pep rally leader shouted to a crowd of five thousand. Perhaps it was indicative of waning antiwar fervor and the quality of Cal football, but of the three, ending pollution drew the loudest cheers.[103] From the moment it was suggested by Senator Gaylord Nelson, Earth Day aimed for and reached the hearts of moderate youth looking for a cause. The outpouring of sentiment all over the country was, much to the chagrin of corporate America, antibusiness, and to the distaste of radical activists, progressive and reformist but not revolutionary. There was a pervasive undercurrent of hostility and contempt toward government and industry at these college demonstrations. Charles Luce, chairman of New York's Consolidated Edison Co., confessed it was "embarrassing to sit there and get booed and laughed at" while he argued for incremental reform. But reporters who looked for signs of radicalism more often found students in suits and ties and focused on education programs. Even in Berkeley, one reporter noted, student environmentalists were more likely to say "'Enjoy the walk,' than scream 'Up against the wall.'"[104]

It was civil rights activists and Berkeley radicals who were most disappointed with the temperate tone of the demonstrations. Environmental awareness appeared to coop antiwar activities or a commitment to civil rights. Black activists held aloof from environmentalism, believing it was a way for whites to avoid dealing with racial problems.[105] The New Left feared the "co-optive potential of ecology" that would divert attention from revolution and Vietnam. And they were right. "I think environment is a bigger issue than the war," one college student remarked, "and I think people are beginning to sense its urgency."[106] A *Ramparts* editorial argued that Earth Day was a trick sponsored by corporate sponsors and establishment elites. Instead they approved of a student-led burning of a Bank of America branch in Santa Barbara following the oil spill. "The students who burned [the bank] will have done more to save the environment than all the Survival Faires and 'Earth-Day Teach-Ins' put together."[107] Ultimately, there were few revolutionary acts. The activities leading up the 11 April 1970 main event focused on renewal and repair of environmental problems.

Earth Day's reasonable tone engendered an unprecedented broadening of the environmental movement. Consumer activists such as Ralph Nader organized student groups to push for environmental legislation. Young attorneys in Long Island formed the Environmental Defense Fund to pursue what one of its founders called the "sue the bastards" strategy.[108] And David Brower's Friends of the Earth acted as the moral conscience of the new movement. The Sierra Club would also pick up support from young people interested in legislative reform. The club sponsored its own "campus program" to recruit college activists. Agreeing with these advocates of a "new environmentalism," Phillip Berry said, "There has to be a change in the whole system. We need a true revolution of ideas."[109]

With diversity would come a diffusion of responsibility and power in the environmental movement. The nuclear issue would not be a debate isolated to Sierra Club board meetings. As the Sierra Club's new executive director, Michael McCloskey, told the board of directors: "The Environmental Movement is coming to be more than a re-labeled Conservation Movement. It is coming to represent an amalgamation of many other movements with the Conservation Movement: the consumer movement, including corporate reformers; the movement for scientific responsibility; a revitalized public health movement; and a diffuse movement in search of a new focus for politics."[110] McCloskey knew the club would have to share power with these other movements.

The club would have its key issues, but it would not be a participant in broad coalition politics that it could not dominate. These coalitions would be especially apparent in the antinuclear battles to come.

Expanding the Movement: Scientists as Activists

If there was any authority capable of speaking out against the voices of Earth Day, it was America's still widely respected scientists. But the profession was showing serious signs of dissent that threatened their fairly unified voice on nuclear power. In fact, the values that had transformed the Sierra Club converted a significant minority of the scientific community to an environmental ethic.

A large majority of the scientific community still supported and publicly advocated using the peaceful atom. In particular, the atomic scientists of the Manhattan Project remained the key champions of nuclear power. Glenn Seaborg was only the most obvious example of scientist who had made the transition from pure research into an administrative position, where he could champion his favorite technology. In stepping into the public arena, such scientists became what one scholar has called "prominators," who through government agencies promoted various technologies.[111] Prominators had brought to policy a faith in the ability of science and technology to solve humanity's problems. Whether analyzing war, the environment, or urban conflict, Seaborg argued, "it is more science, better science, more wisely applied that is going to free us from these predicaments." In the new "scientific age," the AEC chairman predicted, humanity would raise itself to a "new level of mankind." Seaborg envisioned a future without limits if only society would embrace the power of reason. "If we do not at some point— and, admittedly, on faith—trust in the power of reason and act accordingly," Seaborg warned, "we will either end up living under the worst kind of organized tyranny or in a physical and spiritual jungle."[112] Those who questioned the value of nuclear power, Seaborg implied, consigned society to a lower level of existence.

Nuclear advocates believed theirs was a higher calling for the benefit of all. Oak Ridge Laboratory's director, Alvin Weinberg, nuclear power's most eloquent and quotable scientist, argued: "The nuclear community is not working simply for economic power; it is working for a much nobler goal of converting our society to a permanent economy of abundance; of attaining, permanently, [a] better life toward which men and women throughout the world can aspire." To give up on the atom, Weinberg concluded, would force the world to confront a Malthusian nightmare of starvation and poverty. But the choice was not simply between prosperity and poverty. Even nuclear supporters realized that, like the hero in a Greek tragedy, there was a possibly of fatal flaw to nuclear power, but their faith in leadership and science overcame their fears. Alvin Weinberg admitted that his profession had a "moral imperative" to protect the world from the dangers of the peaceful atom: "We nuclear people have made a Faustian compact with society: we offer an almost unique possibility for a technologically abundant world for the oncoming billions, through our miraculous inexhaustible energy source; but this energy source at the same time is tainted with potential side effects that, if uncontrolled, could spell disaster." Nuclear wastes would perhaps require a "priesthood," Weinberg predicted, to prevent their release even as world civilizations collapsed and new ones arose. While Rome burned, apparently, scientists would fulfill their duty to protect society. Antinuclear activists would repeat Weinberg's Faustian tale for the next decade as proof of the folly of nuclear power.[113]

Antinuclear scientists' interpretation of Weinberg's Faust analogy as an example of flawed science revealed a philosophical difference that went to the core beliefs of the atom's friends and enemies. Alvin Weinberg, an ardent fan of nuclear power, had meant Faust to be a challenge to the nuclear industry. The atomic scientist could offer humanity a special gift if humanity was vigilant to its duty to safeguard it. To Weinberg the lesson of Faust was positive. In the most popular version, told by Goethe, Faust bargained his soul to gain greater knowledge. Faust escaped hell and became a better person through the sincerity of his desires to learn and the love of a woman who redeemed him. Weinberg, like Goethe, believed in the capacity of the human will and intellect to do good. Scientists would triumph over the atom's dangers and elevate humanity.

But activists who despised the tyranny of a scientific "priesthood" drew a different conclusion about human will. There was an older, antimodern version of this Enlightenment Faust. The tale, as told in the sixteenth century, had Faust carried off to hell by the devil for trading his soul for wisdom and magical powers. Its moral rejected the Renaissance veneration of the human intellect. Humankind, the argument went, could not ignore God's laws. In the pantheistic religion of the modern environmental movement, "Nature" replaced "God." Nuclear scientists had damned society to misery because they did not respect nature and sought to transcend it. Human reason, in this view, had to accept natural limits.

The lesson of limits attracted a growing community of dissident scientists whose values closely reflected those of the environmental movement. The roots of this community stretched back to the dissident scientists of the Manhattan Project, who formed the Federation of American Scientists and published the *Bulletin of the Atomic Scientists*. There had also been opposition from ecologists such as Barry Commoner, who claimed that scientific arrogance and specialization had caused the present environmental dilemma. In the sixties, there was a notable increase in dissidents who joined Commoner. A new generation of scientists became disillusioned with their work for the military industrial complex. They worried they had "become slaves to a power structure that they do not trust."[114] The catalyst of this new wave of scientific activism was the Vietnam War and renewed fears of the arms race. At a number of research centers around Boston, Los Angeles, and the Bay Area, socially conscious researchers formed groups to protest the dehumanizing aspects of science, that researchers found, instead of helping society, their work was linked to the Vietnam War, military funding of weapons research, and university support for industrial polluters.

Students protested that research fostered by the government, the military, and universities did not address human problems in American society. The most notable demonstration was in March 1969 at MIT, where students and professors staged a one-day work stoppage. Students demanded "science for the people" that responded to "problems of human significance." About thirty universities around the country, including Stanford and Berkeley, witnessed similar demonstrations and symposiums.[115] Rather tame by the standards of the day, these demonstrations had as their lasting legacy, the formation of a permanent group called the Union of Concerned Scientists (UCS). "We are immersed in one of the most significant revolutions in man's history. The force that drives this revolution is not social dissension or political ideology, but relentless exploitation of scientific knowledge." Noting that society had failed to deal with science's "destructive forces," UCS wanted to use the political system to address "survival problems" by which the "misapplication of technology literally threatens our continued existence." Echoing the sentiments of David Pesonen years earlier, UCS claimed that technological decisions with political implications had virtually "no popular participation." The Union of Concerned Scientists called for an alliance of citizens and scientists to look into the social costs of technology. "It is our belief," it continued, "that a strengthening of the democratic process would lead to a more humane exploitation of scientific and technical knowledge."[116] As Vietnam and the military industrial complex waned as a central issue for activists, the Union of Concerned Scientists caught the spirit of Earth Day and turned its attention to environmental issues.[117]

Dissidents such as Barry Commoner, the student protests, and the birth of the Union of Concerned Scientists revealed a new generation of scientist activists who differed with their colleagues more over values than over scientific theory. These scientist activists reached out to other groups who shared their nonmaterialism, notably environmentalists. In conjunction with the Sierra Club, UCS helped lead an attack on the Pilgrim nuclear power plant near Plymouth, Massachusetts.[118] UCS demonstrated the value of having scientists and environmental organizations working together to alter the regulatory system and raise public awareness of technology's darker side. The group was critical in lending credibility to the limits-to-growth debate. UCS would later play an important role in influencing California to move toward greater regulation of nuclear power.

Although West Coast scientists did not form as influential an organization as the Union of Concerned Scientists, their activism followed a similar path. As at MIT, students and faculty with an anti-establishment agenda tried to democratize technological decisions. Concern with the morality of antiballistic missile systems aroused scientists at Stanford and Berkeley to protest.[119] Hoping to raise a broader question about the "social responsibility of the scientist," these activists organized campus classes to discuss career options outside the defense industry and displayed an increasing interest in environmentalism.[120]

The Sierra Club courted these sympathetic scientists, believing they were "pivotal" in justifying the club's policy positions on "survival" issues.[121] The Diablo Canyon controversy had demonstrated the importance of experts, and the Sierra Club determined to use many more. The first Survival Committee meeting discussed electric power issues at length and determined that a first step was to form committees of scientists. "Expertise is widespread," the minutes reported, and "efforts should be made to assemble a panel of experts."[122] By the early seventies, many scientists sat on club committees.

John Holdren was typical of the new breed of scientist activists who hoped to bridge what they perceived as a widening gap between the world of science and the needs of society. Holdren was, to say the least, a precocious teenager. While other adolescents in the fifties indulged in rock-and-roll and hot rods, Holdren recalled that he worried about whether scientists might be "insufficiently attentive to the wider dimensions of what they were doing and in the realm of human well-being." It was no coincidence that he and David Pesonen had the same reading list, which included Harrison Brown's neo-Malthusian book *The Challenge of Man's Future* and Sir Charles Snow's critique of scientific culture, *Two Cultures*. Thus, even before he attended MIT and completed his Ph.D. at Stanford, Holdren had spent a great deal of time wondering "whether technology would invariably come to the rescue" in dealing with the "unlimited growth and material aspirations" of modern society.[123] At Stanford, Holdren met Paul Ehrlich, and the two began a collaboration that would produce a number of articles and books about population, resources, and the limits of technology in solving the world's Malthusian dilemma.

Ultimately, Holdren could not resolve the conflict between his social values and the military demands of his profession. As with most physicists, Holdren's employment came through the military-industrial complex. In 1969, he left Lockheed to work at the California Institute of Technology with his hero, Harrison Brown. There he joined a growing cluster of socially conscious scientists at the Environmental Quality Laboratory and similarly motivated experts at the Rand Corporation in Santa Monica who were committed to democratic control of technology. The Laboratory produced environmentally sympathetic studies in partnership with the Sierra Club. It argued for power plant construction decisions based on the model of "old town meetings" instead of isolated to government authorities and scientists.[124] By the early seventies, John Holdren and a host of other scientists with environmental sympathies were working either in their careers or as volunteers to critique nuclear power.[125] In California's future power battles, this network of scientist activists and environmentalists would be crucial in creating environmentally sympathetic energy legislation.[126]

Formulating an Environmental Energy Policy

It was this coalition of environmentalists and sympathetic scientists who tried to alter thinking about American's growth paradigm. There was no question that the Sierra Club's ideal was to stop growth. But its immediate goal was to limit growth to the "irreducible needs of society."[127] The club had to decide questions such as what power sources it preferred, whether it should advocate lifestyle changes, and how much energy society really needed.

There were significant divisions on power sources. In the coal-plagued Midwest, chapters passed a limited endorsement of nuclear power. But antinuclear sentiment ran high in California chapters, where coal was less of an immediate problem. Rejecting the Midwest resolution, California activists argued that nuclear power's safety hazards were not likely to be solved. But their critique of energy ran deeper to an anticorporate position and a fear that thermal pollution would harm the environment. "Limiting per capita growth [of] power consumption should be the starting point for a permanent solution of the problem."[128]

One of the important contributions scientist activists made was to apply some basic scientific principles to world energy use. John Holdren argued in the Sierra Club's Battlebook *Energy* that the second law of thermodynamics and heat transfer theory put an upper limit on society's use of energy.[129] Energy put into the atmosphere, whether it was hot water from a nuclear plant or greenhouse-producing carbon dioxide from fossil fuels, would eventually overheat the planet and cause environmental catastrophe. How much energy was necessary to cause this, Holdren admitted, was unknown. He called for limits on energy growth until scientists understood the dangers.[130]

Holdren's argument that there was a natural limit to energy consumption had an instant appeal to environmentalists. Thermodynamic arguments began appearing in Sierra Club documents on energy and public advertisements. Not one given to cautionary statements, David Brower embraced the spate of limits-to-growth studies, arguing for "kicking the addiction to growth that's going to kill us all."[131] The Sierra Club was only slightly less dramatic. The club ran an advertisement with a touched-up photo of the Golden Gate Bridge underwater save for the tops of the towers. "We are making environmental changes with consequences we still don't understand or even suspect. Take heat, for example," the caption read. "One day as we approach the global limits, the polar ice caps could begin to melt, flooding some cities of the earth. There are limits to the alterations we can make to our ecosystem. We would do well to slow the pace of change so we can determine these limits scientifically, before we discover them accidentally."[132] The issue of thermal pollution, which had begun as an isolated matter of fish kills, had blossomed into an inquiry into the global consequences of power generation.

The Sierra Club turned to formulating policy recommendations that would reduce energy consumption. The club pursued this course with two ideas that had recently become popular: externalities and conservation. Convinced that most traditional energy sources received unfair subsidies, environmentalists concluded that their elimination and the forcing of "external costs" into the price of energy would drive down consumption. First theorized decades earlier by British economist A. C. Pigou, "externalities" became a rallying cry of environmental policy in many areas.[133] Some costs such as pollution or the destruction of prime wilderness, environmentalists argued, are not reflected in the price of a commodity but are external to it and born by society through a lower quality of life. If regulators forced the costs of clearing up or preserving a prime wilderness area into the economic system with a pollution tax, for example, environmentalists believed energy use would decline.

These economic disincentives were a relatively nonthreatening way of working nonmaterialist values into the market system.

Externalities, though, had the potential to cripple nuclear power. Externalities in the nuclear program were as numerous as fault lines on California's coast. Subsidies for catastrophic insurance, fuel, and research and development gave the peaceful atom the appearance of economic viability.

A second idea for conserving energy emerged in 1972 as the centerpiece of the environmental energy platform. The notion that energy use was fixed forever to a few key variables such as gross national product and population preempted the possibility that society could ever reduce energy consumption without serious lifestyle changes. The Sierra Club's energy conference did much to explore the possibilities of reducing American consumption of energy. Scientists and energy analysts presented new ideas such as appliance efficiency and home insulation standards, a switch to smaller cars, and "total energy systems" whereby waste heat from power plants and industrial processes were used for other purposes.[134]

In sum, conservation, externalities, and Holdren's thermodynamic arguments did not single out nuclear power as the chief problem, but they inordinately affected the image of nuclear power plants in the eyes of environmentalists. They reduced nuclear power to just another problematic energy source. All traditional forms of energy, the Sierra Club concluded, "can only destroy what remains of the beauty and habitability of the earth." As the key to a cornucopian energy future, environmentalists opposed the peaceful atom regardless of its nuclear hazards.[135] Environmentalists had developed a rationale that allowed them to oppose any new energy source, most of which were slated to be nuclear plants.

In October 1972, the Sierra Club was ready to translate these ideas into a broad energy policy statement. Using externalities and conservation as the policy's guiding tenets, the club called for the removal of subsidies "by internalization of environmental and social costs." To protect the poor from these energy increases, the club called for the inversion of the electric rate structure so that large users paid more for their power. The club further argued that "energy conservation must be made a major national goal." This would be accomplished by government legislation and changes in "personal attitudes" to adopt less wasteful living. The resolution adopted a series of conservation ideas as practical goals. While there was growing sentiment to oppose nuclear power in the club, there was no consensus, and the board passed only a resolution noting their concern about the possibility of a radioactive release as long as the Emergency Core Cooling System remained inadequately tested.[136]

With the broad tenets of their energy policy settled, environmentalists turned their attention to a renewed discussion of nuclear hazards. The nuclear test fallout debate had waned in the late sixties after John Kennedy signed the partial test ban treaty in 1963. But scientist activists now found safety problems in civilian nuclear power. The Union of Concerned Scientists, joined by the Sierra Club, Friends of the Earth, and others, had engaged the Atomic Energy Commission in an embarrassing round of hearings on the Emergency Core Cooling System (ECCS), a vital part of a reactor's safety system. As they questioned AEC witnesses, the UCS's champions, Daniel Ford and Henry Kendall, revealed the fears of many scientists that the ECCS was not sufficiently tested to ensure safety in an emergency shutdown condition. The ECCS hearings added a new argument to the antinuclear arsenal of reasons to oppose nuclear energy. The Sierra Club's 1972 resolution regarding the ECCS system had been in direct response to the success of the Union of Concerned Scientists.[137]

Dissident scientists also renewed the debate over low-level radiation exposure. Although extravagant claims of infant deaths had been made by physicist Ernest Sternglass of the University of Pittsburgh, the issue did not receive broad press attention until two Lawrence Livermore scientists began issuing warnings about exposure in 1969. John Gofman and Arthur Tamplin, two senior researchers for the laboratory, predicted seventeen thousand additional cases of cancer if the public received the annual radiation exposure level allowed by the AEC. The two scientists feared irreversible genetic mutation might occur from low doses of radiation. The AEC and the laboratory's efforts to intimidate Gofman and Tamplin made them heroes to the growing community of antinuclear activists and scientists. In 1971, John Gofman founded the antinuclear organization the Committee for Nuclear Responsibility.[138]

The battering of nuclear power's safety reputation eventually helped shift the position of environmental groups regarding nuclear power. The Sierra Club changed its position on nuclear power after an extensive debate especially at the chapter level. Although they supported the Sierra Club's criticism of specific nuclear problems, directors Will Siri and Laurence Moss continued to fight a general antinuclear resolution. But the distinctions Siri and Moss drew hardly mattered. Thermal pollution, the Emergency Core Cooling System, and low-level radiation exposure provided sufficient reason for the club to oppose any nuclear plant, which it did. Even as the club steadfastly argued that it was not opposed to nuclear power per se, it fought a large number of projects.

Between 1970 and 1972, the club supported a four-year moratorium for a nuclear plant in Oregon, demanded repeal of the insurance subsidies in the Price-Anderson Act, and opposed nuclear construction at Calvert Cliffs, Maryland; Davenport, California; Palisades and Midland, Michigan; and Pilgrim, Massachusetts. The most consequential action for California was the club's legal challenge to the Point Arena plant in Mendocino County.

Turning against Nuclear Power: Point Arena

In substance and style, Point Arena was emblematic of the Sierra Club's complete nuclear reversal since Bodega Bay. At an October 1971 press conference, executive director Mike McCloskey announced in a combative speech that the club would oppose construction of a nuclear plant at Point Arena, an isolated and scenic coastal site a few hours north of San Francisco. Until the Diablo controversy, the Sierra Club had planned to work with PG&E and the Resources Agency for approval of Point Arena. But the club now condemned the State of California's Resources Agency's siting committee system as undemocratic, illegal, and antithetical to recent environmental legislation. The Resources Agency's cooperation with PG&E was, McCloskey reported, "an indication of the supine posture the state takes toward utilities. We've had [a] state policy for some time of ignoring environmental questions." McCloskey hinted that the club would file suit to stop the siting committee process.[139] The announcement shocked state officials since it had been club members Will Siri and Richard Leonard who had participated in and encouraged the siting committee process in the first place. McCloskey now claimed that such an elite system was in violation of club principles.

Although the Sierra Club's public objections to Point Arena centered on coastal protection, the club hierarchy evinced a bias against the peaceful atom. They made this clear by the man they selected to fight the plant. At the conference, McCloskey brought along a number of environmental lawyers, but the one who must have made PG&E officials' blood boil was David Pesonen. The nuclear naysayer was back with a law degree and an attitude. Valedictorian of his Berkeley law school class, Pesonen returned a far more formidable opponent than before and determined to torment PG&E for the rest of the decade.

David Pesonen's return indicated how much the Sierra Club had changed. Galling conservatives, Pesonen fought the Point Arena plant using the same combination of safety issues and personal attacks that had brought him condemnation from the club at Bodega Bay.[140] "PG&E is not to be trusted to prevent radioactive contamination of the environ-

ment or to protect public safety in the event of a nuclear accident," Pesonen told the press. "The company is just brutally intent on destroying
the last stretch of undeveloped coastline. The only thing PG&E learned
from the Bodega Head defeat was to dress up its public relations."[141]
Richard Leonard demanded that Pesonen be fired if the club could not
"control" him. But Pesonen was no longer the extremist. It was Leonard
who was out of touch with the club, and president Raymond Sherwin,
who shared Pesonen's safety fears, rebuffed Leonard's appeal.[142]

The Sierra Club's Point Arena offensive showcased the new environmental movement's combination of environmental activism, legal tactics, and sympathetic expertise. Recruiting San Francisco Bay area
scientists, Pesonen used the aesthetic, anticorporate, and safety arguments he pioneered at Bodega Bay. In a pamphlet, "Power at Point
Arena," Pesonen brought together these points and included the new
concerns about thermal pollution and the findings of the Union of Concerned Scientists on the Emergency Core Cooling System.[143]

PG&E halted construction of the Point Arena facility in early 1973. The
decision reflected the Atomic Energy Commission's opposition more
than that of the Sierra Club. Still, the continuing problem of seismic
safety, an issue that Pesonen first raised at Bodega Bay, was the key reason the Point Arena site was such an easy victory. Moreover, the fight indicated to utilities that the Sierra Club would not limit itself in the tactics
or technical arguments it would use to stop power plant construction.
Although the Sierra Club was not yet on record as opposing nuclear
power, there was a clear antinuclear trend within the environmental
movement. And yet the energy debate remained isolated from the lives
of ordinary Americans. The events of 1973, however, forced the country
to confront the energy debate far sooner than anyone had expected.

Point Arena's defeat in early 1973 punctuated the conflict between environmentalists and advocates of energy growth. While it helped preserve California's coastline, it served as an example of the intractable
position of the peaceful atom's opponents. Environmentalists had no intention of shrinking from their commitment to limit energy consumption. Despite the well-publicized battles over power plants that arose
across the nation, the general public hardly noticed the growing
dilemma over energy use. Energy would move to the center of public
debate in 1973 with the Yom Kippur War and the Arab oil embargo.

The Energy Crisis

Although the energy crisis caught most of the public unaware, the utility industry had warned of shortages for years. Demand for electric

power for air conditioning had jumped faster than anticipated. By 1969 power industry officials claimed that the country would face a crisis by the early seventies unless regulators allowed them to accelerate power plant construction. Sympathetic AEC commissioner Wilfred Johnson admonished an industry audience, "Unless a solution is found, the economy and our standard of living may both falter and even decline, and the extent to which this would imperil the fabric of our society and our democratic institutions cannot be exaggerated." A good deal of the blame for this situation, business and industry publications pointed out, lay with the utilities and had little to do with public opposition to nuclear power. It was an industry, *Fortune* said, staffed with "unimaginative men, grown complacent on private monopoly and regulated profits." Poor forecasting, labor disputes, technical problems of nuclear manufacturers, and a proliferation of regulatory standards had utility executives howling for relief.[144]

The utility industry fought back, arguing that its problems were the fault of environmentalists. In advertising, various energy companies forewarned that "The Energy Crisis is threatening your way of Life!" Utilities, one ad declared, had taken adequate precautions to provide power through the seventies and eighties. "But then something happened. Public concern for the environment." A "rash of lawsuits" from environmentalists who had gone to extremes had delayed vital nuclear projects. Most of these delays had more to do with the industry's problems than with environmentalists, but Michael McCloskey warned Sierra Club directors that the industry offensive would stick unless the club could formulate a response and present it to the public.[145]

Exacerbating the energy squeeze was the eroding market control by multinational oil corporations as oil-producing nations increased prices and nationalized production. The Nixon administration gave energy issues high priority as early as 1971. In April 1973, the president called for expanding energy production but did not mention the idea of conserving energy. The conflict between energy companies and environmentalists prevented a consensus on the president's proposals. The energy industry hoped the oil embargo launched in October 1973 would shift the tide in their favor.

The Arab oil embargo was not America's finest hour. "You are going to give me gas or I will kill you," one motorist threatened a gas station attendant. He left with a full tank. Across the country, attendants began carrying guns to work, sometimes fatal fights broke out as motorists waited hours for a few gallons, and tank trucks were hijacked on the streets of New York City. Students wearing mittens and wool hats shivered in their classrooms, industries shut down due to a lack of fuel, and symbols of American luxury, such as recreation vehicles and large cars, went unsold. Those who hoped the crisis would unite the nation were given pause by the Texas bumper sticker that said of all Yankees: "Let the Bastards Freeze in the Dark." Watching the energy panic roil the nation, energy lobbyists joked confidently that the country would keep warm that winter of 1973–1974 by burning environmental protection laws.[146]

Excitement spread among energy companies as they recognized the opportunity to reverse their regulatory burden. Assuming that Americans would come to their senses and rise up in righteous indignation, politicians and lobbyists began drafting legislation that would suspend pollution laws, grant the president emergency powers, and strip away regulations slowing the construction of nuclear power plants. In early November, Richard Nixon proposed "Project Independence" and called for an effort on the scale of the Apollo space program to make the country energy self-sufficient. He called for emergency powers, minor conservation efforts, a relaxation of environmental standards, and increased power for the Atomic Energy Commission so that it could issue temporary operating licenses without public hearings.[147]

The nuclear industry used the crisis to blame environmental legislation for the shortages, even as it predicted another record-breaking year of nuclear orders.[148] "Boy what a field day the oil companies and everybody else were having with us," the Sierra Club's Washington lobbyist Brock Evans remembered. "Finally after four or five years on the defensive they could come back and they were the good people, honest people trying to provide energy supplies, and we were the bad people, extremists. . . . We were just sort of cowering in the trenches while the artillery thundered overhead, and there wasn't a thing we could do about it." Fearful of a public backlash against them, environmentalists tried to appear reasonable and accept short-term variances to pollution laws.[149]

But environmentalists had underestimated public support for their values. By the end of 1974, nuclear supporters were wondering how they had lost their way. Nixon had resigned in disgrace, and his Project Independence was being picked to pieces by various interest groups. No omnibus energy legislation would emerge in either the Nixon or the Ford administration. Proposals to expedite the nuclear regulatory process had fallen flat. Moreover, conservation efforts by Americans proved more effective than anyone had predicted. The public had risen in indignation, not against environmentalists, but against oil companies and the utility industry. Energy industries received the brunt of public anger at their windfall profits and the ratcheting upward of electricity rates. In 1974, plummeting demand and a financial crisis among utilities led them to cancel as many nuclear plants as they ordered. "The sudden and devastating economic crisis of 1974 is the most serious threat the utility industry has ever faced," one executive noted.[150]

As the tide of public opinion turned against corporations, the environmental movement staunched the flood of industry legislation. A Harris poll showed 83 percent of the public laying the blame for the crisis at the feed of oil companies and 75 percent condemning the federal government.[151] Calling the crisis "a plot to rip off the next generation," David Brower spoke for many when he intimated the existence of a conspiracy among industry and politicians. Brower's Friends of the Earth, by now the leading antinuclear environmental organization, charged Nixon with "trying to use the 'energy crisis' to bypass what insufficient legal means exist to protect the environment in order to hasten development of nuclear power."[152] By the end of January 1974, the big guns from consumer and environmental groups such as Ralph Nader and Barry Commoner were alleging oil company conspiracies. Environmental allies loaded Nixon's energy legislation with so many unacceptable provisions that he repudiated the bill.[153]

Even as they were halting industry-sponsored legislation, environmentalists used the energy crisis to promote their own energy policies of conservation, alternative sources, and limited use of nuclear power to the public. There was an assurance among activists that the energy crisis would provide a philosophical breakthrough among policy makers and the public. Alternative energy sources, such as solar and geothermal energy, found large constituencies, and conservation proposals met receptive audiences. Environmentalists called for a "complete reordering of our life priorities and lifestyle" toward conservation and limits.[154] As the Sierra Club noted, "America's attitudes toward energy conservation are changing overnight. . . . New habits of care are emerging; expectations of growth are changing. . . . Reduced energy consumption means less physical impact on the environment. . . . Energy limits may mean an end to the era of an auto dominated culture. What change could be more profound?"[155]

The energy crisis of 1973–1974 provided an opening for environmental laws and values. As Sierra Club president Lauerence Moss told the board of directors in January, Americans had awakened to the conservation ethic, which had worked far better in mitigating the effects of the fuel shortage than anyone had expected. While the federal government stalled on a comprehensive energy policy, activists at the state level were free to try their hand at energy policy. No state would benefit from this situation more than California, where environmental activists stood ready to push new energy legislation. The worst fears of nuclear proponents had been realized. The crisis had encouraged resentment against large corporations, expertise, and government. All these institutions needed credibility if the peaceful atom was to avoid negative scrutiny.

Toward a Nuclear Moratorium

With the public willing to entertain a conservation ethic, the Sierra Club was ready to move a step further against nuclear power. At the January 1974 board of directors meeting, the club debated a resolution to oppose nuclear plant construction until safety and waste disposal problems had been solved. The sides in the debate reflected old divisions. Lauerence Moss and Will Siri argued that the resolution would damage the club's effectiveness in offering alternatives. Dirty coal would simply be used instead of nuclear power. No energy source except for expensive solar power was without problems. Why should environmentalists oppose nuclear power when the alternatives were so unappealing?

Will Siri had prevented antinuclear resolutions in the past with these arguments, but the evolution of the energy debate since Diablo Canyon left him and Moss isolated. The sudden outpouring of antinuclear sentiment by the majority of regional club committees at the meeting surprised Siri. Although the Midwest committee remained opposed to a moratorium, four other committees, including two in California, favored it.

As the leader of Friends of the Earth, David Brower had lobbied the Sierra Club directors hard with moral arguments for a number of years, and these arguments tipped the balance. The most effective reasons opponents adduced were the ethics of leaving wastes and the genetic mutations for future generations.[156] As Edgar Wayburn later recalled of the vote, "The argument [was] made that it's much more dangerous to breathe in the effects of coal. Perhaps it is, in the short haul. . . . But burning coal as far as we know, is not going to affect future generations the way nuclear energy can. . . . I'm afraid for my children's children, for what the eventual fate of the biosphere is."[157] While other energy sources had their problems, nuclear power's long-term danger convinced environmentalists that it was the world's gravest threat.

The resolution of the nuclear issue allowed the Sierra Club to pursue a clear, if not publicly articulated, strategy to oppose nuclear power over all other energy sources. In a confidential memo to the club's executive committee, Michael McCloskey proposed a strategy to defeat nuclear power, accept coal as an interim fuel, and eventually shift the country to alternative energy sources and reduced per capita energy consumption. McCloskey argued that improving safety as advocated by the nuclear moratorium resolution was "too evanescent a goal" for practical politics. He rightly predicted that defining exactly when nuclear power was safe enough was beyond consensus. Externalities, he argued, should be the club's weapon to kill nuclear power first and then coal power: "We should try to tighten up regulation of the [nuclear] industry both to protect the public and with the expectation that this will add to the cost of the industry and render its economics less attractive. Our campaign stressing the hazards of nuclear power will supply a rationale for increasing regulation." As the regulations took their toll, utilities would switch to coal and eventually to alternative energy sources, the executive director speculated. McCloskey thought that the club could then obtain a moratorium against a weakened nuclear industry.[158] Safety demands, then, were intended as much to make nuclear power unattractive as to protect the public.

It was an honest assessment of the club's strategy, too honest and too Machiavellian. President Raymond Sherwin, who did not respect McCloskey, responded in indignation. "The Sierra Club's prosperity has always rested on our conscientious purpose to espouse the facts and the moment we waffle on the basic policy we embark upon a self-defeating enterprise in the wake of Watergate. I cannot think of any more devastating proposal than one that reeks of a conspiratorial campaign."[159]

McCloskey withdrew his memo, but the club unofficially followed his strategy and fought all nuclear power plants. McCloskey also worked with the coal industry and favored it as a "bridge fuel."[160] Moreover, this position became the unstated policy for California regulators by the late seventies.

The antinuclear alliance in California of scientists, consumer advocates, and environmentalists entered the troubled seventies with a clearly articulated rationale for opposing the cornucopian growth philosophy of the nuclear industry. Perhaps most important to this alliance was the power of the Sierra Club. The club was not the earliest antinuclear convert; Friends of the Earth preceded it. But the Sierra Club was the most important for California. It had a growing, activist membership and a capable lobbying team in Sacramento that could fight for energy conservation and antinuclear legislation.

These strengths in advocating energy legislation proved crucial. Environmentalists were more successful at working their nonmaterialist values into the regulatory system in California than in any other state. As a result, sympathetic energy regulation developed alongside the antinuclear movement. In the seventies, the energy bureaucracy and antinuclear movement would nurture and protect each other. Through this supportive relationship, the two would find the strength to confront and ultimately stop the peaceful atom. The evolution of energy regulation in California is the subject of the next chapter.

3

A Backdoor Approach to Nuclear Regulation

The Creation of the California Energy Commission

State regulation of electric power plants had long been a quiet contrast to California's contentious public versus private power debates. Since the twenties, there had been numerous attempts to weaken the private utilities in California with initiatives favoring various forms of public power agencies, and PG&E had fought epic battles with the Bureau of Reclamation over hydro power in the Central Valley. But these conflicts were over the issue of control of transmission lines and power sources. No one particularly cared how or where a power plant was built. The Public Utilities Commission, as was evident at Bodega Bay, had little inclination to question a company's choice of site.[1]

The controversy at Bodega Bay inaugurated a far-ranging transformation in state energy regulation and broke the autonomy of state utilities in building power plants. No one needed to explain to Charles DeTurk, director of California's Department of Parks and Recreation, how much the Bodega Head controversy had humbled the state's utilities; Pacific Gas and Electric would do that for him. In July 1963, the utility requested a meeting with DeTurk. The utility was in the midst of fighting for Bodega's life, but its executives knew the company had paid a price for its secretive methods. In violation of the Brown Act, PG&E

had held closed-door meetings with Sonoma County supervisors and obtained advance approval of Bodega. The company controlled the terms by which it shared land with Parks and Recreation and the University of California. And it had been unwilling to minimize the unsightly appearance of the plant's power lines. When citizens challenged PG&E, its officials had obtained background information on them and encouraged a congressional investigation. Yet it was left with nothing more than a $4 million hole in the ground. PG&E leadership knew they had to change their ways.

Under a new executive, PG&E resolved to compromise on the Nipomo Dunes site. When the ailing Norman Sutherland stepped down, the utility decided to go with leadership more attuned to the art of the deal than the more confrontational style that executives with engineering backgrounds seemed to favor. Robert Gerdes appeared to fit the bill. A lanky attorney with a Jimmy Stewart voice, Gerdes resolved to imbue PG&E with a more conciliatory philosophy. Believing "better a bad settlement than a good lawsuit," Gerdes would make the decision to pull out at Bodega and negotiate with the company's opponents.[2] Hat in hand, the utility would seek state and conservationist cooperation.

Invited to San Francisco, Charles DeTurk entered Robert Gerdes' office to find George Collins and Doris Leonard of Conservation Associates seated with other PG&E executives. Collins and Leonard had been brought in as consultants to advise PG&E how to deal with California agencies and conservation groups. DeTurk could not have been happier at PG&E's new "consciousness" of the siting problem. In the meeting, Gerdes demonstrated extraordinary flexibility by offering to move the proposed plant up to a mile inland to avoid the new park. PG&E's chief executive emphasized his willingness to work with state agencies and conservation groups to form a new partnership in power plant siting. Pleased with the meeting, DeTurk left the office believing he had found a new mechanism to deal with utility, state, and private concerns and resolve them in a quiet cooperative fashion.[3]

Within a year, this new system was formalized as the Resources Agency's power plant siting committee, which included representatives from every department concerned with resource planning and safety. Conservation Associates and the Sierra Club, as the state's leading conservationist group, would also participate in site selection. The state empowered the committee to sign a memorandum of understanding indicating that it accepted a particular site. The state had gained a greater role in plant siting, but PG&E could be pleased that the intrusion into private enterprise was minimal. Utilities would pick sites, and the state would only exercise an informal veto. Planning for the future appeared to remain in the hands of private utilities.

Pacific Gas and Electric's modest request for state assistance in site selection opened the door to a new era of energy regulation. No one in Gerdes' office that day understood that their informal agreement would mushroom about ten years later into a state regulatory body known as the Energy Commission of over five hundred individuals that was philosophically opposed to nuclear power. The new agency was far more powerful in mission, structure, and procedures than the siting committee it replaced. All of its functions aimed to reduce energy consumption and the construction of power plants, increase public participation, and eliminate the utilities' power to control, or "capture," agencies. The power plant siting system of the sixties merely acted as a transition to new environmentally friendly and democratic regulation that compromised and negotiated far less, and litigated more.

The roots of this regulatory transformation lay in an expanding state bureaucracy and the influence of nonmaterial values on state regulators, politicians, and scientists. In particular, the growing capacity of the state in the postwar period made it possible for regulators to act without relying on industry expertise. With expanding state budgets, resource managers could ambitiously broaden their professional jurisdiction over questions concerning land use, recreation, and public safety.[4] Siting of nuclear power plants was part of this general drive by officials to push at the boundaries of state control.

Their new influence, regulators hoped, would also achieve philosophical goals. DeTurk and other officials had sympathized with the preservationist sentiment of conservationists, and they hoped to augment their profession's emphasis on efficiency and economic growth with nonmaterialist values. The resource administrators' prime concern had been the efficient use of resources, such as the coastline, to promote economic expansion. But their new role as environmental "stewards" demanded more attention to quality-of-life issues relative to economic ones. The Bodega controversy and later nuclear projects presented them with the quandary of how to preserve California's coast without crippling economic and energy expansion. Expressing this mixture of professional and personal values, state officials tried the difficult trick of promoting nuclear power as a means to preserve California's coastal beauty. Under the notion of "multiple use," state planners wanted to use the strategic siting of nuclear plants to control population density, open private land for recreational use, and prevent coastal erosion. Ultimately, officials could not carry it off.

Part of the reason for their failure lay in the siting committee's rather retrograde private style of regulation that was typical of Progressive Era and New Deal. It relied on informal negotiations by government and industry leaders.[5] Democratic control of technology, as David Pesonen advocated, was an unthinkable option to state officials. The regulatory system they operated in favored elite negotiation in informal settings. Regulatory agencies had a wide latitude to make public decisions without consulting the public, judiciary or legislature. Resource administrators read public sentiment and acted as their representatives. Including what they perceived to be an uninformed public was redundant and inefficient. Admittedly, the new arrangement was more public than any other mechanism yet seen in the utility industry. The mere presence of conservationists in the meeting was a tacit admission by PG&E that the public could put limits on its siting discretion. But in limiting discussions to conservation elites, the precedent was only a slight tremor in regulation, rather than the tectonic movement toward democracy that followed.

The new regulatory arrangement broke down as it failed to keep pace with shifting environmental values and demands for participatory democracy. When the power plant siting committee tried to promote nuclear power as a recreational resource, those excluded from the decision-making process called for greater democracy and used environmentalism, safety concerns, and fears of overdevelopment to derail its plans. Environmentalists and residents near proposed power plants objected to state planning mechanisms that excluded them in the interest of expedited nuclear construction. Joined by like-minded scientists and politicians, antinuclear groups worked to limit the independence of state bureaucrats who they feared were likely to become "captured" promoters of the industry they regulated.

Typifying the spirit of the "new social regulation" sweeping all areas of environmental and consumer issues in the seventies, California activists proposed a new kind of agency. The California Energy Commission, based on nonmaterialist values of public participation and environmentalism, was a more politically contentious body than the power plant siting committee and provided for ample public involvement.[6] It limited the possibility of agency capture by means of public hearings, equal representation of all interested parties, and an expanded, impartial bureaucratic structure.[7] Most important, the new commission's mission was to halt uncontrolled energy growth and limit its impact on the environment. This attitude would place it squarely in the path of state utilities rushing to build nuclear power plants.

Nonmaterialism affected not only government institutions but the way experts, in and out of government, looked at technical issues. Concerned with placing limits on growth, key experts offered new energy perspectives that supported the environmental view. Some scholars have argued that scientists are motivated by professional interests and respond to the environmental ethic only when goaded by public opinion. The scientific community was, however, no more immune to nonmaterialist values than was the public at large.[8] The environmental sympathies of scientists allowed them to ask questions and reveal problems that the nuclear and utility industry had not addressed. It was neither values nor science alone that spurred this inquiry, but the interaction of the two that was critical.

The ideas of scientists and the values of environmentalists, in turn, found new forums in California politics. Politicians, too, were attracted to the message of antinuclear activists and sought to change the values of regulatory legislation. As the capacity of the Golden State's government and legislature expanded, these politicians no longer needed to rely on industry experts for their information, but could turn to a whole community of dissident experts.[9] Politicians had the resources and expertise to look askance at industry officials pleading for regulatory relief to speed power plant construction. The rise of such a powerful antinuclear network of environmental lobbyists, scientists, and politicians made possible the creation of an agency with nonmaterialistic values.[10]

The victory of environmentalists in energy regulation resulted in a new system that was more legalistic, more subject to judicial review, and more limiting of regulatory discretion than the old. Moreover, in their own view, environmentalists supplanted regulators as guardians of the public interest. The role of regulator shifted to that of an adjudicator who made decisions, not on private negotiations, but on a publicly compiled evidentiary record.[11] The captured agencies and decision-making process that environmental critics derided proved remarkably accessible when challenged.[12]

This transformation of the energy regulation field by 1974 would have profound implications for nuclear energy. Activists had succeeded in writing nonmaterialist values into law. If law is seen as the expression of community will, it was clear that the California public was no longer sure that unrestrained growth was a fundamental right. As the era of resource abundance drew to a close in the seventies, citizens called for greater community involvement in what had been the utility's private decisions over energy and land use. The responsibility for planning was now in the hands of state regulators. This expanded state capacity would provide a new forum for California antinuclear activists. As such, it would be an important force for halting the peaceful atom in the Golden State.

Regulation in the Early Sixties: The State Gains a Role

The early move toward greater state and utility cooperation was dictated largely by the ambitions and philosophy of state regulators. Bodega had cemented the marriage between utilities and state resource planners, but the desire of state officials to assert greater control over nuclear issues emerged earlier, in the late fifties, from the public reaction to atmospheric testing of nuclear weapons and ocean waste disposal controversies. Prior to these episodes, states were interested in sharing regulation of the atom with the federal government in hopes of promoting nuclear power construction. Some states established advisory panels and atomic energy coordinators' offices to investigate atomic issues and act as liaisons with federal agencies to express state concerns regarding nuclear regulation. Moreover, California and other states took advantage of Atomic Energy Commission training to develop their own expertise on atomic issues.

Despite the heightened safety concern, the aim of these early activities was usually to smooth the way for nuclear development. In establishing an advisory panel in 1959, Governor Edmund "Pat" Brown asked the scientists to explore the "mysterious and dangerous maze of atomic progress. . . . I want to be as sure as I can . . . that what we are trying to do is worth it." The panel was instructed to determine if more state regulation was needed to ensure the safety of the state's citizens. The governor also asked it to look into any possible atomic project the state might support. Thus Brown hoped the scientists would calm fears and promote the atom in California.[13]

But at a surprisingly early stage, and well before conservationists in California, state regulators expressed environmental concerns about nuclear power and demanded limits to the growth of radioactive emissions. They protested when radioactive waste disposal containers were dumped beyond the Golden Gate near the Farallon Islands and near Santa Cruz Island in Southern California.[14] Between 1958 and 1961, California officials pressed the AEC to have the dumping take place at depths of two thousand fathoms, beyond the feeding depths of most commercial and game fish. The disposal controversy and a fatal accident at an experimental reactor in Idaho raised important doubts in the mind of state officials as to the adequacy of the Atomic Energy Commission's approved disposal requirements. Recognizing that the amount of waste would expand enormously, the director of the Department of Fish and Game, Walter Shannon, asked California's atomic coordinator, Alexander Grendon, "Is it not unrealistic to assume the oceans have an infinite capacity to dilute [radioactive wastes]?" He warned Grendon, "Somewhere along the way we are going to have to draw the line and say 'This much and no more.'"[15]

The dumping episode declined in importance, in part because the AEC stopped issuing licenses for sea disposal, but the environmental concern of California resource officials endured. Once alarmed by the waste issue, they expanded their inquiry into atomic affairs including human safety. Walter Shannon in particular argued for a holistic view of radionuclides from "fallout, to nuclear vessels, to shore based reactors, to continued waste disposal. It would seem appropriate at this stage of our ignorance, that we assume increases in background radiation are potentially detrimental and that the state should make every effort to control those amounts added to the environment."[16]

State officials turned their attention to the embryonic nuclear industry and expressed their outrage at the failure of utilities and the federal government to consult them on siting decisions. In letters to PG&E and the Department of the Interior, Walter Shannon protested the approval of the small Humboldt nuclear power plant without consulting the Department of Fish and Game and demanded proper consultation before PG&E proceeded with its still nascent plans for Bodega Bay.[17]

These turf wars revealed growing doubts on the part of state officials that the AEC had safety questions in hand, and these questions pushed their way into the emerging siting debate. State officials were irked that the AEC continued to approve reactor sites "before the State has any indication that a site is being considered." Unimpressed with the AEC's vague guidelines for siting and the dearth of clear facts regarding the health and safety risks of nuclear plants, resource administrators determined to establish their own criteria to protect urban areas.[18] The Resources Agency formed an ad hoc siting committee in late 1960 to make recommendations as to what criteria the state should use in determining where nuclear plants should be built. At first, power plant safety was the key concern of the committee. Members gave little consideration to how a plant might impede recreation or coastal access.[19] There was great disagreement among state agencies as to how restrictive siting had to be. Fish and Game led the way, calling for extensive ecology studies and exclusion zones near populated areas. By contrast, the Public Utilities Commission, long considered by critics as an agency captured by utility interests, argued for a "no restriction" policy and accepted designer assurances that a power plant could be built safely in Golden Gate Park. This was far more permissive than the AEC's policy, but was just the position utilities favored. State resource officials, however, were moving closer to the views of Fish and Game. They decided to establish a state policy "covering catastrophic accidents and based on population density, potential land use, and protection of freshwater supplies."[20]

The potential influence of the Resources Agency over nuclear power was great, but it was influence that had almost never been used. Questions of whether wildlife should be protected and whether plants should intrude on state parks of other scenic areas had been left unregulated.[21] The Public Utilities Commission would listen to the concerns of other state agencies, but it was under no obligation to follow their recommendations. The Resources Agency could act as an intervenor in AEC hearings, but there too it had only the right to be heard. The best the Resources Agency could hope for was that if it made its desires known, a utility would be forewarned and the AEC might be inclined to oppose a site.[22]

The nuclear siting issue pointed to a severe land use problem for a state with explosive population growth. California officials had no authority to control development of land that the state did not own.[23] In the early sixties, the right of individuals to develop their land was limited only by local zoning laws. And these restrictions were often by passed by accommodating county or city officials. This posed an insuperable obstacle to rational land policy, since 61 percent of the coast was in private hands.[24]

The Resources Agency's ambitions for land use planning received vital support from conservation groups. A band of San Francisco activists began to write and lobby for broad land management practices. In addition to the Sierra Club's work to create Point Reyes National Seashore, a number of other organizations worked to inspire planning legislation to preserve California's natural beauty. Catherine Kerr, wife of University of California president Clark Kerr, led the drive to stop the filling of San Francisco Bay that culminated in 1965 in the historic establishment of the Bay Conservation Development Commission. The Planning and Conservation League formed in 1965 to lobby for coastal protection legislation in Sacramento. Its work was largely inspired by California Tomorrow, a nonprofit organization that had published the influential work *California Going, Going . . .* , which called for integrated statewide planning to deal with the "hordes of people" who threatened to overrun the state's beauty and resources.[25] The problem was particularly acute on the coast since nearly 85 percent of the state's residents lived within thirty miles of the Pacific.[26]

These planning advocates came from relatively moderate conservation ranks. There were few antigrowth advocates such as David Pesonen. California Tomorrow members, and individuals such as Richard Leonard and Will Siri within the Sierra Club, did not oppose population and economic expansion. Nor did these individuals feel the populist spirit as Pesonen did. While Pesonen railed against specialists and the denial of local control at Bodega, these individuals preferred elite stewardship. They were likely to agree with one AEC official who discouraged broad public participation in hearings, fearing that the proceedings could turn into a "town meeting." It was far better for administrators and managers to conserve, protect, and develop the state's natural resources for the public than to allow the excesses of democracy to ruin rational management.[27]

Elements of this philosophy had been advocated for over a century. Since the Gold Rush, California resource policy and legislation focused almost entirely on promoting economic growth over quality of life. If state officials advocated greater control over resource planning, it was not because of any environmental ethic but because they believed natural resource management was a more efficient and just method of allocating the state's natural bounty. In this tradition, the Resources Agency's first head, William Warne, announced in 1961 that he considered "conservation, efficiency, and economy" its prime objectives.[28]

Inspired by conservationists, however, state resource leaders began reassessing their mission to incorporate new values. In a soul-searching conference in 1964, Resources Agency administrators regretted that their past emphasis on gross productivity had damaged the state's aesthetic resources. They believed the state needed a greater emphasis on public service and quality-of-life values rather that on industry promotion. Expropriating California Tomorrow's dictum, state administrators asked, "What do we want California to be?"[29] Their answer was to propose a master plan for resource use that would preserve environmental amenities while accommodating development pressures.[30] Thus their philosophy had qualitative and quantitative aspects. Electric power plants, and, as will be shown, especially nuclear plants, fell within this new regulatory attitude. But the Resources Agency still needed authority to convince utilities to cooperate with its land use planning objectives.

The Power Plant Siting Committee

Bodega provided just the wedge state officials needed. Scenic, seismic, slated for a park and marine research facility, the Head could not have been a worse location for a power plant short of putting the facility in Yosemite Valley. With the utilities cowed into cooperation after PG&E's debacle and conservationists in the Sierra Club willing to help select sites, the Resources Agency now had the consensus it needed to use power plant siting to achieve its planning goals. Resources Agency improvised in the absence of statutory authority and developed a power plant siting committee composed of representatives of all Resources Agency departments. The committee had the authority to sign a memorandum of understanding with the utility stating that the agency did not oppose a power plant as long as it met certain aesthetic, ecological, and land use restrictions. The agency went further and drafted power plant siting guidelines to direct utilities in their early surveying of prospective locations.[31]

Nuclear power plants seemed a perfect vehicle to effect land use planning. Atomic Energy Commission regulations required utilities to purchase substantial acreage around any site to establish and exclusion zone that limited residential population. Hampered by the rights of private ownership and a lack of funds to purchase beachfront property, Resources Agency officials recognized that utility land could become quasi-public and made accessible for transient populations interested in recreation. The sites could also act as a buffer against residential development and would channel this growth away from state parks or beaches.[32] Patterning their ideas on the "multiple use" management of the national forests, state officials believed that development of nuclear power and enjoyment of the coast could coexist.

Resource officials carefully probed the conservation community in hopes of generating a popular base of support for their policy. They found their audiences willing to accept this type of multiple use of the coastline if it would improve public access and not diminish the aesthetic quality of the area. An ominous dissent was sounded by Pesonen's Northern California Association to Preserve Bodega Head and Harbor, which accused state officials of "scientific prostitution," but generally the officials thought they had developed a policy that would avoid public resistance of the kind evidenced at Bodega and Malibu.[33] Resources Agency administrators might have done well to listen to the Bodega Association's exaggerated accusation of agency capture.

While state agencies had not sold their integrity to the nuclear industry, they were now hitching their agenda to the fortunes of nuclear power. To carry out this coastal policy, the state became promoters of nuclear plants regardless of local objections.[34] And while the siting system was not a captured process, it was inherently undemocratic. Those involved in site selection were not interested in opening up the process to the public. Agency officials, in fact, argued that public opinion had no influence on their decisions.[35] This viewpoint would prove unworkable as the public demanded greater access to such decisions.

Armed with their informal polling of conservationists, state administrators pursued this nuclear-recreation-aesthetic balancing act. The siting committee pressed forward, reviewing a variety of sites along the Pacific coast for plant construction. Through 1969 the Resources Agency entered into ten agreements on proposed sites with every major utility in the state.[36] The Sierra Club participated in the selection of the Diablo Canyon and Rancho Seco nuclear sites.[37] The agency's records demonstrate how state officials sought to use nuclear power to further their land use planning ideas. At Southern California Edison's San Onofre nuclear plant, the Resources Agency negotiated a deal that would expand public access to adjoining beaches. At Point Arena on California's north coast, siting committee officials worked with PG&E, encouraging it to purchase additional lands to preserve scenic coastline and then open it up for recreational use. Near San Diego, state officials encouraged San Diego Gas and Electric to purchase a site near Torrey Pines State Park in hopes that the plant would limit the suburban sprawl inching ever closer to the park. Bolsa Island, a nuclear-powered desalinization project sponsored by every major Southland utility and the Metropolitan Water District, particularly excited officials since it would not use the Southland's coastline and would protect the sands along Sunset Beach from erosion. Moreover, before public fears of thermal pollution overtook the utility, industry, resource officials valued the warm water discharged by power plants since it attracted sport fish.[38]

The siting committee's greatest victory was also its most controversial, Diablo Canyon. PG&E negotiators evinced a great deal of flexibility in their anxiousness that the siting committee be happy with the final arrangement.[39] Robert Gerdes had already resolved to avoid the Nipomo dunes. A senior engineer recalled that company officials had informed Gerdes that "Nipomo would be another Bodega. . . . Gerdes was still bleeding from Bodega and said that if [Nipomo] was trouble, he wanted no part of it."[40] PG&E cast about for other locations in the area. In early October, PG&E asked the siting committee to inspect a site a half mile from Avila Beach and west of San Luis Obispo in Wild Cherry Canyon. The site was privately owned ranch land, and a power plant would open up the land for recreational access. The committee recognized there were potential problems since the area was heavily used for commercial and recreational fishing, but after touring the area the officials enthusiastically recommended that further explorations be done. After settling on the nearby Diablo Canyon site, Fish and Game began explorations to determine how much abalone and kelp would be affected.[41] Satisfied by the inspection, the Resources Agency was ready to sign an agreement.

When officials announced the Diablo compromise in 1966, they hailed it as an example of rational cooperation among industry, state, and "responsible" conservationists toward land use planning goals. It appeared to correct all the problems of the Bodega affair. It preserved Nipomo in its current condition, and opened up formerly restricted land to public access. While there were some minor faults in the plant's sandstone foundation, they had not been active for millions of years, much longer than the Bodega or Malibu faults.

The splintering of the Sierra Club over this issue, however, was a portent of the trouble that this new system would face in winning approval of future plant sites. Although the ejection of David Brower and his disciples seemed to indicate a victory for the conservatives, the controversy within the club changed it forever. The club had broken up because of the undemocratic nature of the Diablo decision. The exclusive style of Will Siri and the Leonards was discarded in the process. The club refused to sanction any more power plants and moved to oppose future projects.

Although the Resources Agency continued to negotiate and sign agreements with the utilities, the loss of conservationist support for the process undermined the siting committee's authority. This was crucial, as one representative admitted, since the authority of the committee was based on a "good faith understanding."[42] As long as the siting system suited the utilities and conservationists, the agreements had meaning. But either side could walk away if consensus was not achieved. By the late sixties, both sides believed the system needed to be changed. A regulatory crisis forced the champions of nuclear power to ask for a new system.

Regulatory Crisis: Bolsa Island

The late sixties were years of optimism for the nuclear industry nationally, but increasing frustrations in California eventually led to a crisis. Reactor orders had skyrocketed nationally as the industry entered what has been called the "great bandwagon market." But in California the number of successful projects was thin. Although nuclear facilities at Rancho Seco, San Onofre, and Diablo all moved forward, the number of proposed and then abandoned sites was larger than this paltry list. In addition to the fatalities at Bodega and Malibu, utilities came up empty at Davenport, Point Arena, Bolsa Island, and Point Conception. And the above listing does not even include sites that were quickly passed up based on the *suspicion* that there would be opposition, such as a site proposed in Orange County. If activists mounted effective opposition, the utilities lost. The power plant siting committee had achieved some success in avoiding Bodega-like controversies, but the shrinking availability of sites due to seismic problems, scientific uncertainty, and citizen opposition dogged the industry.

The best example of continued siting problems was the Bolsa Island desalinization project begun in 1964. The project enjoyed many advantages, but was still canceled. Many officials favored the island concept as an imaginative solution to coastal development pressures. With federal subsidies and the backing of every Southland utility, as well as the Atomic Energy Commission, the Joint Committee of Atomic Energy, the Department of the Interior, and Lyndon Johnson, this demonstration desalinization plant located south of Los Angeles should have sailed through the regulatory process.[43] The utilities involved in the project claimed that they canceled the plant owing to its poor economics. But the economic rationale given to the public masked larger siting problems, including public opposition, seismic design uncertainties, infighting among utilities, and an uncertain regulatory climate.[44] It was a prime example of the failure of science to live up to its image as a solution to social ills.

Advocates touted projects such as Bolsa Island as a positive example of an industry/government partnership of "creative federalism," where federal regulation and promotion of Great Society projects would serve to benefit the public.[45] Bolsa Island was the culmination of proposals begun during the Kennedy administration to solve California and the Southwest's water shortage through desalinization projects funded in part by federal grants. Early projections predicted huge savings if the water was made by large nuclear plants. With an enthusiastic send-off by LBJ, who remarked that the project was a demonstration of the government and utilities' "will and power to act" in a joint endeavor, the project was formalized in November 1967.[46] The Metropolitan Water District would operate the facility in cooperation with the Los Angeles Department of Water and Power, Southern California Edison, and San Diego Gas & Electric. Even before they signed the cooperative agreement, however, some of the utilities were looking for a graceful exit. As at Bodega and Malibu, the role of antinuclear opposition played an important role.

The Department of Water and Power was still recovering from its shellacking at Malibu when it agreed to the Bolsa project. With its hopes for Malibu destroyed, LADWP became desperate to find an acceptable site for nuclear plant construction. But when questions regarding the seismic worth of the Bolsa site surfaced, LADWP reevaluated its commitment. The AEC's divisions over the Mailbu site's seismic hazards did not bode well for Bolsa Island. In private conversations with the staff of the Joint Committee on Atomic Energy, LADWP's chief engineer, Eugene Koffman, noted that a "blue ribbon panel" was ready to conclude that the Bolsa Island plant would need design modifications to withstand earthquake hazards. Some panel members resigned because they did not believe seismic considerations were taken seriously.[47] Koffman and JCAE staff knew the site would be "strenuously contested" since the Sunset Beach Chamber of Commerce was raising money to intervene in PUC and AEC hearings.[48] It was easy to foresee an embarrassing Malibu-like cross-examination of witnesses by intervenor lawyers, headlines discussing differences between experts, and prolonged hearings while the proposal withered. Koffman hinted to the JCAE staff that the utility was looking for a "face-saving excuse" to withdraw from the project.[49]

The project had been a difficult one from the beginning. The rivalry between a municipal utility like LADWP and a private company such as Southern California Edison had made for a tense venture. Government officials complained privately that "none of the participants . . . appear willing to relinquish 1 prerogative to permit the project to go ahead."[50] As much as government and industry liked to think of their relationship as a partnership to further the common good, Bolsa Island indicated that utilities had a hard time overcoming historic rivalries.

Two months after Koffman's conversation with the JCAE, the Department of Water and Power had not yet found the right excuse to withdraw and signed the participation agreement. There they stood at the signing ceremony, various government and utility leaders, all smiles and handshakes. What appeared to be a new era of limitless water supplied by the atom through "creative federalism" was a facade meant to hide the substantial cooperative and technical problems the project faced.[51]

It was practically a relief for the participants when revised estimates in early 1968 showed the project cost had jumped from $444 million to $765 million. The utilities attributed most of the increase to an amazing failure to factor inflation into the original estimate and to the costs of safety redesign and construction. Executives found it hard to explain how some of the largest utilities in the country made this fantastic oversight.[52] The utilities had their face-saving excuse. "Everybody was waiting for the other guy to pull the plug," one observer admitted after Southern California Edison withdrew in August of 1968.[53] Bolsa Island's failure demonstrated that the combination of seismic hazards, coastal development, and antinuclear opposition had created a de facto moratorium on the development of new nuclear power plant sites in California. The use of economic excuses was typical in the utility industry to hide serious technical and organizational problems.[54]

The economic justification for canceling Bolsa Island served to gloss over the economic and regulatory problems the electric utility industry faced. Part of the reason Bolsa Island was too expensive was that safety costs relating to seismic hazards had been forced into the plant's price tag. By demanding greater safety measures, opposition at Bodega Bay and Malibu had a telling effect on the costs of later power plants. It was not recognized or referred to as such, but Bolsa Island was an example of how "externalities" could change the attractiveness of a power source. Environmentalists would later consciously advocate safety measures in part to force up the price of power sources they opposed. The poor economics of Bolsa Island despite significant federal support demonstrated that the postwar alliance of science, government, and industry was not an effective remedy for all of society's problems. California's chronic water shortage defied cost-effective technical solutions.

Rather than recognize this bald reality, nuclear advocates upped the stakes by calling for draconian regulatory reform to crush public opposition.[55] The near certainty that every nuclear proposal would meet with opposition led California congressman Chet Holifield to think about creating a larger superagency that would clear a path through the increasingly complex regulatory thicket.[56] Chet Holifield had more than a passing interest in nuclear power. The leading authority on the Joint Committee on Atomic Energy, Holifield had a passion for nuclear issues that earned him the name "Mr. Atomic Energy." Nuclear power, Holifield believed, was the only way to meet the country's growing needs. The crisis, he wrote to an industry official, "is so clear to me, and it is so urgent that, for the first time in my life, I am aware of the meaning of my age and the shortness of probable time which I have to work on the problem."[57] But he perceived it as a crisis of energy supply only. Convinced energy was necessary to economic health, Holifield did not consider cutting back energy demand. Holifield instead proposed a fantastic project to overcome the "kooks" who were holding up new sites.[58]

Holifield's solution was typical of his New Deal ethos. The grand scale of projects such as TVA, the Manhattan Project, and Hoover Dam impressed him. Holifield proposed some "big solutions to the big problems." If San Onofre was the only site acceptable in Southern California, he reasoned, why not build scores of power plants right there? Holifield offered an idea of establishing a "reactor park," an oxymoron that environmentalists hated. An association of all Southland utilities would own and operate the dozens of reactors in the complex.[59] Holifield and his Republican colleague Craig Hosmer proposed to Governor Ronald Reagan that the state consider establishing a power plant siting authority with greater regulatory teeth than the Resources Agency committee possessed. As the two California congressmen envisioned it, the agency could purchase and develop land for reactor parks and provide a one-stop authority to overcome any conflicts between electrical need and "other public values," including environmental concerns.[60]

But California's major utilities fled from the medicine of Holifield and Hosmer's reactor park proposal.[61] While the idea was helpful to a utility that had yet to find a site, such as the Los Angeles Department of Water and Power, neither Pacific Gas and Electric nor Southern California Edison was anxious to see a quasi-governmental agency take over siting when they had already obtained the best spots on the coast for themselves, or so they thought.[62] Even more disturbing, Edison privately informed Holifield that the price of building nuclear plants was too high. In a 1969 letter, Southern California Edison's president, William Gould, declared that Edison was scaling back its commitment and planning to build only a couple of nuclear plants at San Onofre. The uncertain regulatory atmosphere and rising costs of reactor components, Gould claimed, were no longer conducive to atomic construction.[63]

But elements of Holifield and Hosmer's plan did appeal to the utilities, such as creating a superagency, a "one-stop shopping" concept, capable of expediting site approval over public resistance. The Resources Agency power plant siting committee was unable to quell public dissent, and even the committee opposed some plant proposals because of pollution problems. The utility industry wanted to vest their friend the PUC with the power to overrule the siting committee and other recalcitrant government agencies. The utilities correctly assumed that when asked to choose between pollution standards and building more power plants, the PUC would choose the latter. When an air pollution control board blocked expansion of Southern California Edison's fossil fuel plant at Huntington Beach, for example, the PUC ordered construction anyway, citing dire need for power. This arrangement failed when state courts blocked the PUC order, leaving ultimate siting authority unresolved.[64]

The Failure of Pro-Utility Reform

Having been blocked by the courts at Huntington Beach, utilities needed to obtain legislative relief from its political allies. John Briggs, a conservative Republican assemblyman from Orange County, was chairman of the Joint Committee on Atomic Development and Space and anxious to see Bolsa revived. He drew inspiration from Holifield and Hosmer's proposals. In early 1970 with the support of utilities and the Reagan administration, Briggs's bill AB 818 became the first legislation introduced in California providing statutory authority for the siting process.[65] Although it applied to all types of plants, nuclear power so dominated discussion of electrical power that the press called AB 818 the "nuclear siting bill."

It is indicative of the utilities' desires that Briggs patterned much of the bill's language on the Resources Agency's power plant siting policy standards and added the clause that the PUC would hold preemptive authority over other state agencies. The power plant committee would merely approve or veto sites suggested by the utility and had no authority to determine site location.[66] Thus the origins of state regulation of the atom began as a pro-utility effort to use the state government to speed the regulatory process.

While the bill might have passed in 1964 when only a handful of individuals outside the industry cared about such matters, in 1970 the legislation ran straight into the antigrowth environmental movement. Because of Diablo Canyon controversy, the Sierra Club opposed any legislation that eased developing the California coast. "The Nipomo Dunes controversy quite clearly was the immediate stimulus for advancing the idea" of restricting coastal development, Will Siri recalled.[67] Board members Edgar Wayburn wrote: "The Sierra Club simply cannot agree that power production should take precedence over every other aspect of our coast. For this reason alone we will resist the whole premise of doubling power production every 7 to 10 years. . . . At the present time, the discussion isn't so much over the relative merits and different methods of producing power, but the premise of spiraling power production."[68] Under the Phillip Berry regime, the Sierra Club resolved in May 1970 that the negative influence of power plants was "unmistakable and undeniable." The club opposed the "inevitability of continued escalation of power needs."[69] It did not take an antinuclear position until 1974, but this declaration was a turning point in the club's position on energy use. In the past it had condemned sites only if they threatened scenic areas. The club's 1970 resolution argued that any augmentation in electrical supply was an environmental threat. The club was not opposing nuclear power per se, but by condemning future electrical expansion it would oppose all nuclear construction.[70]

California's other environmental associations also concluded that the peaceful atom was the key threat to the coastline. The nuclear power plants that state officials had promoted as the solution to coastal planning were condemned by California Tomorrow as the "dreariest of manmade monuments." The exponential growth in power plant construction, the Planning and Conservation League feared, would have greater influence on the coast "than any foreseeable development."[71] Wherever they confronted power plants, environmentalists were finding problems. Coal and oil offered unacceptable levels of pollution, and the once promised savior, nuclear power, was running into negative press for the effects of thermal pollution. Environmentalists were coming to realize that there was no escape from the dilemma of growth.[72]

The now substantial environmental lobby in Sacramento rallied its legislative supporters to defeat the Briggs bill.[73] Assemblyman Edwin Z'berg, environmentalists' best ally in Sacramento, denounced AB 818 as "one of the worst environmental bills to come along in many years."[74] The Sierra Club's John Zierold, with the help of engineer Charles Washburn who had helped Fred Eissler during the Diablo controversy, came up with a headline-catching statistic. They showed that current nuclear construction plans would lead to a plant on California's beautiful coast every four miles.[75] At first, environmentalists tried to alter the bill to ensure that aesthetic and environmental values were preserved.[76] The conservative state senate, however, gutted the environmental amendments. But the Sierra Club was able to prevent any revised bill from passing. Armed with threats of political retribution, John Zierold managed to pressure lawmakers to oppose the bill. AB 818 died in committee.

It was a crucial victory, planting a seed of doubt as to the wisdom of the utility industry's plans. Many lawmakers would look askance when later bills tried to rejuvenate the one-stop shopping concept the utilities treasured.[77] Briggs failed at reviving the bill in 1971, even though he eliminated any positive mention of nuclear power. Utilities also asked that power plants be exempt from any coastal siting bill, predicting potential blackouts after 1974 if construction plans were slowed. But politicians no longer accepted the utility industry's dire predictions of electrical shortages at face value. Republican assembly leader Paul Priolo remarked that he had heard the industry's dire warnings before, but was more "educated" this time. Pro-utility bills went nowhere.[78] The industry would never get another chance to tailor a bill to its liking.

Dismantling Pro-Growth Regulation

With public attitudes on their side, environmentalists not only stalled utility legislation, but also launched an offensive to destroy the siting committee and the regulatory philosophy behind it. The Sierra Club's Point Arena offensive had the dual aims of protecting the California coast and exterminating the power plant siting committee. The Sierra Club's suit against the Resources Agency was illustrative of just how much the regulatory climate had changed by the early seventies toward a far less negotiated style. The club's suit against the Resources Agency marked a new period where environmentalists relied on judicial review of regulatory decisions. Until the early seventies, the courts had allowed agencies wide latitude to act in the public interest. Environmentalists were now finding the courts an effective forum when agencies made unsatisfactory decisions.[79] They further maintained that the "citizen law suit" was the best means of obstructing decisions made by captured regulatory agencies.[80]

Seeing itself as the repository of the public interest, the Sierra Club was not willing to tolerate private negotiations between government and industry. Secretary of Resources Norman Livermore admitted that the siting committee was "playing footsie with the utilities" and had a "cozy relationship."[81] But resource officials believed that they had been acting in the public interest, and it disturbed them that environmentalists would not grant them such discretion. David Pesonen discovered that the Sierra Club had genuinely hurt the pride of Resources Agency officials by accusing the agency of having "strayed from its statutory role as the state's official guardian of the environment."[82] Whether the agency had actually strayed was not as important as the painful message that government officials could not be trusted. Such decisions, the club argued, had to be made under the watchful eye of public-minded citizens, preferably with a law degree. The Point Arena suit, Livermore concluded, was "the last gasp" of an exclusive siting committee process.[83]

The Sierra Club won a significant victory in 1972 when a superior court ruling nullified the Resources Agency's agreement with Pacific Gas and Electric. The court agreed with club arguments that the agency was not in compliance with environmental laws, nor had it held hearings on its agreements. The defeat established that any system that replaced the siting committee would have to rely on a publicly compiled record for its decisions. The victory also made a new government siting system a critical need.[84]

The demise of the power plant siting committee system was only part of PG&E's unhappy Point Arena story. PG&E's future construction strategy depended on the nuclear plant's success. As David Pesonen understood, halting Point Arena would exorcise the "growth" demon that had obsessed him and other environmentalists. Pesonen feared that PG&E would build so many plants that the coastline would come to resemble a "picket fence." But if Point Arena could be stopped, the Sierra Club might halt the whole of PG&E's "Super System." It would be nearly impossible to find another site on the coast that could clear the regulatory process. A Sierra Club victory could halt electric growth, and begin the social changes necessary to live with less energy.[85]

The Bodega defeat notwithstanding, PG&E had decided to pursue a strategy of relying almost exclusively on the atom for its new sources of power. There was one point of agreement between Pesonen and PG&E. The fate of the coastal plants would decide "the state's economy, the livelihood of its citizens and the pattern of its growth." The key difference was that PG&E believed growth must continue for the public good. As a result, the utility had been quietly purchasing sites on the coastline for reactor parks.[86] In 1969, PG&E had been so confident that it had locked up the best coastal sites that it had, along with Southern California Edison, spurned Chet Holifield's offer of creating an agency to choose acceptable sites. Its "picket fence" strategy suffered a blow when a proposed site at Davenport near Santa Cruz fell victim to seismic questions and public opposition. Opposition was particularly strong at Davenport, and the site had some unresolved seismic questions. PG&E's investment in the site was fairly small and its withdrawal in 1972 relatively quiet.[87] But the Point Arena site threatened to bring its construction plans to a complete halt.

Its situation acute, PG&E resolved to stand and fight when opposition arose. County supervisors favored the facility, but here too local opposition from conservationists and a nearby Indian reservation quickly coalesced around safety issues and scenic considerations.[88] With the addition of the Sierra Club and David Pesonen to the fray, opposition would be well organized and able to exploit scientific uncertainty regarding the site's earthquake hazards. This time, however, it would not be independent geologists who would force the issue. PG&E encountered hostility from the AEC and the Unites States Geological Survey. Federal geologists, some veterans of the Bodega and Malibu fiascoes, were unimpressed with PG&E's data regarding offshore faulting. They concluded that technology that could adequately determine ocean floor faulting simply did not exist. Ferd Mautz, PG&E's vice president of engineering, flew to Washington to castigate the AEC for interminable delays only to find himself called on the carpet. The AEC was furious to be put in the position of passing public judgment on yet another questionable site offered by a California utility. "They really blistered me," Mautz recalled of the AEC's lecturing him on the poor work the utility had done on the site.[89] In January 1973, the Geological Survey declared that it was not scientifically possible to provide "conservative assurance" of the seismic safety of the site as defined by the AEC. The AEC politely suggested to PG&E that it withdraw its application and consider some other site.[90] It was clear that the AEC had had enough of earthquakes and atoms.

Despite the clear rejection by the AEC, PG&E tried to divert attention from technical problems by blaming the "uncertainties" caused by the recently passed coastal protection initiative, Proposition 20.[92] Pesonen ridiculed this last argument as "a smokescreen addressed to the company's stockholders" to hide its failure to qualify the Point Arena site. But PG&E was close to the mark in expressing the conviction that new coast siting was impossible anytime soon. As Pesonen himself declared, "no more coastal sitings should be permitted in California. PG&E has a duty to explore the technology of alternate sources of energy and alternate inland siting of thermal plants, fossil and nuclear."[92] Events were to show that environmentalists had no intention of allowing nuclear plants inland either; stopping growth did not end at the water's edge. Yet state utilities would pursue this option.

Point Arena brought to a climax the public, scientific, and regulatory crisis in the utility industry. The utilities entered 1973 with no institutional mechanism for siting power plants and no place to put them. The utilities were eager to the point of desperation for energy legislation. Environmentalists were eager for legislation too, but they wanted an agency that would slow growth. Public attitudes, however, favored environmentalists.

Earth Day and Regulation

The moderate tone of Earth Day made environmentalism a respectable issue, and its supporters knew no political boundaries. By 1970 every politician in the state could be found uttering environmental platitudes. As one noted, "There is not a subject more on our minds than the preservation of our environment and the absolute necessity of waging an all-out war against the debauching of the environment. A booming economy and the 'good life' will be no good at all if our air is too dirty to breathe, our water too polluted to use, our surroundings too noisy and land too cluttered and littered to allow us to live decently."[93] Unremarkable words except that these lines came from Ronald Reagan. Reagan, in fact, dedicated almost all of his 1970 state-of-the-state address to environmental issues. It was under this Republican governor, and for a few years a GOP-dominated legislature, that some of the most creative environmental legislation in the country would emerge. The "Earth-Day Zeitgeist," John Zierold recalled, dominated the legislative agenda in Sacramento. By 1974, the legislature had enacted three key pieces of legislation related to power plant siting: the California Environmental Quality Act (1970); Proposition 20 creating the California Energy Commission, (1974); and the Warren-Alquist Act creating the California Energy Commission, (1974). The early years of the 1970s were what one environmental lobbyist recalled as the California equivalent of "Camelot."[94]

Camelot took a few years to arrive. Despite the hoopla of Earth Day, 1970 proved to be a rather meager year for environmental legislation in

Sacramento, considering that the legislature was flooded with 1,100 environmental bills. The most important environmental demand for coastal protection failed in the face of a concerted lobbying effort by utility and development interests and division among environmentalists. As the AB 818 debate showed, environmentalists could stop legislation, but they were a divided lot when trying to pass their own bills. "Last year we booted it real bad," one environmental lobbyist admitted.[95] But the environmental lobby regrouped and pressed ahead. The successful passage of coastal legislation would set important precedents for later energy legislation.

Utility company resistance to the creation of a coastal superagency was for practical and philosophical reasons. By 1972, it was clear the coastline would be regulated on environmentalist terms. Developers and utilities opposed new regulatory agencies that would slow their expansion plans. Utilities had long warned that a coastal commission would mean "power shortages and blackouts" and fought a losing contest for exemptions from any coastal legislation.[96] The Planning and Conservation League and the Sierra Club demanded government agencies with broad powers to regulate and plan future development. These proposals were a substantial incursion on traditional capitalist ideas of property ownership and the utility industry's historic freedom to determine what its customers needed. To the utilities, planning was tantamount to socialism.[97]

The attacks on government intrusion might have worked to stop the creation of a coastal commission, but there was a wide consensus among moderate Republicans and Democrats that the existing system had failed to protect the coast. The behavior of county supervisors in zealously promoting the nuclear plants often over the objections of residents, environmental advocates argued, was typical of how utility companies had captured local governments.[98]

Creation of the coastal commission would eventually come through the voters. When the 1972 bills failed, environmentalists marshaled their sizable forces in the state and qualified Proposition 20 through the Herculean feat of collecting nearly a half million signatures in one month. Utilities, oil companies, and real estate interests mounted a sizeable campaign to defeat the issue, spending a reported one million dollars. Despite being overwhelmed in spending, advertising, and the Nixon landslide, Proposition 20 passed with 55 percent of the vote.[99] Environmentalists had realized their decade-long call for statewide land use planning. Proposition 20 had two effects on power plant construction: it delayed for a few years at least any proposal to build a power plant on the coastline; and its planning ethic filtered into emerging energy legislation.

Despite the environmental tide that threatened to engulf them, utility companies still held one powerful card—electrical demand. Utility and PUC demand projections (there was almost no difference between the two) showed a 6.4 percent annual rate of increase that would double consumption within nine years. The PUC warned that utility reserves would deteriorate by the mid-seventies, creating shortages. It recommended legislation to overcome delays in completing projects and called on public officials and the utilities to warn the public of the crisis.[100]

The utilities attempted to win public support by appealing to faith in growth and technology as the basis for the nation's economic well-being. Growth was inevitable, utility advertising forewarned, and the electricity shortage meant catastrophe for jobs, food, and the environment. PG&E ran a television "Lights Out" advertisement where a commentator turned off a light switch and proceeded to warn from his darkened room that such darkness and unemployment would become commonplace if the utility did not overcome opposition to its construction plans.[101] Southern California Edison used the jobs and electricity theme as well, but also tried to capitalize on the popularity of environmentalism with a "Cleaner Environment" advertisement. The ad claimed that electrical power in the form of nuclear plants was essential if society was to operate pollution control equipment. "Yet every effort by Southern California Edison to obtain permits necessary to build any new major power plants during the past four years has been delayed or blocked," it warned.[102]

Pronuclear advocates presented their rationale in a patented formula in articles, advertisements, or public engagements. The speaker, audience, or issue at hand might vary, but the message did not change. The tenets of this message were thus a valuable insight into the logic of the pronuclear viewpoint. Most speeches began by making the case that electrical growth was so fundamental to society that chaos would result without it. Nuclear advocates warned of ballooning demand, economic depression, and blackouts. The country could not rely on fossil fuel plants, speeches warned, with their limited supply and air pollution. They finished with a rousing pitch for the only alternative that had not been eliminated—clean, safe, cheap nuclear power. But there was one problem, the argument warned: delays were hampering construction. These delays were the result of unnamed "groups" who did not understand nuclear power.[103] If America's postwar expansion was to continue unabated, nuclear advocates predicted, then unrestricted nuclear power was the only solution.

The pronuclear message posed a formidable challenge to power opponents struggling to formulate an energy policy of their own. Pronuclear industrialists and politicians lambasted environmentalists for their obstructionist tactics and their failure to offer alternatives to the impending energy crisis.[104] And so despite the power of the environmental movement, lawmakers could hear an insistent drum from industry and its allies that people would freeze in the dark if they did not act.

Forming a Network: Environmental Politicians and Scientists Join the Debate

The debate and defeat of AB 818 indicated, however, that politicians had developed their own skepticism of the tenets of the progrowth message. Legislators began to question the wisdom of the electric industry's pleas for an expedited regulatory system. Within a few years, a group of politicians and staff transformed themselves into energy experts. They would employ state institutional capacity to transform state regulation along the lines of the legal formalism favored by environmentalists. To understand how this occurred, it is important to understand the evolution of the California state legislature.

By 1970 the personnel and level of expertise the California legislature could bring to bear on the state's problems were surpassed only by those of the federal government and a handful of countries. Just ten years earlier, the badly understaffed and part-time state legislature would have done what the utilities asked simply out of ignorance. But California's state government had expanded rapidly since Pat Brown had taken office in 1958. The number of state employees had jumped by 50 percent during the Brown years and another 21 percent under Reagan. The man who would ride to the White House on the axiom that government was the problem and not the solution increased state spending from $4.6 to 10.2 billion annually.[105] The legislature had benefited handsomely from this trend. Jesse Unruh, assembly speaker through most of the 1960s, resolved to professionalize the legislature and increase staff expertise. The legislature budget leaped 150 percent by the end of the decade. In 1966, California voters had overwhelmingly approved a proposition to switch from a part-time to a full-time legislature. Legislative committees now had the time and resources to create their own options instead of relying on interest groups. These changes were so significant that one citizen committee ranked the California legislature the best in the country. With this new level of independence, legislators refused to take the utility estimates at face value.[106]

It was into this more capable and skeptical state government that utility representatives marched with their graphs, charts, and progrowth message. The utility industry repeated its demand to vest the Public

Utilities Commission with the power to preempt local roadblocks. The agency would provide a "one-stop shopping" location to bypass local officials and expedite construction plans. In the utility version, the agency would have no authority to encourage conservation or develop its own expertise and estimates of state power needs. Instead, the utilities' bloated calculations of electrical demand would form the basis for long-term planning. The industry lobbied Sacramento lawmakers and presented parabolic curves of electrical demand portraying in dire terms the energy predicament the state faced.

In the early seventies, Democrats had gained control of the legislature and decided to take a deeper look at the energy issue. Assembly speaker Robert Moretti assigned committee aide Emilio "Gene" Varanini the task of studying electrical demand. Varanini's experience as a naval academy graduate, training as a general staff officer, and service with the CIA made him ideally suited to integrate technical expertise, policy, and politics. Varanini recognized that information was power. He needed independent expertise to challenge the utilities, and he found it at a cocktail party where he met scientists from the Rand Corporation. With Rockefeller and National Science Foundation grants, Varanini was able partly to sponsor an ongoing study by Rand to study California's energy future.[107] The Rand report was one of the most influential energy studies to emerge in the early seventies by becoming the basis for California energy legislation.

The choice of Rand was significant because its experts had been asking just the kinds of energy policy questions that environmentalists and legislators wanted answered. Rand, a nonprofit think tank whose studies had focused principally on defense issues, had been working its way into the energy debate since 1970. In that year, Rand requested funding from the National Science Foundation for a study called the *The Growing Demand for Energy*. The NSF funding program itself was noteworthy since it came as a result of Congress's impatience with the failure of scientific research to solve social problems. To help spur innovative approaches, the program sought to fund worthy research that did not fit neatly into traditional disciplines.[108]

The Rand proposal was the kind of innovative study wanted by the National Science Foundation. Rand's experts would stand traditional notions of energy supply and demand on their heads. Unlike the utility's "demand accommodation" philosophy that allowed demand and supply to grow unimpeded, Rand's assumption was that there were limits to both. "One cannot take for granted that the future is merely a scaled-up version of the present," as electric companies were wont to do, the proposal warned. It contended that this approach was unmindful of environmental, resource and social limits. The researchers argued that changes in values, namely environmental values, would place "constraints" on consumption that needed to be estimated.

Rand reversed utility priorities. Instead of estimating demand and then finding ways to meet it, Rand put environmental and social limits first and conformed demand to them. This led Rand to a fundamental question: Was "the social well-being of the nation . . . contingent on an inexorable growth of the use of energy?" Rand speculated that a healthy economy might be possible in a "less energy-intensive social and industrial framework."[109] These bland pronouncements were revolutionary stuff; they were the first hints that there were limits to energy supplies and that it might be necessary to reorder social and economic priorities.

If the proposal sounded as if it had been written by a bunch of environmentalists, it was because it had been. The direction of the study came from an internal Rand debate in which scientists who were also members of the Sierra Club sought to guide the study toward environmental questions. Richard Ball, one of the key authors of the California study, worked with another Sierra Club member and Rand employee, Alan Carlin, to focus on how to shape power plant siting regulation in environmentally satisfactory ways.[110] Ball was particularly concerned about regulatory issues since he was a principal Sierra Club activist in Southern California lobbying to create a coastal commission.[111] Ball would eventually lead the section of the Rand study devoted to siting regulation.

Of equal import was the contribution of Rand specialist Ron Doctor, who had originally helped convince Varanini and the state legislature to fund Rand's ongoing study. With a Ph.D. in nuclear engineering and extensive experience in the nuclear industry, Doctor was an unlikely candidate for environmental radicalism. "I was enthusiastic as anyone else [about nuclear power]," Doctor dates his antinuclear conversation to around 1970 when he met Jim Harding, the Friends of the Earth's point man on energy, and Henry Kendall of the Union of Concerned Scientists. He found their data and safety concerns so disturbing that he began to investigate these issues himself and became convinced that safety issues had not been addressed. Under Richard Ball's urging he joined the Sierra Club and scientist activists such as John Holdren centered at the California Institute of Technology's Environmental Quality Laboratory. With Ball, he helped the Sierra Club develop an energy policy. Within just a few years, the nuclear engineer would become, in the words of Gene Varanini, "violently opposed" to the peaceful atom.[112]

Had the Rand report been coopted by environmentalists? Environmental sentiment clearly influenced key authors of the report, but to conclude that the report was unscientific would ignore the academic independence that Rand worked hard to maintain.[113] As Ron Doctor remembered, the report's conclusions had caused some concern within Rand ranks. But while this subjected Doctor and the other authors to further scrutiny, the corporation stood by the results. The values of Doctor and Ball led them to pose new questions and start with opposite assumptions from utilities. In so doing, they revealed legitimate problems that the industry had not dealt with or clearly understood.[114] Accusations of cooptation imply that scientific fact is at odds with environmentalism. Scholars have accepted this arbitrary division between environmentalists and experts.[115] Instead, environmentalism encouraged a broadening of scientific inquiry from simple questions of technical feasibility of energy choices to a legitimate inquiry into limits and wisdom of America's lifestyle choices. By inserting the idea of limits, researchers were altering the scientific debate. Nonmaterialist values thus supplemented material ones in scientific inquiry.

Rand's results were an environmentalist's dream and what one assemblyman called "political dynamite."[116] In 1972, Rand published the devastating *California's Electricity Quandary* report.[117] Researchers considered the utilities' estimates of their needs through the century and, in one of their most memorable conclusions, estimated that California would need 130 1,200-megawatt power plants. Borrowing the Sierra Club's analogy, Doctor concluded that would mean California would have to site a plant along its beautiful coast every eight miles.[118] "This rate of growth cannot continue," the study warned, "for it would theoretically outstrip the ability of society to finance, build, and even find room for the generating facilities—to say nothing of supplying them with fuel nor of their impact non the environment." As for nuclear power, the Rand study maintained that a "headlong rush" to construction was unwarranted in the face of emerging safety and environmental problems. Limiting demand was the most rational solution.[119]

The Rand study was only the first occasion on which the Sierra Club and other environmental groups influenced energy policy through their access to experts who shared their values.[120] The Rand study was the first serious challenge by environmentalists and their scientific allies to the utility industry's cornucopian energy vision. The report served as the rationale for the state to gain control over energy planning and for environmentalists values to filter into policy debate.[121]

For the study to have influence, however, it would need extensive and committed political support. The Rand study won an important convert to the environmental and antinuclear cause in Los Angeles assemblyman Charles Warren. Until 1972, Warren had been an ally of environmentalists, but his prime area of interest was chairing the assembly judiciary committee. But Warren was a politician in search of a mission and a new more meaningful philosophy. In the sixties, he became distressed at the political wars in the state Democratic Party and horrified by what he witnessed at the 1968 Democratic Convention in Chicago. Warren returned to California determined to devote himself to meaningful legislation. He found his cause when he chaired the assembly planning and land use subcommittee hearings on the Rand report.

Charles Warren held hearings on the Rand report with the intention of creating new legislation covering all forms of energy consumption in the state. In these days before the 1973 Arab oil embargo, Warren found the hearings poorly attended; sometimes he sat alone and listened to testimony. But for environmentalists, they could not have had a more important audience. The assemblyman sat "aghast" at the dimensions of the energy growth problem laid out before him.[122] By the end of the six days of testimony, Warren later admitted, "My life was changed." He had become a committed "malthusian" who intended to clamp limits on energy growth.[123] Convinced that growth and the utilities' "demand accommodation" philosophy were a prescription for disaster, Warren immersed himself in the task of creating energy-limiting legislation.[124]

What Warren heard at the hearings did not change the Rand report. In one respect the deck was already stacked in favor of Rand's findings. Warren and Varanini developed extensive interrogatories that asked witnesses to respond to assertions in the Rand study. This demand for specific answers weakened sweeping generalizations that utilities relied on when publicly denouncing Rand's findings. Those assertions that utility witnesses failed to discredit would become part of Warren's legislation. The utilities did not seriously undermine Rand projections of growth. Their new forecasting techniques estimated that demand would not rise as fast as projected. The utilities eventually conceded that Rand demand projections and estimation techniques were "reasonable."[125] They also admitted that conservation could reduce demand, but they countered that significant conservation was not needed since an accelerated nuclear construction schedule would fill the gap.[126]

But antinuclear activists undermined the attractiveness of nuclear power. Ron Doctor and others argued that nuclear reliance was a risky prospect since antinuclear activism and safety questions were likely to increase.[127] The nuclear industry and the Atomic Energy Commission assured Warren that safety issues were well in hand and that nuclear waste disposal problems were of little concern. But Union of Concerned Scientists' representatives Henry Kendall and Daniel Ford impressed Warren more than utility witnesses.[128] After the hearings, Charles Warren reported to Kendall that he found utility efforts to refute the MIT professor's safety studies unconvincing. The Los Angeles assemblyman quickly established a friendship and alliance with Kendall. In the ensuing months, "Dear Henry" and "Dear Charlie" letters crisscrossed the country.[129] Warren's antinuclear conversion and their failure to discredit the Rand study were important setbacks for the utilities. Without an unlimited sanction to play the nuclear card, they would have to find ways for reducing demand instead of increasing supply.

Charles Warren's drafted legislation with "a whole new set of values" that still provided something for environmentalists and the utility industry.[130] The utilities would receive their "one stop" agency with the power to override local agencies. He proposed creating a five-person commission that would be independent of the Public Utilities Commission. With a large staff, it would conduct extensive public hearings, develop and evidentiary record, and issue a site certification. This aspect of Warren's bill was little different from other pro-utility siting bills.

The price for this agency was high—planning.[131] Warren empowered the new energy commission to take the authority for planning and forecasting of state energy needs from the utilities. This was a critical and unprecedented step for the state. California would tell the utilities what facilities they needed and what the demand would be. The state would develop it own expertise and models in forecasting and planning. The legislation authorized the new agency to discourage "wasteful, inefficient, unnecessary, or uneconomical use of electrical energy" with home insulation, lighting, and appliance efficiency standards. These portions of the bill, which encouraged reduced demand, represented the true motives of Charles Warren. "This is really the heart of the approach represented by this bill and represents the first time any governmental agency has recognized its responsibility to reduce the energy-demand curve," Warren wrote.[132] For anyone who doubted Warren's environmental motives, he added funding to promote alternative energy sources such as geothermal and solar power. Thus, three out of the four sections of the bill were antithetical to utility interests: state planning, reducing demand, and searching for alternatives. Environmentalists could hardly have been more pleased.

But what of nuclear power? There was no language aimed at discouraging nuclear construction, but hidden behind the bill's talk of reducing consumption was an antinuclear motive. Warren knew his antinuclear inclinations had no political support. The public only wanted nuclear plants to be safe, and was not ready to shut them down. To write nuclear roadblocks into legislation would have doomed the bill. The Los Angeles legislator would have to capitalize on the limits-to-growth debate to stymie the peaceful atom indirectly. Warren pursued energy legislation that, he explained to Governor Reagan, was neither antinuclear nor antidevelopment, but merely rational management. But Warren knew if he could slow all types of electric power construction plans, which were largely atom plants anyway, he was targeting the nuclear industry.[133]

Warren almost won passage of the bill in 1973. He used his power on the judiciary committee to trade judgeships to send the legislation to the governor's desk. Even without the antinuclear language, Reagan vetoed the measure on 2 October 1973. It is unlikely that Reagan had given much thought to energy issues, and his veto message indicated as much. Reagan did not seem bothered by the bill or its threat to utilities, although he cited "unacceptable details" without naming them. What really irked the scourge of taxation was a provision for a small surcharge on utility bills to raise funds for the new agency.[134] After the defeat, Warren desperately considered introducing antinuclear legislation to raise public awareness of the issue. But Warren's timing turned out to be far better than Reagan's. Four days after the veto, Egyptian forces surged across the Suez Canal and Syrian tanks seized the Golan Heights from Israeli troops on the Jewish holiday of Yom Kippur.[135] By the end of the month, the OPEC cartel had instituted an oil embargo on the United States.

The Oil Embargo and the Creation of the Energy Commission

The Arab oil embargo of October 1973 forced the nation to confront questions of energy, lifestyles, and the environment. But effective policy would not emerge from Washington. The Watergate-crippled Nixon administration failed to pass effective legislation. States had an opportunity to develop their own policy. Because of the well-developed energy debate in California, environmentalists were in a prime position to force through their slow-growth agenda. Now appearing as a prophet ahead of his time, Charles Warren, joined by environmentalists and most of the state press, lambasted the governor for vetoing his energy bill. "Perhaps no gubernatorial veto was ever so unpropitious or innocent of prescience," the Sierra Club gloated.[136]

Ronald Reagan's position slowly bent under this pressure. The governor thundered a progrowth line in his January 1974 message to the legislature. Calling conservation a "short-term solution," he spent most of his speech talking about expanding energy supply including accelerated nuclear power plant construction.[137] But the governor was not about to repeat his October mistake. Correctly reading public sentiment, Reagan called for decisive action and began encouraging conservation measures and even implored Californians not to return to their "wasteful ways."[138]

With little expertise of their own, Reagan's aides turned to Warren to revise the vetoed bill.[139] Other than reducing the tax feature somewhat, the bill was virtually identical to the one that the governor had vetoed in October. Reagan personally worked on the negotiations and became something of a convert to Warren's bill. Reagan demanded that the utility executives support the legislation's final version.[140] Complaining all the way to the signing ceremony about the taxes in the bill, Reagan approved the "compromise" measure, commenting that "the legislature had finally provided the powerplant siting mechanism I have sought for several years."[141]

The environmentalist values of the Rand report thus gained legal expression in the Warren-Alquist State Energy Resources Conservation Act. Warren's legislation gave the utilities one-stop shopping. In return the state wrested responsibility from the industry to manage energy demand, enforce conservation measures, and determine the state's need for new power sources.[142]

The Reagan administration was ignorant of what it had signed. The administration believed it had a nuclear siting bill that gave "the commission some ability to do some conservation," as one Reagan aide argued.[143] They, and even the bill's co-sponsor, Alfred Alquist, believed that the primary mission of the new commission was to expedite power plant construction while giving some attention to reducing demand.[144] For them, the new Energy commission was not radical or different from the power plant siting legislation that they had been proposing since 1970. Expediting supply was their priority; conservation was an afterthought.

The Warren legislation, like the Rand report, had reversed these priorities. Weighing external costs, promoting conservation, and reducing demand were the heart of the new commission; construction was a last resort. While much of the new Energy Commission's philosophy depended on whom the next governor chose as commissioners, the commission's structure had a conservation bias written into it. This bias would eventually emerge, but in the early years of its history, the commission would be an agency with two souls—one favoring growth, the other believing that small is beautiful.

From his perch in the assembly, Charles Warren had no intention of allowing the Energy Commission to expedite nuclear construction. As he confided to Henry Kendall at the time, and admitted later, he intended that the commission have an antinuclear agenda.[145] The Warren legislation worked new nonmaterialist values favoring limited growth into California's legislative framework. With the right leadership, the Energy Commission could force electric companies to pursue slow-growth policies and stop building power plants. Moreover, a legislative framework now existed to regulate nuclear power (later antinuclear legislation was incorporated into the Warren Act). Few outside the energy industry understood Warren's antinuclear and antigrowth motive at the time.[146] Warren bided his time for the chance to expand state control of nuclear power again.

Charles Warren and the environmentalists had brought about a transformation in energy regulation in creating the Energy Commission. The siting committee of the 1960s with its informal procedures and emphasis on negotiation by industry, government, and citizen elites had been replaced by an agency more in tune with environmental concepts of regulation. This highly structured agency had far more public exposure, legalistic hearings, and expanded government power at the expense of the private sector. Environmentalists used these new procedures to rein in the possibility of industry capture. In the process, they demonstrated that the idea of capture needed revision. The system proved flexible and open to nonindustry interests. Environmentalist themselves often did not recognize this fact. When asked in the early eighties whether there was anything to prevent the Energy Commission from capture, John Zierold replied, "No. . . . It's reasonable to assume that. Yes. A game-keeper sometimes turns poacher."[147] But the Energy Commission was not simply a vehicle to be commandeered by any one interest. As time would demonstrate, the new regulatory regime of the seventies would inhibit such attempts just as environmentalists intended.

The creation of the Energy Commission in California portended a shift in the site of the energy and antinuclear debate. With the federal government stymied in developing a coherent strategy, states began asserting their traditional police powers and authority in energy and nuclear regulation. Antinuclear activists would target state action in the years to come as the soft underbelly of the nuclear industry.

Environmentalists demurred at the future electric growth that utility companies declared must occur to stave off social decline. Energy consumption had to come under control, they believed, regardless of the decline in living standards. Although the growth debate had skirted the nuclear issue, concerns about the peaceful atom were at the heart of it. Nuclear power, proponents claimed, would allow America to escape the dilemma of limits and environmental problems. But state politicians, bureaucrats, and nuclear opponents no longer believed this rosy scenario was possible or desirable. Interdependence, not independence, they claimed, was an essential part of the relationship between humanity and nature. The abuse of the environment implied by exploding energy growth had to be curbed. And so this value had been written into the legal system.

The legislative process, however, had pushed the energy issue as far as it could without more dramatic changes in public attitudes. The establishment of the Energy Commission provided expression for many nonmaterialist values, but it did not address the comprehensive critique of American society that the atom's opponents offered. An open hearings process, for example, may have been more in keeping with a democratic spirit, but it was not the same as establishing a democracy where the people decided what technologies they preferred. Nor did the commission's birth deal with the moral and safety issues that concerned antinuclear activists.

The time was now ripe for antinuclear activists to take the nuclear issue to the public, raise awareness, and block atomic development openly. In raising moral, safety, and democratic issues, activists enlarged the antinuclear constituency beyond its core of environmentalists and scientists to include former members of the New Left, peace groups, and religious organizations. Abandoning legislative lobbying, they revived a political tool from California's Progressive past, the voter initiative. Their efforts culminated in the 1976 Proposition 15 initiative, the nation's first public referendum on nuclear power. The largest state in the nation would hold the "town meeting" that the atom's advocates feared.

4

Radical Initiatives and Moderate Alternatives

California's 1976 Nuclear Safeguards Initiative

Edward Teller was furious. With trembling hands and flushed face, the father of the hydrogen bomb confronted two engineers outside a California hearing room. His voice rising as they argued, he finally shouted at them, "you are traitors!" before storming away. Teller had a reputation for a volatile personality. Still, for Sierra Club lobbyist John Zierold who witnessed the exchange, it was unnerving to watch a man of Teller's stature come unhinged in public.[1]

No one present needed to be told what the exchange was about or whom the engineers had betrayed. The sin of these men was quitting their nuclear engineering jobs with General Electric in order to join a campaign for a 1976 voter initiative to halt nuclear plant operation and construction. As threatening as it sounded, Teller's outburst seemed odd considering the initiative's slim chances for success. The nuclear industry had already turned public opinion against the initiative. After the 1973 oil embargo, the idea that voters would shut down nuclear plants was absurd.[2] Under these circumstances, an air of haughty contempt might have been more appropriate from Teller.

Because these engineers came from the nuclear community, however, their decision to join the opposition struck at the public's confidence that the nuclear industry was operated safely. Their resignations had helped elevate the initiative's profile to national and international levels, and made it the gravest threat the industry ever faced. Because of Proposition 15, nuclear power became an issue in the 1976 presidential elections and inspired six similar ballot measures in other states and even Switzerland. Proposition 15's success, industrialists feared, might create an antinuclear domino effect.[3] Teller was petrified. "Goddamn, I've got to defeat the nuclear initiative," the scientist confessed to a reporter.[4] He was not alone in his fears. Adversaries spat on each other, debate flared into shouting matches, and each side routinely branded its opponents as liars. Short tempers abounded in a campaign in which fundamental values were at stake.

Edward Teller, a Hungarian refugee from Nazi Germany, believed technology in a democratic society could elevate civilization to higher levels of dignity and achievement. Nuclear power would create energy abundance, spread American democracy and civilization, and end the "pollution of poverty."[5] Whatever its flaws, scientists and engineers were best off seeking reform within the system rather than engaging in open dissent that could wreck enthusiasm for the peaceful atom.[6]

The engineers had lost Teller's technological optimism. As children of the Cold War, they feared poverty less than they feared a decline in the quality of their middle-class existence and the essential immortality of nuclear power and wastes. Technology, they concluded, had not been the magic solution to their generation's concerns. Government and scientific control of nuclear power appeared to threaten democracy, the environment, and world peace. Unlike Teller, they saw their profession as part of the problem and thought that only open disagreement could solve it.[7]

For the moment, the public decided they still sided with Edward Teller. The nuclear industry breathed easier when Californians rejected Proposition 15 by a 2 to 1 margin in June. Antinuclear initiatives in the other states lost by similar margins six months later. The American people were not ready to turn their back on the country's most highly touted energy option. David Pesonen, leader of the initiative, surmised, "All their lives, people are told to connect the good life with industrial technology. With progress. We threatened all that, we scared them, and they backed away."[8]

Proposition 15 proved to be a mixed victory for the nuclear industry. The defeat was less remarkable than the fact that the election was held at all. A third of the voters wanted to shut down nuclear power, and many more citizens were uneasy about the peaceful atom. And in a clear setback to the industry, antinuclear politicians capitalized on the public dread of nuclear hazards whipped up by the campaign and pushed through three bills expanding the state's power to restrict nuclear plant construction just days before the Proposition 15 vote. This achievement provided a modest alternative to the more radical initiative.

Behind the large pronuclear victory, it was evident that the antinuclear movement had stripped away important and influential support for nuclear power. The initiative was an attempt to challenge the old economic growth paradigm and infuse society with the new values of a nonmaterialist worldview, and in this effort antinuclear activists had particular success. County-level voting patterns indicate that nuclear opposition came from those who had most benefited from the post-World War II expansion in income and education.[9] These voters valued nonmaterial amenities more than economic growth and technological advancement. And as a younger, better-educated generation reached maturity by the seventies, nuclear opposition would only expand into an ever broader coalition opposed to the centers of authority supporting the peaceful atom.

Supplementing environmentalists in the Proposition 15 coalition were progressives such as former New Leftists and peace groups. They cared more about participatory democracy and personal empowerment than about employment and economic growth issues that historically concerned traditional Democratic Party liberals. Progressives expanded objections to nuclear power form the aesthetics and safety issues favored by moderate environmentalists to a fundamental critique of government, industry, and scientific authority. Unwilling to accept risks imposed on them by scientific elites, citizens joined the nuclear opposition to challenge the corporate and federal power structure. For these groups, nuclear power was symbolic of what was wrong with America.[10]

As financially secure as many of its members were, the Proposition 15 coalition perceived a fragile world strewn with perils. In the early seventies, potentially catastrophic problems of economic and environmental decline, a crisis of authority, and weapons proliferation supplanted much of the middle-class and baby boomer concern over the Vietnam War and urban conflict. The country, they believed, was headed toward restricted personal freedom, environmental catastrophe, and possible global conflict. Only new values could alter the nation's direction. When searching for solutions to the harmful effects of modern society, such as pollution, nonmaterialists argued for a return to simpler lifestyles, local amenities, and community power. In the words of Jerry Brown, Americans had to accept "a world with limits to it resources and a country with limits to its power and economy."[11]

Proposition 15 provided a means for Californians to seek basic social change in the wake of the upheavals of the sixties and early seventies.

Not all antinuclear activists were in accord on the degree of change necessary, but an antinuclear initiative offered something for everyone. Moderate groups like the Sierra Club joined the movement because they merely wanted greater public sensitivity to the environment. At the other end of the spectrum, millennial religious groups believed their antinuclear message could create wholesale change and usher in a new age of peace and brotherhood. In between, populists, former New Leftists, and antiwar activists gravitated to nuclear issues to alter public attitudes about corporate power, weapons proliferation, and democratic control of technology.

California's political system held out the possibility of a democratic solution for these seventies activists through a Progressive, and largely western, political device—the citizen initiative, little used until the early seventies. Activists who championed citizen democracy believed the nuclear controversy could further their goals. They challenged scientific authority and nuclear regulation by establishing the average citizen as the arbiter of the once exclusive debate over the atom. Proposition 15 did not achieve the utopian goals of its most zealous allies, but it furthered democratic aspirations, raised public doubts about nuclear safety, and won nuclear legislation that transferred future regulatory control from the federal government to states and localities. Using a radical initiative, activists won moderate reforms.

The legislative victory also followed from the antinuclear movement's control over California's regulatory institutions governing energy use. Environmental activists had allied with a network of Sacramento bureaucrats, politicians, and sympathetic scientists to create the Energy Commission and promote alternatives uses of energy. The antinuclear network used Proposition 15 and state government regulatory capacity to pry concessions from the electric industry and seize a victory from the initiative's defeat. By overcoming the utility industry and passing bills that ultimately forbade future reliance on the atom, antinuclear forces achieved a triumph unmatched in any other state.

The Proposition 15 controversy offers a practical lesson in the interest group politics of the seventies and how new public values are written into law. Antinuclear activists achieved success through the political and bureaucratic resources offered by a dynamic western state. This fusion of grassroots work, political lobbying, and scientific talent created an atmosphere conducive to new legislation. Although they were seen as such, the nuclear bills were not a cynical maneuver to prevent a radical solution from passing. Quite the reverse. The initiative acted as an opening wedge to force on the political order legislation with new values. The older progrowth philosophy had to accommodate nonmaterial values.

Turning to State Solutions

The antinuclear movement turned to the states after generally unsuccessful local interventions and federal lobbying. Activists took heart from the dissolution of the promotional Atomic Energy Commission (AEC) and the creation of the purportedly neutral Nuclear Regulatory Commission (NRC). There had also been scattered victories over power plants, especially in California, but the atom's supporters still won most of the battles. Nuclear proponents were strong enough to prevent further erosion of federal support for nuclear programs. They halted antinuclear attempts to pass legislation such as a construction moratorium, cuts in funding for the experimental breeder reactor, and a repeal of the Price-Anderson Indemnity Act. The latter bill provided special insurance protection to the industry in the event of a serious accident. The AEC and the NRC were making it harder for activists in construction hearings by prohibiting questions on government-subsidized insurance, generic reactor safety problems, and waste disposal. Perennial activists such as David Pesonen, now a San Francisco attorney, had grown cynical about ever stopping nuclear power without some dramatic, general victory.

David Pesonen. Merely to utter his name in the presence of a California utility executive would evoke curses and dread. The state's most persistent nuclear foe was back again. In 1964 Pesonen had reduced the Pacific Gas and Electric Company's Bodega Bay excavation for a nuclear complex to a four-million-dollar duck pond. The utilities might have been relieved when in the mid-1960s Pesonen took a break from hounding them to pursue a Berkeley law degree. But he returned a more formidable opponent. He led the Sierra Club's opposition to PG&E's ill-fated nuclear project at Point Arena and brought antinuclear litigation against the utility. Pesonen, Friends of the Earth executive David Brower noted, was the "only man I know of who has two nuclear reactor skulls hanging from his belt."[12] Pesonen would prove he had no intention of resting on his laurels, and he began casting for some "political device" to stop the nuclear industry.[13]

In 1973, the national leadership of the antinuclear movement convened a summit meeting at the home of MIT physicist and leader of the Union of Concerned Scientists (UCS) Henry Kendall. Representing the key antinuclear groups were consumer representatives from Ralph Nader's organization, public interest lawyers, environmentalists from

Friends of the Earth, and scientists with UCS. Their numbers were small enough to fit in one room. David Comey, an activist from Chicago, joked that they represented the "ruling presidium of the antinuclear cabal." They were a capable bunch, but their past victories would not compensate for what seemed to be an ever growing reactor market in the early seventies. Jim Harding, leader of the Friends of the Earth's antinuclear activities, thought nuclear power was an "unstoppable industry." Most opponents, he recalled, would have "gladly come to terms with [only] 200 reactors" in the United States."[14]

The gathering decided that a state challenge might get at the soft underbelly of federal control. It seemed a desperate strategy since it had already been tried before and failed in federal courts. The 1971 Northern States decision had declared that federal laws preempted the states' police power with respect to setting safety standards for radioactive hazards. Despite this setback, activists thought that perhaps by exerting power over other aspects of nuclear construction and operation ignored by the ruling, states might break through the iron triangles of federal control.[15] Pesonen and Richard Spohn, a California Ralph Nader associate, decided to seek antinuclear legislation in Sacramento.[16]

Pesonen and Richard Spohn approached state assemblyman and environmental ally Charles Warren in early 1973 to persuade him to include restrictions on nuclear power in the legislation he was drawing up to create the Energy Commission. Warren was sympathetic, but told them antinuclear legislation had no public or political constituency. Warren advised the two men to create support by qualifying an antinuclear initiative. An initiative might give Warren a reason to hold hearings, raise awareness, and perhaps even introduce legislative solutions. Pesonen was not thrilled with the suggestion for an initiative, and had considered this difficult and expensive option a last resort. But the two activists agreed to navigate the hazardous waters of California's initiative process.[17]

Pesonen's reluctance to pursue an initiative was justified. California is famous for its ballots stuffed with citizen-generated initiatives, but this was not always the case. By the sixties, this Progressive tool had become a device only wealthy interest groups could afford. Gathering qualified signatures was a bureaucratic nightmare. Few groups could raise the large sums of money for a campaign. When initiatives did qualify, voters, often confused and irked by their complexity, struck them down at a rate of 4 to 1.[18] The advantage of pursuing an initiative, however, was that it would draw peace groups and left-wing populists into antinuclear activism. In the process, these groups would revive the initiative and transform the antinuclear cabal into an expansive movement.

Populists and Peace Activists Join the Movement

When it came to popular democracy, Ed Koupal was a latter-day Tom Paine. Koupal, a disgruntled used car salesmen, revolutionized the initiative system by tapping into a growing egalitarian, anti-authoritarian sentiment in the nation.[19] Concluding he had been betrayed in a local political matter, this Ford dealer from Sacramento decided that politics was a conspiratorial "web of corruption."[20] His transformation was so dramatic that he forsook his career and went to war against the political system. Literally deserting his home and furniture, he moved his family to Los Angeles to be near a population center for signature gathering.[21] Learning from his failures, including an attempt to recall Governor Ronald Reagan, Koupal formed the People's Lobby. Staffed with young activists, People's Lobby launched a successful initiative to simplify laws governing petition gathering. Koupal used his sales ability to pioneer cheap mass signature-gathering methods that became a campaign standard.[22] Without the work of Koupal, an initiative would have been impossible for the antinuclear movement.

In the early seventies, Ed Koupal's democratic instincts led him to join the nuclear power opposition. Unlike most people, Koupal viewed the issue as one not of science and safety, but of political power. Proponents used the aura and mystery of nuclear power, he believed, to mask their usurpation of power.[23] Scientists often thought opposition stemmed from an uneducated public, but often the safety issue was less significant to activists than the right of the people, right or wrong, to decide what risks were worth taking.[24] Koupal wanted to employ this growing skepticism of authority to promote the initiative process. "One of the great things about the initiative," Koupal raved, "is that ordinary citizens can go directly to the people with the great issues of the day, like nuclear power—bypassing the politicians, powerful lobbies, special interest groups, and state legislatures."[25] People's Lobby placed the Clean Environment Act, Proposition 9, on the June 1972 ballot. The omnibus initiative attacked nearly every conceivable polluter and included a five-year moratorium on nuclear plant construction. The initiative created a general panic among business circles. In a prelude of the kind of opposition Proposition 15 would face, nearly every sector of the business community waged a successful campaign against a measure they claimed would strangle economic development, cause massive unemployment, and force citizens back to "the scrub board and laundry tub."[26] Undaunted, Koupal joined the new antinuclear initiative coalition to try again.

Remnants of sixties antiwar activism spilled over into the initiative

Ed Koupal was critically important in reviving the voter initiative in California, and hoped to use the nuclear issue to create a national initiative system. Courtesy Sacramento Archives and Museum Collection Center, *Sacramento Bee* Collection.

as such groups began taking a greater interest in the environmental effects of weapons production and nuclear power. Important in California was Another Mother for Peace. Formed in 1967 by fifteen Beverly Hills women, including actress Donna Reed, Mothers for Peace became a national organization with over 230,000 members in 1971.[27] During anti-Vietnam War activism, the Mothers showed only passing interest in civilian nuclear issues.[28] The war movement's decline encouraged the Mothers to shift its focus to civilian nuclear power, as did the effective lobbying of antinuclear scientist John Gofman. New members, mostly young mothers, expressed concern for the effects of the environmental hazards of weapons production and nuclear power on their children.

The Mothers for Peace rejected nuclear power as an immoral power source. The Mothers differed from environmental organizations in that their history of peace activity steered them to the link between civilian power and nuclear weapons proliferation and the genetic hazards radiation pose to children.[29] They promoted a maternal image in the sixties, and they continued to do so in antinuclear campaigns. The organization had begun with the popular slogan "War is unhealthy for children and other living things." In the seventies, they modified "War" to "Radiation" for antinuclear campaigns.[30] The Mothers joined the antinuclear initiative coalition as protectors of children and generations unborn. The addition of Another Mother for Peace broadened the critique of nuclear power to include moral questions such as its link to war and its threat to the survival of humanity.[31]

Activists worked together to form a state coalition called People for Proof, and went to work on an initiative proposal.[32] The authors first had to overcome the image that moratorium legislation would shut down the entire nuclear industry.[33] Most activists wanted to shut down nuclear power, but they had to balance their own desires with an alternative acceptable to a still pronuclear public. What they needed was a measure ending nuclear power without admitting it. It was not a forthright strategy, but an initiative that openly claimed it would shut down nuclear power seemed doomed to failure.[34] A number of sources also advised the activists to challenge federal preemption through the state's power to control land use within its borders. To win on these grounds required a narrow view of federal authority.

Attempting to incorporate these objectives, the final form of the initiative, later called Proposition 15, took shape in early 1974. In steps, the initiative would halt construction and reduce the operation of existing nuclear plants unless three areas were addressed: federally subsidized accident insurance; reactor safety; and waste disposal. The Price-Anderson Act's ceiling on liability in the event of a nuclear accident had to be lifted by Congress or waived by the utility. This stipulation was especially pernicious since it exposed the industry to unlimited damage claims and nullified a federal law. A second condition required a two-thirds vote by the state legislature declaring reactor safety systems worked. Finally, there had to be a solution to the waste disposal problem. Otherwise, operating reactors would be phased out by 1987.[35] The act seemed fair in that it only specified conditions of operation and did not arbitrarily shut down all reactors without reason. Activists admitted in private, however, that the Price-Anderson waiver in particular could never be met.

With the objective of qualifying the initiative for the November ballot, People for Proof kicked off a campaign in March of 1974.[36] Unlike Koupal in his ill-fated 1972 initiative, organizers had garnered some impressive allies, including Friends of the Earth (FOE), the Sierra Club, Ralph Nader's California Public Interest Group, and Another Mother for Peace. With the support of such major organizations, People for Proof appeared to be a serious threat to the nuclear industry.

The conversion to antinuclear activism by the Sierra Club and the more aggressive Friends of the Earth indicated environmentalists had at last reunited in opposition to nuclear power. Militant environmentalists, after many years, prodded the movement away from aesthetic issues to focus on the human health hazards that industrialism posed through toxins such as radioactive wastes.[37] In 1974, after years of acrimonious debate on nuclear power, the national board of the Sierra Club still refused to take a moral position on nuclear power, but it did pass a pragmatic statement of disapproval until problems with waste and safety were solved. Locally, the leaders of the club's California chapters were more ideologically opposed to nuclear power than the national organization.[38]

Having split with the Sierra Club on nuclear power a few years before, the Friends of the Earth refused to "mistake growth for progress" and assumed a more democratic and moral position. FOE attacked the ethics of nuclear wastes, control of the industry by big business, the links between nuclear power and weapons, and irreversible genetic damage.[39] FOE believed in local control and democratic answers like the initiative. By contrast, the Sierra Club was leery of the poor history of initiatives when it came to withstanding court challenges. It was more comfortable with legislative dealings and was the most effective environmental lobbyist in Sacramento.[40]

But hopes for this coalition proved unfounded. FOE and Sierra Club leaders in California tried to recruit signatures and support, but soon discovered there was no constituency even among their membership. Commitment was high at leadership levels, but below them there was little awareness of nuclear dangers. Without the financial resources for a professional petition drive, they had to rely on volunteers, most drawn from California's counterculture; there were too few volunteers chasing too many signatures. People for Proof suffered from poor accounting practices, and hippies resisted enforced discipline. When Dwight Cocke volunteered to gather signatures, he found the initiative office filled with counterculture types who refused to keep records. When he encouraged them to organize the office, they asked him, "What's your [astrological] sign?" When he told them, they gazed at each other with knowing smiles and went back to the old way of doing things. There was also conflict between Northern and Southern California wings of the movement. San Francisco area activists, the bulk of the organization, resented what they perceived as poor management by southern leadership.[41]

Internal strife opened the door for David Pesonen to take control of the movement. With the signature drive in disarray, some Bay Area volunteers approached Pesonen for advice. Pesonen had helped launch the initiative, but the demands of his law practice limited his involvement in the signature-gathering phase. He convinced activists to scrap the campaign and begin anew with him as the leader. Ed Koupal did not go quietly.[42] Koupal wanted to use the California initiative as a platform for his dream of creating a national initiative process. Through a new group called Western Bloc, Koupal aimed to push antinuclear initiatives in other states and thereby create popular support for this democratic tool.[43] Pesonen, however, was more interested in the immediate goal of passing the initiative in California. Pesonen was determined to squeeze Koupal out of a leadership role in the new effort. In a carefully arranged meeting in August 1975, Pesonen won election as chairman of a newly named organization, Californians for Nuclear Safeguards (CNS), which absorbed People for Proof. To bring better management to the new effort, CNS hired campaign professionals Robert Jeans and Larry Levine. Operating out of Pesonen's law office basement, Dwight Cocke ran the signature drive without relying on the stars for guidance.[44]

Even with the quelling of factional disputes and better organization, Californians for Nuclear Safeguards still faced the basic problems of money and personnel. Pesonen secured $5,000 from the Union of Concerned Scientists (UCS).[45] But with little else, the antinuclear movement was hard-pressed to get the needed signatures. What Pesonen needed was the impossible: a thousand affluent idealistic individuals who saw the antinuclear movement as a religious undertaking. Lucky for him, this was California.

Creative Initiative: A Middle-Class Millennial Movement

Little in David Pesonen's years of activism prepared him for the nonprofit Creative Initiative Foundation (CIF). The Palo Alto-based group was composed largely of wealthy and middle-class professional couples drawn from the San Francisco Bay area's burgeoning white-collar communities. In December of 1974, the leadership of Creative Initiative contacted Californians for Nuclear Safeguards to learn more about its campaign. Without much knowledge of Creative Initiative, Pesonen and other CNS leaders went to Palo Alto thinking it would be a routine pitch to small group. They found themselves on a stage before a thousand of the best-dressed, most attentive activists they had ever seen. *Every* person in the hall took notes. Pesonen was an excellent speaker, but this was like preaching to the choir. The morning presentation ended when Creative Initiative leaders told the members to break for discussion, but to remember that God had called on them to oppose nuclear power. Those who returned to the auditorium would do so as members of a new political organization to oppose nuclear power. Nearly all returned to make large donations. CNS leader James Burch counted the mound of money and checks and uttered, "twenty thousand dollars."[46] Pesonen and his associates gaped at Burch as the audience burst into applause.

The money was only the beginning. Pesonen now had at his disposal a staff of lawyers and advertising executives. The women of Creative Initiatives provided labor critical to the effort. Although many of them held jobs, the majority did not and were willing to devote a great deal of time to the cause. They were eager to learn Koupal's methods and hit the streets in search of signatures.[47] Pesonen drove home with a six-inch stack of checks on the seat next to him trying to figure out what had just happened back there. What made Creative Initiative tick? Members' energy was exhilarating, but their unity was unnerving. They were too naïve, this antinuclear veteran thought, and defeat might crush them. For the moment, however, their optimism wiped away all of Pesonen's fears. He was happier than he had been in months.[48]

David Pesonen was not the last individual baffled by Creative Initiative. Its enemies often described it as a "quasi-religious cult." This label is simplistic, if partly accurate. It was not a formal religion, although its philosophy was an eclectic amalgam of world religions. It was not a cult, but it was committed to building a strong community culture. Intense encounter sessions built a strong group bond and a startling degree of unanimity.

Creative Initiative's members were like many middle-class Americans who in the late sixties and seventies had grown uncomfortable with their lives and experimented with new lifestyles and philosophies.[49] The difference was Creative Initiative's turn to religious millennialism. Elements of the group dated from the 1940's, but CIF's modern form emerged two decades later. In the early sixties, a group of Palo Alto women began discussing their concerns about post-World War II family and society. They had achieved the ideal of the American way of life, but found it empty and threatening. They exemplified Betty Friedan's discontented women in *The Feminine Mystique* who found that family life "wasn't enough" and wanted greater power to influence society. The group tried to reconcile traditional family expectations with their feelings of social responsibility, and to balance male and female roles. Their title (Creative a traditionally feminine quality, Initiative, a masculine one) signified their striving for balance.[50] Balance was also the key to their social goals. Creative Initiative members believed that America's male-dominated society was too enamored of economic growth and that it neglected quality-of-life values. A holistic world-view was needed if civilization was to survive.

The women of the organization resolved to lead a millennial movement to a more moral and peaceful world. Specifically, 1975 and 1976, as the International Women's Year and America's bicentennial, members thought, would usher in a "New Order of the Ages" of racial brotherhood and peace.[51] To achieve this transformation, they sought an issue that affected all levels of society. In the wake of the 1973 oil crisis, the most obvious issue was energy. They were drawn to the "small is beautiful" ideas of economist E. F. Schumacher, whose own opposition to the "ethical, spiritual, and metaphysical monstrosity" of nuclear power derived from religious roots.[52] Schumacher's advocacy of decentralized and small-scale energy sources pointed the way to a safer and more ethical alternative. By contrast, nuclear power represented to them an apocalyptic threat to the world through its link to nuclear weapons and was symbolic of humankind's disregard for future generations and limits.[53] To leave a legacy of toxins represented the ultimate crime against humanity. For Creative Initiative, Proposition 15 was the perfect vehicle toward a more peaceful age.[54] CIF formed a political action organization, Project Survival, to campaign for the initiative.

The women of Project Survival joined the final signature drive in early 1975 and fanned out over the Bay Area and the state's Central Valley cities. They arrived by the carload to work a city's shopping centers and homes. With Koupal's petition methods, they collected nearly 250,000 signatures. The women capped off their drive with a call for hearings on nuclear power. On 5, May 1975, the initiative qualified for the June 1976 ballot with 400,000 valid signatures.[55] Assemblyman Charles Warren kept his word to Pesonen and announced fall hearings on Proposition 15.

Creative Initiative also moved beyond nuclear power to its millennial message to the populace. The educational presentations balanced typically rational "masculine" arguments with appeals to motherhood, future generations, and predictions of catastrophe. One announcement declared, "We are irreversibly committed to one million deaths from nuclear radiation. . . . We must take immediate action. All other problems of human welfare take second place."[56] The "feminine principle must lead," the women announced, as they launched a colorful parade of four hundred "rainbow women" in Sacramento wearing pantsuits in the colors of the rainbow. In a solemn evening "way of the light" ritual, the "warriors of the rainbow," including a multiracial group of women, accepted a covenant to wage a nonviolent war to inaugurate the new age.[57]

Creative Initiative had brought new ideas to the antinuclear move-

In May 1975, the members of Project Survival triumphantly marched at the state capitol in Sacramento, proclaiming their goal of world peace and unity. Courtesy Sacramento Archives and Museum Collection Center, *Sacramento Bee* Collection.

ment. Its moral outrage at what male domination had done to society and a desire for a greater role for women in the movement would expand its appeal. But Creative Initiative had saved the Proposition 15 campaign at a price. Other activists did not always greet it with open arms. These well-to-do members envisioned remaking lifestyles in a manner counterculture activists did not. Their odd mix of conservative lifestyle and group discipline alienated other activists, making cooperation difficult. The Palo Alto group also had difficulty conveying its message to the public. Its displays offended many who thought it s regimentation anathema to an individualistic society, even fascist. CNS leadership quickly moved to tone down Project Survival and persuaded the group to pursue more narrow educational efforts in support of Proposition 15.[58] But it remained a persistent problem for the antinuclear campaign to balance practical needs and public image with the more utopian goals of some of its coalition members.

Assembly Hearings and Legislation: Growth Advocates Lose the Debate

When the initiative qualified, industry-sponsored opposition made its debut. The nuclear industry could count on groups who believed energy and economic growth were necessary to maintain social stability and who trusted scientists and scientific rationality as the means to the common good. It was a traditional coalition of conservatives, business and industry associations, labor organizations, and progrowth politicians. An impressive list of America's scientists signed on to oppose the measure. Proposition 15, they argued, would shut down safe nuclear power, stifle economic growth, cost the state jobs, impoverish the poor, raise utility rates, pollute the air, and increase dependence on Mideast oil. The jobs-and-growth theme attracted Republicans and New Deal Democrats alike.[59] Former governor Edmund "Pat" Brown, long a champion of large government projects, announced he would assume leadership of the opposition: "Let us not forget one key reality: Either we continue to develop our domestic energy sources, or this nation is programmed for economic and eventually social disaster."[60] Despite such posturing, Pat Brown was a politician who knew how to straddle issues.[61] He hinted at some future legislative compromise.[62] In the meantime, the opposition's first task was to prepare for the hearings held by an all too familiar foe, Charles Warren.

By now the most capable energy politician in the state, Warren was poised to use all the resources he had in the new hearings to push his antinuclear agenda. The hearings on Proposition 15 opened in October

The "Way of the Light" ceremony, on the Capitol steps, demonstrated the significant role that women and religion played in Creative Initiative as well as the antinuclear movement. Note the statue of the Virgin Mary on the table. As a millennial movement, Creative Initiative members hoped that Proposition 15 would launch the beginning of a new age for humanity. Courtesy Sacramento Archives and Museum Collection Center, *Sacramento Bee* Collection.

1975, anticipated eagerly by activists, dreaded by the nuclear industry. This was the first public forum devoted to raising awareness of nuclear power issues. The "specter of a nuclear moratorium" had haunted the industry for some time.[63] The fifteen days of hearings took on a life-or-death importance as both sides rushed in "platoons of goons," as Gene Varanini remembered.[64] Publicly, Charles Warren claimed he would not introduce legislation from the hearings and would only create a voter's guide.[65] Industry organizations considered the legislators to be "obviously biased against nuclear power, and . . . sure to make this known, officially or unofficially."[66] Industry officials grumbled that the legislators had "ganged up" on pronuclear witnesses in an "inquisition in which industry is presumed to be guilty."[67]

Analysts, however, faulted the industry for failing to win the hearings debate.[68] Industry spokespersons could not clearly refute the antinuclear witnesses' accusations about poor nuclear safety. What were the assemblymen to think of Edward Teller's championing of nuclear power despite his misgivings about the power plants safety and desire to bury them far underground? And Nobel Prize-winning physicist Hans Bethe admitted he based his support for nuclear power on faith. When asked if the Emergency Core Cooling System was adequate, Bethe remarked: "I do not know, and the people who know much more about it . . . do not know either. [But these experts have] the feeling that it will work. The best you can do is to rely on the feelings of people who have studied it."[69] Some listening were stunned. "My God!—they really don't have the answers, do they?" One woman in the room blurted out.[70] Industry witnesses did convince the committee that Proposition 15 was poorly written, its two-thirds majority vote requirement in the legislature was too harsh; it would have severe economic consequences; and it would shut down nuclear power.[71] But they could not show that reactor safety and waste disposal problems were well in hand. For every industry expert to testify, antinuclear activists presented one of their own. "After listening to 120 learned witnesses who could not agree on the merits of the Initiative or the safety of nuclear power," the committee concluded, "it is clear that no objective conclusion *can* be drawn.[72] Initially, Warren's committee members were uncommitted. By the end, nearly all considered the initiative defective, but they opposed unregulated nuclear power.[73] The hearings neutralized pronuclear expertise and provided a justification for state regulation.

Scientists, motivated by their environmental sympathies, added further ammunition to the Proposition 15 campaign, just as they had in creating the Energy Commission. In one instance, Richard Sextro, a Lawrence Berkeley Laboratory physicist and Sierra Club leader, worked on an Energy Department and Research Administration study of California's energy needs. Sextro was a Sierra Club leader in the Proposition 15 campaign and was morally opposed to nuclear power. Like Ron Doctor, Sextro considered nuclear power a "monster" and rejected nuclear scientists' claims to objectivity and elitism. Other environmental scientists were able to influence an oversight board for a Federal Energy Administration-sponsored study of Proposition 15's possible effects. This expanded access to expertise enjoyed by the legislature and environmentalists is a clear example of how nuclear power was undermined by the formation of ideologically motivated alliances of politicians, scientists, and political activists. These scientists with nonmaterialist values were thus able to provide the factual basis for legislation Charles Warren planned to introduce.[74]

In January of 1976, the Warren committee members determined that the state should move into this technical debate and presented legislation free of the "harsh" provisions and "procedural problems" of the radical nuclear initiative.[75] The four bills restricted the construction of new nuclear plants, but exempted those under construction. Two of the bills forbade new construction until the Nuclear Regulatory Commission found facilities for fuel reprocessing and waste disposal. A third bill prohibited construction for one year while a study looked into Teller's recommendation for burying nuclear power plants. A final bill, which did not survive, required power plant operators to waive the Price-Anderson exemption and assume full liability for any accident. The Energy Commission established under Warren's 1974 legislation would determine whether the NRC and the industry had met the conditions of the bills. The legislature would approve the commission's findings by a simple majority.

The new moderate legislation posed a dilemma for the nuclear industry and a lesser one to initiative supporters. The Proposition 15 forces feared the Warren legislation could end all chances for the initiative. Nonetheless, CNS recognized that the bills were substantive legislation and that passage would represent a victory. CNS decided it could pursue both a radical and a moderate solution. "I think it's courageous of this committee to venture into this area," Pesonen declared in what became its standard response, "but it certainly isn't going to dampen our efforts to campaign for the initiative."[76] A few activists claimed they always intended the initiative to be a radical, provocative way to force the state legislature to act. Most eventually came to a fatalistic understanding of this strategy and accepted it.[77]

Pronuclear forces opposed Proposition 15 because the initiative was extreme in eliminating the nuclear option at a time when the nation needed every energy source it could find. But if they were to use their influence to halt the bills, then Warren's committee and Governor Jerry Brown, who at the time was heating up for a presidential bid, threatened to support Proposition 15. The pronuclear forces therefore decided to keep the bills alive and negotiate changes.[78] Throughout the spring, Warren and environmental lobbyists played on industry fears about Proposition 15 to win concessions. Meanwhile, antinuclear activists had a surprise that scared the wits out of the nuclear industry.

Losing Faith

Project Survival provided the most sensational story of the campaign, and one that best exemplified the clash of old and new values. General Electric nuclear engineers within Creative Initiative had been discussing how the morality of nuclear energy fit into their worldviews. When they joined the field, they had dreamed of bringing a cheap, limitless source of energy to the nation. Now three of them saw greater trouble in the long-term dangers of the nuclear fuel cycle and reactor safety. Could they work for an industry that posed strong intergenerational risks? What could they do about the threat of sabotage and nuclear proliferation? If they stayed with GE, could they help eliminate the risk to reactor safety posed by human error? Dale Bridenbaugh, Gregory Minor, and Richard Hubbard concluded they could not. They would leave the industry. On 2 February 1976, these engineering managers, each the father of three, exited the gates of GE's San Jose plant for the last time. They distributed copies of their resignations to the *San Francisco Chronicle*, the *New York Times*, and the *Los Angeles Times*. Nuclear power, they told the press, was a "technological monster." "The issue we face is not the survival of an industry, rather it is the survival of mankind."[79]

These resignations altered the context of the debate over nuclear power. Activists had other scientific support, but now they could boast of endorsements directly from the nuclear industry. Moreover, these men's motives appeared unimpeachable since they had forsaken their careers for principle. The engineers' decision roiled the nuclear industry well out of proportion to the accusations leveled as rumors spread of other defections. Despite fears that they would tell "where the bodies are buried," the trio offered no damaging information to the Joint Committee on Atomic Energy (JCAE). Their objections centered on what degree of risk was acceptable, possible human error, and a philosophical rejection of a technology that left its problems to be solved by a generation unborn. What made their stand so unnerving was that they had been members of the faith, the nuclear family.[80] How were the true believers to explain this apostasy?

As Edward Teller had done, the atom's defenders branded the men traitors and irrational. Within weeks, the shaken nuclear industry counterattacked by turning the light on the three engineers' affiliation with Creative Initiative. Not everyone found the group enchanting. Many found its close-knit structure and intimacy invasive and intimidating. Former members claimed Creative Initiative insisted on a "party line."[81] Others called CIF a cultlike "force for robbing men and women of their individuality and turning them into willing slaves of the leaders of the group." Pronuclear advocates such as Congressman Mike McCormack claimed the three engineers were "pressured" by CIF in an "orchestrated ploy." He pronounced a decree of excommunication on the three men: "In two years they'll be totally forgotten by the public, frozen out of the industry, and of no further use to the people who exploited them. They'll be dead."[82] McCormack's hyperbole contained an element of truth. Creative Initiative was hamstrung in refuting cult labels because there *was* strong peer pressure. "We were hard on each other. And I think we overstepped boundaries," one member admitted.[83]

The engineers' public resignation had the unintended effect of lowering the level of Proposition 15 debate. From educating the public about nuclear power, it sank into the miasma of ideology and motivations. As the campaign dragged on into the spring, debate degenerated into shouting matches, name-calling, and wild exaggerations of the opposition's position. In the battle of ideologies, CNS's message was at a disadvantage. Nonmaterialism had a distinct following, but the growth ethic still appealed to a wide audience struggling through the economic uncertainty of the seventies. As the country struggled with economic malaise, it was hard for the antinuclear movement to avoid charges of elitism.[84] Pronuclear forces devised their own version of the "people versus elites" theme by portraying the "neo-religious, radical environmentalists" as a "privileged few" willing to let the average citizen freeze in the dark and caring little for blue-collar workers who would lose their jobs from nuclear plant closings.[85] There was some truth to this charge since antinuclear activists and general supporters of Proposition 15 tended to be younger and more educated than the typical "no" voter.[86]

Instead of parrying specific attacks on nuclear safety, which the Warren hearings proved was impossible, the "No on 15" campaign fixed on economics. Proposition 15, in pronuclear ads, became a draconian "shutdown initiative" that would cost the state jobs and domestic product, and the average home owner thousands of dollars in higher electric bills.[87] Still smarting from the shocks of the recent economic downturn and rising fuel prices, most Americans looked toward their immediate problems of jobs and energy. For the average citizen, protecting future generations and a "small is beautiful" message paled before protection of America's energy supply.[88] By the time of the balloting, pronuclear forces gloated that they had thousands of people, journalists, and organizations chorusing: "It's too drastic. it's a shutdown."[89] The American people refused to follow the three engineers in a revolt against nuclear technology. It was a "masterful campaign," CNS media coordinator Larry Levine admitted.[90]

While the pronuclear message stayed on its economic theme, the disparate groups forming CNS failed to speak with the same unity. Scientific authority still carried ample influence among voters, and CNS worked hard for scientific endorsements. It had achieved some notable success in gaining the backing of the liberal American Federation of Scientists, the three GE engineers, and Nobel Prize winners Linus Pauling and Harold Urey. But through this authoritative façade surfaced populist, counterculture, and emotional pleas that appealed only to the converted. An undecided voter was sure to find the pronuclear message "California Scientists Urge No on 15" more convincing than "Why the Doobie Brothers Want You to Vote Yes on Proposition 15." Even when, CNS switched its advertising strategy, it had little influence on opinion. CNS ran photos of children in emotional ads emphasizing nuclear power's long-term hazards. It also contrasted the corporate funding for the "No on 15" campaign with its more populist effort.[91] Voters considered these arguments distractions from a more specific debate over the wisdom of the initiative. In a slow and steady progression, support for the initiative slipped.[92]

Seizing a Victory and Expanding State Power

But the industry strategy of portraying the initiative as extreme left a gap for Charles Warren and the Sierra Club lobbyists to push the nuclear bills through the legislature. While PG&E and other electric companies dragged their feet, Southern California Edison openly supported the bills and offered to work with Warren's committee to insert compromise language.[93] Assembly speaker Leo McCarthey, Charles Warren, and the Sierra Club's gifted lobbyist John Zierold worked in a bruising battle to keep the bills alive.[94] The utilities agreed to remain neutral on the legislation, while Warren, McCarthey, and Brown took a similar position on Proposition 15.[95] With sufficient compromises incorporated into the bills to pacify the utilities, opposition leadership shifted to Democratic senator Ralph Dills for the floor fight. At the top of his lungs,

In this June 1976 demonstration at a national utility conference held in San Francisco, supporters of Proposition 15 prominently featured children to highlight the questionable ethics of leaving nuclear wastes to future generations. Courtesy James Burch.

Dills attacked the "no-growth" philosophy of the bills as so much "gobbledegoo." "Let's do something manly for once," he exhorted his colleagues, "and turn this baby down." The lawmakers ignored this hairy-chested oratory, and the three bills passed the legislature. Governor Brown signed them into law on 3, June 1976, just days before the balloting on Proposition 15. "This kills the initiative," crowed Proposition 15 opponent Lieutenant Governor Mervyn Dymally.[96]

Why did the utilities accept the compromise? Unlike Warren's 1974 energy legislation, these bills offered the utilities nothing to compensate for their concessions. The utilities, observers believed, had the influence to stop the bills. By April, moreover, opinion polls showed growing pluralities against Proposition 15. By June a large "No" vote was certain. Support by Brown and others would help but was unlikely to pass the initiative. The nuclear industry could have had it all—a defeat of both Proposition 15 and the nuclear bills.

The industry believed the future of the atom was at stake. The energy crisis, nonexistent orders for plants, and the burgeoning antinuclear movement had eroded industry optimism. A half dozen antinuclear initiatives in other states awaited utilities in November, and they needed to win them all. Antinuclear elements were planning to move to nonviolent, direct action tactics against nuclear plants.[97] A close victory was insufficient to stem this tide. The industry needed a win, a big one.[98]

The voters appeared to give the nuclear industry their wish in the 8 June primary, striking down Proposition 15 by a 2 to 1 margin. Former congressman and industry lobbyist Craig Hosmer exultantly announced: "We have broken the back of the opponents—that vast collection of food faddists, perennial bitchers, deep-breathers, nature lovers and anti-establishment counter-culturists who came together in California."[99] *Time* called the vote a "go ahead" for nuclear power.[100] In one sense, Hosmer and *Time*'s analyses were correct. Polling indicated that citizens thought the atom was necessary in scarce times and opposed shutting it down.[101] Activists' grand dream of a national moratorium was dead. The public still believed in nuclear power as a savior of the nation's energy future.

Voting patterns, however, indicated a troubling shift by certain sectors against nuclear power, a technology that only a few years before had enjoyed overwhelming public support. Correlations of county-level returns with 1980 presidential voting and census data indicate that the antinuclear movement made its greatest inroads among nonmaterialist voters who were progressive, well educated, and affluent.[102] By contrast, opponents of the initiative scored well among lower economic classes and conservative voters. While counties with heavy Democratic voter registration tended to be antinuclear, a far better correlation was obtained by filtering out conservative Reagan Democrats. Progressive counties that supported Jimmy Carter in 1980 favored Proposition 15 with a correlation of +.62.[103] These voters were not the blue-collar constituencies that Reagan so successfully courted that year. Proposition 15 support was most evident in counties with rising levels of education and per capita income, with correlations of +.443 and +.419, respectively. In all, the three variables account for 76.5 percent of the variation in the voting data, with progressivism contributing the most, education second, and income the least.[104] There was no significant correlation between the vote and a county's share of its labor force in the manufacturing sector or unemployment levels. It would seem that while economic security encouraged antinuclear attitudes, insecurity had no effect. A similar analysis reveal that a county's share of its labor in agriculture was not quite statistically significant, but the correlation was negative as might be expected considering agriculture's historic hostility to environmental issues. Proposition 15 was a decidedly progressive issue.[105]

The Proposition 15 vote lends credence to scholars who argue that the antinuclear movement was a postindustrial phenomenon. It was popular among Americans and Western Europeans who escaped pressing concerns about their material well-being and were instead driven by concerns for quality of life.[106] These were the voters who responded to the "Yes on 15" campaign's advertisements emphasizing personal and environmental safety, moral appeals, and participatory democracy. Nuclear supporters' warnings of economic and social collapse made their greatest mark among the less affluent and educated Californians.

The nuclear industry had achieved its big win, but the margin masked the great inroads the antinuclear movement had made among important sectors of the voting public. A third of the voters were now committed to shutting down nuclear power regardless of the influence it would have on their electric supply. The significance of this fact was not lost on David Pesonen, who told reporters, "A million and a half people were willing to vote to shut down nuclear power. Those people are firm and will not go away."[107] Firmness did not characterize the sentiments of those who rejected Proposition 15, and many were wary of a pronuclear energy policy.[108] Majorities believed the nation was better off investing in alternative energy sources and conservation, even at a risk to living standards.[109] The "shutdown" theme of the pronuclear campaign made the ballot an inaccurate gauge of public concern for nuclear safety and waste disposal. The large no vote represented a desire to protect basic energy supplies and a rejection of a radical proposal.[110] And by putting the issue before the public, the initiative raised public awareness of nuclear safety issues to nearly 95 percent.[111] Voters initiatives in the future were far easier for antinuclear activists to mount as it finally became respectable to question America's commitment to the peaceful atom.

The pronuclear victory also obscured the significant challenge to federal control that the initiative generated. Charles Warren's legislation was a state's rights rebel yell against the federal government's control of the peaceful atom. Richard Maullin, chairman of the California Energy Commission, described the new authority vested in his commission as "a new facet of energy federalism. We will be holding the federal government to the test."[112] This new power was destined at a later date to be tested in the courts. Legal opinion assumed that the initiatives and even Warren's legislature would fall before federal preemption. Nuclear industry lawyers began preparing for a future legal challenge that would ask the courts to take a broad interpretation of federal powers under the 1954 Atomic Energy Act. They asked the justices to declare that the real motive behind the new state laws was to regulate reactor safety, not land use.[113] The lawyers were right, of course, but Gene Varanini had been preparing for a legal challenge too. He wrote the final Warren committee report on Proposition 15 knowing the document would be the focal point of any legal challenge. He gave the safety issue a wide berth and justified California's regulation of nuclear power as an economic necessity. State regulation of nuclear construction was essential, Varanini wrote, because waste disposal problems were "largely economic or the result of poor planning, not safety-related."[114]

Regardless of these notable gains, Proposition 15's large defeat would alter the direction of the movement; it would turn away from moderate elements who had provided it with its political and legal victories. The coalition that came together for Proposition 15 drifted apart as the nuclear industry declined. Peace groups and Creative Initiative moved on to weapons issues in the early eighties. Populist elements within the movement had strengthened the initiative process, but the national initiative dreamed of by Ed Koupal faded with his death in March 1976 and with the defeats of the other state nuclear initiatives. Nuclear power would not be the means to popular democracy or a radical social transformation. Some activists envisioned a radical direction. "We're feeling very disillusioned about the legal and legislative channels for stopping nuclear power," one California activist pointed out. "Our new method is disciplined, nonviolent direct action."[115] These activists would invest their energies in a large but futile movement to stop the already constructed Diablo Canyon nuclear plant.

It has been the failure of the antinuclear movement with Proposition

15, however, and at sites like Diablo Canyon that has led scholars to dismiss its influence. Certainly Proposition 15's large margin of defeat could not be called a victory.[116] But as the rest of this study will demonstrate, Proposition 15's regulatory and attitudinal legacy would solidify with two new California conflicts. The demise of a new project in the eastern California desert would reveal the shift in regulatory power to antinuclear state officials. At the same time, a proposal in the Central Valley would demonstrate how nuclear opposition had spread beyond the ranks of nonmaterialists to become a pervasive attitude even among the most conservative elements of society.

But what had Proposition 15 meant for pronuclear idealists? These apostles had lost much in this fight. They could only watch with alarm as the nation's commitment to their worldview and the respect accorded them, once almost mystical, weakened. What solace could they take in this muddled compromise? There was little for an individual to do but lash out at enemies. When Edward Teller branded the former GE engineers traitors, it was to a vision of the nation fewer individuals accepted. The best label for that vision is an overused term these days: the American Dream. To Teller and many Americans, the dream still meant economic growth, confidence, and a way of life without limits.[117] Because the energy crisis demonstrated the risks of fossil fuels, the peaceful atom appeared to them as the only way to save the dream. The California initiative indicated that Americans were less sure of the old values; new ones had to be found.

5

Frankenstein's Monster Comes of Age

The California Energy Commission
and the Sundesert Project

Frank Fats, a Chinese restaurant at 802 L street in Sacramento and just a couple of blocks from the capitol building, is one of the favorite eateries for state politicians and lobbyists. Since 1939, some of the major political deals in California have been made and written out on its table napkins over wonton and fortune cookies. In the thirties, forties, and fifties, it was the lobbyists who ran Sacramento politics from Fats's tables. Full-time lobbyists exerted considerable influence over the part-time legislators—writing their laws and even obtaining lodging and office space for them. Artie Samish, once dubbed the most powerful man in California by Earl Warren, held court in the real seat of power, Fats's opulent dining room, as legislators came to do his bidding.[1]

Lobbying had gotten tougher since the fifties.[2] The proliferation of interest groups and political reform laws had made it difficult for any industry or lobbyist to control state politics. Lobbyists still gathered at Frank Fats, but the legislators who came no longer trembled before them, and relations with Governor Jerry Brown were cool. The lobbyists assigned to push through approval of San Diego Gas and Electric's Sundesert nuclear plant in California's southeastern desert near Blythe knew they faced a task more difficult than anything Artie Samish ever

confronted. In early 1978, Frank Devore, a vice president and chief lobbyist for San Diego Gas and Electric (SDG&E), and some other utility
employees sat in Frank Fats late one evening after managing to engineer
a bill through the senate that would exempt the project from the limitations of the 1976 nuclear bills.[3] SDG&E needed the exemption because
one of the nuclear bills prohibited construction of Sundesert or any
other new nuclear plant until the Energy Commission certified that the
federal government had found a solution to high-level radioactive waste
disposal problems. There was no hope that would happen. Despite Devore's victory in the state senate, none of the men from SDG&E were in
a celebratory mood. Those gathered knew the project was just one step
from oblivion as a host of California agencies wanted to kill it. The California Energy Commission[4] and the Public Utilities Commission both
had recommended against construction. To bypass them, SDG&E
needed approval for the exemption bill by the liberal state assembly,
where it was locked up in committee. Even if it won a vote by the legislature, Governor Jerry Brown had vowed to veto it. The only chance Devore had was for the state assembly to pass the exemption bill. That
show of political power in an election year might induce the governor
to sign the bill. The governor was the only man with enough influence
to change the minds of committee members who held the exemption bill
hostage. As the utility employees ate their dinner, Jerry Brown, taking
a break from his late-night work habits, walked into Frank Fats for a
meal.

Frank Devore had argued before with Jerry Brown about the project,
but he could not let the opportunity to confront the governor go. He had
been the company's point man for Sundesert since the project's incep-
tion in 1973, and it was consuming his life. "I practically did not get to
raise my two daughters because I was gone [from home] so much," Devore remembered. Devore had come to SDG&E as a ditchdigger with an
eighth-grade education but had risen to the top in Horatio Alger style
with hard work and a reputation for honesty. A practical and outspoken
man, Devore was not impressed with Brown's "no-growth" philosophy
and his opposition to nuclear power. Neither, the lobbyist believed, was
good for the state's business climate. "Governor Brown was never interested in the economics of the state," Devore recalled. Devore was
certain San Diego needed Sundesert's cheap power for its economy and
future generations. He had worked to build a coalition of Southland
cities, chambers of commerce, farm groups, and labor. Now it seemed
the project would not win approval because it was caught up in election
year politics. Brown's growing opposition to nuclear power seemed irrational and unrealistic to a man of Devore's sensibilities. It was more a

play for environmental support in future gubernatorial and presidential races than a sober assessment of state power needs. If the plant was to be built, Devore had to confront the governor and plead his case.[4] As Brown ate his dinner, the two men argued, and a group of legislators and lobbyists joined in. Neither man had much new to say. For years, nuclear opponents and proponents had tossed about the same arguments: the need for the plant, safety, the lack of a waste disposal solution, and the reasonability of energy alternatives. What it would now come down to was political strength. The assembly's floor leader, Lou Pappin, jumped in, arguing that Devore deserved the chance to have the issue brought before the full chamber. But Brown would not hear of it. The exemption bill would not get out of committee, the governor informed the group. He did not want a nuclear plant approved while he was in office, and he would not overrule the Energy Commission. Devore left the governor to finish his dinner knowing he had wasted the last five years of his life. Sundesert was lost and with it the war over nuclear power in California.[5]

It is difficult to exaggerate the stakes that both sides thought they were playing for in the Sundesert controversy. Since California was the trend-setting state for the country, the nuclear industry was convinced that its chances for new nuclear construction rested in Jerry Brown's hands. And so when Brown became the first major politician to use his office to stop a nuclear plant, there was bedlam in California and the nation. Jerry Brown and the Energy Commission were pilloried by a substantial number of politicians and nearly every newspaper in the state. Even Democrats such as Los Angeles mayor Tom Bradley joined in with the plant's supporters in condemning the Sundesert decision.[6] One of the legislators who created the Energy Commission confessed to feeling like "Dr. Frankenstein" for creating the agency most responsible for Sundesert's demise. The national press was critical as well. The *Washington Post* predicted that because of the California governor's action "the next generation is likely to be sitting around in the dark blaming utilities for not doing something this generation's officials wouldn't let them do."[7] "We'll All Freeze in the Dark," prophesized an editorial headline in, of all places, Palm Springs.[8] In the face of mounting fossil fuel costs, there was a consensus outside of antinuclear groups that the decision to forgo the nuclear option was ludicrous.

To those in the Brown administration who engineered the Sundesert defeat, the only thing more satisfying than watching the utility industry eat its words was just how quickly it did so. By 1983, with Three Mile Island, collapsing energy demand, and billion dollar losses accompanying nuclear plant cancellations, SDG&E conceded that the decision to cancel the project had saved it from possible bankruptcy. "We wouldn't want to be in the middle of building Sundesert today," confessed SDG&E's engineering vice president Gary Cotton.[9] A utility spokesperson noted, "The age of the dinosaur—the large central power plant . . .—may have passed."[10] A decade later, SDG&E representatives remained quite relieved they did not build. "I don't think we would build [a nuclear plant] if they gave us the permit and the money [to do it]," SDG&E's lobbyist confessed.[11] In the unfortunate history of the nuclear industry, it was one of the few times when a state regulatory agency stopped a nuclear plant early enough to avert substantial losses. Former adversaries have now joined in looking to alternatives to nuclear power plants.

Why were Sundesert and the whole nuclear industry halted in California? Immediate analysis focused on politics and money. The press credited the governor's presidential aspirations and his desire to court environmental votes. Brown himself bragged, "*I* blocked the Sundesert plant."[12] Still, opposing nuclear construction was a huge political risk for a national politician. Brown halted Sundesert a full year before the accident at Three Mile Island. There was no hue and cry to stop reactor construction. Some scholars favor economic arguments and the role of the Public Utilities Commission. The PUC had argued that SDG&E could not afford to build the plant and denied the utility the rate increase it needed to continue construction.[13] Sundesert was never built because "economically it [made] no sense," contended former public utility chairperson Robert Batinovich.[14] Yet regulators at the time admitted that Sundesert was the most economic and pollution-free option. If money alone had been the problem, SDG&E could have sought more partners in the project to improve financing.

Sundesert was, rather, the logical conclusion of the movement that had begun at Bodega Bay and came to a close in the desert sands near Blythe. The demands by Bodega activists for public participation, environmental consideration, and a whole new set of public and regulatory values had altered the context in which political and economic calculations were made. Jerry Brown's short-term political maneuvers and economic calculations were merely the end result of trends that had been developing for decades.

Sundesert made plain the reciprocal relationship between activists, politicians, and state capacity that had fundamentally changed energy policy over a ten-year period. The state's history of energy policy debate and large economic resources provided the rationale to dramatically change its government structure with the creation of the Energy Commission. The commission and its access to resources in expertise and funding affected the goals, behavior, and accomplishments of activist organizations who were interested in energy policy. Instead of direct-action protest, antinuclear activists could achieve their goals through the accommodating procedures and philosophy of the commission.[15]

The antinuclear movement in turn influenced Energy Commission policy by linking three ingredients: ideology, growing state regulatory power, and energy forecasting that emphasized conservation. Ideology had three important roles. The expanding popularity of a nonmaterialist worldview, especially in the wake of Proposition 15, made for a significant constituency that included sympathetic scientists outside and inside government. Ideology also altered state regulatory power and energy forecasting. Environmentalists understood the importance of the state in opposing nuclear plant construction and had fought hard to create in the Energy Commission a sympathetic institution that would challenge federal control. This worldview also encouraged new views about energy use and forecasting at a time when old ideas that had served utilities for decades were in crisis.

National trends, too, worked in favor of the antinuclear agenda. By 1978, new values, particularly of the environmental movement, had spread throughout the country, fundamentally altering the nature of American society. Moreover, the opposition to Sundesert would not have succeeded if there had not been a legitimate crisis in the nation's economy and utility industry. Nor could it have prevailed without the general expansion of bureaucracy at all levels in the sixties and seventies, of which the Energy Commission was a product. Nuclear opponents outside and within the Brown administration succeeded because an opportunity to promote their views existed, evidence cast doubt on the viability of nuclear power, and there was sufficient state capacity to force new ideas on a reluctant industry.

With regard to state capacity, what is remarkable about the Sundesert story is how a variety of officials, groups, and politicians came together to make the state a stronger player in energy issues. In the process, they circumscribed the power of the nuclear industry, lobbyists, and even other state agencies. Significantly, the Energy Commission marked the fruition of a state rebellion against federal energy and nuclear policy that was influenced to a large degree by the antinuclear movement. Thus California shut out the influence of the federal government in its decisions over nuclear power. The rebellion ensured that if the peaceful atom was to have any future, "energy federalism" would guide America's nuclear policy.

The Early Years of the Energy Commission

Although the Energy Commission developed into an agency friendly to nonmaterialist values, there was no guarantee that this would be the case.[16] The Warren-Alquist Act that created the commission was a compromise between the utility industry's legislative ally, Alfred Alquist, and the environmentalists' champion in the assembly, Charles Warren. The negotiated settlement granted industry the accelerated approval procedures for power plant siting it desired. Environmental groups won an agency with the power to promote energy conservation and alternatives, enact building and appliance codes mandating energy efficiency, and determine how much energy was really needed by the state. They had also secured a commission that provided a more democratic "public process" than California's past power plant siting efforts. The Energy Commission, environmentalists envisioned, would ensure that decisions involving nuclear power would not be left only to scientific experts.[17] Unfortunately, the law institutionalized the battle between industry and environmentalists. Born in the midst of an energy crisis and the nation's electric wars, the commission would have to develop under intense scrutiny by pro and antinuclear factions who looked for any indication of "capture" by the opposition. By legislative fiat, the Energy Commission would have a split personality. It would have the rather undemocratic function of speeding approval of power plants while also trying to expand public access to the debate and discouraging construction of new power plants. The early years would be a contest to see whose commission it would be, Charles Warren's or Alfred Alquist's. Events, some unforeseen, and the bureaucratic evolution of the Energy Commission would ensure that Charles Warren would win.

The first mistake the utilities made was agreeing to the Warren-Alquist compromise in expectation that they could control appointments to the five commissioner seats. In March of 1974, this did not seem an unreasonable assumption since the two leading candidates to fill outgoing governor Ronald Reagan's shoes were Republican Houston Flournoy and assembly speaker Robert Moretti. Moretti had a record of supporting environmental reform, but was a traditional Democrat interested in using the government as a spur to jobs and economic growth. A man who loved the art of compromise and deal making, Moretti could be expected to accommodate nuclear power.[18]

Watergate shocked California politics by rocketing thirty-six-year-old Jerry Brown to prominence and the governorship. Taking advantage of the Watergate scandal, Brown used his position as secretary of state to form a coalition of citizen groups such as Common Cause and Ed Koupal's People's Lobby to sponsor a successful campaign and lobby reform initiative. Brown rode the reformist wave and enjoyed the substantial name recognition of being Pat Brown's son. He won the Democratic nod and then beat Houston Flournoy in a close race in the November 1974 campaign.[19]

It was not obvious what the rise of Jerry Brown meant for the state energy debate. In the election, Brown had cultivated labor support and avoided any controversial ideas. This was in part due to campaign tactics, but on energy issues it also revealed Brown's ignorance. One of his key aides, Richard Maullin, remembered that Brown was completely innocent of the ongoing electric war. The Jerry Brown that would come to national attention in 1976 as an advocate of sparse lifestyles and a "small is beautiful" view of energy problems was hardly visible.[20]

Brown's lack of interest in energy issues showed in his initial appointments to the Energy Commission, and nearly ensured the utility capture of the agency. The reasons for each choice had little to do with administering an effective energy policy for the state. Richard Maullin had been squeezed out of Brown's inner circle and was appointed commission chairperson as a consolation prize. The story had become current that Maullin, a political scientist with the Rand Corporation, and another aide, Thomas Quinn, had "made" Brown and that there was little substance to the new governor. Perhaps insecure of his position, Brown had purged Maullin and Quinn from his inner circle. Maullin was a shrewd strategist who was adept at finding the political center of an issue. It was difficult to know how he would vote, "but he always voted with the majority," one staffer recalled. Despite Maullin's banishment, he was considered a close ally of Brown, and his votes were often a bellwether of the governor's agenda.[21] Over time, Maullin would shift to the antinuclear camp.

Political considerations, rather than energy policy, assured that the Energy Commission would begin with a pronuclear majority. The Energy Commission was a convenient place for vanquished foes. Robert Moretti, once the powerful assembly speaker and now simply a defeated gubernatorial candidate, still had enough friends in Sacramento to make his appointment to the commission a wise choice. Richard Tuttle had been a Public Utilities Commission lawyer, but his primary qualification was his large donation to the Brown campaign. Brown's old college friend Allen Pasternak, a nuclear engineer, became the fourth commissioner. Moretti, Tuttle, and Pasternak formed a pronuclear coalition that controlled the direction of the commission until Tuttle's departure in 1976.[22]

Only the appointment of Ron Doctor pleased environmentalists and antinuclear activists. As one of the key authors of the influential 1973 Rand study that had inspired the creation of the Energy Commission, Doctor brought with him solid expertise as a nuclear engineer, experience in electrical demand forecasting, and an uncompromising opposition to nuclear power. While technically well qualified, Doctor was a newcomer to Sacramento and not as politically aware as Moretti and Maullin. His critics argued that Doctor was arrogant and shrill, and he often alienated those he needed to convert.[23]

This motley assortment of individuals would have been contentious even in an agency with a long history of bureaucratic inertia. Given that they were creating the Energy Commission from whole cloth, the combination was explosive. "These five guys had about as bad a chemistry as you can think of," Gene Varanini recalled.[24] The commissioners quickly grasped that every choice they made—in staffing, developing commission structure, and even selecting energy forecasting models— would have significant influence on the direction of energy use and nuclear power. With no clear lines of authority in the new agency, there were no institutional mechanisms for dealing with dissent. The stage was set for a civil war over the basic nature of the Energy Commission.

The commission's pronuclear majority seemed to have an advantage as a voting bloc and as a result of national trends. The 1973 oil crisis had brought with it proposals for a massive increase in the commitment to nuclear energy. Richard Nixon's Project Independence proposals called for 40 percent of the nation's electricity to come from the atom. Other ideas included rate relief to allow utilities to come up with the massive capital needed to build nuclear plants.[25] Coming just three weeks after the advent of the Arab oil embargo, Nixon's proposals had been little more than a technological enthusiast's knee-jerk response and lacked political support. His, and later Gerald Ford's, sympathetic proposals for the utility industry died in the midst of partisan feuds and Watergate. A comprehensive federal energy policy would not develop until 1978 under Jimmy Carter.

A less obvious but more enduring legacy of the energy crisis was detrimental to nuclear power. The energy crisis opened up for questioning and scrutiny what had been an invisible sector of the economy. Nixon's Project Independence had the unintended effect of bringing together skeptical analysts to look at the utility industry's electricity demand forecasting methods. Utility forecasts repeatedly overestimated growth, and the industry now had to confront experts who used sophisticated analysis that revealed flaws in their methods. The Project Independence team had developed forecasting models that it hoped would become a standard for the country.[26]

The failure to develop a federal policy during the Nixon-Ford administrations left the job of forecasting to innovative states like California. Project Independence employees and other energy analysts in the country created a ready pool of talent for the Golden State. In search of managers to supervise the Energy Commission's five hundred new employees, commissioners found the federal analysts easy recruits. They came for the reasons people had always come: for the sun, the quality of life, and the excitement of living in a land on the cutting edge of innovation.[27]

There was a great social purpose to their mission. It may seem odd that something as mundane as predicting electricity consumption could carry some higher purpose, but one thing that both sides of the electric wars agreed on was that energy was at the root of the nation's social and economic problems. Staffers hoped that the Energy Commission would lead the nation in a quiet revolution just as the Golden State had done in so many other areas.[28] The Energy Commission thus formed an institutional culture friendly to new approaches and an environmental consciousness. The staff was infused with the conviction that they could protect the environment and make better use of its resources, Richard Maullin remembered.[29] There would be a price to pay for idealism. Before it could change the way California and the nation thought about energy, the commission would have to resolve its split personality.

"It was a bloodbath," Ron Doctor remembered of the internecine struggles for the Energy Commission's soul that he participated in. A bit of hyperbole, perhaps, but those who worked for the commission agreed with Doctor's assessment. They found themselves enduring "gut-wrenching, soul-searching, sleepless weeks" trying to come to terms with one question: Which side are you on? Staff members could not feel safe from interference from individual commissioners who did not like their conclusions.[30] It was not unusual for them to be hauled before one or more of the commissioners and grilled to find proof of flaws in their thinking that could be used against them. Maullin remembered the staff being pressed by some of their bosses and commissioners to draw preordained conclusions. "This approach was VERY hard on the staff," Ron Doctor wrote. "Individual staff people usually were being pulled in different directions by Moretti, Maullin and me." In turn, staffers would bypass their immediate division chiefs and even the executive director and appeal to sympathetic commissioners. In the fluid first years of the commission, there were few clear guidelines dictating behavior, and that too contributed to the tensions.[31]

The war of ideology and ethics fought out by the commissioners and staff loyal to them was incessant. On the seemingly innocuous matter of insulation codes for new construction, for example, commissioners disagreed. Was it right for the commission to demand that consumers buy new homes with insulation? For Robert Moretti such a demand was overly intrusive and costly to those who aspired to the American Dream of home ownership. Ron Doctor thought the denial of personal freedom and immediate costs incurred were more than compensated for by eventual savings and need to moderate behavior for the good of the environment.[32] Doctor prevailed. The commission developed effective conservation standard on home insulation and appliance efficiency. "They served as models for other states," Doctor noted, "and in fact were implemented across the country. By the time the nuclear lobby woke up to this it was too late. There was a state-based bandwagon rolling."[33]

The fighting turned ugly and public. In 1975, an early Energy Commission forecast of dubious quality showed demand rising at a rate dramatically below utility predictions. Some staffers feared that the pronuclear commissioners would squelch the report. Commissioners were aware that the report could be used by antinuclear activists who were than at full throttle in pushing Proposition 15. These staff fears appeared warranted when the commissioners ignored the forecast and instead adopted a robust forecast that relied on utility estimates.[34]

For antinuclear activists, the leaking of the original report and the subsequent firing of the chief of the forecasting division were proof that the commission had been "captured" by pronuclear forces.[35] Charging that some of the commissioners had "sold out to the nuclear community," the People's Lobby claimed that the Energy Commission was suppressing the information and serving as a "platform to promote nuclear power regardless of any forecast to the contrary." John Zierold, Sierra Club lobbyist, called the high forecasts "unconscionable," and environmentalists gave the Brown administration a "D" on energy regulation.[36] Conversely, the utility industry was pleased with the Energy Commission's performance, and a spokesperson noted that it was doing a "very good job, considering their [short life]."[37]

The Energy Commission's pronuclear drift could not continue for long. Despite the best efforts of the pronuclear commission majority of Pasternak, Tuttle, and Moretti, a number of trends finally turned the tide against those favoring growth and development of nuclear power.

An important influence that would ensure that the Energy Commission would not be a captured agency was its mandate to promote citizen participation. The commission's public advisor, former community activist Tony Rossman, was charged with seeking public involvement in Energy Commission proceedings and deliberations. Rossman worked hard to make the position as independent of the commissioners as possible and to make his office the "Commission's public conscience," Ron Doctor wrote. The Energy Commission would be a truly public agency whose decisions were closely scrutinized by the public.

Charles Warren and his staff assistant Gene Varanini were also carefully following the direction of the agency they had created. They were intent on forcing the commission to develop its own expertise and capacity to formulate energy policy without relying on the electric industry or unreliable think tanks. When the commission tried to farm out certain studies to independents such as Lawrence Berkeley Labs, Varanini and Warren cut the commission's funding for such projects. Warren and Varanini demanded that the commission do most of its own work. While it may have hurt the quality of work initially, it was the policy that turned the commission into the independent policy maker Warren and environmentalists wanted.[38]

The Warren-Alquist legislation also lent the Energy Commission a structural bias toward conservation, alternative sources, and reduced growth and against new power plant construction. The energy assessment, conservation, and alternatives implementation divisions, by virtue of their mission and staffing, tended to oppose new plant construction as antithetical to their goals. Only the energy facility siting division's mandate of overseeing the approval of specific power plant locations was friendly to new plant construction. It was also the division that employed most of the commission's hirees from the utility and nuclear industry. The siting unit was outnumbered in any decision requiring the full participation of the commission's divisions. It was considered something of a rebel in its philosophy by the rest of the staff.[39] And so the commission had its own philosophy and was not as prone to "capture" by the pronuclear faction as thought had been.[40] As much as pronuclear commissioners wanted to steer the Energy Commission one way, the staff and the commission structure were pulling in a different direction.

This trend was clear in the early conflicts over which method the commission would use to forecast electricity demand. The choice of one model over another would determine whether nuclear plants were needed at all. "Everybody, staff and commissioners, knew that if you came up with a low forecast you would not need nuclear power," Ron Doctor thought. "The forecast became the stand-in for the nuclear power battle itself." If demand grew quickly, only large-scale power plants such as nuclear power would be sufficient to meet the country's needs. Predictions of slower growth would eliminate a large number of power plants from construction planning. Slowed growth would allow smaller alternative energy projects such as geothermal, wind farms, and cogeneration to compete. It would be possible to cobble together a number of small sources and a little enforced conservation to replace the few nuclear plants that might be required. Operating on ground he was expert at, Ron Doctor and the staff developed low forecasting methods that cut much of the need for nuclear power.[42]

New forecasting techniques were already gaining currency nationally as the utilities' methods faltered. The slump in the economy and higher cost of fuel after 1973 had caused utilities to scale back the scope of construction plans, but many assumed that the energy crisis was a temporary setback. They did not rethink their assumptions about energy use. The utility industry clung to the myth that electric growth was directly related to economic growth. Conservation and changing consumption patterns, it believed, altered the equation little. Forecasting had been a simple matter of trend analysis—looking back at the past decade's economic and electric growth, plotting it on a graph, and extending the curve ever upward. The method was similar to trying to determine the grade of the road ahead by looking backward.[41] Effective in periods of stability, it was poor at predicting the bumps ahead; in this case, Americans were about to change their patterns of consumption. By 1979, the electrical industry had admitted its failure, calling forecasting "an annual exercise in futility."[43]

With the utilities in disarray, the Energy Commission staff started formulating a new method of forecasting. At the Rand Corporation, Ron Doctor had done the kind of modeling the commission hoped to do.[44] The commission staff started by asking questions about energy use on a microscopic level. Would households continue to increase electrical consumption at the rate that they had in the past two decades? This was dubious. Much of the past growth came as families bought appliances for the first time. Washers, dryers, electric stoves, refrigerators, and televisions had now saturated the market. New units were usually just replacements, and more efficient ones at that. This was especially true in the wake of the commission's new efficiency standards. New appliances would actually decrease consumption. Would new appliances appear? Well, yes, as the personal computer has demonstrated, but not as often as in the past, and electronics did not use as much power. The net effect of this microscopic analysis, what was dubbed "end-use" forecasting, was to reveal the fat in the utilities' breezy predictions of constant growth. "What made [the Energy Commission's forecasting capability] so important," Doctor recalled, "was that the utilities could no longer hide behind some mystical expertness." The Energy Commission demonstrated that the go-go days of the sixties would not return even if the economy resumed its bullish ways.[45] The age when electricity and the economy grew in parallel was over.[46]

Indicative of the dramatic change in the regulatory climate since the Bodega controversy, Pat Fleming of San Diego Gas and Electric stands next to the 30-volume, multimillion dollar, Environmental Impact Report required for the Sundesert project. The company spent nearly 100 million on the ill-fated power plant. Courtesy San Diego Gas and Electric Company.

It was a substantial victory and an indication of a maturing staff expertise when the commission's model withstood the challenges of the utility industry. With no factual basis to oppose it, the pronuclear commissioners, save Pasternak, voted to accept the staff's model.[47] The utilities lowered their forecasts accordingly, and as one SDG&E engineer admitted, "time has proven they were right." The commission's model was the most developed at that time and portended a national shift to end-use forecasting.[48] The lower forecast wiped away a huge block of California electric industry's plans for nuclear construction. This effective work by the commission made it a leader in the growing state resistance to nuclear power. Ron Doctor and Charles Warren were avidly sought after in like-minded states such as Washington, Minnesota, and even Arizona.[49]

Jerry Brown's Antinuclear Evolution

The greening of the Energy Commission received added stimulus from an environmentalist shift within the Brown administration that would also have implications for the Energy Commission. As Jerry Brown's presidential ambitions heated up in 1976, he began to take a closer look at energy issues and cultivate environmental support both as a voting bloc and for campaign financing. In his presidential bid, he spoke the lingo of the environmental movement, referring to "spaceship earth." As governor, he raised serious doubts about the installation of a liquid natural gas terminal in the state, supported the 1976 nuclear bills, and sought legislation to protect the coast. All of this was anathema to traditional Democrats and conservatives. They accused Brown of placing his presidential aspirations ahead of the state's economic welfare. "If Jimmy Carter says sweet, Jerry Brown says sour," surmised conservative columnists Roland Evans and Robert Novak.[50]

Jerry Brown's ambitions for high office certainly influenced his political decisions, but considering his background and worldview, it would have been amazing if he had not taken a new direction in Democratic politics. Simply put, Jerry Brown was not his father's son. There was more to their differences than generational tension. Pat Brown had been a traditional New Deal liberal in his faith in government and the accommodation of all interests. "I'm an environmentalist but I'm also a builder," the elder Brown once said. "I love to see projects."[51] Jerry Brown was no builder. He had been disillusioned with the failure of sixties liberalism to solve social and economic problems. He was a part of the generation who believed that Vietnam demonstrated the failure of expertise, large-scale projects, and government solutions. It was no accident that in searching for a metaphor to explain the nuclear controversy, he called it the "Vietnam" of the seventies.

The two Browns were different, too, in lifestyle and ethics. Pat Brown had never been as impressed by the ascetic traditions of his Catholic roots as his son. Jerry Brown hoped to bring to politics the ethics of simplicity and frugality and the belief that each person was ultimately responsible for his/her life that he had learned in his brief stint in a Jesuit seminary. It was his Catholic thinking and evangelical desire to create a new spirit, a new man, a more ethical moral person that drove him, surmised Richard Maullin. While Brown's attraction to Zen philosophy caused him to be labeled a New Age[52] politician, it was the similarity between Zen and his own Jesuit experiences of frugality, intuitiveness, and simplicity that struck a chord with him.[53]

Jerry Brown's attraction to environmentalism, then, was much in the religious tradition of one of his heroes, E. F. Schumacher, another Catholic drawn to philosophies of the East. Brown, by 1976, sounded every bit like the British economist who had contended that "small is beautiful." "A simpler view of life is coming upon us. I have no doubt about that," he told William F. Buckley. "The accumulation of possessions and material indulgence is impossible over time because of the ecological limits imposed on this planet."[54]

Brown and his environmental allies aspired to change the nation's faith in growth and disregard of limits. Never before had a band of pessimists approached the task of lowering expectations with such glee. A simpler view. Limits. Small is beautiful. To many, these notions were the ideas of a pessimist and un-American. "Thanks to the triple blessing of the lost cause in Vietnam, the loss of control of the Energy Crisis, and the loss of innocence with Watergate, general prospects for America are now better than they've been in years," exulted the publisher of the *Whole Earth Catalog* and Brown confidant, Stewart Brand. "Three public humiliations in two years has put the country in Learning Mode."[55] A chastened America might finally change on the most essential level— energy consumption.

Brown's longtime allies found themselves shunted aside as the governor sought out New Age messengers not only for intellectual inspiration, but as government administrators. No longer looking in from outside, environmentalists and New Age followers flooded into the Brown administration, filling key posts. They brought with them a new critique of business, lifestyles, and power structures. Spurred on by their experience with Vietnam, the environmental movement, and the energy crisis, these new administrators tried to bring new ethics to energy production. They emphasized reducing consumption, small-scale production facilities, renewable alternatives to traditional energy sources such as nuclear and oil. Advocates of a "soft energy path" such as Amory Lovins argued that ultimately their energy ideas were more democratic and less threatening to human survival than nuclear power. In addition to the dangers inherent in the technology, they feared that continued expansion of the atom would foster nuclear proliferation. thus future world stability depended on the "soft" path. There may not be another chance to turn back, they warned.[56]

The Brown administration became a bazaar for people with ideas on energy alternatives. Whether it was energy from kelp or a solar cow washer, no idea went unsampled by Brown. Some ideas were as nutty as they appeared, and critics dismissed the "woodchips and windmills" approach.[57] But the Brown administration's willingness to consider any alternative proved to be a blessing. In pressing for the Lovins agenda of diverse energy sources, conservation, and smaller power plants in opposition to conventional industry wisdom, the New Agers were onto something. "[Brown] was surrounded by a horde of nontraditional people," noted Jim Cassie, lobbyist for SDG&E. "I hate to say this, they really were on the cutting edge of what we are doing today [in the energy field]."[58]

Jerry Brown's sympathies with environmentalists had immediate influence on the Sundesert proceedings in his appointment of Emilio (Gene) Varanini to replace Richard Tuttle as one of the five energy commissioners. Environmentalists considered the appointment a litmus test of Jerry Brown's seriousness about environmental issues, and cheered the appointment of Charles Warren's key aide from the Assembly Energy Resources and Land Use Committee.[59] Varanini was not a political appointee and was supremely qualified. Varanini's independence of Brown made him acceptable to utilities. Recognizing that there was little chance that Brown would appoint anyone sympathetic to the utilities, industry lobbyists consoled themselves with the notion that Varanini was "not in line with the Governor."[60]

Naval academy graduate, marine officer, lawyer, and assembly staff member, Varanini could claim the Energy Commission as a child of his considerable skill and experience. Having worked with Warren on energy issues before anyone else was thinking about them, Varanini had helped steer the pathbreaking Rand study of 1973 to completion, had written the legislation creating the Energy Commission, and had served a key role in the negotiations over the 1976 bills. What he also brought was a passion for his work, an unpredictable temper, and dogged determination. Unfortunately for the staff, he was very willing to interfere with their work. And when Varanini latched onto an issue he refused to let go of it.

Varanini brought his talents to the Energy Commission's immediate task of evaluating the status of the federal government's long-term nuclear waste disposal program. Without a positive determination by the commission that the federal government had found a solution, the 1976 nuclear bills stipulated that no new nuclear plants, including Sundesert, could be built. Utility executives had accepted the 1976 bills in part because they had received quiet assurances from federal regulators that the waste disposal problem would be solved within a year. If those assurances were true, the legislation would have no real influence on their construction schedules. This concession by the industry was a fatal mistake. "We had them," Varanini recalled in a revealing admission of his antinuclear leanings. "It was clear the feds didn't know what they were doing [with the waste disposal problem]."[61]

Varanini's opposition to nuclear power broke the Energy Commission's pronuclear majority.[62] This became apparent when the Energy Commission adopted its biennial report. The report was not only a projection of state energy use but a statement of the operating philosophy of the commission. With the pronuclear commissioners Pasternak and Moretti in dissent, the commission adopted a program that one industry official described as "almost pure [Amory] Lovins." There was some truth in the official's sweeping conclusion that the New Agers, whom he called "Aquarians," had gained control.[63] While differing in their logic by favoring economic arguments more than Lovins, the commissioners embraced his ideas on alternatives and offering subsidies for their development. They also argued against building large nuclear power plants.[64] It was an indication that the industry had lost the energy war. One nuclear industry official concluded, "while we were winning at the ballot box [during Proposition 15] the Aquarians were consolidating their hold on the energy policy apparatus at the federal level and to a very significant degree in the important state of California."[65]

The shift in the balance of power in the Energy Commission was later confirmed when in early October 1977. Robert Moretti resigned accusing the commissioners of being "no-growth" and the commission of "purposely attempting to stop nuclear power in this state." Moretti's departure signaled that the pronuclear advocates had lost control of the commission.[66] A bid to regain control by preventing Ron Doctor's reappointment failed when legislators dismissed as trivial charges that he had abused state funds in dropping his daughter off at school in a state vehicle.

SDG&E's Nuclear Gamble

If the Aquarian takeover of the Energy Commission and the Brown administration conspired against SDG&E's application, these hurdles did not begin to describe the economic problems the state's smallest private utility faced. Analysts expected the SDG&E's service area would grow faster than any other region in the state. SDG&E's growth predicament was particularly acute in an industry whose fiscal house was in serious disorder. Utility companies' construction needs made them the most capital-intensive industry in the country. The high interest rates of the mid-seventies forced the utilities into a cash squeeze of unprecedented proportions. In general, the electric industry responded to this by demanding more rate increases and legal relief to allow them to raise capital for construction.[68] To finance Sundesert, the small utility had to raise an amount equivalent to the entire net worth of the company. Risking that much money in one project was foolhardy. More unsettling still were SDG&E plans to build four more nuclear plants after Sundesert.[69] All this was enough to make an accountant lose sleep. Believing they had no choice, SDG&E executives were taking a gamble that there would be sufficient demand waiting for the electricity the plant would supply. They were less concerned for the risks of owning a plant that might have runaway construction costs or for the threat posed if demand did not rise as fast as projections. The Energy Commission warned that an emphasis on large power plants might leave utilities with expensive facilities and no customers for their electricity.[70] Recognizing this risk, too, the Public Utilities Commission took a dim view of Sundesert and SDG&E's novel financing schemes.

San Diego Gas and Electric, then, faced four formidable state hurdles to win approval of Sundesert. In the application process (known as the notice of intent), it first had to prove that Sundesert's Blythe site was well qualified to gain approval from the Energy Commission. Even if SDG&E won an endorsement, it was nearly certain that the commission would prevent it from constructing the plant if the nation's waste disposal problem was not solved. A third threat lay in possible actions by the antinuclear governor and his administration to undermine Sundesert. The final threat came from Public Utilities Commission's inquiry into the corporation's financial troubles. These problems would seem to be enough for any utility to pursue some other alternative. Administrators had a hard time understanding SDG&E's eagerness for such a risky project when there were other, less capital-intensive sources than nuclear power, such as oil or coal. Inexplicably, Richard Maullin noted,

SDG&E acted like someone possessed in its passion for Sundesert.[71] But SDG&E was driven by more than the issue of money.

For SDG&E, a nuclear power plant represented freedom from its historic dependence on fossil fuels and on its giant competitor to the north, Southern California Edison. Edison officials had dreamed of swallowing up SDG&E for years.[72] It held the smaller utility under its thumb because SDG&E's power line connections to other utilities ran through Edison's transmission system. This meant the larger utility controlled the price and terms of electricity SDG&E "wheeled in" from other sources. Sundesert could solve this problem too. The power line built from San Diego to the plant would also connect to other transmission systems free of Southern California Edison control. The sheer size of the plant would expand SDG&E's capital base and strengthen the company's expertise in construction and generation. For those in SDG&E who had dreams of turning the company into a utility that might rival others in the state, nuclear power was the answer. Although SDG&E spokespersons trumpeted the economic advantages of Sundesert, the plant had unstated strategic value. As Jim Cassie summed up, "It was our destiny to build Sundesert."[73]

The first stop on that road to destiny was winning popular approval of Sundesert in the Blythe community. It proved an easy task. There was some minor farm opposition since Sundesert was a potential competitor for irrigation water. SDG&E's plan, however, would cool the plant with waste water from farm fields.[74] The wastewater removed from the drain, moreover, would help solve the problems of Colorado River salinity, which was a concern for all downstream farmers.[75]

Just as important to SDG&E's local success was its vice president, Frank Devore. Devore had the common touch. He gained access to Indian reservations when no other utility executive could. He worked the Blythe area relentlessly, meeting with gun clubs, Mexican American groups, farmers, and the business community.[76] Devore and others within SDG&E won the trust of most of the local community.

A further advantage of the Blythe site was that there was no metropolitan area from which to draw a large body of activists to fight the project. In fact, residents were concerned to attract projects such as Sundesert, since most children raised in the area left for opportunities elsewhere. Local opposition was sporadic, poorly organized, and ultimately unimportant.[77] The lesson of Sundesert may be that if you want to gain community support for a nuclear power plant, it is best it have an unstable economy and sparse population.

San Diego Gas and Electric's problems began when it went to Sacramento for the notice of intent site approval proceedings. In the notice of intent hearings, SDG&E acquitted itself well in demonstrating the suitability of the Blythe site, but it had a much more difficult time assuring the Energy Commission of the project's necessity and its own ability to finance it. At hearings before the commission, state regulators expressed skepticism about the need for two nuclear units at Blythe. A number of considerations were raising doubts. The commission's forecast predicted far lower growth than any of the state's utilities; it rightly predicted that all state utilities had overestimated the growth in residential electrical usage. SDG&E admitted as much in December of 1976 by slashing its own estimates. From that point on, SDG&E had the best forecasting record of any state utility.[78] But the downward revisions, commission staffers maintained, meant that SDG&E needed only one unit of the facility.[79] Lower growth, escalating construction costs, and poor operating performance of nuclear plants cast doubt on the wisdom of building Sundesert, or any nuclear plant, to replace existing oil-fired facilities.

As the Energy Commission threw cold water on SDG&E's need for the project, the Public Utilities Commission attacked another weakness of SDG&E—its finances. In late 1976, the commission declared that SDG&E could not afford the 50 percent ownership share of the plant it wanted. The utility simply did not have the earnings to service the debt it would incur from the project. SDG&E objected, arguing that it needed at least 50 percent for future needs, and proposed a financing scheme known as Construction Work In Progress that would increase rates on electricity to finance ongoing projects. The Public Utilities Commission under Brown appointees was hostile to this revenue-raising method since it billed ratepayers for electricity they would not use for decades.[80] In July of 1977, the PUC denied SDG&E's request for $752 million in financing. The PUC further warned that 50 percent participation in Sundesert would put SDG&E "chronically and continuously in a state of financial emergency." This left the utility with the option of stretching out the construction schedule or reducing its 50 percent share of the project.[81] It did neither. Instead, the utility hoped to create a regulatory domino effect by using positive endorsement from the Energy Commission to pressure the PUC into reversing its negative decision.[82]

But SDG&E had trouble winning anything more than a lukewarm endorsement from the Energy Commission. The question of need and financing so concerned the commission that an initial staff report recommended withholding a favorable ruling on the notice of intent until the problems could be addressed. "The record is totally inadequate to support even an initial determination on this [financial] matter," announced the commission's executive director, Lloyd Forrest. Moreover, the commission noted that it was possible that conservation programs could obviate the need for part or even all of the project.[83]

The commission staff could object to Sundesert, but it did not have an alternative to it. The commission had not yet developed enough evidence or expertise to offer a viable substitute to Sundesert. In fact, Varanini was disgusted with the weakness of the commission's staff and felt the commission had preformed poorly in the notice of intent hearings (NOI). The staff offered no coherent program to replace nuclear power. Regardless of their own views, the antinuclear commissioners had to use the NOI record of evidence. And as Maullin argued, this failure to develop an alternative meant that the commission had to accept SDG&E's prediction that it would need about 900 megawatts of electricity by 1985. "Frankly, even with effective energy conservation the future does not look good," Maullin admitted.[84] Noting the possibility of using conservation but despairing at the lack of a program, commissioners Varanini and Maullin concluded in a preliminary report that nuclear energy was probably the best course for new energy. They rejected coal and oil alternatives as not viable for cost and pollution reasons.[85] It was a lukewarm endorsement at best. The commission wanted an alternative.

The Atom's Achilles Heel: Waste Disposal

As SDG&E appeared to be winning the notice of intent proceedings, the Energy Commission's study of waste disposal emerged as the next obstacle to Sundesert. By mid-1977 it was evident that Varanini's study would determine that no federal solution for waste disposal was near. The company launched a campaign to bypass the construction moratorium imposed by the 1976 nuclear bills.[86] SDG&E presented Sundesert as a dire need for Southern California in asking the legislature for an exemption from the bill. Blaming the legislature for the plant's possible demise, Frank Devore demanded that the assembly rush an exemption bill through in the final days of the session or the utility would halt the project. It was an astute gambit. If the assembly failed to act, SDG&E could blame politicians in Sacramento for Sundesert's cancellation. Since there was no alternative proposed by the Energy Commission, the assembly had no basis for standing in the way of a plant whose electricity even the Energy Commission admitted would be needed by 1985. It would be more proof of bureaucratic ineffectiveness at dealing with issues best left to the private sector.[87]

By the late seventies, the Energy Commission had to contend with state and national dissatisfaction with government ineptitude. The Energy Commission's inability to take a definite stance on the Sundesert question hurt its standing with the public and with the legislature. SDG&E, its own dissatisfied energy commissioners, and the press lambasted the commission as typical of bureaucratic excess. SDG&E had found a receptive audience when it blasted bureaucratic delays and poor legislation.[88] Sundesert's biggest fans, the conservative editors at the *San Diego Union*, complained in it editorials about the bias, poor quality, and temporizing of the commission. The paper claimed that Sundesert was "caught in the jaws of a bureaucratic vise that might well squeeze the economic life out of the state." Just before his departure from the commission Robert Moretti had also complained of the time-consuming nature of the Sundesert hearings. Commissioners, the former assembly speaker charged, were holding up the project while they debated the placement of stop signs around the plant instead of acting as the one-stop agency the Warren-Alquist legislation had intended.[89]

The assembly committee could not respond to this pressure and grant an exemption when it would upset its nonmaterialist constituency. This was the committee that created the Energy Commission, and some of the most antinuclear politicians in the state were members. They had authored the nuclear bills, and were in no mood to see their work undone. Moreover, their support came from environmental groups such as the Sierra Club. The club recognized that Sundesert was the decisive battle in California. "Sundesert is more than critical," and internal club paper noted. "If San Diego Gas and Electric is able to win support for and license to build their nuclear plant it will set precedents allowing the construction of . . . other projects now being planned by the Los Angeles Department of Water and Power, Pacific Gas and Electric and other utilities." The club lobbied hard to retain the construction moratorium.[90] Caught between Scylla and Charybdis, the committee needed a compromise.

The cool maneuvering of SDG&E might have worked if not for the equally astute legislative ploy by assembly speaker Leo McCarthey and Gene Varanini to transform the logic of the exemption bill. SDG&E had thus far succeeded in narrowly defining the scope of the debate so that the key question before the Energy Commission was, "Is Sundesert a reasonable means of meeting San Diego's energy needs?" Thus far the commission had no basis for arguing otherwise.[91] The exemption bill, AB 1852, depended on the fact that the Energy Commission had not formulated alternatives to Sundesert. The bill provided the perfect excuse to change the question to whether there were reasonable alternative methods of meeting electricity demand. Varanini and McCarthey changed the legislation to allow an exemption *if* an Energy Commission study determined that there were no viable energy alternatives to Sundesert.[92] McCarthey and Varanini knew it was crucial and deadly amendment for Sundesert. With five hundred Energy Commission staffers eager to explore alternative energy approaches, the study was almost certain to find alternatives.[93]

Varanini and Sierra Club lobbyist Mike Eaton hashed out the legislation's language. Eaton delivered the compromise bill to SDG&E, announcing, "we can live with this." After reviewing the document, Frank Devore knew he had been had. The Sundesert inquiry would turn into an open-ended forum on conservation and alternative sources, and Devore had little doubt the Energy Commission would find alternatives. But he knew fighting the bill was hopeless. The assembly now had the escape they needed to avoid an outright exemption. After huddling over the bill's language, the utility lobbyists emerged and agreed to the compromise.[94] "Very frankly, the bill falls far short of our desire," Devore admitted. "We wanted a decision up or down."[95] Instead, SDG&E was stuck in an even more complex regulatory thicket. Tacked onto the PUC investigation into SDG&E's financial health, Varanini's waste disposal probe, and the Energy Commission's notice of intent plant approval process was now AB 1852's fourth level of analysis into the question of viable alternatives to the Sundesert project. Failure in any of these arenas spelled the plant's doom.

The notice of intent proceedings wound to a close in December 1977 with SDG&E winning a approval of Sundesert. The Energy Commission approved only one of the two Sundesert plants by a vote of 4 to 1. Calling the project "a $3 billion mistake," only Ron Doctor favored outright rejection. Despite the lopsided commission endorsement, the approval was, as Richard Maullin noted, "limited." Tacked onto the decision were forty-nine conditions, including a demand for greater conservation efforts and, because of SDG&E's financial condition, a restriction on the utility to 33 percent ownership in Sundesert.[96] What the Energy Commission gave to SDG&E with one hand, it was already working to take away with the other. Maullin reiterated in announcing the commission's approval that it depended on a finding in its AB 1852 exemption study that "virtually no alternatives existed."[97] This was a finding that Maullin, the commission staff, and the Brown administration were determined against. The blows against Sundesert now followed in rapid succession between January and February of 1978.

Gene Varanini's report on the federal waste disposal program ensured that there would be no easy way out of the nuclear bills for SDG&E. Varanini had formed a task force within the Energy Commission to investigate the federal program. As Varanini would discover, the problems with waste disposal were far graver than anyone had recognized in the mid-seventies. In the final report, released in January 1978, Varanini laid out the story of a twenty-year failure to find an acceptable disposal method. Exploding the myth that there was an easy technical fix for the waste problem, the Energy Commission found that assurances of a viable waste disposal method were based on faith, not field testing. In fact, despite confidence in the technical solutions proposed, all testing had failed. Optimism about future solutions was not warranted, and the time had come for states to demand proof of a solution from the federal government.[98] The commission concluded that it was "even *questionable to assume* that [waste disposal technology] will be demonstrated before the mid 1980s."[99] Varanini's predictions were proven two months later when in March the federal government announced that it would not have a waste disposal site ready by its 1985 target date.[100]

Supporters of nuclear power refused to believe that the nuclear establishment could be wrong. The *San Diego Union* confidently predicted that a solution to the waste question would be found within a year, and charged the Energy Commission with being "grossly irresponsible" for risking the Southland's energy future.[101] Although the report's results were expected, SDG&E claimed it felt like a "prisoner on the racks" and with some justice charged that there was a conspiracy afoot: "It is beginning to seem like there is a plain and concerted effort to not only kill the Sundesert project but to foreclose the nuclear option throughout the state."[102] With the possibility of a federal waste disposal solution foreclosed, the Energy Commission's AB 1852 study of Sundesert alternatives would be the key to determining whether SDG&E won its coveted release from the restrictions in the 1976 nuclear bills.

The Energy Commission staff well understood that they, as much as Sundesert, were on trial in the AB 1852 study. The commission had been created in part because of a sense that the federal government had not done enough on energy issues and that there was an essential state role to be played in energy planning. AB 1852 was the culmination of that logic. A state agency was about to tell a utility that its choice of energy production was ill conceived and that other sources were better. The commission would tell SDG&E what to build. That was a role that few state agencies had ever assumed for a private utility. If the study was flawed, the embarrassment would jeopardize the commission's future. Already politicians in the legislature were warming up bills to dissolve the Energy Commission, including one by its founder Alfred Alquist. The Energy Commission had to be credible to survive. Staffers launched a frenzied period of work that forced them to work through weekends, Christmas, and New Year's Day.[103] The January report was, in the words of the commission, "the most intensive independent analysis of a power plant project anywhere in the United States."[104]

Including expertise from all Energy Commission departments assured that the "Lovins" philosophy would emerge in the report. The commission's bias in favor of alternatives left it open to attacks that it was twisting facts to support its antinuclear proclivities. But in this volatile period of energy consumption there was no clear body of facts favoring nuclear or nonnuclear technologies. As commission staffers noted, "We have observed in our work that it is possible to [favor any energy technology] merely by choosing an appropriate set of individually reasonable (and arguably consistent) set of assumptions."[105] With this much latitude, the commission's philosophy played a crucial role in the conclusions.

The Energy Commission's report was a direct challenge to the idea that large centralized power facilities were the most economic form of electric generation. The commission cobbled together a combination of conservation, geothermal energy, and efficiency improvements of existing oil plants, and proposed the construction of a 475-megawatt coal plant—enough energy to equal Sundesert's output. As the Commission pointed out, these more modest proposals would relieve SDG&E of its capital requirements—a point the Public Utilities Commission was sure to endorse.[106]

Coal and oil! The Energy Commission's proposal seemed incredible. Up to that point the entire direction of energy use in the country had been away from these costly and dirty alternatives. The Carter administration's energy plan had called for a shift away from oil. Air pollution problems seemed to rule out coal, especially in Southern California. Yet here was a state agency trying to reverse course. The commission was lambasted in the press. But the utility had a hard time refuting the staff's conclusions in five days of vituperative hearings during January. Despite the best efforts of SDG&E's talented counsel, Jack Newman, who had demolished many commission staff witnesses during the notice of intent hearings, the Energy Commission proved equal to the task and the report remained virtually unchanged.[107] In public, SDG&E attacked the "unproven, ill-conceived and poorly thought-out plans." But the survival of the commission findings meant that SDG&E would have to return to the legislature and demand a new exemption bill. The legislators would now be asked to ignore a government agency's findings and declare that their understanding of future energy consumption patterns was better.[108]

Bypassing the Energy Commission might still have been feasible had it not been for the Brown administration's concerted campaign to stop

Sundesert that began in late 1977. Previously, Jerry Brown had remained aloof from the Sundesert controversy. He had begun to speak out against nuclear power in general, but there was no indication that he intended to move specifically against Sundesert. Brown appeared to be mouthing little more than platitudes about the need to rein in the atom. By 1977, Brown's green shift was making itself felt in his appointments to administration posts, and they in turn prodded the administration in a New Age, antinuclear direction. The official most important in pushing Brown into direct opposition to Sundesert was his choice for the new secretary of the Resources Agency, Huey Johnson.

New Age Politics and Nuclear Power

Huey Johnson is best understood by his office chairs. Most individuals in a position similar to his opted for the corporate suite styles of fine leather when selecting office furniture. Suspended from the ceiling in Johnson's office in the huge Resources Building were two canvas and chain contraptions that looked like swings. Chic at the time, they would later be dismissed as typical of the cheesey styles of the seventies. None who left Johnson's office forgot their swing in those chairs. "The man in the black canvas bucket," one reporter mused, probably spent most of his time in those chairs in meditation and philosophical dreaming. Johnson argued that his meditation was just a break to relax his mind. But Huey Johnson was a visionary who had never done anything in his life the conventional way. He rode his bicycle eight miles to work every day, a substantial departure from the limousine days of the Reagan administration. After a successful stint as a salesman for Union Carbide, Johnson had left the job to travel the United States and Pacific rim to expand his mind. He had worked as a garbage collector, a teacher, a buyer at a salmon cannery, and an assistant at a ski resort in New Zealand. When he returned he was fully infused with an environmental ethic, and in 1970 put forth his brand of environmentalism in *No Deposit—No Return*. Johnson went to work on environmental issues as the director of the Nature Conservancy and later the Trust for Public Land, which set aside parcels as open space preserves in natural and urban settings. He campaigned heavily in Marin County in support of Proposition 15.[109]

It was popular to dismiss Johnson and others as mystical dreamers whose ideals stemmed from foreign concepts. The reality was that Eastern philosophies were a way of giving expression to impulses that were thoroughly American in origin. Like Jerry Brown, Johnson was attracted to certain Buddhist teachings because they resonated with his personal experiences. Johnson cited the Zen credo "to live well with less, to live close and in touch with the earth" as complementing his environmentalist ethic.[110] Coming from different moral bases, Johnson and Brown dabbled in Eastern philosophies to give expression to their complementary views of the world. It was this common interest in Zen that would allow Brown and Johnson to cross paths. Johnson first met Brown at the San Francisco Zen Center, where over dinner he dazzled the governor with his futuristic thinking. So impressed was the governor that he asked Johnson to join his administration. Johnson declined initially, but Brown later appointed him to the Resources post in late 1977.[111]

More than most political appointees, Johnson brought political and ethical philosophies to bear on the way he carried out his job. Years later he summed up his approach, "My preference is looking to the future in 100-year segments."[112] To Johnson this meant focusing on efforts whose significance might not be understood for years. For legislators who thought a visionary thinker was someone who looked past the next election, such a view was outlandish. Some within the environmental movement contended that Johnson's style was ineffective and unrealistic. "There was such a vast difference between Huey and the legislature: the legislature working at the lowest of abstraction levels and Huey working at the highest," the Sierra Club's lobbyist and Johnson critic John Zierold remembered. "As a result he didn't get done nearly as much as he wanted to do."[113] But such unconventional thinking had direct implications for the Sundesert proceedings. Even more than his antinuclear inclinations, it was this search for permanence and transformative actions that led Johnson to seize on the idea of defeating Sundesert. It was a way of changing forever the state's energy consumption patterns.

Johnson recognized that if Jerry Brown was going to feel comfortable in loudly opposing Sundesert, he, as Resources secretary, would have to take the lead and show that it was politically feasible. Johnson tried to bring his entire agency's capacity to bear against Sundesert by developing a campaign for alternative electric sources.[114] As he recognized, the nuclear debate had been constructed on terms favorable to the industry. The choice was depicted as nuclear power or no-growth. Through national policy and pollution restrictions, coal and oil had been eliminated from serious consideration. In private discussions, Resources Agency officials admitted that SDG&E had succeeded in showing that Sundesert was the only "concrete proposal for a substantial block of base load electric power by the mid eighties." They recognized that developing alternatives was not simple. To be credible, the alternatives would have to be available by the mid-eighties at a reasonable price. Energy from kelp, solar power from satellites, and other exotica would not suffice.[115]

A collection of nine departments and agencies met in December 1977 and developed a series of alternatives that on paper would meet a feasibility test. Energy conservation, coal, and geothermal energy were the immediate options they chose, with solar, biomass, and other options ready for use later. The gathering also planned to increase the state's commitment to fund and search for alternative sources. Never again, they resolved, should the state be in a position of not having an alternative to a nuclear plant.[116]

The results of this meeting were immediately evident in the behavior of state agencies who suddenly took an interest in energy options long thought unworkable in the Golden State. In late December 1977, Priscilla Grew, director of the State Department of Conservation, issued a letter to Governor Brown calling for a greater commitment of state resources to develop the state's "extraordinary geothermal potential," of which she estimated nearly 1,200 megawatts could be developed by 1985.[117]

Tom Quinn, chair of the Air Resources Board, in a policy reversal that left the utilities dumbfounded, announced in a letter to the Energy Commission that "new fossil fuel power plants can be built in many parts of California without causing environmental damage." The letter further recommended a coal plant as an alternative to the Sundesert project. An exasperated Frank Devore argued that the letter "flies in the face of the national energy policy." A true assertion, but it was increasingly evident that California was staking out its own energy vision. The similarity between the letter and Energy Commission policy was not a coincidence. Maullin, hoping to lay the groundwork for a coal alternative in the Energy Commission's AB 1852 study, had worked out the letter in advance with Quinn.[118]

With this green light given to the coal option, the utilities could have seen the next move coming. The Department of Water Resources (DWR), another branch of the Resources Agency, had a partial interest in the Sundesert plant, which was to supply power for the Central Valley Water Project. DWR director Ron Robie had come under administration pressure to back out of the DWR's commitment to Sundesert since it gave the project the imprimatur of state approval. Robie had resisted since it would force the DWR into electric purchase agreements with utilities at unfavorable rates.[119] Brown, however, intervened. Robie recalled, "The governor said, 'I want the Department of Water Resources to build a coal plant.' So we embarked on the planning of a coal plant." A polluting coal plant in the ecologically sensitive desert was, Robie later admitted, "just a dreadful prospect." Dreadful or not, Robie and Huey Johnson announced at a press conference in March 1978 that "coal technology has come a long way" and that the DWR would build its own facility of nearly a thousand megawatts. Citing the Air Resources Board's new flexibility in air quality standards, Johnson declared that the Resources Agency was "assuming the leadership role in this effort to meet our future energy needs and to demonstrate that there are reasonable alternatives to nuclear energy."[120] But by 1979, after Sundesert's demise, the Energy Commission and the Air Resources Board had changed again and were looking askance at the coal alternative.[121]

The effort to advocate alternative energy sources certainly raised the level of debate on such sources, but it also came at the cost of making the Brown administration appear to be manipulating the state bureaucracy. The California press laid the primary blame for SDG&E's fate at the feet of the governor. Depicting him as controlling officials and agencies as if they were marionettes, all the major papers tried to demonstrate that Brown had reversed the bureaucratic machinery of the Energy Commission, the PUC, and the Air Resource Board and turned it against nuclear power. The antinuclear effort, politicians such as assemblyman Alister McAlister asserted, was "instrumented and orchestrated by the Governor for his own reasons. It obviously had nothing to do with the merits of the case."[122]

There was truth in this assertion. Those who ran these agencies were Brown appointees, and they were responsive to the governor. But these were individuals who had come to their conclusions from their own experiences, ideology, and research. No one needed to instruct staffers at the Energy Commission Ron Doctor, Gene Varanini, or Huey Johnson on how to act. Even Richard Maullin, considered the most devoted to Jerry Brown of the commissioners, refused to compromise the independence of the Energy Commission and spurned a private request from Brown for an outright rejection of the Sundesert application. Maullin was intent on using the evidence presented at the notice of intent hearings, and he refused to stand the process on its head.[123] Sundesert's misfortunes were not entirely the result of some grand scheme. They stemmed from legitimate technical and economic problems with nuclear energy, a band of skeptical government administrators, and a growing state capacity to formulate energy policy independently.

Against this broad political assault on Sundesert, SDG&E and its allies launched an effort to bypass the Energy Commission's decision by organizing a Southland coalition to pressure the Brown administration. Labor representatives who were growing sour on Brown's environmental leanings called the energy alternatives he supported "a hysterical search for backyard megawatts."[124] Even Southern California Edison joined in supporting SDG&E's position. Bipartisan backing from Mayors Tom Bradley of Los Angeles and Pete Wilson of San Diego strenuously argued in favor of the project. Wilson's letter argued that only Sundesert could prevent "massive unemployment" and blackouts in the 1980s. Declaring the Energy Commission's action "irresponsible" and its touting of alternatives little more than a pretext by which to halt nuclear power, Southland politicians called for the passage of an exemption bill introduced by Senator Alfred Alquist's committee.[125]

Alfred Alquist's efforts to bypass the Energy Commission indicated just how far the agency had strayed from his original one-stop shopping concept. "I feel like Dr. Frankenstein," Alfred Alquist confessed. "[The Energy Commission's] decisions are made to serve the Governor's political ambitions rather than the people of this state." Alquist had grown increasingly skeptical of the Energy Commission, and Sundesert was the last straw. He had thought to create a commission to expedite plant construction. Instead, the commission had failed to approve any site in three years.[126] Now pronuclear hopes depended on discrediting the commission and convincing the legislature that Sundesert was vital.

Sundesert's supporters tried to generate popular demand for Sundesert, with little luck. Committing a quarter million dollars to a local campaign, SDG&E collected nearly a hundred thousand signatures supporting Sundesert. Reiterating the link between jobs and energy, the utility passed out literature and "Don't Be Powerless Speak Up for Sundesert" buttons. Such "grassroots" efforts had mixed results. Polling in San Diego indicated a majority supported the construction of Sundesert, but it also showed that support for nuclear power in general was soft. Twice as many residents favored alternative sources of power, and 64 percent worried about the nuclear waste problem.[127] Brown and the Energy Commission's position favoring alternatives appeared to fit well between these results. The Brown administration also relied on the landslide results of the March 1978 Kern County vote against the San Joaquin Nuclear Project. As the vote indicated, people might support nuclear power in the abstract, but such support was weak and changed the closer an individual lived to the plant. There was little political damage to opposing Sundesert.[128]

These indications of public opinion, Huey Johnson's efforts, and the position taken by the Energy Commission provided Jerry Brown with sufficient political cover to take an unusually strong position against Sundesert.[129] Citing the Energy Commission's position, Brown declared that he would not overrule his own commission. After SDG&E won passage of the exemption bill in the state senate, Brown vowed to veto any exemption bill that came across his desk. "[Sundesert] is as dead as it can be," the governor declared on a swing through San Diego. "I don't see any reason why we ought to give a special privilege, an ex-

In an effort to launch a pronuclear movement, employees at San Diego Gas and Electric collected 130,000 signatures in support of the Sundesert project. Courtesy San Diego Gas and Electric Company.

emption [to SDG&E]."[130] In another interview Brown told reporters, "My own person belief is that California has a unique place on this planet. It's been a place of dreams. We can pursue a path of benign energy that will set an example that will protect future generations. I will do everything I can to bring that about."[131]

Jerry Brown remained true to his word and fought alongside Sierra club lobbyists and antinuclear activists to shore up opposition in the Assembly Energy Resources and Land Use Committee to kill the exemption bill. Brown's lobbying had the desired effect, and the committee showed no sign that it was ready to consider an exemption. In April 1978, the resources committee held emotional hearings on the exemption legislation. Business and labor leaders begged for a vote by the entire assembly. Senator Newton Russell, the bill's author, called on the committee to "vote with the businessmen, the working people and the consumers of Southern California, who will be the prime beneficiaries of the Sundesert project." Others labeled the Sundesert conflict an "ideological" confrontation in which the workers of the Southland would be made the victims of antinuclear apocalyptic fears. The energy = jobs argument had worn thin. The assembly was in no mood to listen to these warning or the witnesses' confidence in waste technology. One union official declared that "I'd bet my life that there will be some place to dispose of [nuclear waste]." "That may be exactly what we'll be betting," assemblyman Barry Keene shot back.[132] On 13 April 1978, the legislators refused by a 9–4 margin to allow the exemption bill out of committee. Sundesert was dead.

The official end of the project would come at the California Public Utilities Commission. The commission had changed much since its blind approval of the Bodega project. Under Jerry Brown's appointees, the PUC had become progressive and, in the words of the *Wall Street Journal* "a positive villain to utility executives."[133] It had been the first public utility commission to institute "lifeline rates" to help the poor pay utility bills, and now it would become the first to stop a nuclear power plant. SDG&E's poor finances finally caught up with it as the PUC issued a rejection of a rate increase request that the utility needed to continue the project. Robert Batinovich argued that SDG&E was "over their heads" in planning to double its capitalization within only seven years. In an ex parte contact with SDG&E's president, Robert Morris, Batinovich laid out this fact and told Morris that SDG&E needed to pursue alternative power sources. On 3 May, the PUC rejected the rate increase. SDG&E's board of directors immediately followed with the official cancellation of the plant. Sundesert had come to a halt after over $100 million had been spent by the partners in the project.[134]

Some scholars have incorrectly contended that the Public Utilities Commission's action was the key reason for Sundesert's demise.[135] This implies that the 1976 nuclear bills, the Energy Commission, and Jerry Brown's efforts were unnecessary. PUC chairperson Batinovich, who had opposed Sundesert from the beginning, has also embraced this argument. This is a self-congratulatory view because the commissioners' decision was provisional at best. Batinovich had to work for nearly two months before he could get a bare majority to sign the PUC order. Even then, one commissioner declared that the order in no way prevented a different consortium of utilities from building the project. It was an invitation for a utility such as Southern California Edison or the Los Angeles Department of Water and Power to take a larger interest in the project and for SDG&E to reduce its share. This was an arrangement that lobbyist James Cassie later admitted made a great deal of sense. But with the project hung up at the Energy Commission, there was no point in pursuing other financing options. By the time of the PUC order, SDG&E had already concluded that the project could not win approval. But it needed someone to give an official "no" to the project. To have simply canceled the project without any government agency ordering them to would have forced stockholders to assume the loss. The PUC decision allowed them to recoup most of their investment a few years later.[136]

An Ambiguous Future

Sundesert's termination touched off a chorus of calls for the Energy's Commission's head and attacks on Jerry Brown. Alfred Alquist led the charge in promoting a bill to break down the commission and redistribute its functions among the more conservative Public Utilities Commission and a new Department of Energy. Brown's political enemies laid the cancellation of Sundesert at his feet. Brown faced a reelection bid that year, and Republican challengers hoped to use nuclear power as an issue in the election. Other issues would overtake nuclear power later, such as the state's Proposition 13 vote indicating citizens were more interested in property taxes and the size of state government in than nuclear power. But in May 1978, the consensus among the governor's critics was that Brown was using Sundesert for his presidential ambitions: "Brown's strategy is to win the New Hampshire primary by taking [the votes of] all the fuzzy-headed people who say, 'stop Sundesert, stop Sundesert,'" assemblyman Larry Kapiloff surmised.[137] Mayor Peter Wilson of San Diego proposed sacking all four energy commissioners who had used the nuclear issue to their political advantage.[138] State attorney general and gubernatorial candidate Evelle Younger predicted that "The lights are going to go out and we're going to have a major depression in California in the 1980's."[139] The predictions of doom were overblown since even SDG&E conceded that blackouts were only a remote possibility.[140] Pronuclear forces did not give up their campaign to topple the Energy Commission, however, until the accident at Three Mile Island killed any hope of a nuclear resurgence.[141]

Saving the Energy Commission did not resolve the issue of states' rights. The 1976 nuclear bills were only a part of a larger Energy Commission challenge to federal nuclear authority.[142] In 1977 when the Nuclear Regulatory Commission's siting procedures conflicted with the Energy Commission's jurisdiction, Maullin demanded that the NRC modify its procedures to comply with Energy Commission requirements. If the NRC and the commission failed to reach an agreement, Maullin threatened, the Energy Commission would bypass the federal agency and propose new legislation to force compliance.[143] Although the two agencies settled this jurisdictional dispute, Maullin's effrontery testified to the magnitude of California threat to federal nuclear omnipotence.[144]

Nuclear boosters hoped to head off California's insurrection by returning power to the Nuclear Regulatory Commission. This required invalidating the 1976 nuclear bills. Over the objections of his staff whose opinion he ordered revised three times, Attorney General Evelle Younger declared the bills unconstitutional. Federal authority, he argued, dominated state claims.[145] Younger's nonbinding legal opinion shifted the battle to the arena where it had always been fated to end, in court. On this decision hinged the demands of antinuclear activists for greater citizen involvement and state authority over energy.[146] Without this legal sanction of state power, all the hopes and effort antinuclear activists had invested in passing the nuclear bills and supporting the Energy Commission would mean nothing. As a pronuclear president took over in Washington in 1981, it was an open question as to whether the California revolt would succeed. But a controversy in the Central Valley that developed in parallel to Sundesert indicated that nuclear resistance had already spread far beyond the fuzzy-headed thinkers in nonmaterialist ranks to become a widely shared public attitude. The nuclear opposition was about to be transformed from a movement of the left to a general public ethos.

6

Stick It in L.A.!

Community Control and Nuclear Power in the Central Valley

"It was a civil war," farmer Jim Neufeld recalled of the revolt he helped lead against a proposed nuclear power plant near the tiny town of Wasco in California's Central Valley and just northwest of Bakersfield. "The scars between the two opposing sides are the same or worse than Vietnam. . . . I couldn't possibly talk to some of [the plant's supporters about the issue] today. . . . They thought of us as conniving. Yeah, we were conniving. We wanted that thing out of here."[1]

When construction plans were announced in 1973, the San Joaquin Nuclear Project (SJNP) split Wasco into two factions. Some so feared that the project would destroy agriculture and steal their water that they put aside their farming for a season to campaign against it and boycott supporters' businesses. Eventually the community more or less united in opposition to the project and its sponsor, the Los Angeles Department of Water and Power (LADWP). Toward the end of the conflict in 1978, incidents of vandalism had been reported against LADWP equipment. Farmers harassed plant construction workers so much they could not enter local restaurants without a confrontation or feel safe leaving their vehicles unattended. If the Department of Water and Power had not canceled the plant's construction, Neufeld is convinced his allies in agriculture would have resorted to violence.[2] Illegal measures proved unnecessary as the farmers' political campaign succeeded in shifting public opinion. In March of 1978, 70 percent of the citizens of Kern County voted to reject the SJNP. It was the first time that citizens anywhere in the nation canceled a nuclear power plant.[3]

The successful campaign against the San Joaquin Nuclear Project tells a great deal about how antinuclear attitudes toward nuclear power moved out from their nonmaterialist base to convert traditionally pronuclear blue-collar constituencies. The antinuclear movement had never seen the kind of opposition to a nuclear plant as was organized in Kern County. Previously, when Californians voted on the Proposition 15 antinuclear initiative in 1976, the support for it came from progressive, affluent, and educated counties. And typical antinuclear activists came from elements of the left wing of the Democratic Party such as environmental, remnant New Left, and peace groups. But Bakersfield was a long way from San Francisco. Voting analysis suggests that while the antinuclear movement retained progressive voters, the new strength against the San Joaquin Nuclear Project come from conservative farmers and whites at the lower end of the economic ladder who traditionally opposed environmental issues and would later vote for Ronald Reagan. These Reagan Democrats responded to an antinuclear message that was framed in conservative populist rhetoric. There were some environmental activists in the movement, but they played only a supporting role. Conservative agribusiness led the defeat of LADWP's construction plans in league with suburban Bakersfield residents and environmentalists. It was a pragmatic coalition that agreed on little other than a commitment to preserving the county's agriculture and independence from Los Angeles. By overcoming their differences, this movement encouraged one of the major changes of the last twenty-five years, the resurgence of local politics.

To gain a perspective on the basis for this movement, it is best to head west from Wasco about twenty miles to where Interstate 5 bisects California's fifty-thousand square-mile Central Valley. The Valley *is* California, author Joan Didion maintained, but the one never seen.[4] Urbanites from the Southland descend out of the Tehachapi Range, a physical divide between the Valley and the Los Angeles basin, on their way to a weekend in San Francisco or skiing at Lake Tahoe. It is a joyless drive through the flat, treeless Valley, and they will remember only how they shaved fifteen minutes off their record for the journey. Urban Californians tend to think of the Valley, if they think of it at all, in Southern Gothic stereotypes; one San Francisco reporter labeled it the state's

"Bible Belt." The Valley has been made a "scapegoat," one literary observer complained, by other Californians for racism, violence, and re-
actionary political views. The area has provided material for comics
and the public who are convinced it is a land filled with Okies, farms,
and oil rigs even if they have never been there. "People here . . . just [got]
really angry about Johnny Carson making fun of Bakersfield," one resident remembered. Recently when Fox television ran an abortive sitcom
about a small California town's police force filled with oddballs, they
called it "Bakersfield P.D." As advertising executives admit, they face a
hard sell in luring business to Kern because of this stereotype. "When
was the last time people in L.A. really thought seriously about moving
to Bakersfield?" one Los Angeles columnist asked. "Seattle, yes. Oregon,
sure. Good God, people even go to Vegas. But Bakersfield?"5

The truth is that the Valley has been inundated with a diverse immi-
grant population for some time, but Bakersfield's backward image persists among some residents of the Southland. In 1994, Los Angeles
mayor Richard Riordan heard a commercial promoting Bakersfield, an
effort by the county to overcome its backward image, and remarked, "I
hope you all [in L.A.] agree with me that Bakersfield is boring." The re-
mark caused little notice in the Southland, but touched off a firestorm
in Kern County, including bumper stickers that pleaded, "Bakersfield is
NOT boring." But in Los Angeles the pundits and the mayor merely
laughed. One Los Angeles Times columnist chortled, "If you're an Ange-
leno, it's good to be reminded that things could be worse. The City of
Angels has its flaws—earthquakes, riots, fires, crime and such—but at
least it's not Bakersfield." Other municipalities have heaped indignities
on Kern County, including Santa Barbara, which once suggested shipping its homeless population to Bakersfield.6

Few Angelenos ever confront their Valley stereotypes since I-5 acts as
a cultural divide. The highway avoids the agricultural communities
such as Modesto, Turlock, Fresno, and Kern's county seat, Bakersfield,
strung out along state Route 99. The only hint of the Valley's occupants,
and to Angelenos it is not a good one, comes as drivers scan the radio
vainly for something other than country music, Gospel hour, or Spanish language stations. The drive to Kern is about ninety minutes, but
culturally it is as far as Oklahoma and more inhospitable. "Everybody
in Los Angeles seems to remember going through Bakersfield when
they were 7 years old and it was 100 degrees outside," one resident
complained. It is a land to be endured and ignored, not understood. As
the lights of Bakersfield spread out to the east, people's only thoughts
are to keep going and drive faster.7

Bakersfield's citizens respond to the attitudes and lifestyles of Southlanders with resentment, an important element in this story. Los Angeles has its own worn stereotypes, and Valley residents watching this northward parade of Southlanders embellish their decadent reputation and hurl barbs at the city's urban problems such as smog, clogged highways, and riots. Local leaders get a lot of mileage out of references to Los Angeles as the land of the "three-hour lunch crowd" filled with "every kook imaginable." L.A. wealth comes not through honest labor, but by controlling and foisting its problems on its neighbors.[8] "Hey, we got lots of reasons not to like L.A. They think we should be their dumping ground," complained one of Kern's leading politicians and a power plant opponent. "Every problem they got, they want to haul all their garbage to us. . . . We don't like that."[9]

Los Angeles' despotic rule of the Southland was legendary as it bested smaller counties and even nearby states for resources, land, and industry, but especially water.[10] Nuclear energy and water issues intertwine in this story since the proposed nuclear plant needed water to cool it. There was only one source for that much water. In their northward rush to more advanced civilizations, Angelenos may not have noticed the California Aqueduct paralleling the highway. When it comes to resources, the aqueduct water is one thing Kern County and the Southland have in common. Both depend on this state-sponsored project for their livelihood. Built in the sixties, the California Water Project delivers abundant winter runoff from northern Sierra sources to Central Valley agribusiness and the Southland. Kern had done well in negotiating rights to over one million acre-feet of state- and Los Angeles-subsidized water.[11] But looking at the huge pipeline tentacles running through the Tehachapis and south to Los Angeles, Valley residents wondered when the city would grab the rest of their water. "Without that [aqueduct] water, Kern County has nothing, we're a desert," an agribusinessman admits.[12]

The community wrapped itself in the myth of its autonomy even as government subsidized water forced upon it the reality of dependence. "Kern County is a very conservative county," assemblyman Trice Harvey contended. "They don't believe in taking your money and spending it on a lot of social issues, and they don't believe in taking anybody else's money."[13] In the power plant vote, reality lost again to the potent and visceral myths and stereotypes of Kern's conservative political culture. But in acting on their myths, residents made them more politically real than dependence. Framed as an agrarian-versus-urban conflict, the election offered a choice between two competing worldviews: an expansive, cosmopolitan ideal, or a provincial attitude that was suspicious of outsiders, valued community ties and local control, and projected its

economic resentments against its more successful urban neighbors. Ker-
nites justified their choice of the latter through the rhetoric of a nationally ascendant right-wing populism.[14]

Since the end of World War II, Populism had made an ideological
journey from its leftist roots to a favored place in conservatism's rhetorical arsenal. The national sources of the shift were numerous. Cold War
anti-Communism, liberal government policies that appeared to favor
undeserving minorities over working whites, the loss of government
and scientific credibility, the expansion of middle-class communities,
and the resurgence of evangelical churches allowed a series of conservatives such as Joseph McCarthy, George Wallace, Richard Nixon, and
Ronald Reagan to capture Populist rhetoric and win a national following.[15] Previously, Populism had served to justify federal protection of
the working class from large business and financial combinations. By
the seventies, conservative populism was defending the value of religious, hardworking communities against the destabilizing policies of
government elites, their allies in minority communities, and cosmopolitan culture that it considered anti-American.[16] It was Wallace
who got so much political mileage out of Populist suspicions of outsiders, such as the "left-wing pinko liberals" at Harvard, "bureaucrats,"
and urban "pseudo-intellectuals" who undercut the "workingman."
"[The suspicion of outsiders] was part of the psyche that defeated the
power plant," one activist claimed. "Here was L.A. coming in and
telling us what a good deal they were giving us."[17]

Western conservatives in places like the Central Valley led the rise of
the "New Right" that produced national figures like Ronald Reagan
and Barry Goldwater. The latter called his crusade against the eastern
establishment "our new populist movement."[18] In the face of an increasingly organized and centralized society, the economically pros-
perous postwar West retained its regional identity and mythic religion
of rugged individualism.[19] The Central Valley was one of the seedbeds
of western populist sentiment. As chroniclers of the Okie experience in
California have shown, the Depression's rural migration pushed rightward the political culture of the Valley. Even non-Okies assumed the
values of evangelism, a producer ethic, anti-elitism, ethnocentrism, and
individualism. The migrants changed the Valley through their religious
institutions, political rhetoric, and music.[20] Responding to the sixties
political and social turbulence, blue-collar Americans gravitated to the
angry country music ballads of the Valley's Merle Haggard, the "poet
laureate" of the working class. Haggard became the top star of country
music on the popularity of songs such as *Okie from Muskogee, Fightin-
Side of Me,* and *Working-Man Blues,* in which he attacked lazy, pot-smok-

ing "hippies up in San Francisco," antiwar traitors, and welfare parasites of the patriotic working man.[21]

The shift rightward was not much of a trip for Valley residents. They were an awkward fit in the Democratic Party. Okie immigrants had not been good recruits to the labor movement, and their social conservatism was at odds with San Francisco progressives. And as the dominant national themes of America shifted from economic to cultural issues, the region turned dramatically to the right. It is now home to a strong militia movement and intense antigovernment attitudes. Biting the hand of Governor Pat Brown, who fed them massive water projects, county voters responded to Ronald Reagan's promise to get rid of welfare cheats, suppress college radicals, and return law and order by giving him a majority in his 1966 bid for governor. These themes worked the same magic for Richard Nixon's and George Wallace's presidential bids. State initiatives on marijuana legalization, gun control, and labor union issues fared poorly. Popular were measures favoring the death penalty and opposing school busing.[22] One Bakersfield politician noted that these issues had become popular elsewhere: "All those people who've been snickering at us should take another look. . . . There is nothing peculiar or backward about Kern County or its politics. We're the future."[23]

That future swept Kern and the rest of the nation in 1980 when Reagan even carried precincts in the predominately Okie districts of Oildale and the farm communities despite their overwhelming Democratic registration. These Reagan Democrats responded to his antigovernment and socially conservative themes, but with a far more serious edge that has given Oildale, in particular, a reputation as a "crucible for fascism." Right-wing signs regularly dot Highway 99 like "Less Government, More Body Bags" and "I.R.S. in Range to Shoot." The farm town of Delano sports a radical right radio station, and Kern is a favorite place on the citizen militia lecture circuit. Over one thousand people attended a meeting featuring the head of the Michigan paramilitary organization.[24]

There were three components of Kern's conservative populism that were important to this story: a producer ethic that once exalted common labor and that now included the entrepreneurialism of agribusiness; economic anxiety and grievances that manifested themselves in resentment of un-American government and cosmopolitan elites; and a reverence for agrarian communities filled with hardworking, independent people.[25] Bakersfield's mayor put it best: "I think Merle Haggard summed up our philosophy here. We respect and love America, its flags and its symbols. We believe in paternalism, a strong family . . . and the merits of good old hard work. That's all—nothin' very sophisticated about it."[26]

The populist veneration of agricultural labor helped burnish the image of corporate farmers. In the forties, Carey McWilliams detailed the rise of "farm fascism" among agribusinessmen, the antithesis of the agrarian culture that their farm laborers held. "The distinction between farm and city is practically meaningless in California," he wrote. A contemporary Wasco farmer agreed, telling a sociologist, "Farming in this country is a business, it is not a way of life." This agrarian populism, however, softened the self-image of agribusiness and the general community. By the seventies, farming was still a business, but its practitioners displayed the religious and social values of their Okie neighbors. Large operators referred to themselves as "family farmers" and extolled the joys of getting "mud between my toes" and hard work. Interstate 5 in Kern County is dotted with signs trumpeting the contributions of its "family farmers" while failing to mention that many of them own tens of thousands of acres and employ hundreds of laborers.[27] The agrarian, family rhetoric successfully linked agribusiness to an image of hardworking Americans. When residents of Kern implored officials "to do something about all those people eating at the trough" of government, they did not mean agribusiness. Kern County stood with agribusiness even to the point of subsidizing it themselves. As one farmer noted, the entire county was "agrarian" in sentiment, and would instinctively form a united front to protect its identity. The controversy became one of "L.A.'s nuclear plant" against the "farmers and all the good, hardworking people in the towns and cities in this county."[28]

Populism offered a protective language for local interests, sanctifying existing community bonds and an independent image. The contrast between a hardworking, moral community and a depraved, parasitic urban culture helped define the nuclear plant as a threat. Residents imagined themselves to be rooted in the soil, fiercely independent, and a little closer to God than their counterparts in the Southland and other urban areas. In a different context, one Central Valley native summed up this rural provincialism: We thought of ourselves as "the best Americans in the world. To our people, their way of life was America. New York isn't America . . . we were America."[29] Populism negated Los Angeles' appeals that Kern citizens accept the plant for the good of a more broadly defined community of all Californians. Community loyalties took precedence over the state and nation.

Populist rhetoric without political weapons, however, would not have reconfigured the balance of power between federal, state, and local entities. Communities had resisted outside development interests before and failed, but a transformation in political tools and regulation strengthened their position. The most obvious device available was the referendum. The use of the initiative system had been dramatically energized by Ed

Koupal and Proposition 15. For citizens to pass judgment on a technology was no longer a far-fetched notion.[30] The idea of a plebiscite on nuclear power, an unimaginable prospect just ten years earlier, testified to the increasing community control over regulatory decisions.

Environmentalists and their ilk possessed legal skills and a growing constituency that agribusiness initially lacked. Kern environmentalists used legal weapons created by a national reform movement to democratize regulation, including most notably Ralph Nader's public interest organizations and environmentalists. Patterned after the National Environmental Policy Act, the California Environmental Quality Act empowered citizens to demand public scrutiny of any development project. Environmentalists provided the legal and technical expertise to their conservative allies in agriculture to stall construction and rally opposition.

Agribusinessmen had historically proven adept at manipulating the political system and relied on local quasi-governmental water districts. The water district was born in the late nineteenth century as a means for farmers to protect water rights, distribute water from federal projects, and raise funds for local water projects. In their more modern form, the districts played a role in setting resource policy, protecting agricultural interests. Any project touching on water use in the Central Valley came under scrutiny by water districts.[31] Water districts contradicted the authority of state resource institutions. While large-scale water projects offered the means to centralize resource planning, water districts undercut such state authority by protecting local agribusiness interests.[32] The agribusiness faction opposed to the power plant used this contradiction to undermine state water agencies, business, and agribusiness leadership who wanted the economic incentives offered by the power plant.

For agribusiness and blue-collar whites to join environmentalists in supporting an antinuclear campaign was an astounding turn of events. Kern County's environmentalists hold a niche, a reporter noted, once given to "cattle rustlers and horse thieves." "Environmentalism is not all that popular in Kern County," a leader of the local Sierra Club admits with considerable understatement. In the seventies, environmental initiatives fared poorly in Kern as a whole and were routed in white, working-class, and agricultural communities. The same initiatives picked up support among well-educated, wealthier districts and those outside of the Central Valley.[33] The drive against environmental protection has intensified in recent years. When an agribusinessman was prosecuted for killing the endangered kangaroo rat, Kern farmers turned out on hundreds of tractors and crop-dusting planes to hold a huge rally of support. They came replete with signs reading "Fight or lose your job to the

BureaucRATS," while the local assemblywoman suggested they "barbecue the [endangered] Mojave ground squirrel" to feed their families.[34]
But Kern County was not a monolithic block of conservatives. The national evolution of the nuclear issue and demographic diversity of the Central Valley made a minority of the Valley more open to an antinuclear message. Apart of a post-World War II middle-class expansion, urban growth in Bakersfield brought on a migration of individuals who joined a service sector of young, well-educated professionals and environmentalists who wanted to protect their environment, community, and quality of life.[35] They participated in the state and national debate on the atom, canvassed their neighborhoods, and raised local awareness of nuclear dangers. In the years before the Kern ballot on the San Joaquin Nuclear Project these activists had already undermined the credibility of the nuclear community and shifted public opinion.[36] For reasons of ideology and quality of life, environmentalists favored maintaining Valley agriculture as a buffer to Los Angeles-style development. The nuclear plant, they feared, would eliminate agriculture and encourage industrial expansion and pollution.[37] Community empowerment, they believed, could preserve agriculture and serve environmental ends.

And so two different ideologies united on the one issue they could both agree on, community power, even if their notions of community were quite different. The San Joaquin Nuclear Project's demise was not an isolated case.[38] In the seventies and eighties, diverse coalitions embraced Populism and the new grassroots political weapons to gain local control over new technology, busing, MX missile basing, low-income housing, waste disposal, and development projects. The loss of faith in the nation's elites and the expansion of public participation in government decisions permanently expanded community control over nuclear and a host of other issues where citizens did not want to negotiate or compromise.

Utilities Turn Inland

Hostility toward the environmentalist and antinuclear agenda in Kern County had not been enough to lure utility companies to the region. For technical reasons of plant efficiency, utility companies preferred coastal sites. But there had been so many false starts that by the seventies electric companies had given up on this option. Bodega, Malibu, Bolsa Island, Davenport, and the final straw, Point Arena, had made it clear that the desirable option was politically impossible. A combination of seismic problems, scenic considerations, and population densities led to state and federal policy that restricted nearly the entire coast from further power plant construction.[39] After Pacific Gas and Electric's defeat at Point Arena, David Pesonen announced, "it is clear that no more coastal sitings should be permitted in California. PG&E has a duty to explore . . . alternate siting of thermal plants, fossil and nuclear."[40] The utilities took Pesonen's advice.

There were also good political reasons for avoiding inland sites. Agribusiness and inland communities ferociously defended their water supplies. Even residents in the Owens Valley, a region Los Angeles ruled like a fief, slapped back LADWP's tentative bid to locate a power plant there.[41] The demand for Sierra waters from powerful Golden State agriculture exceeded developed supply, and locating a large number of power plants in the Central Valley would have brought certain opposition from the Farm Bureau. PG&E and LADWP were not averse to steamrolling their opposition, as they demonstrated at Bodega Bay and Malibu, but agribusiness was a formidable opponent.

Help came from an ally of farming interests—the Department of Water Resources (DWR). The irrigation water from sources such as the Central Valley Project and ground water had turned California agriculture into an international force, but brought with it a potentially catastrophic problem. In areas of low rainfall such as Bakersfield, salts have little opportunity to leach from the soils. Irrigation waters draw the salts to the roots where they threaten to kill crops unless the water is properly drained off. Failure to remove the wastewater eventually renders the land unsuitable for agriculture. Nearly four hundred thousand acres of the San Joaquin Valley were threatened in 1981. Solutions to this potential self-imposed disaster included a proposal that the government build a huge master drain network to dump the wastewater in the San Francisco Bay three hundred miles to the north, an idea sure to meet the wrath of environmentalists. They, too, pressured the DWR to find solutions to municipal and industrial wastewaters. State utilities proposed building massive drainage systems that would route all wastewater to a nearby power plant for use. The department appropriated substantial funding increases for research to evaluate this proposal.[42]

With their choices constrained by nature, citizens, and environmental policy, agriculture and the electric industry started the technical ground work for a wastewater alliance.[43] As the state moved forward with studies on using wastewater for cooling, the electric companies searched for inland sites. Southern California Edison looked into a site in the Mojave Desert, while PG&E and LADWP scoured the San Joaquin Valley for appropriate locations. The companies assumed that small amounts of inland water could be appropriated for one or two sites. The Metropolitan Water District in Southern California, despite its misgivings about using fresh water instead of the Pacific Ocean, agreed to supply a hundred thousand acre-feet of fresh water (an acre-foot is the amount of water needed to cover one acre to a depth of one foot) from its Colorado River and State Water Project allotments. Utility officials assumed that using MWD water would limit objections by agricultural interests to inland siting since it would be Los Angeles water allocated for the project and not that of Central Valley farmers. By the time they needed more power plants, the utilities assumed wastewater technology would be ready.[44]

The Los Angeles Department of Water and Power located a site after some controversy. A location in the county of Tulare proved to have seismic uncertainties and large local opposition, and in 1972 the Department of Water and Power explored sites in Kern County.[45] In July of 1973, LADWP announced that it was moving forward with more definitive studies and commitments on a site thirty miles northwest of Bakersfield near Wasco. The proposal was big. Four Westinghouse reactors would churn out 5,200 megawatts of electricity—the world's largest complex to date. LADWP would be the operator and own 40 percent of the complex, but every major private and public utility in the state would own a share. LADWP officials expected to begin construction in 1976, with operation of the first unit to start in December of 1981.[46]

The LADWP package offered an answer to every possible objection. Addressing the Kern County board of supervisors, LADWP officials stressed the economic, agricultural, and safety benefits of the $2 billion project (the number later ballooned to $6 billion). While the plant would draw some water from the California Aqueduct, officials assured the supervisors that wastewater use would compensate for the loss. LADWP argued that radiation from the plant was "negligible" and that the plants "can't blow up." With such assurances, the supervisors appeared satisfied.[47]

The scarcity of citizen opposition encouraged LADWP officials. In an informal newspaper poll of some residents, the "what nuclear power plant?" responses ran a tight race for first place with those who favored the project. No one opposed the plant, thinking it would refill the declining school enrollments and "bring more progress." Merchants salivated at the potential for business, and the local head of the chamber of commerce spoke avidly of how the project would reduce unemployment and raise tax revenue. Locals resented the conservationist voices who questioned the plant. Wasco's mayor spoke for many: "I'm a great conservationist too. But we're going to have to find a balance if we're going to maintain our method of living. We're going to have to find some way of getting the power."[48]

Conceived of as a massive four-reactor complex with twelve cooling towers, the San Joaquin Nuclear Project would have dominated the landscape in the Central Valley. To assuage the opposition, the proposal was cut to just two reactors before it was finally scrapped in March 1978. Courtesy Los Angeles Department of Water and Power.

The Emerging Opposition

In time, the perceived threat to agriculture undermined community support for LADWP's plan. The economic advantages of the project were not sufficient to entice some to leave farming who saw it as a way of life. James Payne, an Okie migrant turned agribusinessman, leased farmland on the proposed site. As a renter he had no right to reparations, but LADWP agreed to compensate him anyway. Despite the offer, Payne's identity was bound up in his land. Coming right out of the pages of *The Grapes of Wrath*, he argued, "Everything in my life is tied up in this farm. That's what makes it so hard. I don't need no piece of paper to tell me, after all these years, that this land is mine."[49]

Los Angeles' history of abusing its neighbors helped arouse the suspicions natural to Kern citizens when dealing with outsiders. "The whole psyche of Kern County," Joseph Fontaine recalled, "is to be very conservative, to be suspicious of outsiders, not wanting anyone telling us what to do.'" There had been no egregious crime committed against the Central Valley, but the "rape" of Owens Valley served as a reminder of Los Angeles' avariciousness. In that turn-of-the-century episode, the Department of Water and Power used underhanded tactics to acquire rights to the Owens River water and shipped it to Los Angeles via an aqueduct. The feat crippled the eastern Sierra community.[50] "We all knew the history of Owens Valley. When it was the LADWP," agribusinessman Jim Neufeld thought, "these can't be good guys." With the release of the movie *Chinatown* in 1974, a movie loosely based on the Owens Valley story, the Valley's "rape" was elevated to a public symbol.[51]

Kern's citizens thus regarded Southland incursions with a hypersensitivity bordering on paranoia. "We [in agribusiness] always had a certain [fear of] being attacked [by outsiders]," Neufeld recalled. Neufeld carried the responsibility of a family farming tradition that ran back to czarist Russia. He knew cheaper nuclear power would hold down his $10,000-per-month pumping costs on his two-thousand-acre spread.[52] But he and other residents thought the briefcase-toting "slick public relations experts" sent up from Los Angeles were "smug" and displayed a "steely arrogance" and a hidden agenda. Neufeld sensed "[that LADWP] had the attitude that 'you hicks out here really don't know very much and we're going to educate you on this.'" But when technical explanations about the wastewater system did not make sense, the farmers became suspicious that Los Angeles would need fresh water that normally would go to Kern farms. "I realized this was a P.R. job. . . . They weren't negotiating for wastewater," Neufeld concluded, "they were after [our] fresh water." Kern County would be just another slave to Los Angeles, as Owens Valley had become. The project was a Trojan horse. Fontaine thought that the average citizen began to see the project as "a power grab by Los Angeles to take over Kern County."[53]

Up and down the Central Valley, towns reacted with alarm to the LADWP proposal. Far to the north, the *Stockton Record* warned its readers that with its "political clout" Los Angeles was certain to build other power plants and take more Valley water. Nightmarish images of Valley towns being "gobbled up" by the behemoth from the south seemed to haunt those worried about the Wasco plant. The SJNP was fifteen years dead when Neufeld was interviewed in 1993, but his fear of a Los Angeles takeover remained vivid: "[If the plant was built] we knew we weren't running anything. . . . We were going to lose jurisdiction over our territory. That was the real threat. . . . Once they got their foot in here, we knew this thing was just going to run over us. This thing was just too huge not to run over us."[54] As one farmer told a public forum, Kern's government agencies would be "forever more subservient to the nuclear plant."[55]

Neufeld resolved to organize the farm community and fight the plant on issues important to Kern residents. At a Wasco tavern meeting in July of 1974, local farmers elected Neufeld to head an opposition group.[56] Neufeld and his associates worked the local communities in speeches to chambers of commerce, the Rotary, town boards, and LADWP hearings. At these meetings they showed no interest in safety issues, radiation, or the genetic threat to humankind that dominated antinuclear circles. "We downplayed that," Neufeld said, because the county was simply too conservative to build an antinuclear majority. The farmers focused on themes with a local and populist appeal. Discussion turned on the plant's effect on farming, the economic costs to the county, and possible job losses. Playing on the county's "mistrust," as Neufeld recalled, of Los Angeles, speakers repeatedly insinuated that Los Angeles had ill motives. LADWP's wastewater plan was "manipulated . . . to disguise the fact" that "somebody is going to get shorted" of water, Neufeld told audiences. That would result in "irreparable damage to agriculture in the San Joaquin Valley." What were Los Angeles' true motives, Neufeld and other speakers asked. They had a two-word answer: Owens Valley. Los Angeles would control Kern the way it did Owens if it established this beachhead. "We in Kern County are determined not to be another Owens Valley," Neufeld wrote. Another farmer disrupted a utility forum and warned an audience that the LADWP were "invaders who will destroy Kern County if we don't start acting now!"[57] The farm group had good press, but Neufeld was aware that this small band of malcontents and their speeches counted for little if they did not win some substantive battles. The group searched for issues, allies, and legal weapons to fight the plant. In the process, they connected with a larger movement for citizen empowerment.

Environmental Laws Slow Construction

Without the regulatory revolution that accompanied the environmental movement in the late sixties, halting the SJNP at the local level would have been impossible. The environmental movement of the late sixties and seventies encouraged state and local governments to balance pollution and quality-of-life concerns with their historically prodevelopment attitudes. California moved forcefully into environmental and nuclear regulation, but other states, particularly Minnesota, New York, and Massachusetts, also acted with vigor. Activists often found state governments allied with them in challenging federal promotion of nuclear power.[58] Part of the "new social regulation" sweeping consumer issues in the seventies, environmental activists opened up regulation to citizen involvement through litigation and legislation.[59] The state's best legal tool was the 1970 California Environmental Quality Act, a tougher companion to earlier national legislation. The Wasco farmers were lucky that Bakersfield was not a conservative ideological monolith. There was a committed core of environmentalists already using the state environmental impact report (EIR) process to stop proposed projects.

The environmentalist core in Kern came from the same sources as elsewhere—the professions, especially medicine, law, and education.[60] Among them were Frederic Lane, an anesthesiologist, and his wife, Joy, who was a law student. "We had both experienced smog in Los Angeles," Joy Lane remembered. "We came to Bakersfield hoping to have clean air." To their surprise, Bakersfield was a smog-filled community that was turning into the Los Angeles sprawl they had fled. The Lanes concluded that the agricultural land in the Valley acted as a buffer to the overpopulation and pollution endemic to Los Angeles. The Lanes allied with the local Sierra Club chapter and its leader, Joseph Fontaine, a local science teacher who had fought clear-cutting forests and land development in Kern. He was typical of the well-educated professionals who generally joined the club chapter. Fontaine believed that until the problems of "nuclear waste and plant safety" were resolved, construction should be delayed, especially with Bakersfield being "downwind" of any "radioactive cloud." The Lanes and Fontaine formed a legal response team to file suits that would slow development projects by demanding they adhere to EIR procedures. This alliance helped stop a large housing development at the huge Tejon Ranch.[61]

In the period between 1974 and 1976, the Lanes and the Sierra Club led the most effective legal opposition to SJNP and threatened to file suit unless the Department of Water and Power filed an environmental impact report.[62] The county board of supervisors and the farming community had been hostile to environmental studies. But Joy Lane overcame their resistance by appealing to agrarian sentiment and community preservation. Claiming that the nuclear plant would be the beginning of the Valley's transformation into "one large urban-industrial" sprawl, Lane skillfully mixed agricultural, health, and environmental themes as she warned: "Our lands and growing conditions for the production of food and fiber are not duplicated anywhere else in the world. Once lost, this land can never be reclaimed for agriculture. Our valley weather, air quality, and water constraints cannot withstand the stress of intensive urbanized or industrialized use without endangering the health and safety of people."[63] Kern residents did not want to become like Los Angeles, and even the Farm Bureau joined environmentalists in demanding an EIR to review the wastewater plan.[64]

The EIR episode indicated that there was common ground between farmers and environmentalists on development issues and local autonomy. Agribusiness was not interested in Fontaine's antinuclear issues, but Lane's call to preserve agriculture was more appealing. City expansion of Los Angeles and Bakersfield threatened to crowd out agriculture physically, through urban sprawl, and environmentally, through pollution and greater use of water. The Sierra Club agreed with the farmers, Fontaine noted, that "agriculture [should] remain the key linchpin of the economy." Despite their historic suspicion of environmentalists, Fontaine noted, "we formed a coalition with a lot of the farmers. We all worked together and they didn't have any problems working with the Sierra Club." For a brief moment in their long-running dispute, farmers and environmentalists had a common enemy in development, and saw a common solution in pushing local control. The California Environmental Quality Act would be the means to merge the disparate groups and officials around goals of local autonomy and agricultural preservation.[65]

In the past, LADWP had ignored the objections of its recalcitrant neighbors, but several provisions of the EIR empowered communities. The utility was required to hold extensive hearings on the project, thus exposing itself to extensive press coverage. LADWP, also, could not begin construction until an acceptable report was written. If the EIR it issued was unacceptable to Kern County, it could sue and stall construction. Writing the EIR would probably take less time than a losing court battle. The *Los Angeles Times* reacted with alarm and encouraged LADWP to appease Kern County. "This heavily populated region," it wrote, "must reach out into the thinly populated areas for safe and acceptable nuclear power." LADWP agreed to delay construction while writing the EIR and to cancel the project if Kern County did not want it.[66]

But expressions of goodwill could not counter the project's flaws exposed by the environmental impact report hearings conducted by LADWP. With the local media following every turn in the hearings, activists, including environmentalists like Joy Lane, and agribusiness representatives like Jim Neufeld raised questions ranging from the inadequacy of the wastewater plan to radioactive contamination of crops, and even increased ground fog. Activists also drew on the community of experts from China Lake Naval Weapons Research Center, who tended to support environmental issues. Pierre St.-Amand, a veteran of the Bodega Bay and Malibu controversies, helped the opponents raise issues of seismic safety. Substantiating criticisms, the researchers hired by the county found the report lacked analysis and was weak in evaluating radiation hazards to farms. County officials, citing "major deficiencies," requested that LADWP withdraw the EIR for revision.[67]

While the Department of Water and Power's performance appears inept, it must be remembered that new environmental laws—of the "new social regulation"—demanded an unprecedented level of analysis of projects. LADWP could point proudly to the massive final six-volume version of the EIR that was a foot and a half thick, but it was still not sufficient for its critics. LADWP found that any impact such as traffic, crop losses, and population increases became "environmental" and had to be addressed.[68] To underscore how the EIR had shifted power to localities and citizens, it is instructive to compare the painstaking county scrutiny of the San Joaquin Nuclear Project with the rapid approval given to Pacific Gas and Electric's Bodega Bay nuclear complex just fifteen years earlier. Unencumbered by environmental regulations, county supervisors disregarded public protests and approved the Bodega application without hearings or asking the most rudimentary questions such as whether the plant was to be nuclear or fossil fueled.[69] Lawsuits failed to stop the project, and only the revelation of seismic safety problems halted construction. The incident was one of many that helped force the regulatory changes that the SJNP confronted. To prevent such a rapid, ill-considered approval in the future, the environmental community changed regulation nationally by creating the Environmental Protection Agency and at the state level the antinuclear California Energy Commission and EIR. Citizens had the legal power to force a review of a development project.

The project had stalled at an unfortunate time for LADWP; after years of near universal support for nuclear power, public sentiment for it underwent a general decline in the mid-seventies. Nuclear power depended on confidence in the nation's regulatory institutions for public support. This decline was, in some measure, part of a general decline in respect for American institutions that followed in the wake of Vietnam, Watergate, and the economic malaise of the seventies.[70] But atomic energy officials had their own credibility problems. Beset by internal schisms and outside critics with established scientific credentials, the Atomic Energy Commission saw its impartial image and lock on nuclear expertise unravel in the seventies. The promise and safety of nuclear power had been oversold, and public attitudes turned against the atom as safety and economic problems became apparent. The revelation of scientific divisions on nuclear safety left much of the public wary and unsure of nuclear technology.[71] As debate on the Wasco plant heated up in 1976, the nuclear industry was vulnerable and its support tenuous.

This decline in support for scientific authority played right into the dominant antigovernment ethos of Bakersfield and the economic uncertainty it endured in the seventies. Federal regulation of pesticides, a cause locally championed by agriculture's nemesis, the United Farm Workers, had created tension between agribusiness and federal environmental experts in the Environmental Protection Agency. It was a burden to private operators like Neufeld and James Payne. To many, experts from outside the county just did not understand county needs.[72] The lingering recession of the mid-seventies also fed a general anxiety about the economic stability of the county. Its unemployment generally remained above the national average, and a severe drought in California increased economic anxiety. The less affluent white voters who responded to this populist campaign and voted against the power plant were, as one native Kern writer noted, "people floundering at the bottom . . . frustrated by and angry at a world that offers them only blue-light specials." This frustration could easily be directed against experts representing an outside government interest like LADWP. Politicians in Kern County, Joseph Fontaine noted, did well "demagoguing 'we don't want the state or federal government or any big organization coming in and telling us what to do.'" The antiplant movement could win by doing the same.[73]

The suspicion of government and expertise made county residents receptive to the message of antinuclear activists, which gathered significant strength in just a couple of years. When the plant was first proposed in 1973, nuclear power opposition was still a scattered movement of living-room activists. In 1974, Ralph Nader brought together the disparate elements at the first Critical Mass conference, and two years later nuclear power was one of the most debated issues in America as the California antinuclear initiative, Proposition 15, captured the public spotlight. Activists later pushed similar measures in six states for the November 1976 election.

The initiatives failed, but the extensive national coverage was corrosive to nuclear power's public support statewide and in Kern County. Project Survival, the antinuclear religious sect from San Francisco, campaigned heavily in Kern County, and SJNP opponents in the farm community donated money and campaigned for the measure as well. An antinuclear campaigner admitted that the defeat of Proposition 15 indicated that the public would not reject nuclear power outright, but attitudes toward local reactors had changed dramatically. "We created enough of an awareness that nobody wanted one of the damn things [near them]." This analysis was particularly accurate in Kern County. A poll of residents showed that a majority still favored nuclear power in general, but rejected a nuclear plant in the county by a margin of 43 to 29 percent.[74] Overall, Proposition 15 garnered only 37 percent county approval, but this was higher than in comparable conservative counties. Nearby Kings County gave the initiative just 28 percent of the vote, and Orange County trounced the initiative 4 to 1.

Despite the conservative image, a substantial minority in Kern County opposed the power plant for antinuclear reasons. County women in particular spoke out on these issues. "The women as a whole absolutely did not like the smell of [the nuclear issue]," Neufeld found in campaigning. Coming from the Audubon Society, Project Survival, and the American Association of University Women, female activists stressed the health threat of nuclear waste disposal to generations unborn, the risk posed by low-level radiation, and the susceptibility of nuclear plants to terrorism.[75]

But the real inroads made by the Proposition 15 campaign among Kern voters were not among antinuclear voters, but among populist ones. The economic threat of the plant and resentment of Los Angeles recruited voters in farm communities and blue-collar whites who were usually contemptuous of environmental issues.[76] Regression analysis indicates that statewide there were positive correlations between income and education and support for Proposition 15. This was typical of most environmental campaigns. The same pattern had hitherto held in Kern County. In a 1973 coastal protection initiative, for example, wealth positively correlated to initiative support in largely white precincts. But in the Proposition 15 campaign, exactly the opposite pattern resulted in Kern County. Decreasing affluence correlated to increasing antinuclear votes.[77] The unusual emphasis on nonnuclear issues in the Kern campaign had recruited a different set of votes.

Business and Labor Fight Back

For supporters of the nuclear plant, there was still a chance to use the same populist language in their favor. Less affluent whites and farm communities were hostile to and suspicious of the purveyors of environmentalism. If supporters could tag the antiplant movement with being elitists, outsiders, and enemies of the workingman, they might yet win back the voters they had lost to Proposition 15. Labor, business, and even some agricultural interests bridled at the small "clan of anti-nuclear supporters" composed of "sinister" "no-growth" environmentalists. Labor unions reacted with alarm to the rising antiplant chorus, since they expected 25 percent of all plant jobs would go to county residents.[78]

Robert Carter, head of the Kern, Inyo, Mono Labor Council, would seem to have been the perfect representative to lead the pronuclear fight. He fled his Oklahoma town in the Depression by hopping a freight train to San Diego. A pipe fitter by trade, Carter spent his life as a Kern County labor organizer. To a man from a humble background, "quality of life," a favorite environmental buzzword, meant a secure job. This LADWP—not environmentalists—offered.[79] Carter, in populist fashion, claimed opposition was a conspiracy between "big oil" interests in the county and environmentalists from outside the county, the hippie sons and daughters of the rich, who had flooded Bakersfield to deny the workingman a job. "Every kooky, long-haired environmentalist in the world showed up at that damn thing!" Carter exclaimed in a thick Oklahoma accent. "Oh Lord, they hitchhiked in from everywhere. I mean they swarmed [Bakersfield]!"[80]

Carter discovered an array of progrowth economic interests that had endorsed the power plant, including the chambers of commerce in Arvin, Bakersfield, Taft, and Tehachapi; the Bakersfield Board of Realtors, Kern County Builders Exchange, the Association of California Water Agencies, the Rotary, and a host of leaders of various water and irrigation districts. Despite the objections of Wasco farmers, many very large agribusinessmen actually favored construction. One such leader was George Nickel, an inheritor of the nineteenth-century Miller and Lux ranching kingdom. Where Wasco farmers saw a threat, Nickel envisioned opportunity. The plant's promised wastewater solution was crucial to save Nickel's Lost Hills area lands on the western side of the county. By campaigning for the project, Nickel hoped to curry favor from Pacific Gas and Electric for a joint venture in developing his property and water rights. The state utilities gave a substantial bankroll to the proplant coalition to hire and executive director and staff.[81]

Well financed and organized, the proplant coalition won an early victory by offering moderate presentations and assailing extremism. Members jammed public forums maligning environmental "detrimentalists" and "kooks." "Let the people know the truth and we'll shut the environmentalists up once and for all," Carter predicted. Another speaker argued, "If people don't work there will be trouble. There's no worse environmental impact than unemployment." Impressed by the turnout, county supervisors dismissed Joy Lane and the Wasco farmers. "These people have taken a position that regardless of anything, they oppose it," one supervisor accurately surmised.[82]

Agriculture Leads Plant Opposition

The ad hominem attacks on the part of Carter's coalition presented a possible populist counterattack. By cloaking themselves in the image of protectors of workingmen and women and dismissing the opposition as outside elites in environmental groups, nuclear proponents had seized the initiative. "This thing could have easily flopped off into a completely environmental war, and I knew we were going to lose that one," Jim Neufeld recognized. For the plant opposition to win, it too had to use the language of populism. "As long as we could [portray the power plant] as an invasion of our territory then I knew we had a chance." That meant cutting out the public role of antinuclear activists. Jim Neufeld and James Payne had worked well with local environmentalists, but they knew agribusiness in general would not understand why they were in the campaign. Neufeld told Friends of the Earth and Ralph Nader's California organization that they would give the Kern opponents a poor image. The news was disappointing to Nader's organization since it hoped to organize local antinuclear citizen coalitions. But Nader's left-wing populism with its antibusiness sentiment and large urban constituency was inappropriate for the county. "I didn't want [the Nader representative] anywhere near [Bakersfield]. . . . He was an outsider." And despite the antinuclear motivations of some activists in Bakersfield, they knew the dangers of involvement with their own kind. Warning away a fellow environmental activists, Pauline Larwood, a college student, wrote, "[We feel] that our farmer supporters would drop out if we became known as environmentalists."[83]

Still, the participation of environmental and urban activists from Bakersfield was essential. The trick was to reduce their visibility. These activists could communicate with elements more attuned to the nonmaterialist cultural changes that had swept the county in the sixties and seventies. By the seventies, Kern County hosted a large professional class among whom the threat from nuclear power hazards was an important issue. Bakersfield had a large academic community with a two-year college and state university in town. Physicians such as Frederic Lane and Thomas Larwood were active in opposition to the plant.[84] These organizers expressed concerns about the environment, and safety, and a mistrust of such an elite technology. Like the farmers, many were good Republicans, but their concerns for quality of life and the health and well-being of their families tempered probusiness attitudes.

The nonmaterialists and the farmers gathered at a meeting in September of 1976 to determine whether or not a more unified effort was feasible. There were divisions of interests. The farmers present expressed their concerns about water and crop yields threatened by the plant. They had "no concerns" about nuclear power itself but only about the influence of the plant on agriculture. Others were more interested in plant safety. But "we all recognized that we all came from different backgrounds, probably could never get together on any other issue. And that was fine," one Bakersfield attorney noted. What did unite them, he remembered, was a "natural" conviction that the nature of their community depended on preserving agriculture. "All of us [in Bakersfield] have a general respect for agriculture. We know that our livelihoods are based on oil and agriculture. If you are new to the area, you may not recognize that, but all of us who grew up here know that." Urban activists understood that to convert voters, water and agricultural themes were more viable than an antinuclear agenda.[85]

As antinuclear activists stepped back from the spotlight into rank-and-file positions, agricultural interests took center stage. The Wasco farmers avoided image problems by recruiting bipartisan agricultural leadership. Dave Bryant was the most significant convert. A successful agribusinessman who operated a ten-thousand-acre enterprise near Delano, Bryant was a formidable player in county and state Democratic politics. Dave Bryant's political skills and contacts with Pat Brown's son, Governor Jerry Brown, were just what the Wasco farmers lacked. He was a crack organizer and a superb negotiator.[86]

Bryant designed an aggressive plan to defeat the power plant based on populist imagery. The agrarian style was evident in the group's new name, the Agricultural Protection Council. Its agrarian and avowedly NIMBY (Not In My Back Yard) mission was "to preserve our water and the agricultural base of our economy by diverting the proposed San Joaquin Nuclear Project from our Valley."[87] To shed the antinuclear label, the organization openly advocated nuclear plants in coastal locations, and even testified in favor of the Diablo Canyon Nuclear Power Plant. It targeted Los Angeles as the intrusive outsider by keeping the Owens Valley story before the public. Advertisements and bumper stickers reiterated consistent themes, "Remember Owens Valley" and "Stick It in L.A.!" The issue was so well known that no one had to ask what the "it" was.[88]

The valuable addition of Democrat Bryant had to be balanced by Republican leadership. The county was closely wedded to California's weak party system and nonpartisan elections. Bipartisan coalitions were valued and easily formed in Kern, where politicians run on nonpartisan slates. Citizens prided themselves on "voting the man" even if in practice Republicans won most elections. SJNP opponents needed someone to represent the conservative, individualistic nature of the county. Jack Pandol was a natural choice.

The parking lot of the Pandol Brothers enterprise in Delano explains as well as anything produced by Dorothea Lange or Carey McWilliams the difference between farming and agribusiness. Scores of workers operate the company's processing center and huge loading dock. Tractor trailer trucks move through the complex in a constant stream to pick up Jack Pandol's grapes and citrus. The offices are filled with employees on the phone with customers not just in San Francisco or New York, but cities in Asia and South America. It is a "family farm," as Pandol likes to emphasize, with over $100 million in annual sales. Pandol built his fortune with a capitalist's zeal for hard work, government-subsidized water, and deal making.

On the wall of his office, next to the photo of him shaking hands with General Pinochet of Chile, is a crowbar mounted on a plaque reading "The day we held the line." Delano is the birthplace of Cesar Chavez' labor activism, but Pandol does not have fond memories of the father of the United Farm Workers. Stripped of his shotgun by police, Pandol stood with the crowbar, on a farm road between the newly organized farmworkers, twirling it in the air in defiance, to protect his nonunion workers. He is reviled by union leaders as a "labor-hating bastard." But in an area where respect is given in proportion to business success, Jack Pandol had earned a substantial community standing and had been active in GOP county politics. When he spoke on an issue, no one called him a kook.[89] While Bryant was the political brains behind the effort, Pandol was its populist voice.

That a man like Pandol could fill this role was indicative of how populism had been remade in a conservative form. He was a man who could step off a plane after a business trip to Asia or lecturing at the Harvard Business School and speak convincingly like a humble farmer. If this seemed contradictory, it was not. In economic matters, conservative populism praised the rugged individualism and entrepreneurialism of agribusinessmen. But Pandol derived his identity from agrarian values. Pandol had an almost mystical religious attachment to his land. He converses in paternal language, describing the land in feminine terms and calling his grapes his "children." The land in Delano was desert when his family settled it, and he saw firsthand how irrigation transformed it. He did not trust anyone who put limits on access to water. Pandol despised government, distrusted Los Angeles, and embraced an agrarian community ideal.[90]

Pandol's opposition had nothing to do with nuclear safety questions or environmental concerns. "That didn't affect me," he remembered. "I had an agenda." That agenda was water. More than a commodity, however, water had a cultural value by turning the Valley into a Garden of Eden. "Should we allow this [construction] to happen," he remarked, "on my tombstone they would probably put, 'The fool that allowed . . . a desert in the land of plenty.'" To Pandol, water was essential to community survival.[91]

With his common touch, Pandol was adept at fanning populist resentment of elites. And with the brutal drought and the economic slump that followed in 1976 and 1977, he had an ideal weapon to fan outrage at LADWP's "stealing" of Kern's water. After apologizing for not "having something fancy" for a speech, Pandol attacked Los Angeles' "silver-tongued orators."

> You should warn some of these guys from LA, you know, these silver-tongued orators, that they can go to hell for lying. . . . The jackasses in Los Angeles . . . waste our water, and they still take five gallons to flush down a pint of pee, let them take that diluted water and drink it or run their own nuclear plant. . . . If Los Angeles really loves us they ought to prove it by giving us this extra water. . . . If someone paid me out of Los Angeles enough and my morals slipped a little bit, hell, I'd come up here too and tell you how wonderful it's going to be to have that power plant up here.[92]

Hammering away at county suspicions of Los Angeles, Pandol argued, "Los Angeles has never done anything for us and they never will unless they slit our throats."[93] Pandol was so effective that he became the plant opposition's favorite public speaker, and they proudly used his endorsement in their ads.

The verbal offensive said more about Kern County's attitudes than about the reality of its relationship with Los Angeles. It was a popular argument to charge the Southland with wasting Kern's water. The charge, however, simply was not true. Since 1973, the Metropolitan Water District released its unused entitlement from the California Aqueduct as "surplus water" for agricultural use at fire sale rates. Los Angeles ratepayers doled out $170 million to cover the capital costs and interest on water they never received. Pandol's attacks, coming as they did in 1977, the worst drought year in California history, were galling. To help with Central Valley support in its conflict with the Owens Valley, MWD cut its use of the Aqueduct to a trickle. They drew from the Colorado River basin aqueduct, giving Kern agribusiness access to thousands of acre-feet of surplus water. The subsidies and drought aid by the city did nothing, however, to endear the Southland to Kern. MWD's surplus water had become a right instead of a privilege to growers who called it "our water." They resisted any attempt to "steal" some back.[94]

But Pandol's rhetoric was an accurate portrait of the mind of Central Valley residents. The resentment he stirred up spilled over in public forums where residents hurled insults at LADWP's "robber barons," "Caesars," and the "power hungry, multi million-dollar public utility cartels with their well-heeled lobbyists." Kern residents believed that denizens of Los Angeles viewed them as bumpkins and fools. "You figure you come to Kern County, we're just a bunch of hicks, we'll let you in. . . . It won't be that easy," one speaker warned LADWP officials. But one image dominated: "Los Angeles has a reputation for . . . raping the Owens Valley," one speaker said. "We don't want that to happen to the San Joaquin Valley." The use of rape imagery was no accident. Since Populists days, female icons had been metaphors for rural virtue, purity, and vulnerability. The virtuous had to guard against the urban "invaders," who were rapists, slicksters, and seducers.[95] The *Californian* stated these themes baldly in a dramatic front-page editorial after Bryant secretly secured its support.

They raped the Owen Valley and bled Inyo County dry.
Now it's Kern County's turn?
Comes the Los Angeles Department of Water and Power, bearing gifts and smiling seductively.
We should at least get a kiss beforehand.
Yes we are skeptical. . . .
Wouldn't Los Angeles County residents welcome jobs and burgeoning tax revenues promised by the merchants of nuclear power?
Apparently not. . . .
Kern County's . . . water is the gold ring. But it's far too dear to trade for vague promises.
Some go so far as to call them lies. . . .
Let LADWP go where sea water abounds.
Stick it up in El Segundo.[96]

This clinging to the myth of rural virtue and continued resentment of the Southland in the face of substantial relief from Los Angeles point to the skewed, but culturally necessary, nature of Kern perceptions. Lacking a history with a clear violation of their sovereignty by Los Angeles, Kern residents imported one from the valley on the other side of the Sierra: "Remember Owens Valley." It provided a populist tradition of grievances to justify their independence and water rights. They were the common folk, the producers of food, who stood in danger of enslavement by the wealth and power of Los Angeles.[97]

Against this level of mistrust, the parade of LADWP and Nuclear Regulatory Commission experts were powerless. An exhaustive four-hour presentation in Wasco by LADWP experts fell on deaf ears. One politician noted, "I don't think they've changed the minds of the people here. I don't think they could with another four hours."[98] The nuclear experts were well prepared and knowledgeable, but as government and, especially, Los Angeles representatives, they lacked the credibility to overcome the barbs of Pandol and others.

Breaking Up Plant Support: Water Districts

In tandem with their rhetorical war, the Agricultural Protection Council worked to break up plant support by Kern government institutions.

The key agency to neutralize was the Kern County Water Agency, since it was working with LADWP to design a workable wastewater system for the nuclear plant. The council decided to organize a revolt within water districts against the water agency's plans.[99] Some water districts were not hard to convert, since the agency was selling a wastewater solution to a problem besetting only some water districts. Individualistic farmers were not willing to endorse projects in which they had no stake. The Wasco area's water district bluntly told the agency that until the problem affected Wasco, it would not participate in any program. "The farmer will not put out one nickel [for the plan] unless he has to. It's in his nature," one said openly. "He ain't gonna do it until it hurts, until he sees the boll fall off his cotton before his own eyes." It was greed, perhaps, but the farmers could hardly be blamed for avoiding installing drains costing $275 per acre.[100]

Bryant's strategy had the desired effect. The water districts pressured the Kern County Water Agency to back away from wastewater negotiations with Los Angeles. And with it the political support that LADWP had so carefully stitched together slowly ripped apart.[101] The towns of Shafter and Delano passed antiplant resolutions. Wasco's city council reversed its resolution endorsing the power plant. Council members broke after suffering under a boycott of their businesses.[102] And the state Department of Water Resources, which had once encouraged inland siting, now called the Wasco plant an unwise use of fresh water.[103]

The Farm Bureau proved to be similarly porous. Large operators who ran the Farm Bureau were generally agreeable to the power plant. Less provincial in their outlook, they did not fear being overrun by Los Angeles, and many of the large farms owned land in salt-threatened areas.[104] Jim Neufeld, however, used his position as bureau director to poll its membership. An overwhelming 86 percent of the Farm Bureau's rank and file opposed the plant. Neufeld rigged the result through leading questions, but it was such a crushing margin that few doubted the result. When bureau directors tried to suppress the poll, Neufeld leaked the results to the *Californian*. The headline, "Bureau Clamps Lid on Poll Opposing A-Plant," embarrassed and limited the bureau's influence on the issue.[105]

The success Bryant's farmers had in neutralizing the influence of the Kern County Water Agency, the Farm Bureau, and other institutions point to how the structure of welfare state institutions shaped the direction of the controversy and the fortunes of the Wasco plant. KCWA was a product of California-sponsored water projects, but provided new opportunities for the expression of local autonomy. Utilities usually

Local opinion was rapidly turning against the San Joaquin Nuclear Project by the fall of 1976. In a Wasco town meeting, residents overwhelmingly voted against the nuclear plant. The signs refer to power plant supporter George Nickel who plant opponents believed would receive an economic windfall with the wastewater plan. Courtesy *Bakersfield Californian*.

won county approval of a power plant by cultivating approval from the board of supervisors and by a few words to the chamber of commerce. State resource management changed that equation by creating agencies that were easily accessible to local agribusinessmen who disagreed with Farm Bureau leadership.

This all added up to a disintegration of the pluralistic politics county leaders relied on to make decisions. By generating a vocal debate, forcing county officials to use the EIR to conduct an extensive examination of the project, and stripping away institutional support, plant opponents turned the spotlight on the board of supervisors, who had thus far managed to avoid taking a position. Supervisors argued that their role was to ensure that the Department of Water and Power abided by county procedures and issued a proper EIR. With all regulations met and extensive institutional support, a supervisor would have been safe approving a construction permit. Without the endorsements, the supervisors were at the mercy of constituent opinion. In the November elections of 1976, the Agricultural Protection Council went after the supervisors themselves.

A Kern County supervisor seat is usually a secure job. Those who sat on the board in 1976 had decades of experience, and so the idea of bringing one down on the issue of a nuclear power plant was a long shot. But Dave Bryant had just those ideas. Even so, Gene Tackett was an unlikely choice as a candidate for the office. He had the advantage of being the son of an Okie ditch (canal) tender. But Tackett did not have the usual pedigree expected of politicians in Kern. A fairly liberal Democrat, Tackett had spent much time out of the county attending college and working in the Peace Corps. Against the incumbent, Tackett could count on minority voters and Okies in farm communities and Oildale, but he needed some issue to expand his voting base. Tackett saw an opportunity to bring in new backers when his opponent remained neutral on the Wasco power plant issue. Tackett was naturally attracted to what he believed was a populist issue that pitted smaller farmers against corporate interests. Dave Bryant brought Tackett to a meeting with the Wasco farmers. The interview was short. Where do you stand on the SJNP? Tackett told them as supervisor he would vote against the power plant. In short order, his campaign had $7,000 in contributions.[106]

Tackett won the November election with 57 percent and large majorities in the farm communities.[107] Republican Trice Harvey joined Tackett as a new supervisor and an opponent of the SJNP. Like Tackett, Harvey came from an Okie farm family and was determined to preserve Kern's agriculture. What was the wisdom of "siting a nuclear power plant right in the middle of the richest agricultural land in the world," Harvey argued. The Agricultural Protection Council now had two of the three votes it needed. The remaining supervisors faced hazardous choices. Taking a stand against the plant was not easy. There were powerful players who favored the plant, including former presidents of the Farm Bureau, the Kern County Water Agency, water districts with wastewater problems, bank presidents, and representatives of real estate firms. These were not groups a politician could afford to offend.[108]

In 1977 there would be no way to avoid the issue. LADWP planned to file for a construction permit as its long-delayed EIR took shape. Gene Tackett repaid his political debt to Dave Bryant and the farmers and introduced a resolution at a February supervisor's meeting opposing the Wasco plant and favoring coastal nuclear plants. The three uncommitted supervisors resorted to stalling by arguing that Tackett's resolution was "poorly timed and premature." With shouts, catcalls, and chants of "recall" rising to a din, the resolution failed by a 3 to 2 vote.[109]

Proposition 3

The supervisors needed an expedient way to "get off the hook," as Trice Harvey remembered. On 20 December 1977, with the worst dust storms in memory swirling outside, they unanimously resolved to conduct an advisory election in March of 1978. The ballot for "Proposition 3" would read, "Shall a nuclear power plant be located near Wasco in Kern County?" All supervisors save Gene Tackett pledged to honor the results when they voted on a construction permit.[110] From outside the county, Dave Bryant quietly brought in the antinuclear organizers of California's 1976 initiative campaign to coordinate the "No on 3" crusade.

The Agricultural Protection Council faced a daunting campaign of taking on the financial resources of the nation's nuclear industry and state utilities. The industry had never lost a major antinuclear initiative campaign. The drubbings had been so bad that Ralph Nader's organization had retreated from its populist goals and stopped encouraging initiatives. In fact, the proplant coalition was so sure of victory after the overwhelming defeat of antinuclear initiatives in 1976 that it was the one that proposed the advisory election. Anyone who had watched the way the 1976 initiative had been picked to pieces could only shudder at the thought of taking on all that power.[111]

The pronuclear forces misread the 1976 results; Americans, it was true, would not shut down nuclear power, but they wanted the final say. They did not trust the construction, operation, and safety of nuclear plants to government and electric utilities. The unprecedented public vote on nuclear technology was proof of the eroding trust in government and expert authority. Nationally, the public demanded a voice in nuclear decisions they had once left to experts. In the four years after the 1976 initiatives, antinuclear measures in Montana, Hawaii, and Oregon gave construction veto power to the state legislature or the public. The trend accelerated in the eighties as hundreds of communities demanded similar power over choosing nuclear waste disposal sites.[112] The economic resentments that Kern activists used had worked well in a successful 1976 Missouri initiative. The initiative forbade utilities from charging ratepayers for construction costs before operation. By combining nuclear safety with issues of local control and economics, activists shed the antinuclear label and won the support of conservatives, consumer groups, environmentalists, the Democratic candidate for governor, and Missouri's leading newspaper.[113]

Kern activists created a grassroots campaign using scores of neighborhood canvassers and advertisements stressing populist themes. Activists made the fantastic claim that the plant would cost the county

5,660 jobs and that the county would somehow lose money by the project.[114] This dubious argument worked because they were able to couple economic arguments to an evil, outsider image that destroyed the LADWP's credibility. Employing local resentment of cosmopolitan and government domination, the "No on 3" campaign easily dismissed the proplant "slick" "consortium" of experts from industry and government. "[We] want our agricultural economy to remain strong and fear that *outside interests* such as the Los Angeles Department of Water and Power do not have Kern County's interests in mind," Neufeld warned residents. Advertisements argued that voting "yes" would turn power over to officials in Sacramento and Washington: "We don't want state and federal bureaucrats making the decision for us!" The "No to 3" ads also warned that "L.A.'s power grab" would turn Kern County into a huge waste disposal site for the city: "LA wants us to take the risks while they take the power. LA wants to gobble up our valuable farm land and water and leave us with the wastes! If having a nuclear plant in your own backyard is such a great idea, why don't they keep it?" The message was simple: "People who care about Kern County say 'No on L.A.'s plant!'" Every ad ended with the damning "L.A.'s nuclear plant . . . the more you know about it the less you like it!"[115]

In conjunction with this Los Angeles-as-octopus imagery, the opposition presented Kern as an ideal community by connecting it to as agrarian tradition and emphasizing how it would be disrupted by the power plant. Our theme, Neufeld noted, was that "we were fighting for the farm." Advertisements warned residents, "In Kern County, when you threaten agriculture, you threaten us all!" Opposition advertisements claimed "families with deep roots" would be displaced, disruption the entire pattern of the county's "schools, businesses, and community life." "It is a question of whether we are going to stick together here in Kern County and help out neighbors and ourselves, or whether we're going to let the Los Angeles Department of Water and Power come up here and divide us." Photos of an idyllic farm community showed prolific fields of fruit trees, busy agricultural workers, and local business helping farming operations. The pictures underscored the intimate lines of dependence threatened by the plant. Much of the land to be taken for the plant was not farmland but alkaline flats. But factual arguments could not compete with these simple appeals to preserve what the community imagined itself to be.[116]

The campaign found surprisingly strong support in lower-class white districts that should have sided with Bob Carter and his pronuclear allies. Canvassers in Oildale found near unanimous opposition to the power plant. Almost entirely blue-collar and white, Oildale, as one resident noted, "has been to Bakersfield as Bakersfield is to California." That is, a stereotype of a poor, white, racist community.[117] Its oil field workers should have avidly responded to Carter's pronuclear, jobs message. But by stressing that it was L.A.'s nuclear plant, activists found their other arguments a relatively easy sell.

Plant supports tried to overcome the anti-L.A. and economic themes of the opposition by painting a rosy future with the atom and a literally dark one without it, Nuclear power was clean, safe, and cheap. The plant would serve the county's future filled with "new people, newly formed families, new business, new farms, and new factories." Supporters had their own bleak image of an atomless California. Ads warned of blackouts, householders freezing in their unlit homes, and a dependence on "Arab oil" and "the whims of Arab sheiks." Hoping to combat images of Los Angeles as the evil outsider, they printed cartoons of sheiks on camels wearing "No on 3" signs.[118] They asked county residents to think of their allegiance and responsibility to a larger community of citizens and not to retreat into "isolationism." Los Angeles gave them water during drought years, they reminded readers. "If we are unwilling to share our good fortune with others," advertisements warned, "we are in trouble and the state is in trouble."[119]

The statement of interdependence was true enough, but county residents did not accept facts not in accord with their myth that they were self-sufficient producers forced to support a parasitic urban culture. Supervisor Trice Harvey was typical: "When Los Angeles and San Francisco say 'I can produce the food for my table' then I'll talk about providing their power. Let them do something for us." Local autonomy and community character were the key issues. As the director of the "Yes on 3" committee admitted, "The opponents had a much more easily salable line: it's Los Angeles' plant, it's going to take water. It was something that seeped into the people's thinking long before our campaign become organized."[120] It was more accurate to say that these themes had seeped into the local culture decades ago.

In early March 1978, 70 percent of the county made a statement of independence and struck down the San Joaquin Nuclear Project. The county supervisors, relieved to have had their decision made for them, unanimously decided against a permit for the project and received a standing ovation. LADWP, citing insurmountable "obstacles," canceled the project.[121]

What was most notable about the returns was that this was largely a community vote, rather than one of interest groups. There was little variance between urban and rural areas. Bakersfield, with greater antinuclear sentiment, registered the highest "no" vote with 72 percent. But all district margins were greater than 66 percent. Thin majorities in only 8 of over 230 precincts surveyed voted "yes," and a number of those were precincts with less than ten voters. Rich or poor, black or white, people voted against the power plant.

Analysis of what variation there was, however, indicates that the anti-Los Angeles theme of the campaign created a geographic polarization of the votes in Kern County, Those living in the Central Valley and identifying with it were more likely to be antiplant voters. Nearly all of the proplant precincts were in supervisorial districts outside the Valley and in communities the *Californian* dismissed as physically and "culturally close to Los Angeles' influence." These communities, such Frazier Park, Mojave, and Edwards Air Force Base, had no identification with the Bakersfield community or the Central Valley.[122] The Central Valley voted as a community against Los Angeles.

While all sectors of the Valley's voters cast majorities against the power plant, the populist themes of the campaign produced some class and racial variations. Economic anxiety and resentment of Los Angeles' urban culture influenced voting patterns. Regression analysis of fifty-six precincts indicates that opposition to the power plant rose at the low end of the socio-economic ladder. When precincts outside of the Central Valley are excluded, the economic correlation dramatically improves and is even better than the correlation in the Proposition 15 vote. The agrarian theme also influenced voting patterns in the farm districts. Farm communities, especially those close to Wasco, opposed the plant in higher numbers than did the county as a whole. The precincts in Shafter, Ford City, Maricopa, and Buttonwillow often registered over 80 percent opposition. Wasco, the town with the most to gain and lose, remained a little more divided than other farm communities and voted against the plant by 70 percent, or the same as the county as a whole.[123] Race was less of a factor in voting patterns. While the more liberal minority communities of Bakersfield historically supported environmental issues, the dramatic conversion of lower-class whites and farm communities to plant opposition minimized racial variation. There is a slightly positive correlation with Hispanic precincts and plant opposition, but it is not statistically significant. The small number of black precincts had relatively large antinuclear votes in the Proposition 15 contest, but voted against the plant by the same percentages as the rest of the county. White precincts were slightly more likely to support the plant, but again the data are not statistically significant.[124] The key gain for plant opponents over earlier environmental campaigns was, then, from the less affluent white districts and farm communities that have never supported environmental issues before and never have since.

Kern had voted to affirm its identity as a populist, agrarian community. In a result contrary to studies that depict community power declining in the face of twentieth-century "mass society," a confluence of changes in local society, culture, and government institutions strengthened local control. If community exists when rights are fought for and won, Kern County qualified.[125] Environmentalists and more conservative activists agreed that this was a healthy sign that locales had regained some control from the federal government in power plant siting decisions. Los Angeles officials would have to respect locales it once ignored. It was no idle boast when a local editor asserted that "L.A. has been described as a hundred suburbs in search of a community. Bakersfield is a community."[126]

But what kind of community was this? Community has as much to do with local ties as with an assertion of home rule. In this regard, Bakersfield was not the community envisioned by left-wing community activists. They envisioned relationships based on economic democracy and tolerance of individual differences. Flocking to Bakersfield, antinuclear activists had cut their hair and worked anonymously for the Proposition 3 campaign in hopes of learning how to construct a similar coalition.[127] They were no doubt pleased at the result, but what did they make of this alliance? The more conservative farmers had allied with environmentalists and liberal activists, but denied their existence. Cooperation in this movement was achieved not through an open acceptance of different perspectives, but by maintaining a front of ideological homogeneity. The collaboration evaporated as farmers and urbanites returned to their livelihoods.[128]

The paradox inherent in the Proposition 3 campaign was that despite the rhetoric, it had been a vehicle not to foster community cooperation but to protect a community founded on social conservatism and private interest. While the left believed it was championing economic democracy and toleration, it did not realize that a populist defense of community could be culturally exclusive. In the aftermath of the sixties, there was too much polarization on social issues for local citizens to overcome cultural division in a manner romanticized by left-leaning "new populists." Neither urban elites, environmentalists, nor their minority allies were acceptable to conservative populist discourse. Noticeably, absent from the controversy was the opinion of the county's large Mexican American community. There was little that localism could offer minorities to counter the region's legendary racism when, as one politician admitted, "Kern County has a vested interest in keeping people where they are, especially racially."[129] Left to their own devices, political and business leaders in Kern ignored the problems of marginal groups.

Populism also served to foster personal economic freedom and property rights, not an economic democracy.[130] It is unlikely that Oildale residents gained anything from voting against the nuclear plant other than some feeling of solidarity. Although some plant opponents romanticized this conflict as one between small farmers and larger corporate agribusiness and urban elites, it was successful agribusinessmen who gained the most. Conservative populism ennobled and justified individualistic pursuit of wealth.

Bakersfield was a community, but it was an economically and socially conservative one. It was the New Right that mobilized this community discourse in coming elections. First under Ronald Reagan and then in later elections, citizens demanded local control to limit the intrusion of unpopular federal programs and the cultural decline of America's moral communities.[131] Kern's populism had counterparts throughout the country. While it was not always possible to find the same combination of agrarian images, rural/urban conflict, and water-obsessed farmers, communities combined elements of populism to justify their own rejection of intrusive federal programs, corporate domination, and cultural decay. Populism served particularly well for communities fighting the "greed and power" of "government bureaucrats" and, to a lesser degree, "large corporations" sponsoring waste disposal development. While agrarian myths would not work in urban areas, religious expressions of community stressing the sacredness of a neighborhood or region proved invaluable to Italians and Jews in Brooklyn fighting liberal sponsorship of neighborhood and school integration. In Boston, Catholic women reciting rosaries marched to "preserve neighborhood schools" against the "judicial tyranny" of forced busing. Even the military was not immune. MX basing in Utah ran into Mormons and Shoshone Indians who believed the region's sacredness prohibited its sacrifice for military purposes.[132] After a fifty-year period in which the Depression and the Cold War created a consensus for government domination of programs such as nuclear power, the public had lost faith and reasserted a measure of local control.

Even among architects of conservative populism, the flood of community revolts was a troubling confirmation of a declining national will. Commentator Kevin Phillips mourned that Great Society failures and debacles in Vietnam and Watergate had destroyed institutional and leadership credibility. Americans turned to "less exalting forms of self-identification: ethnicity, regionalism, selfish economic interest, sects, and neighborhoods."[133] Phillips' assessment was largely correct. But the change must have been due to more complex and permanent causes than individual government failures, or new leadership could have recouped these setbacks. With old identities and faith in disarray, populism and new grassroots weapons allowed the public to create and maintain new allegiances to their locales, which crippled the government's ability to implement policy over the objections of localities. Politics in the seventies permanently disintegrated into a fractured, disordered process that relied more than ever on direct public consent. For good or ill, thinking locally reversed the decline in community power at the expense of the state and federal government. It would be more difficult to compromise or negotiate on future development issues for the common good.[134]

Critics decried that in refusing to accept a power plant, citizens had retreated from responsibility and the common good. The Agricultural Protection Council's NIMBYism argued for putting the plant anywhere but in the Valley. It was questionable ethics when plant opponents called for seismically risky coastal sites beyond the Tehachapis just to protect crops.[135] The Valley's NIMBYism might have been a serious threat if there had been a real crisis, but electric companies overestimated the need for electricity and the value of nuclear power. As the eighties would prove, alternative sources such as natural gas, power-pooling arrangements, and conservation were far more economical than the peaceful atom. In defeating the plant, the farmers actually did LADWP a favor that saved billions of dollars. Cancellation of the Wasco plant at a later date is certain since the nation's utilities scrapped all nuclear projects begun in the late seventies. This would have left a half-finished plant sitting by Interstate 5 as a reminder of a failed dream.

The lesson in the Kern vote was political rather than economic. Nuclear power had no future in California or the rest of the nation as long as there was no local consensus on the atom's value. Ultimately, the breakdown in public confidence in utility experts, the nuclear industry, and public officials ensured that citizens would take back this authority.[136] No longer isolated to environmentalists, opposition now included cross-ideological groupings, and the language of populism spread to other antinuclear revolts. Native Americans found similar allies in the Southwest against uranium mining. Farmers, too, brought their populist message to antinuclear groups three thousand miles away at the Shoreham facility on Long Island and in Minnesota and Wisconsin.[137] "When the farm community, which is the conservative bedrock of America, almost solidly opposes nuclear power, it's clear times have changed," concluded one New York farm representative.

"They [New York utilities] don't know it . . . yet, but nuclear power is dead."[138] Three Mile Island was still one year distant, but state and local resistance had taught California utilities that nuclear power could not be saved. But nationally, utility executives still clung to their once grand hopes of locating hundreds of nuclear plants in America. There along the shores of the Susquehanna River the nuclear industry would learn its final lesson.

Conclusion

California Goes National

In the years following the 1978 cancellations of Sundesert and the San Joaquin Nuclear Project, the political and economic landscape changed for the nuclear industry and the antinuclear movement. Nuclear power was in a death spiral from Three Mile Island, skyrocketing construction costs, and collapsing electricity demand. The economic losses were titantic. New plants coming on line often cost two or three times a similarly sized coal plant. The economics of nuclear power were so poor that sometimes completing a plant that was almost finished made no sense. With cancellations and bankruptcy pulling down utilities, the business community offered the most critical assessment. The nuclear industry, *Forbes* thundered, "ranks as the largest managerial disaster in business history, a disaster on a monumental scale. And only the blind, or the biased, can now think that most of the money has been well spent. . . . For the U.S., nuclear power is dead—dead in the near term as a hedge against rising oil prices and dead in the long run as a source of future energy."[1] These well-documented economic causes offer a compelling explanation of the nuclear industry's demise in the eighties.[2] While the antinuclear movement had impressive victories in California, it only managed to save California utilities from the economic horrors that engulfed the nu-

243

clear community elsewhere. The national movement was not a principal cause of the wave of plant cancellations.

California's nuclear opposition exerted its national influence in the drift toward decentralization in American politics and culture. Antinuclear activism helped instigate this trend by infusing new nonmaterialist values into society, by challenging government and expert authority, and by weakening a sense of national purpose and strong federal leadership that surrounded the atom's promotion. Decentralization led to a shift in loyalties and a revitalization of state and local power, concepts of community, and democratic forms of political expression. Despite the high hopes of nuclear advocates for political salvation, decentralization short-circuited the Reagan administration's efforts to revive nuclear power.

The California Energy Commission's decision on Sundesert and its condemnation of the federal waste disposal program sent shock waves through the nation's capital. The nuclear bills were not hollow political stunts after all. In 1978, worried United States senators hauled Gene Varanini before a committee hearing and asked him to declare whether California considered itself "supreme" over the federal controls. "In California we reserve the right to choose our technology and our destiny," Varanini told the senators with a flourish. "It is a moral issue that . . . is superior to national problems."[3] John C. Calhoun could not have asserted states' rights better. If the nuclear industry was to avoid a revolt against the atom, federal authority had to preempt this challenge.[4]

California utilities filed two separate suits, one through a conservative legal foundation and a second brought by Pacific Gas and Electric arguing for federal preemption of the nuclear bills.[5] A federal district court ruled in favor of the utilities by nullifying seventeen of the state's power plant siting laws, including the Warren-Alquist Act. The ruling, however, was too sweeping to survive appeal. It was more befitting an earlier Cold War period where national security interests and the complexity of nuclear power dictated the need for federal authority. By the seventies, centralization had lost much of its justification, since California and other states had built up their own energy-planning capability. Moreover, with the consensus on the value of nuclear power breaking down, the preemption doctrine forced states into what the Energy Commission's lawyer argued was a "nuclear straightjacket."[6] A state and its citizens would not be able to stop an unwanted nuclear power plant if a utility desired to build one. The public would never accept this, one federal official admitted. "The public was willing to be told what to do [in the sixties] when it came to nuclear energy. Now they want more of a say in decisions."[7]

The California Energy Commission responded to the utility suits by hiring Harvard law professor Laurence Tribe and cooperating with environmental lawyers to mount a response.[8] In 1981, the ninth circuit court in a consolidated case overturned the lower courts and held that California's laws were not in conflict with the objectives of the Atomic Energy Act. The appeals court argued that the Atomic Energy Act was not intended to interfere with the traditional right of states to regulate power plants for reasons not related to radiation hazards.[9]

One sentence can mean so much. The ruling hinged on a 1976 assembly report justifying the nuclear bills, in which Gene Varanini argued that California's intent in regulating nuclear wastes was "economic not safety related." Had the utility lawyers convinced the court that the intent behind the laws was a concern for safety, the justices could have struck them down as interfering with federal regulatory power over nuclear safety. But the court crippled the utilities' case by refusing to look into legislative intent. Varanini had inserted the economic justification in the study in anticipation of a court fight. He knew that safety regulation was clearly the province of the federal government, and that economics was not. But as was evident in the drafting of the nuclear bills, legislative intent rested on antinuclear motives.[10]

In April 1983, the Supreme Court accepted this sleight of hand with its unanimous decision supporting the constitutionality of the nuclear bills. It sustained the reasoning of the appeals court in making a distinction between radiological and nonradiological issues. Justice Byron White argued that nonradiological matters such as the need for power, reliability, economics of various options, land use, and rates were the province of state regulation. The Court accepted Varanini's rationalization, arguing that "inquiry into legislative motive is often an unsatisfactory venture."[11]

The decision held serious implications for the future of the peaceful atom. Industry analysts soft-peddled its gravity, arguing that if the federal government finally found a waste solution, state sovereignty over new construction would disappear.[12] But the decision depended on a false distinction between radiological and economic considerations. Waste disposal along with a number of other issues is related to both safety and economics.[13] There are a multitude of issues that might stem from a safety concern but that could be justified by an economic rationale. Since the courts refused to look at legislative motives, the states had a carte blanche, short of outright lying, to justify safety opposition to nuclear plants as long as they said it was due to economics.

Those who hailed the decision as a new period of cooperative federalism failed to recognize that what had really occurred was a coup.[14]

States were not interested in sharing power; they wanted and received a veto over the peaceful atom. States had taken a less compromising position with the federal government. The pronuclear Reagan administration, in a revealing brief by the solicitor general, admitted that the states would halt nuclear power if given the chance since over thirty states filed supporting briefs for the nuclear bills before the Court. The Justice Department correctly warned that if the nuclear bills survived, other states would surely copy them, resulting in the "virtual elimination of nuclear power as a potential energy source."[15] This proved prescient as many states passed imitating legislation and acted to block nuclear projects. Energy federalism gained permanent legal sanction.

The eighties were not all bad news for the industry. The industry's self-destruction also demolished the national antinuclear movement. The industry's ruin took the immediacy out of the nuclear issue. Between 1979 and 1983, a huge nonviolent direct-action movement assaulted power plant barricades and fire hoses, called for anarchic forms of community, and then vanished. Its remnants could be found in weapons protests against the Reagan administration's military programs.[16] Even committed groups such as the Union of Concerned Scientists and Creative Initiative dropped nuclear power in favor of weapons protest. And with no new plants to fight, battles shifted to waste disposal, emergency evacuation planning, and utility rates. Nuclear power opposition returned to its sixties form of decentralized scattered groups.

The loss of public interest in energy issues also clouded the future of the industry's most formidable institutional enemy, the Energy Commission. Utility companies and conservative politicians conceded the wisdom of the commission's actions in the seventies but shifted their argument for scraping the commission. They argued that changes in industry and the markets rendered the commission's planning and forecasting duties unnecessary. No one better exemplifies this neat switch than Pete Wilson, who had opposed the existence of the Energy Commission in the seventies. As governor, Wilson argued that the emergence of open competition between utilities and independent producers of electricity made the market a more perfect instrument to deal with electricity demand than planning.[17]

Wilson's proposal might be dismissed as a political ploy in an election year. As some of its own staff conceded, however, the commission had lost its reputation for innovation. Part of this was a result of the commission's philosophy as it was conceived in the seventies. Nonmaterialism served the commission well in opposing Sundesert and some other key decisions for which it has more than paid back the taxpayers of California for its budget. Its arguments against large centralized power facilities, encouragement of diversity, and methods of forecasting resulting in reductions proved prescient.[18] But the antinuclear movement and the commission's emphasis on renewable alternatives was less successful. Although many energy alternative advocates blamed this ineffectiveness on the cuts in funding for research, these technologies also fell victim to some of the same forces that destroyed nuclear power. The collapse in oil prices, the availability of new sources of natural gas and oil outside OPEC countries, and a surplus of electricity supplies have created an energy world in the nineties still dominated by fossil fuel sources. "That world has killed renewable [energy sources] just as profoundly as it did nuclear," Jim Harding admitted.[19] Committed to a renewable alternatives approach, the Energy Commission, staffer Seymour Goldstone complained, did not shift its focus accordingly. It risks its own future in failing to adapt.[20]

To the nuclear industry's misfortune, its loss of public support neutralized any gains it might have realized from the antinuclear movement's decline. The movement's demise did not end opposition; resistance to the atom simply entered the public mainstream. That is the most important legacy of the antinuclear movement. Antinuclear activists helped change values, democratic aspirations, politics, and attitudes about energy use in the general public. By the eighties, nonmaterialist values, once the province of the young and educated, spread to every age group and sector of society.[21] This shift may not have brought the revolution in energy use environmentalists hoped for, but it did win the war for conservation, mistrust of expertise, and fear of nuclear hazards. As a result, a solid majority of Americans now oppose any nuclear construction. Overwhelming local opposition obviated the need for a national movement.

The disintegration of the nation's patriotic enthusiasm for nuclear power and faith in its experts allowed the populist emotions of conservative communities like Kern County to turn against the peaceful atom. In the decade after Proposition 15, fourteen referendums were held on nuclear issues. Waste dumps and escalating nuclear costs were particularly inviting targets for the populist resurgence that united businessmen, farmers, and home owners in locations such as Louisiana, Washington, Kansas, and Arkansas. These battles allowed participants to give full vent to their resentment of government bureaucracy and uncaring experts. Protecting the sacred deal of community dominated opposition rhetoric. Like their counterparts in Kern County, these activists invoked agrarian and sacred images of the land they protected from a violation of "rural values."[22]

Broad public disenchantment with the atom translated into widespread official state and local resistance.[23] Local activists allied with state and local officials willing to support their causes. Following the California model, state officials and governors elsewhere worked with and often usurped the role of citizens as leaders against nuclear projects. Governors such as Richard Celeste of Ohio, Mario Cuomo of New York, and Michael Dukakis of Massachusetts took a page from Jerry Brown's game plan in highly visible protests against evacuation plans of local nuclear plants.

The chief casualty of the antinuclear movement was the nation's technology enthusiasm for the atom. Utopian notions that nuclear energy would create a golden age without poverty and ignorance had been an important justification for its rapid development through the sixties. By the eighties such passions were impossible to maintain. Nuclear power's promise of freeing the world's impoverished turned into the threat of bankrupting the country. The combination of economic and safety fears was enough for Americans to shed their childlike fascination with the atom. Instead they accepted arguments by skeptics such as Richard Maullin who argued for cold logic in energy sources. Energy options, he told a Bakersfield audience, were not football teams whose fate demanded blind support.[24] A new generation of utility executives agreed. By 1996, only 2 percent of the utility executives said they would consider ordering a new nuclear power plant. They shared none of their predecessors' philosophical attachment or technological enthusiasm for nuclear power and concluded that the best way of meeting energy demand was to reduce it. If this meant shutting down an expensive nuclear plant, so be it.[25]

The best example of this new attitude about nuclear power and the democratic takeover of technology lay just outside Sacramento. In 1989, California was home to another first in the history of nuclear power. Voters in the Sacramento Municipal Utility District voted to shut down the troubled and poorly operated Rancho Seco nuclear power plant. This referendum, however, was not patterned after the 1976 initiative. Voters were antinuclear, but it was a hard thing to ask them to shut down an operational plant. Poor economics and operating history of the plant tipped the balance. It was actually cheaper to buy the power from outside sources than to keep the plant going. This time there was no talk of lost jobs, blackouts, or saving the poor with nuclear power. Nuclear power was simply a bad deal.[26] Private utilities followed suit and shut down outmoded nuclear reactors, most recently the Connecticut Yankee plant at Haddam Neck.

One of nuclear power's greatest champions, Alvin Weinberg, conceded the devolution of control over nuclear power to the states and the public. Nuclear power would not return, he noted, until the public recovered its faith in the nuclear community. The power to effect that recovery rested with environmentalists and other nuclear opponents.[27] Weinberg's was a telling admission. In just twenty-five years, nuclear power had gone from a fledgling technology protected by the federal government to a moribund industry whose fate rested with its enemies at the state and local level.

California had paved the way for this turn of events back in the seventies when most states were unwilling to challenge Washington or the nuclear industry. Institutionally, what is significant about California's antinuclear episodes—Proposition 15, the San Joaquin Nuclear Project, and Sundesert—is how thoroughly state regulators and citizens usurped the federal government's control over the energy debate.[28] As a hybrid of national and local patterns, California's opposition was not an isolated regional phenomenon, but a political style and culture to be shared with other states and activists who chose to challenge federal authority. Democratic control of nuclear power, state resistance, and skeptical evaluation of energy options became the national norm in the eighties.

One warm and magnificent August day in 1994, I went back to Bodega Bay. The community had changed since Alfred Hitchcock had made his visit. A quick stroll around the village today reveals a number of real estate developments and vacation homes. The local chamber of commerce recognized that Bodega's political impotence and isolation during the controversy made it an easy target for industrial development. That isolation had to end. To provide a viable alternative to industrialization, local boosters actively promoted Bodega Head's beauty as a tourist attraction.[29] Yet with a population of only 950 souls, Bodega's charm survives.

I found the schoolhouse where Hitchcock filmed some of the most terrifying scenes in *The Birds*. The schoolhouse was now privately owned, run down, with roosters and chickens running around the yard. Still, it was a busy tourist attraction. The hole in the Bodega Head too had gone to seed. It had filled in with fresh water from the underground streams and was host to seagulls and other shorebirds. It had to be fenced in, though, since the first step into the water is seventy-three feet deep. There had been a sign identifying it, I was told, but it had disappeared.

But the Bodega story lived on. A multigenerational group approached the fence. I expected them to be puzzled by a fenced-in pond, but to my surprise the children started telling the story of Bodega to those around them. PG&E was going to build a nuclear power plant here, they explained. Such a beautiful site, others wondered, how could they? But the people of Sonoma had fought Pacific Gas and Electric and won, someone added. All were genuinely pleased at the thought. They had discovered an earthquake fault through the site, a boy volunteered. All shook their heads at the folly of it. The parents and grandparents started to fill in the details. There was a woman, they said, who had lived on the Head and had fought the plant. What was her name? They tried but could remember only her courage.

I asked them what their feelings on the issue had been at the time. One bystander replied that she had assumed the plant was necessary; she always trusted what her government told her. "You just did what you were told back then." She looked down and smiled at her naiveté. Her husband had fought in World War II, she explained, and this had helped them believe in their leaders. But then she had learned from the activists that the fallout might land on her hometown. Since then she had changed her mind about a lot of things. Her son had come back from Vietnam and had told a very different story of the country's leaders. It was evident her children were not going to have the same trusting attitude about government and experts she had.

The group spoke avidly about citizen efforts to stop a nearby housing development project promoted by county leaders. To these people the citizen activist had become more respectable than any public official. I left them still looking at the pond and drove back over the road PG&E had built to the Bodega site. The townspeople had lost their fight to stop the route from wiping out a beach and some clam beds. The road, I realized, was a fitting symbol of the fight between growth-oriented and nonmaterial values. Built for industrial purposes, it now served as the entrance to the state park.

The emanations of Bodega endured. Nuclear fear, distrust of experts and government leaders, environmental concerns, and a desire for popular democracy, all had become part of an American spirit.

Notes

Index

Notes

Introduction

1.   Terry Lodge, interview by author, 8 July 1989, Toledo, Ohio, tape recording; and Thomas Wellock, "The Light That Failed: A History of Controversy and Opposition to the Davis-Besse Nuclear Power Station," M.A. thesis, University of Toledo, 1989. The image of a federal government that would stop at nothing to promote nuclear power is one of the most common themes of antinuclear tracts. It is probably best exemplified by Daniel Ford, *Meltdown: The Secret Papers of the Atomic Energy Commission* (New York: Simon and Schuster, 1986); Ralph Nader and John Abbotts, *The Menace of Atomic Energy* (New York: W. W. Norton,1979); and John W. Gofman and Arthur R.Tamplin, *Poisoned Power: The Case against Nuclear Power Plants* (Emmaus, PA: Rodle Press,1971).

2.   James Jasper, *Nuclear Politics: Energy and the State in the United States, Sweden, and France* (Princeton: Princeton University Press, 1990), 217. There are few histories of nuclear opposition. But recent studies of antinuclear battles indicate that such a conclusion of powerlessness is only partly true. On the intractable nature of conflicts at Seabrook, New Hampshire, and Shoreham, New York, see Henry F. Bedford, *Seabrook Station; Citizen Politics and Nuclear Power* (Amherst: University of Massachusetts Press, 1990); and David P. McCaffrey, *The Politics of Nuclear Power: A History of the Shoreham Nuclear Power Plant* (Dordrecht: Kluwer Academic Publishers, 1991) For more successful opposition episodes, see Dorothy Nelkin, *Nuclear Power and Its Critics: The Cayuga Lake Controversy* (Ithaca: Cornell University Press, 1971); and Daniel Pope, "'We Can Wait. We Should Wait.' Eugene's Nuclear Power Controversy, 1968–1970," *Pacific Historical Review* 59 (1990): 349–73. For a study that attributes too much influence to the antinuclear movement, see Jerome Price, *The Antinuclear Movement* (Boston: Twayne, 1990).

3.   Nader and Abbotts, *Menace of Atomic Energy,* 13.

4.   Brian Balogh, *Chain Reaction: Expert Debate and Public Participation in American Commercial Nuclear Power, 1945–1975* (Cambridge: Cambridge University Press, 1991).

5.   Quoted in William H. Chafe, *The Unfinished Journey: America since World War II* (New York: Oxford University Press, 1986), 186, 196; Balogh, *Chain Reaction,* 16; and Glodfrey Hodgson, *America in Our Time: From World War II to Nixon* (New York: Vintage Books, 1978), 67–98.

6. Control of the atom was part of a tremendous expansion of the power of the executive branch over security and the economy. In 1946 and 1947, the Employment Act, the Atomic Energy Act, and the National Security Act created the Council of Economics Advisors, the AEC, and the National Security Council from which presidents could direct policy.

7. George T. Mazuzan and J. Samuel Walker, *Controlling the Atom: The Beginnings of Nuclear Regulation, 1946–1962* (Berkeley: University of California Press, 1984), 277–303.

8. As the AEC's mandate was limited to regulation of nuclear safety, such limitations on the hearing process were perhaps justifiable, but it left opponents few forums to question issues such as nonnuclear pollution, land use, or community impact.

9. John Gofman to Robert Head, 3 July 1973, John Gofman papers, Bancroft Library, University of California, Berkley, carton 14.

10. There is a substantial body of literature contending that the late sixties and early seventies represent a new regulatory era. In general, see Hugh Helco, "Issue Networks and the Executive Establishment," in *The New American Political System*, ed. Anthony King (Washington: American Enterprise Institute, 1978); James Q. Wilson, *The Politics of Regulation* (New York: Basic Books, 1980); David Vogel, "The 'New' Social Regulation in Historical and Comparative Perspective," in *Regulation in Perspective: Historical Essays*, ed. Thomas K. McCraw (Cambridge: Harvard University Press, 1981); and Richard A. Harris and Sidney M. Milkis, eds., *Remaking American Politics* (Boulder: Westview Press, 1989). In resource management, see Arthur F. McEvoy, *The Fisherman's Problem: Ecology and Law in the California Fisheries, 1850–1980* (Cambridge: Cambridge University Press, 1986), 227–57; and Hoberg, *Pluralism by Design: Environmental Policy and The American Regulator State* (New York: Praeger, 1992).

11. See Nader and Abbotts, *Menace of Atomic Energy*.

12. Dan M. Berkovitz, "The Role of the States in Nuclear Regulation," in *Controlling the Atom in the 21st Century*, ed. David P. O'Very, Christopher E. Paine, and Dan W. Reichter (Boulder: Westview Press, 1994): 127–54; and Joseph P. Tomain, *Nuclear Power Tranformation* (Bloomington: Indiana University Press, 1987), 14–19.

13. On the trend toward open planning and consensus building in utility regulation, see Dennis W. Ducsik, ed., *Public Involvement in Energy Facility Planning; The Electric Utility Experience* (Boulder: Westview Press, 1986); and Jonathon Raab, *Using Consensus Building to Improve Utility Regulation* (Washington: American Council for an Energy-Efficient Economy, 1994).

14. U.S. Office of Technology Assessment, *Nuclear Power in an Age of Uncertainty* (Washington: Government Printing Office, 1984), 124–27; Irvin Bupp and Jean-Claude Derian, *Light Water: How the Nuclear Dream Dissolved* (New York: Basic Books, 1978); and Charles Komanoff, *Power Plant Cost Escalation: Nuclear and Coal Capital Costs, Regulation, and Economics* (New York: Van Nostrand Reinhold, 1981).

15. On the nuclear industry's poor technological choices, see Joseph G. Morone and Edward J. Woodhouse, *The Demise of Nuclear Energy? Lessons for*

Democratic Control of Technology (New Haven: Yale University Press, 1989). On the institutional differences between the United States and European countries, see Jasper, *Nuclear Politics*; John L. Campbell, *Collapse of an Industry: Nuclear Power and the Contradictions of U.S. Policy* (Ithaca: Cornell University Press, 1988); Christian Joppke, *Mobilizing against Nuclear Energy: A Comparison of Germany and the United States* (Berkeley: University of California Press, 1993); and Dorothy Nelkin and Michael Pollak, *The Atom Besieged: Extraparliamentary Dissent in France and Germany* (Cambridge: MIT Press, 1981).

16. For the studies that see policy as a cause of the antinuclear movement, see Campbell, *Collapse of an Industry*, 9, 89–91; and Morone, *Demise of Nuclear Energy*, 85–103. For a similar argument that the environmental movement as a whole was a result of policy shifts, see John Walton, *Western Times and Water Wars: State, Culture, and Rebellion in California* (Berkley: University of California Press, 1992), 238.

17. Balogh, *Chain Reaction*.

18. This is not to imply that scholars have ignored the antinuclear movement or the values it espoused. But scholars have not done sufficient local research and thus fail to recognize how the movement influenced regulation or the roots of opposition. See Jasper, *Nuclear Politics*, 187–217; Elizabeth Nichols, "U.S. Nuclear Power and the Success of the American Anti-Nuclear Movement," *Berkeley Journal of Sociology* 32 (1987): 167–92; Campbell, *Collapse of an Industry*, 9, 89–91; and Morone, *Demise of Nuclear Energy*, 85–103. Christian Joppke's study of Germany and the United States is unusual in its effective synthesizing of the national and local values and trends that decentralized nuclear regulation. See Joppke, *Mobilizing against Nuclear Energy*.

19. On this point see Chafe, *Unfinished Journey*.

20. Samuel Hays, *Beauty, Health, and Permanence: Environmental Politics in the United States, 1955–1985* (Cambridge: Cambridge University Press, 1987), 1–39, 490, 527–43. Social scientist have provided proof to parts of Hays's thesis. See Conrad L. Kanagy, Craig R. Humphrey, and Glenn Firebaugh, "Surging Environmentalism: Changing Public Opinion or Changing Publics?" *Social Science Quarterly* 75 (December 1994): 804–19. Others have discovered similar trends for most Western nations. The pioneering work in this area was Ronald Inglehart, *The Silent Revolution: Changing Values and Political Styles among Western Publics* (Princeton: Princeton University Press, 1977), and Inglehart, *Culture Shift in Advanced Industrial Society* (Princeton: Princeton University Press, 1990). See also Lester W. Milbrath, *Envisioning a Sustainable Society: Learning Our Way Out* (Albany: State University Press of New York, 1989), and Daniel Yankelovich, *New Rules: Searching for Self Fulfillment in a World Turned Upside Down* (Toronto: Bantam Books, 1982).

21. By the eighties, however, scholars have noted a broad-based shift toward nonmaterial values among all age groups. Kanagy et al., "Surging Environmentalism," 804–19.

22. I use "peaceful atom" throughout without intending any irony. Many activists argued that there was no such thing as a peaceful atom because of the possibility of reprocessing nuclear fuel for weapons production. But the term

had been in common use since the Eisenhower administration's Atoms for Peace program and is simply a convenient reference to the civilian nuclear power industry.

23. Progressivism has become a popular term, especially among San Francisco politicians, to describe what is usually thought of as the "liberal" wing of today's Democratic party. I prefer "progressive" to "liberal" since the meaning of the latter term was undergoing significant change in the sixties and seventies. Liberal is particularly confusing for this story because avid supporters of nuclear power, such as Edmund "Pat" Brown, considered themselves liberal in the older sense of the term. Previously, the liberal coalition included progrowth politicians, labor unions, and business elites that supported development projects, but these groups rarely opposed nuclear power.

24. David Pesonen to James B. Muldoon, 24 December 1962, Joel Hedgpeth papers, Bancroft Library, University of California, Berkeley, box 1; and David Pesonen to Edgar Wayburn, 26 September 1963, Sierra Club Bay Chapter records, Bancroft Library.

25. The link between the rise of a postindustrial society, nonmaterialist values, and intolerance for involuntary risk is detailed by Mary Douglas and Aaron Wildavsky. These new values encouraged a suspicion of authority and involuntary risks, such as nuclear power, imposed by institutions. Only voluntarily assumed hazards are acceptable. The public must therefore have a voice in assuming all risks. See Douglas and Wildavsky, *Risk and Culture: An Essay on the Selection of Technological and Environmental Dangers* (Berkeley: University of California Press, 1982), 158–60. See also Michael Thompson, Richard Ellis, and Aaron Wildavsky, *Cultural Theory* (Boulder: Westview Press, 1990).

26. Hays, *Beauty, Health, and Permanence,* 7 and 490. Other studies that share the people versus the experts thesis are Jasper, *Nuclear Politics,* 19; Campbell, *Collapse of an Industry,* 78–81; Nelkin and Pollak, *Atom Besieged,* 1–7, and Joppke, *Mobilizing against Nuclear Energy,* 57–90. An exception to this view is Brian Balogh, who demonstrated that there was fluid cooperation between dissenting insiders and antinuclear activists. Environmentalism became the language that fused these two groups. However, in his account, the values of scientists remain wedded to their scientific disciplines and are rarely motivated by antinuclear sentiment. He thus misses the important role nonmaterial values played in motivating experts in controversies such as Bodega Bay. For example, compare chapter 1, below, Balogh, *Chain Reaction,* 240–54.

27. This is not to argue that scientific disciplines did not have a powerful influence on their members' attitudes. Studies demonstrate that scientists and engineers had very different attitudes about the safety of nuclear power than did the public and the media. Often these attitudes were driven by ideological considerations. A significant dissenting minority among scientists pursued agendas reflecting their environmental and moral leanings. On the different attitudes among the public and science, see Stanley Rothman and S. Robert Lichter, "Elite Ideology and Risk Perception in Nuclear Energy Policy," *American Political Science Review* 81 (June 1987): 383–404.

28. Samuel P. Hays, "Environmental Political Culture and Environmental

Political Development: An Analysis of Legislative Voting, 1971–1989," *Enviro-mental History Review* 16 (1992): 1–22; and Hays, *Beauty, Health, and Permanence*. A study that deals specifically with these social patterns in San Francisco is Richard Edward DeLeon, *Left Coast City: Progressive Politics in San Francisco, 1975–1991* (Lawrence: University Press of Kansas, 1992).

29. Theda Skocpol, *Protecting Soldiers and Mothers: The Political Origins of Social Policy in the United States* (Cambridge: Harvard University Press, 1992), 41. See also Peter V. Evans, Dietrich Rueschemeyer, and Theda Skocpol, *Bringing the State Back In* (Cambridge: Cambridge University Press, 1985).

30. Even before there were controversies over nuclear power, state regulators had moved aggressively to assume responsibility for radiation regulation and monitoring. See Mazuzan and Walker, *Controlling the Atom*, 277–303.

31. A notable exception, was the intractable conflict at Diablo Canyon. But it was an early case where the plant was approved before the state became active in regulation. The dearth of political outlets for anti-Diablo activists encouraged extralegal tactics such as nonviolent direct action protest favored by former members of the New Left.

32. Maurice R. Stein, *The Eclipse of Community: An Interpretation of American Studies* (Princeton: Princeton University Press, 1960).

33. The conservative turn in populist notions of community is detailed in Michael Kazin, *The Populist Persuasion: An American History* (New York: Basic Books, 1995).

34. Hays, "Environmental Political Culture," 1–22; Hays, "The Environmental West," *Journal of Policy History* 3 (1991): 223–48; and Kanagy et al., "Surging Environmentalism," 804–19.

35. While the generally liberal governors such as Mario Cuomo, Michael Dukakis, and Richard Celeste copied Jerry Brown, conservative politicians have joined the opposition. See Gerald Jacob, *Site Unseen: the Politics of Siting a Nuclear Waste Repository* (Pittsburgh: University of Pittsburgh Press, 1990), 237–63.

Chapter 1. The Battle for Bodega Bay, 1958–1964

1. Alfred Hitchcock to J. B. Neilands, 28 May 1962, Jean and Karl Kortum personal papers, San Francisco (hereinafter cited as Kortum papers).

2. Hitchcock to Neilands, 28 May 1962, Kotum papers.

3. Most movie reviewers were at a loss to explain the meaning of the bird attacks. But for those who drew the vengeful nature moral, see review in *America* 108 (20 April 1963): 589; *Saturday Review* 46 (6 April 1963): 39; and *Commonweal* 78 (12 April 1963): 73–74.

4. Quoted in "Fine Feathered Fiends on a Rampage," *Life*, 1 February 1963, 68. For recent interpretations, see Robin Wood, *Hitchcock's Films Revisited* (New York: Columbia University Press, 1989), 152–72; and Donald Spoto, *The Art of Alfred Hitchcock: Fifty Years of His Motion Pictures* (New York: Anchor Books, 1992), 328–38.

5. Bodega was the first citizen-led power plant controversy, but a short-

lived intense reaction to nuclear waste disposal sites erupted in 1959 at various locations throughout the country. See George T. Mazuzan and J. Samuel Walker, *Controlling the Atom: The Beginnings of Nuclear Regulation, 1946–1962* (Berkeley: University of California Press, 1984), 355–66.

6. Ralph I. Smith to Dr. Wayburn, 26 April 1958, Sierra Club San Francisco Bay Chapter records, Bancroft Library, University of California, Berkeley (hereinafter cited as Bay Chapter records). During the course of my research, the Bancroft Library reorganized the Sierra Club's collections and changed all carton designations. Because the library did not correlate old carton numbers with the new ones, there is no way to match my older notes with the new carton numbers. The change affects the citations in chapter 1 and some of chapter 2. I have removed carton designations from these notes.

7. Smith to Wayburn, 26 April 1958, Bay Chapter records.

8. Karl Kortum, diary entry, 25 February 1962, Kortum papers.

9. "Corporations: Expand or Expire," *Time*, 10 January 1964, 63–64; and Sidney P. Allen, "Battle of Bodega Head," *Public Utilities Fortnightly* 73 (18 June 1964): 37–40.

10. On postindustrialism see Daniel Bell, *The Coming of Post-Industrial Society: A Venture in Social Forecasting* (New York: Basic Books, 1973), 127–29. Scholars have criticized the accuracy and scope of postindustrial social analysis. Many of the trends cited by Bell and others were not new or as pervasive as Bell thought. Postindustrial society has much in common with its industrial predecessor. See Krishan Kumar, *Prophecy and Progress: The Sociology of Industrial and Post-Industrial Society* (Middlesex: Penguin Books, 1978); Jonathan Gershuny, *After Industrial Society? The Emerging Self-Service Economy* (Atlantic Highlands, NJ: Humanities Press, 1978). For a recent reformulation of postindustrial ideas, see Fred Block, *PostIndutrial Possibilities: A Critique of Economic Discourse* (Berkeley: University of California Press, 1990).

11. Samuel Hays, *Beauty, Health, and Permanence: Environmental Politics in the United States, 1955–1985* (Cambridge: Cambridge University Press, 1987), 1–39, 490, 527–43; and California, Department of Natural Resources, Division of Beaches and Parks, *California State Park System: Five Year Program* (Sacramento: Division of Beaches and Parks, 22 November 1954).

12. Ronald Inglehart, *The Silent Revolution: Changing Values and Political Styles among Western Publics* (Princeton: Princeton University Press, 1977); Inglehart, *Culture Shift in Advanced Industrial Society* (Princeton: Princeton University Press, 1990); and Daniel Yankelovich, *New Rules: Searching for Self Fulfillment in a World Turned Upside Down* (Toronto: Bantam Books, 1982). A word on "quality of life" is in order. Quality of life is a protean term that defies a clear definition. When the Environmental Protection Agency convened a conference on the subject, participants could not agree on what it meant. What seemed to describe it was a cluster of variables relating to health and the environment called "amenities." Amenities increase physical or spiritual comfort, but their monetary value is unclear. They include greater personal freedom and expression, a balanced and protected ecosystem, a healthy world free from pollution, and an aesthetically pleasing environment. See United States, Environ-

mental Protection Agency, *The Quality of Life Concept: A Potential Tool for Decision-Makers* (Washington, D.C.: Environmental Protection Agency, 1973).

13. The link between postindustrial society, liberal groups, and intolerance for involuntary risk is detailed by Mary Douglas and Aaron Wildavsky. See Mary Douglas and Aaron Wildavsky, *Risk and Culture: An Essay on the Selection of Technological and Environmental Dangers* (Berkeley: University of California Press, 1982), 158–60; and Michael Thompson, Richard Ellis, and Aaron Wildavsky, *Cultural Theory* (Boulder: Westview Press, 1990).

14. James Q. Wilson, *The Amateur Democrat: Club Politics in Three Cities* (Chicago: University of Chicago Press, 1962).

15. David Pesonen to Edgar Wayburn, 26 September 1963, Bay Chapter records.

16. Scholars usually trace New Left influence to the late sixties and early seventies. For example, see Etahn M. Cohen, *Ideology, Interest Group Formation, and the New Left: The Case of the Clamshell Alliance* (New York: Garland, 1988), 3–4.

17. J. Samuel Walker, "Reactor at the Fault: The Bodega Bay Nuclear Plant Controversy, 1958–1964—A Case Study in the Politics of Technology," *Pacific Historical Review* 59 (1990): 323–48; Dorothy Nelkin, *Nuclear Power and Its Critics: The Cayuga Lake Controversy* (Ithaca: Cornell University Press, 1971), 9–10; Gerald H. Clarfield and William M. Wiecek, *Nuclear America: Military and Civilian Nuclear Power in the United States, 1940–1980* (New York: Harper & Row, 1984), 355–56; Sheldon Novick, *The Careless Atom* (Boston: Houghton Mifflin, 1969), 34–50. For works that recognize the political aspects of the controversy, see Richard L. Meehan, *The Atom and the Fault: Experts, Earthquakes, and Nuclear Power* (Cambridge: MIT Press, 1984), 1–20; and Brian Balogh, *Chain Reaction: Expert Debate and Public Participation in American Commercial Nuclear Power, 1945–1975* (Cambridge: Cambridge University Press, 1991), 242–54.

18. As one study showed, such community intervenor groups tended to have no interest in using nuclear power to further democratic aspirations. Interests were usually confined to protecting property values, community impact, and safety. See Douglas and Wildavsky, *Risk and Culture*, 141.

19. Edgar Wayburn, interview by author, 27 March 1990, San Francisco, tape recording. For a study of Bodega Head's ecosystems, see Michael G. Barbour, *Coastal Ecology Bodega Head* (Berkeley: University of California Press, 1973).

20. David R. Brower to Joseph R. Knowland, 20 August 1958, Bay Chapter records.

21. Michael Cohen, *The History of the Sierra Club, 1892–1970* (San Francisco: Sierra Club Books, 1988), 89.

22. J. W. Hedgpeth to R. E. Burns, 20 September 1958, Joel Hedgpeth papers, Bancroft Library, box 1. (hereinafter cited as Hedgpeth papers).

23. Wayburn, interview; and Edgar Wayburn, "Sierra Club Statesman, Leader of the Parks and Wilderness Movement," interview by Ann Lage and Susan Schrepfer, 1976–81, Bancroft Library, University of California, Berkeley, 59.

24. Division of Beaches and Parks *California State Park System*, 12.

25. California, Sonoma County Planning Commission, *Master Plan of De-*

velopment for Bodega Bay (The Commission, 1956), 13; and *San Francisco News,* 12 September 1958, 1, 2.

26. *Santa Rosa Press Democrat,* 24 July 1959, 1 (hereinafter cited as *SRPD*).

27. County officials admitted to these secret meetings, but claimed they had made no deals. They did, however, tell state agencies that they favored the power plant over all other developments. James M. Miller to R. J. Stull, 15 November 1957, University of California Archives, Bancroft Library, University of California, Berkeley, CU-149, box 45.

28. *SRPD,* 15 January 1960, 12.

29. David E. Pesonen, *A Visit to the Atomic Park* (by the author, 1962), Bancroft Library, University of California, Berkeley, 8.

30. Pesonen, *Atomic Park,* 13.

31. There were two key use permits required. The first, passed in 1959, authorized the construction of power lines through Doran Park. In February 1960, the supervisors issued a second permit for installation of the power plant. Pesonen, *Atomic Park* 13–15.

32. Quoted in Pesonen, *Atomic Park,* 9; and Meehan, *Atom and the Fault,* 6.

33. J. W. Hedgpeth to George Dusheck, 21 September 1958, Hedgpeth papers, box 1.

34. Everett McKeage to Edgar Wayburn, 15 June 1961, Sierra Club records, Bancroft Library, University of California, Berkeley. "Aesthetic Considerations Not Sufficient to Bar Construction of Transmission Line," *Public Utilities Fortnightly* 71 (20 June 1963): 74–75.

35. Clem Miller to Joel W. Hedgpeth, 30 April 1959, Hedgpeth papers, box 1. Hedgpeth's other effort to recruit an ally was with the University of California. The university's expressed interest in Bodega as a marine research station should have made it willing to fight PG&E. In November 1957, six months before PG&E publicly admitted its stake in Bodega, the university withdrew. Berkeley chancellor Clark Kerr claimed that the university's desire to locate the station at Bodega was only the expressed opinion of some faculty members. Hedgpeth knew Bodega had been the prime site in the university's plans and suspected that offical vacillation was due to the fact that PG&E's "tentacles go deeply into the University." *San Francisco News,* 12 September 1958, 1; and J.W. Hedgpeth to Geo[rge] Dushek, 21 September 1958, Hedgpeth papers box 1.

36. Hazel Mitchell, interview by author, 7 July 1991, Bodega Bay, tape recording.

37. Charles Coleman, *P.G. and E. of California: The Centennial Story of Pacific Gas and Electric Company, 1852–1952* (New York: McGraw-Hill, 1952), 320–30.

38. In the seventies, access to production facilities became the key issue in the public power debate as Northern California municipals filed a number of antitrust challenges to PG&E projects demanding a share in project ownership. Marc J. Roberts and Jeremy S. Bluhm, *The Choices of Power: Utilities Face the Environmental Challenge* (Cambridge: Harvard University Press, 1981), 122–24; and Coleman, *P.G. and E. of California,* 331–40.

39. Mazuzan and Walker, *Controlling the Atom,* 118–20; J. Samuel Walker, *Containing the Atom: Nuclear Regulation in a Changing Environment, 1963–1971*

(Berkeley: University of California Press, 1992), 35–36; and Richard Wayne Dyke, *Mr. Atomic Energy: Congressman Chet Holifield and Atomic Energy Affairs, 1945–1974* (New York: Greenwood Press, 1989), 279–81. For a contemporary comment on this link between the public power wars and nuclear power, see Francis X. Welch, "American Electric Utilities Set World-Wide Records," *Public Utilities Fortnightly* 71 (6 June 1963): 6, 8.

40. Central Surveys, Inc., *Nationwide Public Opinion Survey* (Shenandoah, Iowa: Central Surveys, Inc., 1967), 22.

41. Coleman, *P.G. and E. of California*, 333–34.

42. Mazuzan and Walker, *Controlling the Atom*, 19.

43. Pacific Gas and Electric, press release, 27 February 1963, Rodney Southwick to those listed below, 27 February 1963, United States Atomic Energy Commission/Nuclear Regulatory Commission, docket 50–205 (Bodega Bay), microfiche; and David E. Pesonen, *Power at Point Arena* (San Francisco: Sierra Club, July 1972).

44. The "economically competitive" claim was not as groundbreaking as PG&E led the public to believe. In a remote spot like Bodega, and at the even more isolated Humboldt Bay project, the utility argued that nuclear power was competitive with other energy sources. PG&E estimated Bodega would deliver power at only 6.2 mills/kwh, well below their average system cost of 8 mills/kwh. But PG&E assumed it could operate its "relatively simple" General Electric reactor at a virtually unobtainable 90 percent capacity factor. Today, G.E. reactors have some of the worst capacity factors in the industry. PG&E, press release, 28 June 1961, and Joseph Fouchard to Rodney L. Southwick, "Summary of Hearing before California PUC on PG and E Application for Certification of Bodega Bay Nuclear Power Plant," 10 March 1962, AEC/NRC docket 50–205; and Public Citizen, "Nuclear Lemons: An Assessment of America's Worst Commercial Nuclear Power Plant" (Washington, 8 July 1993). The AEC was similarly enthusiastic about Bodega's economics. In a report to President John Kennedy, the AEC cited the Bodega facility as proof of the improved economics of nuclear power. See Atomic Energy Commission, *Civilian Nuclear Power . . . A Report to the President* (Washington: The Commission, 1962), 30.

45. As Spencer Weart has observed, the White City was a utopian notion where technology made possible a clean, healthy metropolitan environment with beauty and art. The White City was not invented by atomic promoters. Its appeal existed throughout most of America's industrial boom. It became popular after the 1893 Chicago International Exposition where just such a utopia came temporarily to life. Spencer R. Weart, *Nuclear Fear: A History of Images* (Cambridge: Harvard University Press, 1988), 7–10, 296; and William Cronon, *Nature's Metropolis: Chicago and the Great West* (New York: W. W. Norton, 1991), 341–69.

46. Pacific Gas and Electric Co., statement by Stan Barton before the Public Utilities Commission, 21 May 1962, Kortum papers.

47. "'Don't Build Here,' Cry Conservationists," *Electrical World* 163 (5 April 1965): 51–54.

48. Joel Hedgpeth to the Public Utilities Commission, 14 March 1962, Bay Chapter records.

49.   Samuel H. Ordway, Jr., *Resources and the American Dream, Including a Theory of the Limit of Growth* (New York: Ronald Press, 1953); Fairfield Osborn, *Our Plundered Planet* (New York: Little, Brown, 1948); and Harrison Brown, *The Challenge of Man's Future* (New York: Viking Press, 1954).

50.   Peggy and Edgar Wayburn, "Our Vanishing Wilderness," *Sierra Club Bulletin* 42 (January 1957): (hereinafter cited as *SCB*).

51.   David Brower, "The Sierra Club on the National Scene," *SCB* 41 (January 1956): 3; and David R. Brower, diary entry, 15 November 1960, David Ross Brower papers, 1933–1977, Bancroft Library, University of California, Berkley, carton 5 (hereinafter cited as Brower papers).

52.   Phillip Berry, "Phillip S. Berry, Sierra Club Leader, 1960–1980s: A Broadened Agenda, a Bold Approach," interview by Ann Lage, 1981, 1984, Bancroft Library, University of California, Berkeley, 22; and Brower, diary entry, 15 March 1961, Brower papers, carton 5.

53.   David R. Brower, "Wilderness—Conflict and Conscience," *SCB* 42 (June 1957): 4,5,10.

54.   Richard M. Leonard, "Mountaineer, Lawyer, Environmentalist," interview by Susan R. Schrepfer,1975, Bancroft Library, University of California, Berkley, 161.

55.   "The Fifth Biennial Wilderness Conference," *SCB* 42 (June 1957): 82.

56.   David Brower, "How Effective Is the Conservation Force?" *SCB* 46 (March 1961): 2.

57.   Meeting minutes, Board of Directors, 5 December 1959, Sierra Club records, (hereinafter cited as minutes).

58.   Brower, diary entry, 15 November 1960, Brower papers, carton 5.

59.   Philip S. Flint to Glenn Seaborg and Edmund Brown, 3 December 1960, Bay Chapter records.

60.   Lewis F. Clark to Edgar Wayburn, 3 February 1961, Bay Chapter records.

61.   Kortum's diary has to rank as one of the great ones. Daily entries often running numerous typed single-spaced pages contain a richness of detail that will make it a valuable addition to San Francisco history.

62.   Karl Kortum, interview by author, 30 August 1994, San Francisco, tape recording; and William Murray, "King of the Dock," *California* 7 (August 1982): 66–70.

63.   Karl Kortum, interview; and Murray, "King of the Dock," 66–70.

64.   Karl Kortum, interview.

65.   Karl Kortum, interview; and Kortum, diary entry, 25 February 1962, Kortum papers.

66.   Karl Kortum, interview.

67.   *San Francisco Chronicle*, 14 March 1962, 34 (hereinafter cited as *SFC*).

68.   Rodney L. Southwick to Joe Fouchard, 21 September 1962, AEC/NRC docket 50–205.

69.   Neilands' petition activity, at the suggestion of Kortum, indicates that much of the "public" response to Kortum's letter was orchestrated by plant opponents. This would be a common tactic throughout the campaign. J. B. Neilands, memo, 22 November 1964, Kortum papers.

70.   *SRPD*, 8 June 1962, 1; and Pesonen, *Atomic Park*, 22.

71.   Pesonen, *Atomic Park*, 27; and *SRPD*, 10 June 1962, 10, and 8 June 1962, 1.

72.   Phillip S. Berry to Mr. Leonard, 26 September 1962, Sierra Club records; and *SRPD*, 8 June 1962, 1. Berry and Pesonen believed the utility and the AEC had pressured the university to accommodate the plant and that the university was, in turn, preventing the faculty from speaking out against the plant. Their suspicions were reinforced by the fact that Chancellor Glenn Seaborg had been named commissioner of the AEC following John F. Kennedy's election as president of the United States. The university's spokesman maintained the plant would pose no harm to the marine station. This flew in the face of faculty reports that urged the university to oppose plant construction because of the hazard it posed.

73.   Bestor Robinson to Edgar Wayburn, 22 January 1963, Kortum papers; and W. H. Nutting to Edgar Wayburn, 28 May 1962, Bay Chapter records.

74.   Berry, "Phillp S. Berry, Sierra Club Leader," 21–22.

75.   Richard Leonard to Phillip S. Berry, Bay Chapter records; Phillip S. Berry to [Richard] Leonard, 26 September 1962, and Dick Leonard to David Brower, 8 October 1962, Sierra Club records..

76.   Leonard, "Mountaineer," 431.

77.   David R. Brower, "Environmental Activist, Publicist and Prophet," interview by Susan Schrepfer, 1974–78, Bancroft Library, University of California, Berkley,198–99.

78.   Minutes, 14 October 1962, and Dave [Brower] to Dick [Leonard], 2 October 1962, Sierra Club records..

79.   Phillip Berry to [Richard] Leonard, 26 September 1962, Sierra Club records.

80.   Bestor Robinson to Edgar Wayburn, 22 January 1963, Kortum papers.

81.   Richard M. Leonard to Phillip S. Berry, 8 October 1962, Sierra Club records.

82.   Minutes, 7 September 1963.

83.   Earlier citizen activism had focused on broad issues when organizing on a community level. See Saul Alinsky, *Reveille for Radicals* (Chicago: University of Chicago Press, 1945), 80–81.

84.   David E. Pesonen, "Outdoor Recreation for America," *SCB* 47 (May 1962): 8; and David E. Pesonen to James B. Muldoon, 24 December 1962, Hedgpeth papers, box 1.

85.   Pesonen to Muldoon, 24 December 1962, Hedgpeth papers, box 1; and David Pesonen to Edgar Wayburn, 26 September 1963, Bay Chapter records.

86.   Dave [Pesonen] to Joel [Hedgpeth], 2 December 1962, Hedgpeth papers, box 1.

87.   David Pesonen, interview by author, 5 March 1990, Oakland, CA, tape recording.

88.   As Neilands later noted, Pesonen spent "no time whatsoever" at the lab, and Neilands, fearing an investigation, had to fire him. Pesonen found another position in the forestry department. J. B. Neilands, memo, 22 November 1964, Kortum papers.

89. Pesonen, *Atomic Park*, 30, 31.

90. *Petaluma Argus-Courier*, 15 May 1963; *SRPD*, 19 March 1963, 7, and 21 May 1963, 6.

91. James M. Miller to R. J. Stull, 15 November 1957, University of California Archives, Bancroft Library, University of California, Berkeley, CU-149, box 45.

92. For a complete overview, see University of California Archives, Bancroft Library, University of California, Berkeley, CU-149, box 45, file: 8. See especially J. D. Frauchy and D. L. Inman to Roger Stainer, 14 June 1960, James Moulton to Glenn T. Seaborg, 1 August 1960, and Thomas Cunningham to Glenn T. Seaborg, 23 August 1960.

93. Pesonen, interview.

94. David Brower to each member of the Executive Committee, 7 November 1962, Sierra Club records.

95. Harold [Bradley] to Dave [Brower], 8 January 1963, Bay Chapter records.

96. Dave Pesonen to Joel [Hedgpeth], 25 November 1962, Hedgpeth papers, box 1.

97. Susan Schrepfer, *The Fight to Save the Redwoods: A History of Environmental Reform, 1917–1978* (Madison, University of Wisconsin Press, 1983), 174.

98. Speech by D. B. Luten, "A Geographer Looks at the Future of Sonoma County," 10 November 1962, Bay Chapter records.

99. Speech by [David Pesonen], [10 November 1962], Bay Chapter records.

100. Luten, "Geographer Looks at the Future."

101. Doris Sloan, interview by author, 30 April 1990, Berkeley, tape recording; and Joel Hedgpeth to William C. Bricca, 20 November 1962, Hedgpeth papers, box 1.

102. Speech by [Pesonen], [10 November 1962].

103. *SFC*, 10 November 1962, 1.

104. *SFC*, 1 December 1962, 44; *SRPD*, 12 December 1962, 1, and 15 January 1963, 9.

105. Karl Kortum, diary entry, 18 April 1963, Kortum papers; and Dave Pesonen to Joel [Hedgpeth], 25 November 1962, Hedgpeth papers, box 1.

106. *SFC*, 17 April 1963, 1.

107. *Guernerville (CA) Times*, 22 May 1963, 1.

108. Sloan, interview.

109. *Petaluma Argus-Courier*, 9 April 1963.

110. Sloan, interview.

111. Malvina Reynolds, "Take It Away," *Broadside* 19 (1963); Northern California Association to Preserve Bodega Head and Harbor, *Newsletter* 9 (9 January 1964): 2, 3; Magrita Klassen, interview by author, 1 July 1991, Sonoma, CA, tape recording; Doris Sloan, interview; and David Pesonen to John Lear, 30 September 1963, Bay Chapter records.

112. See statement of Marin Branch of the Women's International League for Peace and Freedom, 5 February 1963, attached to Robert Lowenstein to Carol Gold, 11 March 1963, AEC/NRC docket 50–205.

113. Sloan, interview.

114. Northern California Association to Preserve Bodega Head and Harbor,

"The Problems of Industrial Fallout: A Brief Review," 3 January 1963, Bay Chapter records; and Rachel Carson, *Silent Spring* (New York: Houghton Mifflin, 1962), chap. 3.

115. [Joel Hedgpeth] to Jack [Spencer], 26 March 1963, Hedgpeth papers, box 1. The farm community was already sensitive to any appearance of contamination of food through pesticides and radioactive fallout. See "Dairymen Take Action against Fallout," *Farm Journal* 86 (October 1962): 31, 64; and "You're Accused of Poisoning Food," *Farm Journal* 86 (September 1962): 29, 52.

116. Klassen, interview; and Robert Gottlieb, *Forcing the Spring: The Transformation of the American Environmental Movement* (Washington: Island Press, 1993), 231.

117. Hays, *Beauty, Health, and Permanence*, 28, 54.

118. *Somona County, Index-Tribune,* 11 April 1963, 3: and *New York Times* (West), 28 February 1963, 3.

119. Weart, *Nuclear Fear,* 199–214; Reynolds, "Take It Away."

120. Quoted in Sheldon Novick, *The Electric Wars: The Fight over Nuclear Power* (San Francisco: Sierra Club Books, 1976), 241.

121. For similar conversion experiences, see Gail Sheehy, *Pathfinders* (New York: William Morrow, 1981).

122. "Nuclear Foes—Not New or Local," *Berkeley Tocsin,* 7 August 1963, 4; and *SFC,* 14 September 1963, 1, 7, and 8 August 1963, 4.

123. Department of Justice, Federal Bureau of Investigation, San Francisco Division, Central Records, "Northern California Association to Preserve Bodega Head and Harbor," 1990, file no. 190-SF-91003.

124. In response to a phone call from PG&E's chief investigator, Robert Lawrence, JCAE staff member John Conway wrote, "If you or your Company have any information reflecting on the good faith or proper motives of these people, I will be pleased to receive the information." Lawrence responded, "My telephone call to you was prompted by our having heard you wanted to know the background of some of the people who were protesting the construction of our proposed Bodega Bay Atomic Park. In the spirit of cooperation it was agreed I should proceed to Washington to pass on to you orally our observations about some of those persons who have uttered protests. These observations could form the basis for any additional inquiry you might wish to initiate." Nothing public was done with the information. See John T. Conway to Robert E. Lawrence, 26 June 1963, papers of the Joint Committee on Atomic Energy (JCAE), record group 128 (Records of the Joint Committees of Congress), National Archives, Washington D.C., carton 543; (hereinafter cited as JCAE papers) and Robert E. Lawrence to John Conway, 28 June 1963, JCAE papers, carton 573.

125. Although the Sierra Club would not cooperate with the Bodega Association on safety issues, it did provide some legal help in litigation where the issue was restricted to aesthetics. D[avid Pesonen] to Joel [Hedgpeth], 20 December 1962, Hedgpeth papers, box 1.

126. Frederick M. Wirt, *Power in the City: Decision Making in San Francisco* (Berkeley: University of California Press, 1974), 65–100; William Issel and Robert W. Cherny, *San Francisco, 1865–1932: Politics, Power, and Urban Development*

(Berkeley: University of California Press, 1986), 213–18; and Richard Edward DeLeon, *Left Coast City: Progressive Politics in San Francisco, 1975–1991* (Lawrence: University of Press of Kansas, 1992), 13–39.

127. For the birth of California Democratic Clubs, see Francis Carney, "The Rise of the Democratic Clubs in California," in *Cases on Party Organization*, ed. Paul Tillet (New York: McGraw-Hill, 1963), 32–63; and Wilson, *Amateur Democrat*.

128. Carney, "Rise of the Democratic Clubs," 42, 46.

129. Wirt, *Power in the City*, 65–100.

130. Wirt, *Power in the City*, 184–214. Karl and Jean Kortum would go on from the Bodega affair to lead fights against high-rise construction and freeways. In 1966, Jean Kortum led a successful coalition that stopped the construction of the Golden Gate Freeway. The proposed highway was slated to slam through some of the most attractive sections of the northern and eastern section of the city. See Gray Brechin, "Progress in San Francisco: It could Have Been Worse," *San Francisco* 25 (October 1983): 58–63; and Murray, "King of the Dock," 66–70, 126, 128.

131. Mildred Hamilton, "Champion for City's Rights," *San Francisco*, 20 July 1969, sec. Women Today, 3.

132. Jean Kortum, interview by author, 20 April 1994, San Francisco, tape recording; Carney, "Rise of the Democratic Clubs," 45, 47; and [Jean Kortum] to Mel [Tatsapaugh], May 1963, Kortum papers. The role of women in the postwar resurgence of the California Democratic Party has begun to receive more notice from scholars. See Jacqueline R. Braitman, "Elizabeth Snyder and the Role of Women in the Postwar Resurgence of California's Democratic Party," *Pacific Historical Review* 62 (May 1993): 197–220.

133. Jean Kortum spent most of her time avoiding public identification with Bodega. She believed that it was more effective to organize others to act and thus give the public appearance that "massive" oppostion had emerged spontaneously.

134. [Jean Kortum] to Dave [Pesonen], 18 July 1963, and [Jean Kortum] to Bill [?], 15 July 1963, Kortum papers.

135. "Big Hurdle for A-Power: Gaining Public Acceptance," *Nucleonics* 21 (October 1963): 18; Karl Kortum, diary entry; 1 April 1963, California Democratic Council, "CDC Issues Program 1963: Natural Resources," 29 March 1963, Kortum papers; and *SRPD*, 1 April 1963, 1.

136. Tom B, Carvey to Lyndon B. Johnson, 15 August 1964, Glenn M. Anderson to Glenn T. Seaborg, 13 August 1963, AEC/NRC docket 50–205; *Petaluma Argus-Courier*, 13 May 1963, 1; *SFC*, 18 July 1963, 7, and *San Francisco Examiner*, 18 July 1963.

137. The AEC understood all too well the growing stature of the Bodega Association. See Dale J. Cook to Joe Fouchard, 30 August 1963, AEC/NRC docket 50–205.

138. Jean Kortum to W[illiam] A. Van Allen, 15, 17, and 25 May 1963, and New America Democratic Club to Pierre Salinger and Stewart Udall, 18 May 1963, Kortum papers.

139. Stewart Udall, *The Quiet Crisis* (New York: Avon Books, 1963).

140. Harold Gilliam, interview by author, 8 March 1993, San Francisco, tape recording.

141. Carr's harping on land-use planning itself was an indication of Gilliam's influence. Gilliam had championed land-use planning, and the lack of adequate planning was his prime objection to the power plant. Gilliam, interview; and *SFC*, 28 February 1963.

142. Harold Gilliam remembered Carr as the chief influence on Udall regarding Bodega. Udall was less certain but concluded that Gilliam was "probably right." Gilliam interview; and Stewart L. Udall to the author, 7 August 1993.

143. Stewart Udall to Kermit Gordon, 18 February 1963, Department of the Interior, Office of the Secretary files, Washington, D.C., accession number 69A-2058, box 55.

144. The author would like to thank J. Samuel Walker for generously placing the primary source material for his book *Containing the Atom* in the Nuclear Regulatory Commission's public documents room in Washington, D.C. (hereinafter cited as Walker files). Glenn T. Seaborg to Stewart L. Udall, 8 March 1963; and Lester Rogers to Harold Price and others, 13 June 1963, Walker files.

145. Secretary of the Interior to Assistant Secretary Fish and Wildlife and others, 25 April 1963, Office of the Secretary files, box 55.

146. Joel Hedgpeth to Harold Gilliam, 16 and 17 April 1963, and Dave [Peaonen] to Joel [Hedgpeth], 15 May 1963, Hedgpeth papers, box 1.

147. David Pesonen's photo caption notes, 1989, Kortum papers.

148. *West Sonoma County Paper*, 1–7 October 1987, 7; *SRPD*, 29 August 1963, 1; R. S. Boyd and R. H. Wilcox to files, 15 August 1962, AEC/NRC docket 50–205; and Karl Kortum, diary entry, 16 April 1963, Kortum papers.

149. *SRPD*, 29 August 1963, 1.

150. Pierre St.-Amand to Harold Gilliam, 19 April 1963, AEC/NRC docket 50–205.

151. Robert H. Rose to James C. Rettie, 14 May 1963; Director, Bureau of Mines to J. C. Rettie, 13 May 1963; and Director, Geological Survey to Assistant Secretary of Interior, 20 May 1963, AEC docket 50–205.

152. Stewart L. Udall to [Glenn] Seaborg, 20 May 1963, AEC/NRC docket 50–205; *San Francisco Examiner*, 22 May 1963, 1; *San Francisco News-Call Bulletin*, 21 May 1963,1; and *SFC*, 22 May 1963, 2.

153. Walker, *Containing the Atom*, 91.

154. See letters to Udall in Office of the Secretary files, box 55; Karl Kortum, diary entry, 23 May 1963, Kortum papers; *Congressional Record*, 10 June 1963, A3692; and Craig Hosmer, "The Atom 1963,"address to the American Nuclear Society, 18 June 1963, Chet Holifield papers, Doheny Memorial Library, Department of Special Collections, University of Southern California, Los Angeles, carton 15. Kortum's letter-writing campaigns did have influence. When questioned by politicians about his strong stand, Udall was quick to cite the two hundred letters he had received in support of his position as proof of "widespread concern" over reactor safety. Stewart L. Udall to John F. Shelley, 28 June 1963, Office of the Secretary files, box 55.

155.   H. L. Price to Chairman Seaborg and others, 13 September 1963, L. Kornblith to R. H. Engelken, 15 September 1963, United States, Department of the Interior, "Geologic and Seismic Investigations of a Proposed Nuclear Power Plant Site on Bodega Head, Sonoma County, California: Part II Seismic Hazards Evaluations," September 1963, AEC/NRC docket 50–205; *San Francisco News-Call Bulletin*, 4 October 1963, 1; and Walker, "Reactor at the Fault," 335, 337–41.

156.   Quoted in Meehan, *Atom and the Fault*, 13; and Roberts and Bluhm, *Choices of Power*, 154.

157   *SFC*, 7 May 1964, 2.

158.   *Oakland Tribune*, 28 January 1964; and *SFC*, 30 January 1964.

159.   *SFC*, 15 April 1964, 40.

160.   Merle Miller, *Lyndon: An Oral Biography* (New York: Ballentine Books, 1980), 452; and Royce D. Delmatier, Clarence F. McIntosh, and Earl G. Waters, *The Rumble of California Politics, 1848–1970* (New York: John Wiley & Sons, 1970), 351–53.

161.   *SFC*, 14 April 1964, 1, 10.

162.   *NYT* (West), 21 February 1963, 1.

163.   Walker, *Containing the Atom*, 100–01.

164.   United States, Department of the Interior, "Engineering Geology of the Proposed Nuclear Power Plant on Bodega Head, Sonoma County California," October 1964, Herbert Kouts to Glenn T. Seaborg, 20 October 1964, and Atomic Energy Commission, "Summary Analysis by the Division of Reactor Licensing in the Matter of Pacific Gas & Electric Company Bodega Head Nuclear Power Plant," 26 October 1964, AEC/NRC docket 50–205, and Walker, "Reactor at the Fault," 343.

165.   Pacific Gas and Electric Company, press release, 30 October 1964, AEC/NRC docket 50–205 and *Sacramento Bee*, 28 October 1964, 2.

166.   Sierra Club, press release, 31 October 1964, Bay Chapter records.

167.   These efforts by California resource officials are discussed in Chapter 3.

168.   *Sonoma County Index-Tribune*, 12 November 1964, sec. 4–2.

169.   *SRPD*, 18 June 1964, 6.

170.   Jules M. Eichorn to Edgar Wayburn, 14 May 1963, Sierra Club records.

171.   Fred Eissler to David Brower, 31 July 1963 Bay Chapter records.

172.   Doris [Leonard] to Will [Siri], 7 April 1966, Sierra Club records.

173.   William E. Siri to Hugo Fisher, 8 December 1964, Sierra Club records.

174.   Minutes, 7 May 1966, Sierra Club records.

175.   For a study of the shift in the Sierra Club's position on nuclear power, see Brock Evans, "Sierra Club Involvement in Nuclear Power: An Evolution of Awareness," *Oregon Law Review* 54 (1975): 607–21.

176.   Hays, *Beauty, Health, and Performance*, and Cohen, *History of the Sierra Club*, 457.

177.   Richard G. Lillard, *Eden in Jeopardy; Man's Prodigal Meddling with His Environment: The Southern California Experience* (New York: Alfred A. Knopf, 1966), 189.

178.   While it may seem axiomatic that a nuclear plant would lower property values, this is not the case in many suburban and rural areas of the country. Often towns that benefit from the taxes of the power plant enjoy high home

values, as is the case in Waterford, Connecticut, or Oak Harbor, Ohio. Where an area enjoying high aesthetic value combines with a heightened awareness of nuclear dangers, however, a nuclear plant may be a liability.

179. Mike Davis has made this argument for the broader homeowner activism in Southern California. See Mike Davis, *City of Quartz* (New York: Vintage Books, 1992), 170.

180. "The Harnessed Atom," *Newsweek*, 84–86.

181. Herbert Kouts to Glenn T. Seaborg, 15 July 1964, F. A. Gifford to Glenn. T. Seaborg, 4 April 1962 and 14 November 1962, and Samuel B. Nelson to Robert Lowenstein, 26 October 1961 and 25 April 1962, AEC/NRC docket 50–214 (Malibu).

182. "Big Hurdle for A-Power," 17–24.

183. Meehan *Atom and the Fault*, 41–42; and "'Don't Build Here,' Cry Consultants" *Electrical World* 63 (5 April 1965): 54.

184. Byron and Terry McLaughlin to Glenn Seaborg, 20 October 1963, AEC/NRC docket 50–214. For other examples of resident sentiment see letters to the AEC in the Malibu docket 50–214 from Marie Peckinpah, 17 October 1963; Valerie Raymond, 29 October 1963; John W. May, 12 November 1963; Nina Druckman, 15 November 1963; M. Klien, 17 November 1963; William and Lillain Knowles, 22 and 24 October 1963; Glen D. Robertson, 29 October 1963; and Clyde and Margaret Denham, 29 October 1963.

185. Merrit H. Adamson to Alphonzo Bell, 29 October 1963, AEC/NRC docket 50–214.

186. *Los Angeles Times*, 5 November 1963, I-1, 8 (hereinafter cited as *LAT*).

187. Burton W. Chace to Craig Hosmer, 7 April 1964, and Hosmer to Chace, 9 April 1964, Craig Hosmer papers, Doheny Memorial Library, Department of Special Collections, University of Southern California, Los Angeles, carton 184. See also *LAT*, 8 April 1964, II-2; and telegram from Samuel B. Nelson, 8 April 1964, JCAE papers, carton 140.

188. *Santa Monica, Evening-Outlook*, 24 March 1965; George Murphy to Glenn Seaborg, 10 March 1966 and 21 November 1966, JCAE papers, carton 140; and Murphy to Harold Price, 18 May 1966, AEC/NRC docket 50–214.

189. *LAT*, 26 March 1965, I—36. See also *LAT*, 24 March 1965; and *Santa Monica Evening-Outlook*, 26 March 1965.

190. Harold Price to Chairman Seaborg and others, 17 November 1965, Walker files, item 135.

191. See transcripts of Atomic Energy Commission, "In the Matter of: Department of Water and Power of the City of Los Angeles," 14 September 1965, docket 50–214, pp. 4543–4567; and *Santa Monica Evening-Outlook*, 15 September 1965, 31.

192. "The Principal Issues Involved in Locating the LADWP Nuclear Power Plant in Corral Canyon: Summary of Staff Position," [19 May 1966?], and "Initial Decision in the Matter of Department of Water and Power of the City of Los Angeles (Malibu Nuclear Plant Unit No. 1)," 14 July 1966, AEC/NRC docket 50–214. Hosmer quote in *Santa Monica Evening-Outlook*, 21 July 1966.

193. Gerald F. Hadlock to separated legal files, 12 May 1966, and Gerald

Hadlock, memorandum to files, 15 August 1966, Walker files, items 137 and 139; and Walker, *Containing the Atom*, 107.

194.   It should be noted, however, that as the promises of nuclear power proved exaggerated when compared with the utopian images of the fifties, the public generally lost interest and articles devoted to civilian nuclear power declined. When interest revived, however, the media focused on the negative aspects of it. See Weart, *Nuclear Fear*, chap. 11 and 15.

195.   "Post-Mortem on Bodega Bay," *Electrical World*, 9 November 1964; and Walker, *Containing the Atom*, 107.

196. *SFC*, 22 November 1964, sec. This World, 28.

Chapter 2. The Rise of Environmental Opposition to Nuclear Power, 1964–1974

1.   Harold Peterson, "Brower Power Awaits the Verdict," *Sports Illustrated*, 14 April 1969, 41; and John McPhee, *Encounters with the Archdruid* (New York: Noonday Press, 1971) 208–9.

2.   The phrase is Susan Schrepfer's. See Schrepfer, "The Nuclear Crucible: Diablo Canyon and the Transformation of the Sierra Club," *California History* 71 (Summer 1992); 212–37. On the Sierra Club's internal schisms, see Michael Cohen, *The History of the Sierra Club, 1892–1970* (San Francisco: Sierra Club Books, 1988).

3.   William E. Siri, "Reflections on the Sierra Club, Environment, and Mountaineering, 1950s-1970s," interview by Ann Lage, 1979, Bancroft Library, University of California, Berkeley, 157.

4.   Samuel P. Hays, *Beauty, Health, and Permanence: Environmental Politics in the United States, 1955–1985* (Cambridge: Cambridge University Press, 1987), 13–39; and Robert Gottlieb, *Forcing the Spring: The Transformation of the American Environmental Movement* (Washington: Island Press, 1993), 7–8.

5.   One scholar's study of the Sierra Club found that the membership remained through the sixties "successful, upper middle-class, highly educated professionals living in the San Francisco Bay area" with "only token lower white collar and blue collar representation." William B. Devall, "The Governing of a Voluntary Organization: Oligarchy and Democracy in the Sierra Club," Ph.D. diss., University of Oregon, 1970, 182. For general studies that document the influence of age, class and affluence on nonmaterial sentiment, see Hays, *Beauty, Health, and Permanence;* Conrad L. Kanagy, Craig R. Humphrey, and Glenn Firebaugh, "Surging Environmentalism: Changing Public Opinion or Changing Publics?" *Social Science Quarterly* 75 (December 1994): 804–19; and Ronald Inglehart, *Culture Shift in Advanced Industrial Society* (Princeton: Princeton University Press, 1990).

6.   Siri, "Reflections on the Sierra Club," 29, 39.

7.   Quoted in "The Harnessed Atom: 'It's a Business Now,'" *Newsweek*, 18 April 1966, 84–86; Tom O'Hanlon, "An Atomic Bomb in the Land of Coal," *Fortune* 74 (September 1966): 132–33; and "Switching to the Atom," *Time*, 14 Octo-

ber 1966, 100. On the early predictions of a miraculous atomic age, see Paul Boyer, *By the Bomb's Early Light: American Thought and Culture at the Dawn of the Atomic Age* (New York: Pantheon Books, 1985).

8.   For example, between March 1966 and February 1967 the *Readers Guide to Periodical Literature* lists eighteen articles under the headings of "Atomic Power Plants" and "Atomic Power—Economic Aspects," all of which have positive titles. Articles in the following year were similarly supportive. It was not until the latter half of 1968 that coverage turned sour.

9.   Daniel Luten, "The Electrical Power Industry: Its Prospects for Growth," June 1970, Sierra Club, member papers, Bancroft Library, University of California, Berkeley, carton 174 (hereinafter cited as member papers).

10.   There is probably no more dramatic way to understand why the public was so supportive of New Deal-style programs than to read Robert Caro's narrative on LBJ's efforts to electrify the Texas hill country. Robert A. Caro, *The Years of Lyndon Johnson: The Path to Power* (New York: Alfred A Knopf, 1982), 502–28. On Lilienthal and the TVA, see Philip Selznick, *TVA and the Grass Roots: A Study of Politics and Organization* (Berkeley: University of California Press, 1984).

11.   Lyndon Johnson, "Nuclear Power: Key to a Golden Age of Mankind," *Department of State Bulletin* 57 (25 December 1967): 862–63.

12.   Quote by Seaborg in Atomic Energy Commission, "Construction Hearings: Pacific Gas and Electric Co. (Diablo Nuclear Power Plant)," 20 February 1968, Atomic Energy Commission/Nuclear Regulatory Commission docket 50–275 (Diablo Canyon), microfiche. See also Glenn T. Seaborg, "Nuclear Energy and the Generation of Power," remarks before the National Association of Manufacturers, 7 June 1966, member papers, carton 189.

13.   "Mother Lives Easier . . . ," *Public Utilities Fortnightly* 71 (6 June 1963): 35; and Walter Bouldin, "Age of Unlimited Energy," *Public Utilities Fortnightly* 73 (4 June 1964): 35–38.

14.   William E. Siri to Frederick Eissler, 16 May 1966, member papers, carton 189.

15.   F. F. Mautz to C. C. Whelchel, 20 September 1963, member papers, carton 189.

16.   Sierra Club, Board of Directors, meeting minutes, 7 September 1963 and 9 June 1963, Bancroft Library, University of California, Berkeley (hereinafter cited as minutes).

17.   Marc J. Roberts and Jeremy S. Bluhm, *The Choices of Power: Utilities Face the Environmental Challenge* (Cambridge: Harvard University Press, 1981), 156; and Jenness Keene, "Solving Reactor Siting in California," *Nucleonics* 24 (December 1966): 53–55, 68.

18.   Kathleen Jackson to George Marshall, 5 August 1966, member papers, carton 189.

19.   Richard M. Leonard, "Richard M. Leonard: Mountaineer, Lawyer, Environmentalist," interview by Susan R. Schrepfer, 1975, Bancroft Library, University of California, Berkeley, 284, 294.

20.   Doris Leonard to Will [Siri], 7 April 1966, member papers, carton 189.

21.   Leonard, "Richard M. Leonard," 315.

22. Conservation Associates, "Power Plant Sites on San Luis Obispo County Coast: Inspection—July 8, 9, and 10, 1964," 14 July 1964, member papers, carton 190.

23. Doris Leonard to Will [Siri], 7 April 1966, member papers, carton 189.

24. J. Michael McCloskey, "Sierra Club Executive Director: The Evolving Club and the Environmental Movement, 1961–1981," interview by Susan R. Schrepfer, 1981, Bancroft Library, University of California, Berkeley, 93.

25. Siri, "Reflections on the Sierra Club," 102.

26. Quote is from Kathy Jackson to William E. Siri, 22 November 1964; and see Fred Eissler to Will Siri, 19 October 1964, member papers, carton 189.

27. For a discussion of the sectarian personality see Mary Douglas and Aaron Wildavsky, *Risk and Culture: An Essay on the Selection of Technological and Environmental Dangers* (Berkeley: University of California Press, 1982), 102–51.

28. Fred Eissler to Will Siri, 19 October 1964; Fred Eissler to Will Siri and Dave Brower, 23 November 1964; and Eissler to Will Siri, 21 January 965, member papers, carton 189.

29. William E. Siri to Frederick Eissler, 24 January 1965, and see press release attached to Kathy Jackson to Charles Judson, 16 November 1964, member papers, carton 189; William E. Siri to Frederick Eissler, 22 June 1966, member papers, carton 190, and William E. Siri to Margaret B. Porter, April 1966, Sierra Club records, Bancroft Library, University of California, Berkeley.

30. *Paso Robles Press*, 11 February 1965.

31. *Santa Maria Times*, 10 February 1965, 1.

32. *San Luis Obispo Telegram-Tribune*, 14 June 1965, 1; *Paso Robles Press*, 14 June 1965, 1; *Santa Maria Times*, 10 June 1965, 14, and 2 April 1965, 13.

33. Kathleen [Jackson] to Will [Siri], Brower, 2 June 1966, member papers, carton 189. Martin Litton and Fred Eissler later argued that they too had been isolated from the decision-making process on Nipomo. Siri and Leonard denied this, but there is indication that they made no effort to keep them informed of the evolving negotiations. In a letter to Will Siri, Kathy Jackson asked if copies of her Nipomo correspondence should go to Doris Leonard, Randall Dickey, and David Brower. There is no reply from Siri, but after that copies went only to Leonard and Dickey. Kathleen Jackson to William Siri, 24 January 1965, member papers, carton 189.

34. Kathleen Jackson to William Siri, 14 June 1966, member papers, carton 189.

35. Minutes, 7 May 1966; and Fred Eissler to William Siri, 29 April 1966, member papers, carton 189.

36. William E. Siri to S. L. Sibley, 6 May 1966, Richard M. Leonard to Shermer L. Sibley, 4 July 1966, member papers, carton 189; S. L. Sibley to William E. Siri, 12 May 1966, and S. L. Sibley to George Marshall, 12 May 1966, member papers, carton 190.

37. Albert J. Gustus to Kenneth J. Diercks, 3 June 1966, member papers, carton 189.

38. George Marshall to Doris Leonard, 28 May 1966, member papers, carton 189.

39. George Marshall to William E. Siri, 28 May and 11 July 1966, and George

Marshall to Doris Leonard, 28 May 1966, member papers, carton 189. Although Siri claimed in an interview that he was aware of the correct location of the power plant and that he had told board members, there is no clear evidence of this in the 7 May minutes. Siri, "Reflections on the Sierra Club," 104.

40.　Charles Washburn to George Marshall, 26 June 1966, member papers, carton 189.

41.　George Marshall to Doris Leonard, 28 May 1966, and George Marshall to William E. Siri, 28 May and 11 July 1966, member papers, carton 189.

43.　Cohen, *History of the Sierra Club*, 155–56.

44.　Martin Litton, untitled essay, [1968?], member papers, carton 88.

45.　Peterson, "Brower Power Awaits the Verdict," 41.

46.　Litton, untitled essay.

47.　Martin Litton, "Martin Litton: Sierra Club Director and Uncompromising Preservationist, 1950s-1970s," interview by Ann Lage, 1981, Bancroft Library, University of California, Berkeley, 97.

48.　Martin Litton to Hugh Nash, 7 October 1966, member papers, carton 87; and Alex Hildebrand to Ansel [Adams], 4 December 1966, member papers, carton 1.

49.　Siri, "Reflections on the Sierra Club," 108.

50.　Litton, "Martin Litton," 105.

51.　Martin Litton to Shermer L. Sibley, 13 June 1966, and Martin Litton to Robert B. Marre, 10 June 1966, member papers, carton 189.

52.　Kathleen Jackson to William Siri, 14 June 1966, member papers, carton 189, and Siri, "Reflections on the Sierra Club," 105.

53.　Kathleen Jackson to Will Siri, 2 June 1966, member papers, carton 189.

54.　Ansel Adams to Martin Litton, 23 June 1966, member papers, carton 189.

55.　Martin Litton to Ansel Adams, 1 September 1966, and Adams to Litton, 7 September 1966, member papers, carton 189.

56.　Minutes, 17–18 September 1966.

57.　Minutes, 17–18 September 1966.

58.　The feelings of betrayal by club members were genuine but unwarranted. PG&E had been very clear in its intentions to Doris Leonard, Will Siri, and Kathy Jackson. Edgar Wayburn, interview by author, 27 March 1990, San Francisco, tape recording.

59.　Minutes, 7 January 1967.

60.　Minutes, 7 January 1967; and Siri, "Reflections on the Sierra Club," 109.

61.　Alan P. Carlin, William Hoehn, and Laurence I. Moss, "Nuclear Power Plant Site Selection for the PG&E System," 18 February 1967, member papers, carton 190; and minutes, 18 February 1967.

62.　Mark Evanoff, "Boondoggle at Diablo: The 18-Year Saga of Greed, Deception, Ineptitude—And Opposition," *Not Man Apart* 10 (September 1981): D-2.

63.　Siri, "Reflections on the Sierra Club," 101–2, 106.

64.　Dick [Leonard] to Will [Siri] and George [Marshall], 20 February 1967, member papers, carton 189.

65.　There is no way of knowing how a vote simply on the merits of the Diablo site would have turned out. But Will Siri and Phil Berry both noted that

274 Notes to Pages 87–89

conservatives like Tom Jukes were not a persuasive force to most members who were philosophically closer to David Brower. Siri, "Reflections on the Sierra Club," 37; and Phillip S. Berry, "Phillip S. Berry, Sierra Club Leader, 1960s–1980s: A Broadened Agenda, a Bold Approach," interview by Ann Lage, 1981, 1984, Bancroft Library, University of California, Berkeley, 25 and 63. As an example of the conservative opposition to Brower in the club, see Tom Jukes to members of the Sierra Club, 17 March 1967, and Robert Marshall to Phillip Berry, 18 March 1967, member papers, carton 189.

66.   It is unlikely that the club vote hinged on nuclear power or the merits of the Diablo site. A later vote by the club showed most members viewed the conflict between the two factions as one over responsibility. See Devall, "Governing of a Voluntary Organization," 235–37; and Schrepfer, "Nuclear Crucible," 226.

67.   "Club Elections Results," *Sierra Club Bulletin* 52 (March 1967): 2; and Martin Litton to Kenneth Anglemire, 17 January 1968, Litton to Betty Hughes, 20 November 1967, and Litton to Alexander T. Boregas, 22 May 1967, member papers, carton 87.

68.   Martin Litton to Eliot Porter, 26 January 1996, Litton to Betty Hughes, 20 November 1967, and Litton to Alexander T. Borgeas, 22 May 1967, member papers, carton 87.

69.   Will Siri argued that it was Diablo that was the immediate stimulus for environmentalists to push for greater planning to limit growth on the coast. Siri, "Reflections on the Sierra Club," 186.

70.   At the 1965 Wilderness Conference, for example, club members advocated putting nuclear plants near cities to protect wilderness areas. *San Francisco Chronicle*, 3 April 1965, 1.

71.   John Holdren, interview by author, 17 November 1994, Berkeley, tape recording; and Paul Ehrlich, *The Population Bomb* (New York: Ballantine Books, 1968), 13–14, 154–57.

72.   On the critical damage the thermal pollution issue did to nuclear power's image, see J. Samuel Walker, *Containing the Atom: Nuclear Regulation in a Changing Environment, 1963–1971* (Berkeley: University of California Press, 1992), 272–95. The peaceful atom's poor record on thermal pollution was not lost on the coal industry. Coal representatives encouraged dissident scientist Barry Commoner to take a stronger position against a nuclear station at Calvert Cliffs, Maryland. Joseph Moody to Barry Commoner, 31 July 1967, and Commoner to Moody, 1 September 1967, Barry Commoner papers, Library of Congress, Washington, D.C., carton 189.

73.   *Sports Fishing Institute Bulletin*, nos. 193 and 198, April and September 1968.

74.   Walker, *Containing the Atom*, 272–95.

75.   Of nineteen articles listed in the 1968 version of the *Readers Guide to Periodical Literature*, thirteen focused on nuclear power problems. This was true regardless of the publication's political orientation. See, for example, "Atom Power Plant in Hot Water," *Business Week*, 29 June 1968, 69–72; "Nuclear Power Setback?" *Forbes* 102 (15 November 1968), 57–58; "Cayuga's Waters," *Nation* 207 (30

December 1968): 709; "Nuclear Power—Not So Fast," *Nation* 207 (23 December 1968): 677–78; and "Nuclear Power—Rosy Optimism and Harsh Reality," *Science* 161 (12 July 1968): 113.

76. David Brower to Edgar Wayburn, 29 April 1968, member papers, carton 121; and Brower to Wayburn, 11 June 1968, member papers, carton 189.

77. Executive Director to the Board, 10 September 1968, member papers, carton 87. In 1968, the Sierra Club passed a resolution calling for the Federal Water Pollution Control Administration to maintain thermal pollution standards. "Board of Directors Meets September 14–15 at C.T.L.," *Sierra Club Bulletin* 53 (October 1968): 3–4.

78. David Brower to Edgar Wayburn, 29 April 1968, member papers, carton 121; and Brower to Wayburn, 11 June 1968, member papers, carton 189. The Sierra Club picked up on this statistic of water flow, and such descriptions of the size of thermal pollution would be cited often. *Sacramento Bee*, 26 December 1968, A13.

79. See comment by Brower in margin of a Department of the Interior news release on thermal pollution, 6 August 1968, member papers, carton 190.

80. Minutes, 14 December 1968; and Schrepfer, "Nuclear Crucible," 227.

81. *Palo Alto Times*, 11 February 1969.

82. David Brower to George Marshall, 6 March 1967, member papers, carton 189.

83. Peterson, "Brower Power Awaits the Verdict," 41.

84. For an analysis of the club vote, see Devall, "Governing of a Voluntary Organization." 217–38.

85. Richard Leonard and Ansel Adams still feared that somehow Brower would rise from the dead if the staff and board were not cleansed of "Brower-washed" supporters. Leonard told his allies that they would sack all senior staff except their Washington lobbyists and Michael McCloskey, who would become the next executive director. Richard Leonard to CMC Directors, 20 April 1969, in Richard Leonard, "Richard M. Leonard," 451–52; Ansel Adams to Dick Leonard, 10 May 1969, and [Richard Leonard] to Anne Van Tyne, 27 July 1969, member papers, carton 83.

86. Minutes, 3–4 May 1969. John McPhee captured the drama of the board meeting. See McPhee, *Encounters with the Archdruid*, 208–18.

87. McPhee, *Encounters with the Archdruid*, 216–17.

88. Schrepfer, "Nuclear Crucible," 237.

89. Quoted in Schrepfer, "Nuclear Crucible," 230.

90. The portrayal of the Sierra Club as a stodgy organization caught wholly unawares by the new environmental movement is common. See Gottlieb, *Forcing the Spring*, 85–86, 107–8, and 148–49.

91. Friends of the Earth, *Muir and Friends* (January 1970), Bancroft Library, University of California, Berkeley, 1.

92. David Brower, "Rambouillet Meeting Proposes Nuclear Moratorium," *Not Man Apart* 1 (April 1971): 7–8; and Amory Lovins, "Roslagen Energy Statement," *Not Man Apart* 1 (December 1971): 2.

93. See Phil Berry's introduction in Siri, "Reflections on the Sierra Club," i.

94. Berry, "Sierra Club Leader," 64.

95. By contrast, FOE's organization gave Brower and other leaders far more discretion to make policy and act without input form members.

96. "Sierra Club Annual Organization Meeting May 3–4," *Sierra Club Bulletin* 54 (May 1969): 3; minutes, 21–22 June 1969; and Berry, "Sierra Club Leader," 25, 36–37.

97. Attached testimony to memo of Peter Borelli, 1 April 1971, Sierra Club records, carton 147.

98. "Sierra Club Mounts a New Crusade," *Business Week,* 23 May 1970, 64; and Berry, "Sierra Club Leader," 54.

99. Phillip S. Berry to Wes Foell and others, 16 July 1970, Sierra Club records, carton 53; and Berry, "Sierra Club Leader," 60.

100. Jeremy Main, "A Peak Load of Troubles for the Utilities," *Fortune* 81 (November 1969): 119; and Main, "Conservationists at the Barricades," *Fortune* 82 (February 1970): 145.

101. Berry, "Sierra Club Leader," 61; Siri, "Reflections on the Sierra Club," 159; and Richard Cellarius to Sierra Club Environmental Survival Committee, 29 October 1970, Sierra Club records, carton 53.

102. Quoted in Cohen, *History of the Sierra Club,* 442.

103. *New York Times,* 30 November 1969, 1 (hereinafter cited *NYT*).

104. Steven V. Roberts, "The Better Earth," *New York Times Magazine,* 29 March 1970, 8.

105. Barry Commoner, "Beyond the Teach-in," *Saturday Review,* 4 April 1970, 52; and Roberts, "Better Earth," 8.

106. *NYT,* 30 November 1969, 57.

107. Editorial, *Ramparts* 8 (May 1970): 8–9.

108. "Ecology: Give Me That New-Time Religion," *Nuclear News* 13 (March 1970): 31–32.

109. Minutes, 6–7 December 1969; and "Sierra Club Mounts a New Crusade," *Business Week,* 23 May 1970, 65.

110. Minutes, 2–3 May 1970.

111. Brian Balogh, *Chain Reaction: Expert Debate and Public Participation in American Commercial Nuclear Power, 1945–1975* (Cambridge: Cambridge University Press, 1991).

112. Glenn T. Seaborg, "Science Technology, and the Citizen," *Vital Speeches* 36 (15 October 1969): 5–10; and Seaborg, "Toward a New Scientific Era," *Vital Speeches* 35 (15 January 1969): 230–40.

113. Alvin Weinberg, "Nuclear Energy and the Environment," *Bulletin of the Atomic Scientists* 26 (June 1970): 69–74; and Weinberg, "The Moral Imperatives of Nuclear Energy," *Nuclear News* 14 (December 1971): 33–37.

114. Union of Concerned Scientists, "Beyond March 4," Union of Concerned Scientists, office files, Cambridge, Massachusetts, folder Reactor Safety, History I (hereinafter cited as UCS office files). See Also Don Lombardi and others, "Preliminary Draft," 26 January 1970, UCS office files, folder Nader.

115. "M.I.T.'s March 4: Scientists Discuss Renouncing Military Research," *Science* 163 (14 March 1969): 1175–78; "A West Coast Version of the March 4

Protest," *Science* 163 (14 March 1969): 1176–77; and Dorothy Nelkin, *The University and Military Research: Moral Politics at M.I.T.* (Ithaca: Cornell University Press, 1972), 150–52.

116.   Union of Concerned Scientists, "Beyond March 4," UCS office files, folder Reactor Safety, History I; and Lombardi, "Preliminary Draft," UCS office files.

117.   Union of Concerned Scientists, Committee on Environmental Pollution, 26 February 1970, UCS office files, folder Reactor Safety, History I.

118.   UCS and the Sierra Club would continue their collaboration in critiques of AEC safety studies. See Henry W. Kendall and Sidney Moglewer, "Preliminary Review of the ACE Reactor Safety Study," November 1974, UCS office files.

119.   One such group was based at Stanford, but national in its scope, Scientists and Engineers for Social and Political Action. See its *Newsletter* in UCS office files.

120.   Scientists and Engineers for Social and Political Action, *Newsletter* 4 (June 1969): 7, and (December 1969): 1, UCS office files.

121.   Phillip S. Berry to Wes Foell and others, 16 July 1970, Sierra Club records, carton 53.

122.   D. B. Luten to Conservation Research Committee, 5 January 1970, Sierra Club records, carton 53.

123.   John Holdren, interview; Harrison Brown, *The Challenge of Man's Future* (Boulder: Westview Press: 1984[1954]); and C. P. Snow, *The Two Cultures and A Second Look* (Cambridge: Cambridge University Press, 1964).

124.   *NYT*, 12 December 1971, 66; Environmental Quality Laboratory, *People, Power, Pollution: Environment and Public Interest Aspects of Electric Power Plant Siting* (Pasadena: California Institute of Technology, 1971); and John P. Holdren, *Uranium Availability and the Breeder Decision* (Pasadena: California Institute of Technology, 1974).

125.   It was usually the nonmaterialists values of the Sierra Club's scientists that led them to look closer at energy issues. For example, Richard Sextro, a Lawrence Berkeley physicist, had joined some of his colleagues on the club's San Francisco Bay chapter's energy committee after working for lesislation to preserve the California coastline. This work alerted him to the dangers posed by power plant construction. Sextro was soon preoccupied with the entire issue of power growth. The energy problem, in turn, brought Sextro in confrontation with nuclear power. Sextro's own investigations would convince him that nuclear power was a "monster" that had to be stopped. Rich Sextro to Lowell Smith and Sid Moglewer, 22 December 1973, Rich Sextro personal files, Berkeley; and Richard Sextro, interview by author, 17 June 1992, Berkeley, tape recording.

126.   On the construction of other issue networks on nuclear power, see Balogh, *Chain Reaction*.

127.   Keith Roberts to Sierra Club Board of Directors, 29 November 1970, Sierra Club records, carton 133.

128.   Henry Romer and David Rubin, "An Initial Reaction to 'A Report by the Sierra Club Midwest Regional Conservation Committee Power Production

Task Force,'" 28 February 1971, George W. Pring to Board of Directors, 1 May 1971, and Sierra Club Northern California Regional Conservation Committee, "Preliminary Report , Toward an Energy Policy," 5 June 1971, member papers, carton 190.

129. John Holdren and Philip Herrera, *Energy: A Crisis in Power* (San Francisco: Sierra Club Books, 1971), 72–73, 94–98. A similar study popular at this time that used thermodynamic arguments was Howard T. Odum, *Environment, Power, and Society* (New York: Wiley-Interscience, 1971), chap. 2.

130. Holdren himself would eventually realize that warm water, unlike carbon dioxide, was an insignificant addition to global warming. But Holdren's argument was part of a large body of literature that used systems theory and ideas of limits to project future catastrophe if civilization did not limit its population and demands on earth's resources. The classic neo-Malthusian tract is the report by the Club of Rome. See Donella H. Meadows et al., *The Limits to Growth: A Report for the Club of Rome's Project on the Predicament of Mankind* (New York: Universe Books, 1972).

131. Minutes, 6–7 May 1972.

132. Sierra Club, "A Probability Report," [1972?], Sierra Club records, carton 165. Position papers by the club's energy activists now argued that all power plants should be opposed until research removed reasonable doubt thermal affects. See, "On Energy," paper attached to George W. Pring to members, Board of Directors, 27 September 1971, and Sierra Club, "Preliminary Report," 5 June 1971, member papers, carton 190.

133. A. C. Pigou, *The Economics of Welfare* (London: Macmillian, 1952).

134. David B. Large, "A Report on the Sierra Club's Conference on the Electric Power Industry," 26 January 1972, Sierra Club records, carton 165.

135. Minutes, 2–3 May 1970. For the way activists and scholars used the limits-to-growth argument against nuclear power, see Meadows et al., *Limits to Growth*, 131–33; Odum, *Environment, Power, and Society*, 48, 134–36; and Herman E. Daly, *Steady-State Economics: The Economics of Biophysical Equilibrium and Moral Growth* (San Francisco: W. H. Freeman, 1977), 132–34.

136. Sierra Club, "Energy Policy," 21 October 1972, member papers, carton 190; and June Viavant to those in attendance, 25 October 1972, member papers, carton 193.

137. For the story of the Union of Concerned Scientists success in exposing flaws in the ECCS systems, see their own version in Daniel Ford, *Meltdown: The Secret Papers of the Atomic Energy Commission* (New York: Simon & Schuster, 1982), 83–130; and Joel Primack and Frank von Hippel, *Advice and Dissent: Scientists in the Political Arena* (New York: Basic books, 1974), 208–38.

138. On the Gofman-Tamplin controversy, see Walker, *Containing the Atom*, 331–62.

139. *San Francisco Examiner*, 27 October 1971, 1.

140. *San Francisco Chronicle*, 28 October 1971, and 29 October 1971, 2; *Sacramento Bee*, 27 October 1971, A 4, and 28 October 1971, A 4. The Sierra Club published a pamphlet written by Pesonen documenting safety concerns and raising questions as to PG&E's monopolistic motives. Executive Director Mike Mc-

Closkey also questioned the safety of the Point Arena plant. See David E. Pesonen, *Power at Point Arena* (San Francisco: Sierra Club, July 1972), Bancroft Library, University of California, Berkeley; and Michael McCloskey to Don B. Curran, 18 April 1972, AEC/NRC docket Nos. 50–398 and 50–399 (Mendocino Power Plant Units 1 and 2).

141. Sierra Club, press release, 15 September 1971, Sierra Club records, carton 147; Sierra Club, press release, 9 February 1972, Sierra Club records, carton 166; and Sierra Club, press release, 22 December 1971, member papers, carton 190.

142. Richard Leonard to Donald Harris, 12 August 1972, in Leonard, "Richard M. Leonard," 461a and b; and Raymond J. Sherwin to Richard M. Leonard, 21 August 1972, Sierra Club records, carton 166.

143. Pesonen, *Power at Point Arena.*

144. Main, "Peak Load of Troubles," 118; "Something to Cheer About," *Nuclear Industry* 17 (February 1970): 20–22; "Face-to-Face with the Power Crisis," *Business Week,* 11 July 1970, 52; "Why Utilities Can't Meet Demand," *Business Week,* 29 November 1969, 48–62; "How Wrong Forecasts Hurt Utilities," *Business Week,* 13 February 1971, 44–46; Lawrence A. Mayer, "Why the U.S. Is in an Energy Crisis," *Fortune* 82 (November 1970): 74–77, 159–66; and Harold B. Meyers, "The Great Nuclear Fizzle at Old B&W," *Fortune* 81 (November 1969): 123–25, 164, 168, 172.

145. Michael McCloskey to Board of Directors, 23 August 1972, member papers, carton 174. See advertisements attached to letter.

146. "The Coldest Winter?" *Newsweek,* 31 December 1973, 6–9; "Conserving to Learn," *Time,* 7 January 1974, 45; "A Global Deal on Prices?" *Time,* 14 January 1974, 15–16; and "Losses—and Gains— for the Environment," *Time,* 4 February 1974, 37–38.

147. *NYT,* 3 November 1973, 1, 26, and 8 November 1973, 1, 33. For an overview of the Nixon energy policy, see Neil de Marchi, "Energy Policy under Nixon: Mainly Putting Out Fires," in *Energy Policy in Perspective: Today's Problems, Yesterday's Solutions,* ed. Craufurd D. Goodwin et al. (Washington: Brookings Institution, 1981), 395–474.

148. "Another Peak Year," *Nuclear Industry* 20 (January 1974): 3–6.

149. "Where the Tradeoffs Come in the Energy Crisis," *Business Week,* 17 November 1973, 66–67; Brock Evans, "Environmental Campaigner: From the Northwest Forests to the Halls of Congress," interview by Ann Lage, 1982, Bancroft Library, University of California, Berkeley, 177.

150. From very early in the energy crisis, the public tended to blame politicians and industry. Environmentalists' reputation held up well. See "Congress Greets the Energy Crisis," *Sierra Club Bulletin* 59 (February 1974): 13; and "The 21st Year: Looking Ahead," *Nuclear Industry* 20 (November 1974): 14–17.

151. *Sacramento Bee,* 7 February 1974.

152. Conspiracy theories among environmentalists, consumer groups, and the public were widespread in 1973 and 1974. See Friends of the Earth, "Nixon's New Emergency Energy Program," [21 November 1973?], Friends of the Earth records, Bancroft Library, University of California, Berkeley, carton 41; Brock

Evans, "Oilgate: Or, Is the Fuel Shortage Contrived," Sierra Club records, carton 181; and *NYT,* 9 November 1973, 27.

153. Martin Melosi, *Coping With Abundance: Energy and Environment in Industrial America* (Philadelphia: Temple University Press, 1985), 285.

154. Bill Press et al. To participants in January 23 Energy Convocation, 28 January 1974, Friends of the Earth records, carton 41.

155. "Where We Are in the Energy Crisis," *Sierra Club Bulletin* 59 (January 1974): 10; and Sierra Club, *Capitol Calendar,* 4 January 1974, Bancroft Library, University of California, Berkeley.

156. See David Brower's appeals to the Sierra Club in Minutes, 6–7 June 1972.

157. Edgar Wayburn, "Sierra Club Statesman, Leader of the Parks and Wilderness Movement," interview by Ann Lage and Susan Schrepfer, 1976–81. Bancroft Library, University of California, Berkeley, 60–61. Because of arguments like Wayburn's, those who voted with Siri later argued that the vote was "political" and not based on scientific evidence. In fact, the club's national energy committee opposed the moratorium vote. Scientists like Siri and engineers like Moss appeared to be arrayed against a nonscientific, emotional opposition. There is some truth in this stereotype, but it would be misleading to see club positions as one of science arrayed against Luddites. The crossover of dissident scientists to outright opposition was crucial in shifting the club's position. J. William Futrell, "Love for the Land and Justice for Its People: Sierra Club National and Southern Leader, 1968–1982," interview by Ann Lage, 1982, Bancroft Library, University of California, Berkeley, 57; and Siri, "Reflections on the Sierra Club," 167–69.

158. Michael McCloskey to Board of Directors, 11 June 1974, member papers, carton 176.

159. RJS [Raymond Sherwin] to Board of Directors, 1 June 1974, member papers, carton 176.

160. Quoted in Gottlieb, *Forcing the Spring,* 150.

Chapter 3. A Backdoor Approach to Nuclear Regulation: The Creation of the California Energy Commission

1. The public-private wars in California and the nation would continue into the sixties and seventies over access to nuclear power sources and the ability to "wheel" power into a service area. Marc J. Roberts and Jeremy S. Bluhm, *The Choices of Power: Utilities Face the Environmental Challenge* (Cambridge: Harvard University Press, 1981), 119–24. On the changing nature of utility regulation, see Douglas D. Anderson, *Regulatory Politics and Electric Utilities: A Case Study in Political Economy* (Boston: Auburn House, 1981).

2. Quoted in Roberts and Bluhm, *Choices of Power,* 133; "Utilities: Gerdes for the Battle," *Newsweek,* 1 July 1963, 54–55; and "Corporations: Expand or Expire," *Time,* 10 January 1964, 63–64.

3. Charles A DeTurk to Hugo Fisher, 26 July 1963, California, Department of Fish and Game papers, California State Archives, Roseville, Marine Resources Branch files, Radioactive Material, 1960–63 (hereinafter cited as F&G papers).

4.   My ideas on the importance of government capacity have been influenced by state-centered theory. In particular, the creation of a governmental structure to independently analyze, recommend, and implement energy policy (a capacity that no other state government had to the same degree as California) was a key component that allowed regulators and politicians to question the wisdom of electrical growth. There is now a large body of work on state-centered theory, some specifically dealing with the role of government structures in the nuclear controversy. See Theda Skocpol, *Protecting Soldiers and Mothers: The Political Origins of Social Policy in the United States* (Cambridge: Harvard University Press, 1992); Peter V. Evans, Dietrich Rueschemeyer, and Theda Skocpol, *Bringing the State Back In* (Cambridge: Cambridge University Press, 1985); James M. Jasper, *Nuclear Politics: Energy and the State in the United States, Sweden, and France* (Princeton: Princeton University Press, 1990); and Christian Joppke, *Mobilizing against Nuclear Energy: A Comparison of Germany and the United States* (Berkeley: University of California Press, 1993).

5.   The following discussion of the New Deal regulatory regime is drawn from George Hoberg, *Pluralism by Design: Environmental Policy and the American Regulatory State* (New York: Praeger, 1992), 19–38.

6.   David Vogel, "The 'New' Social Regulation in Historical and Comparative Perspective," in *Regulation in Perspective: Historical Essays,* ed. Thomas K. McCraw (Cambridge: Harvard University Press, 1981), 155–86.

7.   There is a substantial body of literature contending that the late sixties and early seventies represent a new regulatory era. In resource management, see Arthur F. McEvoy, *The Fisherman's Problem: Ecology and Law in the California Fisheries, 1850–1980* (Cambridge: Cambridge Univeristy Press, 1986), 227–57; and Hoberg, *Pluralism by Design.* More generally, see Vogel, "'New' Social Regulation"; and Richard A. Harris and Sidney M. Milkis, eds., *Remaking American Politics* (Boulder: Westview press, 1989).

8.   Samuel P. Hays, *Beauty, Health, and Permanence: Environmental Politics in the United States, 1955–1985* (Cambridge: Cambridge University Press, 1987), 390, 540–53.

9.   Brian Balogh, *Chain Reaction: Expert Debate and Public Participation in American Commercial Nuclear Power, 1945–1975* (Cambridge: Cambridge University Press, 1991).

10.   The emergence of the Energy Commission is an example of how environmentalists created their own "issue network." Issue networks consist of a broad number of participants from government, science, and activist groups who seek to influence policy. The expanded access to expertise by the legislature and environmentalists supports Brian Balogh's argument that the decline of nuclear power was caused by the formation of issue networks of politicians, scientists, and political activists. Contrary to Balogh's argument, however, science and environmentalism did not develop along separate paths that eventually joined. Scholars must avoid such polarization, since science often reflected social developments as much as it did internal professional debate. See Balogh, *Chain Reaction,* 19.

11.   Hoberg, *Pluralism by Design,* 8–9.

12.   Typical of the capture theorists were Grant McConnell, *Private Power and American Democracy* (New York: Vintage Books, 1966); and Theodore Lowi, *The End of Liberalism: Ideology, Policy and the Crisis of Public Authority* (New York: W. W. Norton, 1969).

13.   *San Francisco Chronicle*, 7 October 1959, 8 (hereinafter cited as *SFC*).

14.   George T. Mazuzan and J. Samuel Walker, *Controlling the Atom: The Beginnings of Nuclear Regulation, 1946–1962* (Berkeley: University of California Press, 1984), 287; W. T. Shannon to Alexander Grendon, 22 July 1960, James S. Leiby to Alexander Grendon, 16 August 1960, F&G papers, carton F3498:362; and *SFC*, 14 February 1957, 1, and 8 April 1958, 8.

15.   Mazuzan and Walker, *Controlling the Atom*, 355; W. T. Shannon to Alexander Grendon, 22 July 1960, and William W. Steffan to Departmental Coordinating Committee, 17 April 1961, F&G papers, carton F3498:362.

16.   W. T. Shannon to Alexander Grendon, 22 July 1960, F&G papers, carton F3498:362.

17.   W. T. Shannon to James B. Black, 15 February 1960; Richard S. Croker to Director, 28 October 1960, Alexander Grendon to Fred Seaton, 31 October 1960, W. T. Shannon to Alexander Grendon, 18 January 1961, F&G papers, carton F3498:362; and Ross Leffler to Alexander Grendon, 22 December 1960, United States Department of the Interior, Office of the Secretary files, Washington, D.C., accession number 69A-2058, box 55.

18.   Steffan to Departmental Coordinating Committee, 17 April 1961, F&G papers, carton F3498:362.

19.   Members actually contended that nuclear plants had no influence on recreation values. Harold Bissell to Director, 13 April 1961, F&G papers, carton F3498:362.

20.   William W. Steffan to Departmental Coordinating Committee, 17 April 1961, F&G papers, carton F3498:362.

21.   W. T. Shannon to Alexander Grendon, 18 January 1961, F&G papers, carton F3498:362.

22.   William W. Steffan to Departmental Coordinating Committee, 17 April 1961, F&G papers, carton F3498:362.

23.   Charles DeTurk noted this linkage between land use and nuclear power, commenting that state officials had no authority and recommending they request legislative clarification. The Resources Agency would adopt a more informal arrangement to deal with the legislative difficulties. DeTurk to Fisher, 26 July 1963, F&G papers, Marine Resources Branch, Radioactive Material, 1960–63.

24.   Stanely Scott, *Governing California's Coast* (Berkeley: Institute of Governmental Studies, 1975), 7.

25.   John Zierold, "Environmental Lobbyist in California's Capital, 1965–1984," interview by Ann Lage, 1984, Bancroft Library, University of California, Berkeley, 3–4; Rice Odell, *The Saving of San Francisco Bay: A Report on Citizen Action and Regional Planning* (Washington: Conservation Foundation, 1972); and Samuel E. Wood and Alfred E. Heller, *California Going, Going . . . Our State's Struggle to Remain Beautiful and Productive* (Sacramento: California Tomorrow, 1962), 7, 63.

26. Scott, *Governing California's Coast*, 5.

27. California, Resources Agnecy, *A Study of Resource Policy Directions for California* (Sacramento: Resources Agency, December 1965), 1–12; "AEC Wants Licensing Hearings to Have More Public Appeal," *Nuclear Industry* 15 (August 1968): 41; and Richard M. Leonard, "Richard M. Leonard: Mountaineer, Lawyer, Environmentalist," interview by Susan R. Schrepfer, 1975, Bancroft Library, University of California, Berkeley, 161.

28. California, Resources Agency, *The Story of the Resources Agency of California: Organized for Conservation, Economy, Efficiency* (Sacramento: Resources Agency, November 1961); and William Warne, "Opportunities and Goals of the Resources Agency of California," 16 November 1961, Water Resources Center Archives, University of California, Berkeley. On California's tradition of resource regulation to spur economic growth, see Gerald D. Nash, *State Government and Economic Development: A History of Administrative Policies in California, 1849–1933* (Berkeley: Institute for Governmental Studies, 1964); and Scott, *Governing California's Coast*, 301–3.

29. [Walter Shannon?], handwritten notes of Resources Agency Conference, 23 May 1964, F&G papers, carton F3498:142; and Resources Agency, *Second Annual Resources Agency Conference: Proceedings* (San Francisco, The Agency, 22–23 January 1965), 168. California Tomorrow asked state citizens, "What do you wish this state to be like tomorrow?" Quoted in Samuel Hays, *Beauty, Health and Permanence*, 389.

30. Resources Agency, *A Study of Resource Policy Directions for California*, (Sacramento: The Agency, December 1965), 23.

31. Resources Agency, *Resources Agency Policy on Powerplants in California*, 21 July 1965, and Resources Agency, "News Release," 13 July 1965, F&G papers, Director's administrative files, California State Agencies, Resources Agency, May–August 1965.

32. *Sacramento Bee*, 31 January 1965, D 4.

33. Harold D. Bissell to Hugo Fisher, 25 February 1965, F&G papers, Director's administrative files, California State Agencies, Resources Agency, Jan.–April, 1965; and *Sacramento Bee*, 31 January 1965, D4.

34. There was no justification for state administrators to oppose nuclear construction. Legislation dating from the fifties and unanimously renewed thereafter put the state on record as favoring nuclear plant construction. The Resources Agency had dutifully incorporated this mandate into their power plant siting policy stating that it would "encourage" the use of nuclear power whenever possible. California Senate, Resolution No. 168 (1967); California, Assembly, Resolution No. 217 (1967); and Resources Agency, *Resources Agency Policy on Powerplants in California*, attached to Hugo Fisher to Walter T. Shannon, F&G papers, Director's administrative files, California State Agencies, Resources Agency, May–Aug., 1965.

35. Janness Keene, "Solving Reactor Siting in California," *Nucleonics* 24 (December 1966): 55.

36. Resources Agency, *Siting Thermal Power Plants in California* (Sacramento: The Agency, 15 February 1970), appendix 4.

37. Lloyd Fergus to Paul E. Shaad, 11 February 1967, Sierra Club records, Bancroft Library, University of California, Berkeley carton 166.

38. Hugo Fisher, statement by Hugo Fisher before the San Diego Regional Water Pollution Control board, 30 March 1964, California State Library Sacramento; Harold D. Bissell to Administrator of Resources, 14 September 1965, F&G papers, carton F3498:342; and Hugo Fisher to Shermer Sibley, 20 July 1966, F&G papers, carton 3498:148; and Pacific Gas and Electric Company, "Summary of Ecological Studies and Agreements between California Resources Agency and Pacific Gas and Electric Company for Thermal Power Plants" (San Francisco, March 1969).

39. "Official Minutes of Meeting Held Between Representatives of the State Resource Agency and Pacific Gas and Electric," [October 1964], Department of Water Resources Central Records, Sacramento, file code 089.2

40. Quoted in Roberts and Bluhms, *Choices of Power*, 156.

41. California, Department of Water Resources, "Existing and Planned Uses of Avila Area," October 1964; and "Official Minutes of Meeting Held between Representatives of the State Resource Agency and Pacific Gas and Electric" [October 1964], Water Resources Central Records, file code 089.2; Harold Bissell to Hugo Fisher, 14 December 1964; P. L. Clifton to L. W. Carter and others, 21 December 1964, Water Resource, Central Records, file code 089.2.

42. Testimony of Paul Clifton before California Senate Public Utilities and Corporations Committee, *Hearing on Power Plant Siting* (Sacramento: The Senate, 10 February 1972), 5.

43. *New York Times*, 19 December 1964.

44. Some who supported the project never expected this demonstration project to be economic. Stewart Udall, for example, did not stress the project's economic advantages or its contribution to the water problem, but hoped for technological breakthroughs. See Udall's remarks in United States, Department of Interior, press release, 20 November 1967, Craig Hosmer papers, Doheny Memorial Library, Department of Special Collections, University of Southern California, Los Angeles, carton 179, (hereinafter cited as Hosmer papers); Glenn Seaborg and Udall to Joe Jensen, 23 April 1968, papers of the Joint Committee on Atomic Energy (JCAE), record group 128 (Records of the Joint Committees of Congress), National Archives, Washington D.C., carton 651 (hereinafter cited as JCAE papers); and Edward J. Bauser to John T. Conway, 22 September 1965, JCAE papers, carton 650.

45. Quoted in David Vogel, *Fluctuating Fortunes: The Political Power of Business in America* (New York: Basic Books, 1989), 25.

46. Department of the Interior, press release, 20 November 1967, Hosmer papers, carton 179.

47. Charles F. Richter to Frank C. Di Luzio, 23 May 1966, JCAE papers, Carton 651.

48. William T. England to John T. Conway, 25 June 1966, JCAE papers, carton 651.

49. England to Conway, 28 July 1967, JCAE papers, carton 651. For a rather frank assessment of the seismic problems of Bolsa Island, see England to Con-

way, 21 January, 27 May, 25 June 1966, and 12 October 1967; Edward J. Bauser to files, 31 May 1966; and Chairman, Advisory Committee to Evaluate Geologic-Seismologic Factors Pertaining to Siting of Nuclear Power-Desalting Plants to Secretary of the Interior, 22 July 1966, JCAE papers, carton 651.

50.   Edward J. Bauser to files, 26 March 1968, JCAE papers, carton 651. AEC director Milton Shaw provided Cher Holifield a laundry list of problems facing the project that ran thirteen pages. See Milton Shaw to Chet Holifield, 3 October 1968, Chet Holifield papers, Dohney Memorial Library, Department of Special Collections, University of Southern California, Los Angeles, carton 45 (hereinafter cited as Holifield papers).

51.   Department of the Interior, press release, 20 November 1967; and United States Atomic Energy Commission, press release, 20 November 1970, Hosmer papers, carton 179.

52.   Utility officials later admitted that they knew the price tag for the project would rise when they signed the contracts. *Los Angeles Times*, 23 November 1969, 1, 5 (hereinafter cited as *LAT*); and Public Relations Committee, Bolsa Island Nuclear Power and Desalting Plant, press release, 5 April 1968, Hosmer papers, carton 179.

53.   *Nucleonics Week*, 9 (1 August 1968), 1.

54.   Economic excuses also hid serious technical problems and AEC opposition to the Ravenswood project in New York. Balogh, *Chain Reaction*, 228.

55.   For a discussion of the crisis in science policy, see Bruce L. R. Smith, *American Science Policy since World War II* (Washington: Brookings Institution, 1990), 73–107. The regulatory crisis and the decline in public trust in business are detailed in Vogel, *Fluctuating Fortunes*, 37–92.

56.   Similar activity occurred at the federal level. Senator Edward Kennedy had offered siting bills that the industry did not like in 1968 and 1969. Nuclear advocates began offering federal siting bills in the early seventies, although no significant legislation ever passed in Congress. See "New Kennedy Siting Measure to Eliminate Nuclear Penalty," *Nuclear Industry* 16 (January 1969): 49–51; and "Congress Tackles Siting," *Nuclear Industry* 16 (August 1969): 13–19.

57.   Quoted in Richard Wayne Dyke, *Mr. Atomic Energy: Congressman Chet Holifield and Atomic Energy Affairs, 1945–1974* (New York: Greenwood Press, 1989), 233.

58.   Chet Holifield to William E. Warne, 12 September 1969, and Holifield to Samuel B. Nelson, 16 October 1969, Holifield papers, carton 46.

59.   Chet Holifield and Craig Hosmer to Floyd Goss, 1 April 1969, Holifield papers, carton 48; "Holifield, Ramey Urge Long-Range Power Plant Site Selection Activity," *Nuclear Industry* 16 (August 1969): 14; and "State Siting Authorities," *Nuclear Industry* 16 (December 1969): 4.

60.   Craig Hosmer and Chet Holifield to Ronald Reagan, 5 August 1969, Holifield papers, carton 47.

61.   Holifield would continue to work toward a federal siting bill for the rest of his career, but would never produce a bill acceptable to industry and environmentalists. Dyke, *Mr. Atomic Energy*, 245–55.

62.   William Warne to Robert H. Gerdes, 25 August 1969, Warne to Chet Holifield, 22 September 1969, Holifield papers, carton 46; and "State Site Ac-

quisition and Environmental Review Bills Examined," *Nuclear Industry* 17 (March 1970): 29–34.

63.   William Gould to Chet Holifield, 9 June 1969, JCAE papers, carton 139.

64.   Testimony of Paul Clifton and Walter Cavagnaro, *Hearing on Power Plant Siting.*

65.   John V. Briggs, "Notice of Public Hearing on November 18 and 19, 1969," Hosmer papers, carton 179; Briggs to Ronald Reagan, 5 December 1969, and Briggs to James T. Ramey, 4 August 1969, Holifield papers, carton 47; and California, Resources Agency, 9 March 1970, F&G papers, carton F3498:182.

66.   California, Assembly, *California Bills* (1970), AB818.

67.   William E. Siri, "Reflections on the Sierra Club, the Environment, and Mountaineering, 1950s–1970s," interview by Ann Lage, 1979, Bancroft Library, University of California, Berkeley, 187.

68.   The Sierra Club would begin informal working groups in 1970 to discuss forming a policy on electric power. See Edgar Wayburn to William D. McKee, 7 July 1970, Sierra Club records, carton 133, and extensive correspondence on Sierra Club policy in carton 133.

69.   "Power Consumption," *Sierra Club Bulletin* 55 (May 1970): 3.

70.   At the May meeting, Sierra Club directors passed resolutions opposing two nuclear power plant projects, one in Davenport, California, and the other outside of Eugene, Oregon. "Power Projects," *Sierra Club Bulletin* 55 (May 1970): 22.

71.   George Barrios, "The Wasteland Playground," *Cry California* 3 (Fall 1968): 17; and Charles A. Washburn, *Powerplant Siting and California's Coastal Environment* (Sacramento: Planning and Conservation League, [1971?], 12. California Tomorrow had never shared state officials' infatuation with the idea of using nuclear or fossil plants to effect land use planning. See Karl Way, "The Beach at San Onofre," *Cry California* 1 (Fall 1966): 34; Ronald Loveridge and Larry Yount, "The Towering Stack of Morro Bay," *Cry California,* 2 (Fall 1967): 33–38; and Barrios, "Wasteland Playground," 17–19.

72.   For a history of how thermal pollution damaged nuclear power's environmental image, see J. Samuel Walker, *Containing the Atom: Nuclear Regulation in a Changing Environment, 1963–1971* (Berkeley: University of California Press, 1992), 267–96.

73.   "Power Plant Siting," *Sierra Club Bulletin* 55 (May 1970): 22.

74.   *Sacramento Bee,* 4 August 1970, A 14.

75.   Assembly, *California Bills* (1970), AB 818; and Washburn, *Powerplant Siting and California's Coastal Environement,* 15.

76.   Assembly, *California bills* (1970), AB 818.

77.   *San Francisco Examiner,* 11 July 1970, 3; and Zierold, "Environmental Lobbyist," 93–94.

78.   *San Diego Union,* 15 Aril 1971, B3; and Assembly, *California Bills* (1971), AB 818.

79.   Legal activism by the Sierra Club increased accordingly. The club did not even file a suit until 1969, but then litigation jumped to about seven suits each year in the early seventies. Hoberg, *Pluralism by Design,* 65.

80.   Raymond Sherwin, "Speech Given to Policy Conference on Electric Power," 15 January 1972, Sierra Club records, carton 165.

81.   Norman Livermore, "Man in the Middle: High Sierra Packer, Timberman, Conservationist, and California Resources Secretary," interview by Ann Lage and Gabrielle Morris, 1981–182, Bancroft Library, University of California, Berkeley, 158–59.

82.   David E. Pesonen to files, 22 May 1972, Sierra Club records, carton 166.

83.   Livermore, "Man in the Middle," 159.

84.   "Sierra Club Wins Round against Power Plant," *California Journal* 3 (October 1972): 314–15.

85.   David E. Pesonen, *Power at Point Arena* (San Francisco: Sierra Club, July 1972).

86.   Shermer L. Sibley, "Pacific Gas and Electric: Utility Challenges in the Nuclear Age," *Nuclear News* 10 (June 1967): 29–33.

87.   Richard L. Meehan, *The Atom and the Fault: Experts, Earthquakes, and Nuclear Power* (Cambridge: MIT Press, 1084), 47.

88.   *Ukiah Daily Journal*, 1 December 1971, 1; and testimony of Citizens for Clean Energy, California Assembly Committee on Planning and Land Use, *Special Hearing on Power Plant Siting* (Sacramento: The Assembly, 18 November 1971), 30–31.

89.   Quoted in Meehan, *Atom and the Fault*, 48.

90.   V. E. McKelney to John S. O'Leary, 8 January 1973, R. B. McMullen to Roger S. Boyd, 3 October 1972, and Edson G. Case to Frederick T. Searls, 19 January 1973, AEC/NRC docket 50–398 and 50–399.

91.   F. T. Searls to John F. O'Leary, 19 January 1973, AEC/NRC docket 50–398 and 399, microfiche.

92.   *SFC*, 20 January 1973, 1.

93.   "Reagan State-of-the-State: Full Text," *California Journal* 1 (January 1970), 15.

94.   Zierold, "Environmental Lobbyist," 79; and Michael Eaton, interview by author, 19 June 1992, Sacramento, tape recording.

95.   *LAT*, 27 November 1970, II-1; "Momentum Builds for Coastline Preservation Bill," *California Journal* 2 (April 1971): 109; and "Environmental Lobby Suffers Second Year of Defeat for Its Major Proposals," *California Journal* 2 (November 1971): 296- 99.

96.   *San Diego Union*, 15 April 1971, B 3.

97.   The socialism charge would be leveled during the energy commission debates. See "Concession or Compromise? How the New Energy Act Should Work," *California Journal* 5 (July 1974): 239.

98.   Scott, *Governing California's Coast*, 120.

99.   For the history of the legislative battles regarding the California Coastal Commission, see Scott, *Governing California's Coast*, 287–364.

100.   California, Public Utilities Commission, *Report on Ten-Year and Twenty-Year Forecasts of Electric Utilities' Loads and Resources* (San Francisco: The Commission, 25 July 1972), 3, 20.

101.   Description of commercial found in Michael McCloskey to Don B. Curran, 18 April 1972, AEC/NRC docket 50–398, 399.

102.   See appendix B of Sierra Club, "Media Access Project's 1973–74 'Energy Crisis' Environmental Advertising Program," 8 May 1973, Sierra Club records, carton 181.

103.   For example, see Chet Holifield and Craig Hosmer, [Press Release], [1969], Holifield papers, carton 47; "Nuclear Power and the Environment," *Nuclear News* 13 (August 1970): 44; testimony of Barton W. Shackelford and David Fogarty, California Assembly Committee on Planning and Land Use, *Special Hearing* (Sacramento: The Assembly, 18 November 1971), 1–6, 69–82; testimony of John Landis, California, Legislative, Assembly Committee on Planning and Land Use, Subcommittee on State Energy Policy, *State Energy Policy Hearings* (Sacramento: The Assembly, 16 February 1973), 170–77; and David J. Fogarty, "Keeping Pace with New Energy Demands," *California Journal* 4 (June 1973): 198–99.

104.   California, Senate, Public Utilities and Corporations Committee, testimony of Jim Reed, *Hearings on Power Plant Siting* (Sacramento: The Senate, 10 February 1972), 47–59.

105.   Lou Cannon, *Reagan* (New York: G. P. Putnam and Sons, 1982), 185.

106.   The professionalized legislature has been said by some to be ineffective in recent years, but has generally been considered a modest success story. See Charles G. Bell and Charles M. Price, "20 Years of a Full-Time Legislature," *California Journal* 18 (January 1987): 36–40; A. G. Block and Robert S. Fairbanks, "The Legislature's Staff—No. 1 Growth Industry in the Capitol," *California Journal* 14 (June 1983): 214–19; and Citizens Conference on State Legislatures, *The Sometimes Governments: A Critical Study of the 50 American Legislatures* (New York: Bantam Books, 1971).

107.   *San Diego Union,* 15 April 1971, B3; and Emilio Varanini, interview by author, 2 July 1992, Sacramento, tape recording.

108.   Smith, *American Science Policy,* 78–79; and Ronald D. Doctor to the author, 15 March 1994, copy in possession of the author.

109.   Rand Corporation, Research Proposal for *The Growing Demand for Energy* (Santa Monica: Rand Corporation, May 1970), 3–5.

110.   Carlin also leaked internal Rand documents to the Sierra Club's executive director in late 1970 when the club was also trying to get Rand to do a similar study for them. See three memos dated the same day from Alan Carlin to Michael McCloskey, 23 December 1970, Sierra Club records, carton 136.

111.   Scott, *Governing California's Coast,* 324–25; and Gilbert E. Bailey and Paul S. Thayer, *California's Disappearing Coast: A Legislature Challenge* (Berkeley: Institute of Governmental Studies, University of California, 1971), 54.

112.   Varanini, interview; and Ronald Doctor, interview by author, 13 December 1993, telephone tape recording.

113.   When the Sierra Club first began to inquire in 1970 as to whether Rand would do a study for them, Alan Carlin warned Mike McCloskey that Rand would not be lackeys for the club. He indicated that Rand had maintained similar independence when working for the Department of Defense and would not change. See Alan Carlin to Michael McCloskey, 23 December 1970, Sierra Club records, carton 136.

114. California utilities admitted that there was much they did not understand about consumption patterns. "What Kind of Energy Policy for a Fast Growing Economy?" *Nuclear Industry* 19 (Nov.-Dec. 1972): 59.

115. This instance points to the difficulties of evaluating environmental conflicts as Samuel Hays does by polarizing them between people and experts or as Balogh does by focusing on professional specialization. Experts brought with them perspectives from outside their professions, and these attitudes influenced their position in public debates. In doing so, they blurred the line between the "insider" perspective of experts and the "outsiders" in social movements such as environmentalism. The weakness of this popular distinction is best typified by a response Sierra Club lobbyist John Zierold made in an interview. When asked how the club had managed to "infiltrate" the Rand Corporation, Zierold replied that he wished that he could claim such a coup, but "those people [Doctor and Ball] were already there and happened to have been active in the Sierra Club." John Zierold, "Environmental Lobbyist," 96–97.

116. *LAT,* 17 October 1972, I-1.

117. Rand Corporation, *California's Electricity Quandary,* 3 vols. (Santa Monica: Rand Corporation, 1972).

118. Rand Corporation, *California's Electricity Quandary,* vol. 3: *Slowing the Growth Rate,* by R. D. Doctor et al., vi.

119. *California's Electricity Quandary,* vol. 1, v.

120. *California's Electricity Quandary,* vol. 3, vi. Sierra Club scientists also gained access to the energy debate during later antinuclear campaigns through other studies. Zierold, "Environmental Lobbyist," 96–97; William E. Siri et al., *Impacts of Alternative Electrical Supply Systems for California,* and *Analysis of Supply-Demand of Electricity for the Twelve Western States, 1973 to 1990* (Lakewood, CO: Western Interstate Nuclear Board, 1976); Center for Energy Studies, *Direct and Indirect Economic, Social, and Environmental Impacts of the Passage of the California Nuclear Safeguards Initiative* (Austin: University of Texas, April 1976), 29; and Balogh, *Chain Reaction,* 19–20 and 149–50.

121. Rand closed its pitch for conservation by estimating that state-sponsored conservation measures would have little impact on the growth of *per capita* state product. *California's Electricity Quandary,* vol. 3, 105.

122. *LAT,* 4 March 1973, II-1.

123. Charles H. Warren, "From the California Assembly to the Council on Environmental Quality, 1962–1979: The Evolution on of an Environmentalist," interview by Sarah Sharp, in *Democratic Party Politics and Environmental Issues in California, 1962–1976,* Bancroft Library, University of California, Berkeley, 1986, 19–21.

124. Varanini, interview; and Warren, interview by author, 2 July 1992, Sacramento, tape recording. Warren's conversion to an environmentalist ethic was complete. He was troubled by the disparities between Western nations and the Third World consumption. Even as a state assemblyman, he viewed his legislation in international terms and tried to bring holistic management practices to issues such as food supplies, natural resources, and energy consumption. He became a committed "Malthusian," believing growth itself was the

enemy. Warren thus opposed nuclear power construction in part because of the expanded consumption it would encourage. Charles Warren, "Parsons Malthus Tolls the Bell," *Sierra Club Bulletin* 60 (March 1975): 7–10, 24, 31.

125. Testimony of Barton Shackelford and David J. Fogarty, *State Energy Policy Hearings*, 15 February 1973, 50 and 58.

126. Supplements to testimony of Barton Shackelford, *State Energy Policy Hearings*, 162–64.

127. Testimony of Ronald D. Doctor, *State Energy Policy Hearings*, 16 February 1973, 7.

128. See entire day of testimony, *State Energy Policy Hearings*, 16 February 1973.

129. For the development of Warren's relationship with the antinuclear movement and his intentions in writing state energy legislation, see his correspondence with Kendall in the Union of Concerned Scientists Archives, Institute Archives and Special Collections, Massachusetts Institute of Technology, Cambridge, Massachusetts, carton 33, folder California Assembly Hearings (hereinafter cited as UCS Archives). See especially Charles Warren to Henry W. Kendall, 16 May 1973; Warren to Kendall, 21 November 1973; and Kendall to Warren, 6 December 1973.

130. Warren, "From the California Assembly," 25.

131. Nationally, utilities were so horrified at such government invasion that they told environmental lobbyists that they would block all federal siting legislation, friendly or not. Richard Lahn to Larry Moss, 3 August 1973, Sierra Club records, carton 180.

132. Charles Warren, "An Assemblyman's View: A Legislative Response to the Energy Crisis," *California Journal* 4 (June 1973): 197.

133. Charles Warren to Henry W. Kendall, 16 May 1973, and Charles Warren to Ronald Reagan, 13 July 1973, UCS Archives, carton 33.

134. *LAT*, 3 October 1973, 1. Although there was speculation that Reagan had vetoed the bill because of utility pressure, not an unreasonable assumption, it seems that his lifelong antipathy for taxes was also a legitimate motive. Norman Livermore recalls that there was much discussion regarding the tax issue in the administration before the veto. See Livermore, "Man in the Middle," 166.

135. Gary D. Simon to Henry W. Kendall, 5 October 1973, UCS Archives, carton 33; and Varanini, interview.

136. Sierra Club, *Capitol Calendar*, 4 January 1974, Bancroft Library; and Charles Warren, "A State Legislative Response to the Energy Crisis," 15 November 1973, Sierra Club California Legislative Office records, Bancroft Library, University of California, Berkeley, carton 1. For editorial opinion, see *Sacramento Bee*, 11 November 1973, 2, and 13 December 1973, A13; *LAT*, 4 October 1973, II-6; 15 November 1973, II-6; 3 December 1973, II-6; and Maureen Fitzgerald, "Who Does What in the Energy Crisis," *California Journal* 4 (December 1973): 407–9.

137. "Complete Text of Governor Reagan's State-of-State Message," *California Journal* 5 (February 1974): 64–67.

138. *Sacramento Bee*, 7 February 1974, C 3, and *LAT*, 20 March 1974, I-3.

139. Varanini, interview.

140. Warren, interview.

141. *Sacramento Bee*, 22 May 1974, 1.

142. "Concession or Compromise? How the New Energy Act Should Work," *California Journal* 5 (July 1974), 239; and Varanini, interview.

143. "Concession or Compromise?" 240.

144. Alquist, whose district included General Electric's nuclear division, had always envisioned a bill that was heavy on siting and light on conservation. In 1972, he remarked that the state needed an agency "that will satisfy our ever-growing need for more power and at the same time provide a little environmental protection to meet the concerns of the conservationists who have been making a very loud protest in this area." See Senate Public Utilities and Corporations Committee, *Hearings on Power Plant Siting*, 1.

145. Warren, "From the California Assembly," 25; and Charles Warren to Henry W. Kendall, 17 May 1973, UCS Archives, carton 33.

146. Warren himself believes that the industry was the only entity that understood what his agenda was. See Warren, "From the California Assembly," 25; and "Interview: A Legislator, an Industry Spokesman, and a Conservationist Discuss the Energy Problem," *California Journal* 4 (June 1973): 203–8.

147. Zierold, "Environmental Lobbyist," 101.

Chapter 4. Radical Initiatives and Moderate Alternatives: California's 1976 Nuclear Safeguards Initiative

1. John Zierold, interview by author, 23 June 1992, telephone tape recording; and anonymous source, telephone interview by author, 8 June 1993, handwritten notes.

2. William L. Rankin, Stanley M. Nealey, and Barbara D. Miller, "Overview of National Attitudes toward Nuclear Energy: A Longitudinal Analysis," in *Public Reaction to Nuclear Power: Are There Critical Masses?* ed. William R. Freudenburg and Eugene A. Rosa (Boulder: Westview Press, 1984), 41–68.

3. *Nucleonics Week* 17 (6 May 1976): 7, and 17 (27 May 1976): 2.

4. *San Luis Obispo Telegram-Tribune*, 20 October 1975.

5. *San Luis Obispo Telegram-Tribune*, 18 October 1975, 1.

6. Edward Teller, *Energy from Heaven and Earth* (San Francisco: W. H. Freeman, 1979), 155, 158–67, 310–12.

7. The link between ideology and scientists has been described in Stanley Rothman and S. Robert Lichter, "Elite Ideology and Risk Protection in Nuclear Energy Policy," *American Political Science Review* 81 (1987): 396–97.

8. *Los Angeles Times*, 10 June 1976, 1 (hereinafter cited *LAT*).

9. Samuel Hays, *Beauty, Health, and Permanence: Environmental Politics in the United States, 1955–1985* (Cambridge: Cambridge University Press, 1987), 1–39, 490, 527–43. Other scholars have more generally demonstrated Hays's thesis for the United States and most Western nations. Ronald Inglehart, *The Silent Revolution: Changing Values and Political Styles among Western Publics* (Princeton: Princeton University Press, 1977), 3; Inglehart, *Culture Shift in Advanced Indus-*

trial Society (Princeton: Princeton University Press, 1990); and Daniel Yankelovich, *New Rules: Searching for Self Fulfillment in a World Turned Upside Down* (Toronto: Bantam Books, 1982).

10.   The link between nonmaterialist values and intolerance for involuntary risk is detailed by Mary Douglas and Aaron Wildavsky. See Mary Douglas and Aaron Wildavsky, *Risk and Culture: An Essay on the Selection of Technological and Environmental Dangers* (Berkeley: University of California Press, 1982), 158–60. See also Michael Thompson, Richard Ellis, and Aaron Wildavsky, *Cultural Theory* (Boulder: Westview Press, 1990).

11.   Peter N. Carroll, *It Seemed Like Nothing Happened: America in the 1970s* (New York: Holt, Rinehart, and Winston, 1982), 323.

12.   Friends of the Earth, *Not Man Apart*, July 1973, 9.

13.   Quoted in William J. Lanouette, "The Nuclear Power Issue," *Commonweal* 103 (30 July 1976): 489; and Gene [Coan] to Mike [McCloskey], 15 May 1974, Sierra Club records, Bancroft Library, University of California, Berkeley, carton 191.

14.   Jim Harding, interview by author, 1 January 1994, El Cerrito, California, tape recording.

15.   *Northern States Power Co. v. Minnesota*, 447 F 2d (8th Cir. 1971).

16.   David Pesonen, interview by Ann Lage, rough draft of transcript, used by permission. This idea eventually evolved into the goal of using California and possibly other state initiatives to force the passage of national moratorium legislation by America's bicentennial. See "Summary of Organizational Meeting of October 26–27, 1974," Sierra Club records, carton 119.

17.   Charles Warren, interview by the author, 2 July 1992, Sacramento, tape recording; and Pesonen, interview.

18.   "Initiative Makes a Big Comeback as Groups Seek to Bypass Legislature," *California Journal* 3 (August 1972): 229–30.

19.   For a discussion of the importance of Ed Koupal to the modern initiative process see David D. Schmidt, *Citizen Lawmakers: The Ballot Initiative Revolution* (Philadelphia: Temple University Press, 1989), chap. 3.

20.   Schmidt, *Citizen Lawmakers*, 42.

21.   Diane Koupal-Hyde, interview by author, 7 June 1992, Santa Rosa, tape recording.

22.   One of Koupal's star pupils was Howard Jarvis who would lead California's Proposition 13 tax revolt. Koupal's methods are best described in People's Lobby, *National Initiative and Vote of Confidence (Recall): Tools for Self-Government* (Los Angeles: People's Lobby Press, 1977); and Schmidt, *Citizen Lawmakers*, chap. 9.

23.   Koupal believed a "nuclear web" of conspiracy existed to thwart citizen efforts to control the atom. People's Lobby even drew this web illustrating the ties of influence between politicians and the nuclear industry. Koupal thought this web was a chance creation "by the circumstances of finances and employment, and in some cases, marital and nepotistic ties." Because of these links elected officials become "contemptuous of voters and disdainful of the public at large." *People's Lobby Newsletter*, Nov.-Dec. 1975; and quoted in Jerome Price, *The Antinuclear Movement* (Boston: Twayne, 1982), 101.

24. An example of this inability to understand the motivations of the opposition occurred when scientist Hans Bethe, speaking before a California audience, compared favorably nuclear power hazards to automobile deaths in a public lecture. A woman in the audience responded, "But we choose, we the people choose, to drive automobiles, and we choose not to have nuclear power!" "Hans Bethe Recounts Some Frustrations as a Nuclear Spokesman," *Nuclear Industry* 22 (November 1975): 20. See also Spencer Weart, *Nuclear Fear: A History of Images* (Cambridge: Harvard University Press, 1988), 339–43; and Douglas and Wildavsky, *Risk and Culture*, 126–51.

25. Quoted in McKinley C. Olsen, *Unacceptable Risk: The Nuclear Power Controversy* (New York: Bantam Books, 1976), 12; and *San Francisco Chronicle*, 7 April 1975, 9 (hereinafter cited as *SFC*).

26. "How the Pollution Initiative Affects You," pamphlet, Craig Hosmer papers, University of Southern California, carton 197 (hereinafter cited as Hosmer papers). For business opposition to Proposition 9, see Felix Owen to Garland C. Ladd, 8 September 1971, Hosmer papers, carton 194. Schmidt, *Citizen Lawmakers*, 51; Richard Spohn to Ralph Nader, 4 July 1974, Union of Concerned Scientists Archives, Massachusetts Institute of Technology, Institute Archives and Special Collections, Cambridge, MA (hereinafter cited as UCS Archives), carton 33.

27. See untitled description of the group dated 11 October 1972; Another Mother for Peace, "Look What We Did Together in 1970–71," July 1971; and "Look What We Did Together in 1971–72," July 1972, Another Mother for Peace records, Swarthmore College Peace Collection, Swarthmore, PA, box 1 (hereinafter cited as AMP records).

28. Dorothy B. Jones to Elizabeth [Hogan], 23 March 1970, AMP records, box 3.

29. See correspondence between Dorothy Jones, John Gofman, and Elizabeth Hogan between 1970 and 1973 in AMP reords, box 3; and AMP, "The Nuclear Presence in Los Angeles County," March 1976, AMP records, box 1.

30. AMP, "Another Mother for Peace Newsletter," December 1972 and Winter 1974, AMP records, box 1.

31. AMP, "Another Mother for Peace Newsletter," Winter 1974, AMP records, box 1.

32. Pesonen, interview; Ilene Lengyel to friends, 3 April 1973, UCS archives, carton 33; and Alvin Duskin, interview by Yuko Hirabayashi, 16 June 1992, San Francisco, tape recording.

33. The idea of a moratorium was popular for some years in antinuclear circles. The citizens of Eugene, Oregon, passed a four-year ban on construction in 1970. This victory inspired some national activists like John Gofman, and some efforts were made in 1972 to pass moratorium measures. The general assessment was that "moratorium" was too closely associated with Vietnam peace campaigns. See Olsen, *Unacceptable Risk*, 13; Daniel Pope, "'We Can Wait. We Should Wait.' Eugene's Nuclear Power Controvesy, 1968–1970," *Pacific Historical Review* 59 (1990): 349–73; John W. Gofman and Arthur R. Tamplin, *Poisoned Power: The Case against Nuclear Power Plants* (Emmaus, PA: Rodale Press, 1971), 227–42; Rich Sextro to Lowell Smith and Sid Moglewer, 22 December 1973, Richard Sextro personal files (hereinafter cited as Sextro files).

34. Handwritten notes, "Moratorium Group Meeting," 2 December 1973, UCS Archives, carton 33; Pesonen, interview; and Larry Levine, interview by author, 24 June 1992, telephone tape recording.

35. The best explanation of the mechanics of Proposition 15 is John H. Barton and Charles J. Meyers, "The Legal and Political Effects of the California Nuclear Initiative," in *The California Nuclear Initiative: Analysis and Discussion of the Issues*, ed. W. C. Reynolds (Stanford: Institute for Energy Studies, Stanford University, April 1976), 1–36.

36. *LAT*, 12 March 1974, II-1.

37. Hays, *Beauty, Health, and Permanence*, 173, 205.

38. "Club Board Adopts New Policies: Nuclear Power, Oil Shale, Energy," *Sierra Club Bulletin* 59 (February 1974): 15. For a discussion of the Sierra Club's evolution on nuclear policy see Brock Evans, "Sierra Club Involvement in Nuclear Power: An Evolution of Awareness," *Oregon Law Review* 54 (1975): 607–21.

39. Hugh Nash, ed. *Progress As If Survival Mattered* (San Francisco: Friends of the Earth, 1977), 7–10, 25–62. See also "15 Reasons to Vote Yes on 15," *Not Man Apart* (June-mid-June 1976); Sheldon Novick, *The Electric Wars: The Fight over Nuclear Power* (San Francisco: Sierra Club Books, 1976), 184–95; Egan O'Connor, "Moratorium Politics," *Not Man Apart* (May 1973): 10–11; Eugene Coan et al., "Nuclear Power and the Sierra Club," November 1977, pamphlet.

40. The Sierra Club's national position on nuclear power was more conservative than that of the local California chapter leadership. California activists especially in the San Francisco and Los Angeles areas moved to endorse the initiative very early in 1974, while the national board of directors would not do so until 1976. Richard Sextro, interview by author, 17 June 1992, Berkeley, tape recording; Ted Trzyna to SCRCC members, 18 January 1974, Sierra Club records, carton 191; various material in Sextro files; and Joseph Fontaine and Phillip Berry, "Nuclear Safety Initiative," *Sierra Club Bulletin* 61 (March 1976): 21–22.

41. Gene [Coan] to Mike [McCloskey], 15 May 1974, Sierra Club records, carton 191; Richard Sextro, interview; and Spohn to Nader, UCS Archives, carton 33; Dwight Cocke, interview by author, 21 July 1992, San Francisco, tape recording; Schmidt, *Citizen Lawmakers*, 51; and Pesonen, interview.

42. Duskin, Cocke, and Pesonen, interviews.

43. Schmidt, *Citizen Lawmakers*, 59; "Citizens Organize Western Bloc," *Critical Mass* 1 (August 1975): 1 4; and Laura Tallian, *Direct Democracy: An Historical Analysis of the Initiative, Referendum, and Recall Process* (Los Angeles: People's Lobby Press, 1977), 111–19.

44. "Minutes of Steering Committee Meeting," 23 August 1975, 21 September 1975, and 25 October 1975, Sextro files; Pesonen and Cocke, interviews.

45. Rob Duboff to all participants of organizational meeting of October 26–27, 1 November 1974, Sierra Club records, carton 119; and Pesonen, interview.

46. Pesonen, interview; James Burch, interview by author, 17 June 1992, Palo Alto, tape recording; Wileta Burch, Beverley Sorensen, Jane Kroll, and Fredricka McGlashan, interview by author, 1 July 1992, Palo Alto, tape recording (hereinafter cited Creative Initiative, interview); and Cocke, interview.

48. Pesonen, interview.

47. Novick, *Electric Wars*, 242–49; Pesonen, Burch, Creative Initiative, and Cocke, interviews.

49. For a discussion of the shifting cultural patterns in the seventies, see Yankelovich, *New Rules*, and Inglehart, *Silent Revolution*.

50. Creative Initiative, interview. For a detailed history of creative Initiative, see Steven M. Gelber and Martin L. Cook, *Saving the Earth: The History of a Middle-Class Millenarian Movement* (Berkeley: University of California Press, 1990).

51. Creative Initiative program "The Time is Now," attached to Paul C. Valentine to J. Anthony Kline, 13 May 1975, Governor Edmund G. Brown, Jr. papers, Doheny Memorial Library Department of Special Collections, University of Southern California Archives, Los Angeles, carton E-26–10 (hereinafter cited as Brown papers).

52. E. F. Schumacher, *Small Is Beautiful: Economics As If People Mattered* (New York: Harper & Row, 1973), 145.

53. Creative Initiative and Burch, interviews; and Novick *Electric War*, 242–49.

54. "The Time Is Now," Brown papers.

55. *LAT*, 6 May 1975, 24, and 9 May 1975, iv-1; and Creative Initiative, interview.

56. Quoted in Gelber and Cook, *Saving the Earth*, 256.

57. "The Time Is Now," Brown papers; and Creative Initiative, interview.

58. Cocke, interview.

59. No on 15 Committee, *California Energy Bulletin* (Spring 1976): 1.

60. *LAT*, 7 May 1975, II-1.

61. Pat Brown's ability to shift his position on issues was legendary. See Roger Rapoport, *California Dreaming: The Political Odyssey of Pat and Jerry Brown* (Berkeley: Nolo Press, 1982).

62. Bruce Keppel, "Nuclear Power: California's Next Big Initiative Battle," *California Journal* 6 (June 1975): 202–3; and "A Labor Committee against Proposition 15," *Nucleonics Week* 17 (22 April 1976): 7.

63. "Nuclear Power in the U.S.: Chaos Reigns Supreme as 1975 Opens," *Nucleonics Week* 16 (16 January 1975): 1.

64. Emilio Varanini, interview by author, 2 July 1992 and 12 December 1993, Sacramento, tape recording.

65. "The California Initiative Organizers Filed Some 500,000 Signatures," *Nucleonics Week* 16 (10 April 1975): 8.

66. Atomic Industrial Forum, "Report on Warren Committee Hearings," 14 and 15 October 1975, from the personal files of James Burch (hereinafter cited as Burch files), copy in possession of the author.

67. Atomic Industrial Forum, "Report on Warren Committee Hearings," 21 and 22 October 1975, and 4 and 5 November 1975, Burch files.

68. Even industry publications admitted industry witnesses fared poorly. See *Nucleonics Week* 17 (15 January 1976): 2; and James K. Staley, "California Initiative Hearings: Industry's Showing Faulted," *Nuclear Industry* 23 (January 1976): 9–11.

69. Edward Teller and Hans Bethe, Committee on Resources, Land Use, & Energy, *Hearings on the Nuclear Initiative*, 22 October 1975, vol. 4, 16 (hereinafter cited as *Assembly Hearings*).

70. Staley, "California Initiative Hearings," 10.

71. Michael Peevey, *Assembly Hearings*, 2 December 1975, vol. 12, 46–56; and Katherine Dunlap, *Assembly Hearings*, 10 December 1975, vol. 15, 58–60.

72. See especially *Assembly Hearings*, 28 and 29 October 1975, vols. 5 and 6; and California, Assembly, Committee on Resources, Land Use & Energy, *Reassessment of Nuclear Energy in California: A Policy Analysis of Proposition 15 and Its Alternatives*, 10 May 1976, 4.

73. Staley, "California Initiative Hearings," 10.

74. Rich Sextro to Lowell Smith, Sid Moglewer, 22 December 1973, R. Sextro files; Varanini, interview; John Zierold, "Environmental Lobbyist in California's Capital, 1965–1984," interview by Ann Lage, 1984, Bancroft Library, University of California, Berkeley, 96–97; William E. Siri et al., *Impacts of Alternative Electrical Supply Systems for California*, and *Analysis of Supply-Demand of Electricity for the Twelve Western States, 1973 to 1990* (Lakewood, CO: Western Interstate Nuclear Board, 1976); Center for Energy Studies, *Direct and Indirect Economic, Social, and Environmental Impacts of the Passage of the California Nuclear Safeguards Initiative* (Austin: University of Texas, April 1976), 29; and Brian Balogh, *Chain Reaction: Expert Debate and Public Participation in American Commercial Nuclear Power, 1945–1975* (Cambridge: Cambridge University Press, 1991), 19–20 and 149–50.

75. *SFC*, 23 January 1976, 6. At least one scholar has seen the bills as a conspiratorial effort to coopt the antinuclear movement's agenda and forestall the victory of the initiative. This interpretation fails to consider the motives of Charles Warren or other committee members. See Price, *Antinuclear Movement*, 99–104.

76. Pesonen, interview; and *SFC*, 23 January 1976, 6.

77. Duskin and Levine, interviews.

78. Charles Warren hinted publicly and told the Winner/Wagner campaign managers in private that he would support the initiative if the bills failed. PG&E concluded that Brown, Warren, assembly speaker Leo McCarthey and a number of newspapers would have changed their position on Proposition 15 if the utilities "killed" the surviving bills. See Warren, interview, and Pacific Gas & Electric Co., "Proposition 15: The What and Why of Its Defeat," Burch files.

79. Dale Bridenbaugh to N. L. Felmus, 2 February 1976; Richard B. Hubbard to Abdon Rubio, 2 February 1976, copies of letters in the possession of the author. The story of Dale Bridenbaugh's decision is detailed in Gail Sheehy, *Pathfinders* (New York: William Morrow, 1981), chap. 16.

80. "Four Resignations Radically Change Complexion of the Nuclear Fight," *Nucleonics Week* 17 (12 February 1976): 1–2; and "Debate on Safety Stirs Senate," *Nuclear Industry* 23 (February 1976): 2–5.

81. *SFC*, 12 February 1976, 1.

82. McCormack's prediction proved wrong. The three engineers formed the consulting firm MHB Associates, which is a substantial success. *Portland Oregonian* 17 March 1976; *Spokane Chronicle*, 27 February 1976; and "Creative Initiative Foundation: An Enigma against Nuclear Power," *Nucleonics Week* 17 (11 March 1976): 9; and Gail Sheehy, *Pathfinders*, 373.

83. Creative Initiative, interview.

84. No on 15 Committee, "Why We Oppose Proposition 15" (n.d.), pamphlet, Sextro files; *SFC*, 7 June 1976, 32; *California Energy Bulletin* (Spring 1976): 3.

85. *Santa Rosa Press-Democrat*, 18 March 1976, 4; No on 15 Committee, *Californian Energy Bulletin* (Spring 1976): 1–8; John Simpson testimony, *Assembly Hearings* 14 (9 December 1975), 10; and "Annual Banquet Speech Is a Stem-Winder by Mike McCormack," *Nuclear Industry* 22 (December 1975): 3–5.

86. Alexander J. Groth and Howard G. Schultz, "Voter Attitudes on the 1976 Nuclear Initiative in California," *Environmental Quality Series* 25 (Davis, CA: Institute of Government Affairs, December 1976): 20–21.

87. "$40 Billion Cost, $7,500 per Family, Seen for California," *California Energy Bulletin*, (Spring 1976): 1; and *SFC*, 31 March 1976, 13.

88. A good example of the nuclear experts' prophecy of doom is an article by Hans Bethe that the pronuclear forces referred to often in the Proposition 15 campaign. Bethe warned that nuclear power was the "only source" available to meet most of America's energy needs. Without rapid expansion the country faced "unemployment and recession, if not worse." H. A. Bethe, "The Necessity of Fission Power," *Scientific American* 234 (January 1976): 21–31.

89. Pacific Gas and Electric, "Proposition 15: The What and Why of Its Defeat," Burch files.

90. Pesonen later admitted that "much of the public saw us as dishonest . . . and it hurt." PG&E, "Proposition 15: The What and Why of Its Defeat"; Levine and Pesonen, interviews.

91. *SFC*, 4, 6, and 7 June 1976); *LAT*, 7 June 1976; Project Survival, "The People Are for Yes on 15 Big Money Is against Yes on 15," pamphlet, Sextro files; "15 Reasons to Vote Yes on 15," *Not Man Apart* (June and mid-June 1976); and see Proposition 15 literature in Sierra Club, San Francisco Bay Chapter records, Bancroft Library, University of California, Berkeley, carton 9.

92. Rich Sextro meeting notes, Sextro files. The proportion of yes to no voters dropped from 48 to 45 percent in March to 27 to 54 percent in June. *SFC*, 4 March, 16 April, 4 June 1976.

93. *SFC*, 9 March 1976, 6.

94. Governor Jerry Brown was supportive of Warren's efforts, but did not become involved in the legislative negotiations. He and his aides, in the words of Charles Warren, did "absolutely nothing" to assure passage of the legislation. "Brown and Nuclear Safety," *Yodeler* (June 1976; Varanini, Zierold, and Warren, interviews.

95. "California Utilities Appear to Be Able to Live with the Three Nuclear Bills," *Nucleonics Week* 17 (10 June 1976): 3.

96. *SFC*, 12 and 13 May, 1 and 2 June 1976; Warren picked up key support by exempting the proposed Sundesert project from the underground reactor feasibility study. See Warren-Alquist State Energy Resources Conservation and Development Act, § 25534.1–5.

97. "California: One Down, Many to Go," *Nuclear Industry* (23 June 1976): 32; and *Nucleonics Week* 17 (1 January 1976): 1–2, and 17 (8 April 1976): 3.

98. Utilities outside California subscribed to this view, especially those with initiatives in their states in the fall. Robert T. Person to shareholders of Pub-

lic Service Corp. of Colorado, 17 May 1976, Sierra Club records, carton 20; and *New York Times,* 23 May 1976, sec. 3, 1.

99. Tim Nicholson, "No Truce in the New A-War," *Newsweek,* 21 June 1976, 61.

100. "A Go-Ahead for Nuclear Power," *Time,* 21 June 1976, 62.

101. Deborah R. Hensler and Carl P. Hensler, *Evaluating Nuclear Power: Voter Choice on the California Nuclear Energy Initiative* (Santa Monica: Rand Corporation, 1979), 10.

102. Data for income, education, and manufacturing and agricultural labor shares were derived from the 1980 Census. U.S. Department of Commerce, Bureau of the Census, *Census of Population (1980). Social and Economic Characteristics,* California (Washington, DC: Government Printing Office, 1982). For employment figures for 1975 and voter registration figures, see County Supervisors Association of California, *California County Fact Book* (Sacramento, 1975 & 1977).

103. All correlations cited were significant at the %1 level or higher. The 1980 voter returns are a better measure of liberalism than Democratic voter registration (which was also positively correlated to the vote, but less so), since many Reagan Democrats had not yet changed party affiliation.

104. An interesting outlier was well-educated and affluent Orange County. This conservative stronghold with its heavy reliance on defense industries rejected Proposition 15 by nearly 4 to 1. Thus ideology and personal involvement in the military/industrial complex tended to offset socio-economic factors. Excluding just this one county from the analysis improved the correlation of education and income to +.485 and +.500, respectively.

105. Social scientists have obtained similar results for education levels in studies of the 1976 Nuclear Safeguards initiatives in Ohio and Oregon. See Lettie McSpadden Wenner and Manfred W. Wenner, "Nuclear Policy and Public Participation," *American Behavorial Scientist* 22 (Nov./Dec. 1978): 277–310. The results found in California have not been universally confirmed. Daniel Pope found no correlation with education and income in his analysis of the safeguard vote in Washington state and a positive correlation to the proportion of labor involved in manufacturing. Daniel Pope, "Anti-Nuclear Activism in the Northwest: WPPSS and Its Enemies," in *The Atomic West,* ed. John Findlay and Bruce Hevly (Seattle: University of Washington Press, forthcoming).

106. Inglehart, *Silent Revolution* and *Culture Shift.*

107. Atomic Industrial Forum, *Info* (June 1976): 1.

108. Groth and Schultz, "Voter Attitudes," 11, 15.

109. Groth and Schultz, "Voter Attitudes," 37.

110. *LAT,* 10 June 1976; Hensler and Hensler, *Nuclear Power,* 10; and Groth and Schultz, "Voter Attitudes," 10.

111. "California: One Down," 8.

112. Quoted in Mary Ellen Leary, "California's Nuclear Initiative: The Best Possible Defeat," *Nation* 223 (14 August 1976): 104–7.

113. ". . . But Lawyers Predict Anti-Nuclear Bills Face Court Upsets," *Nuclear Industry* 23 (January 1976): 11–13.

114. Varanini, interview; and Assembly, *Reassessment of Nuclear Energy,* 18.

115. Carroll, *It Seemed Like Nothing Happened,* 321.

116. James M. Jasper, *Nuclear Politics: Energy and the State in the United States, Sweden, and France* (Princeton: Princeton University Press, 1990); Elizabeth Nichols, "U.S. Nuclear Power and the Success of the American Anti-Nuclear Movement," *Berkeley Journal of Sociology* 32 (1987): 167–92; and Pope, "Anti-Nuclear Activism in the Northwest."

117. Edward Teller's view of the link between ample energy and the American Dream is best illustrated in *Energy from Heaven and Earth*, chap. 10.

Chapter 5. Frankenstein's Monster Comes of Age: The California Energy Commission and the Sundesert Project

1. For the history of Artie Samish's reign, see Elmer R. Rusco, "Machine Politics, California Model: Arthur H. Samish and the Alcohol Beverage Industry," Ph.D. diss., University of California, Berkeley, 1960.

2. The following incident at Frank Fats' has been drawn from Frank Devore, interview by author, 3 January 1994, telephone tape recording; and Gary Cotton, interview by author, 28 December 1993, telephone tape recording.

3. These were the nuclear safeguards bills passed during the Proposition 15 campaign. See chapter 4.

4. The commission's formal name was the California Energy Resources Conservation and Development Commission, although from the start it was commonly referred to simply as the Energy Commission. The official name was later shortened to Energy Commission, and the shorter version will be used in this chapter.

5. Devore, Cotton, interviews.

6. *San Francisco Chronicle*, 7 September 1978, 16 (hereinafter cited as *SFC*); *Energy Users Report*, 9 January 1978; Tom Bradley to Edmund G. Brown, Jr., 16 January 1978, Governor Edmund G. Brown, Jr. papers, Dohney Memorial Library, Department of Special Collections, University of Southern California Archives, Los Angeles, carton C-3-7 (hereinafter cited as Brown papers). See also Pete Wilson and others to Edmund G. Brown, Jr., 30 January 1978, Brown papers, carton A-13-7; Alfred E. Alquist to Edmund G. Brown, Jr., 28 April 1978, Brown papers, carton F-31-9; and John Stull to Edmund G. Brown, jr., 25 January 1978, carton A-13-7.

7. *Washington Post*, 27 November 1977. The condemnation by state papers was even more strident. For example see *Sebastopol Times*, 15 December 1977; *Glendale News-Press*, 26 December 1977; *Hayward Review*, 29 December 1977; *Fontana Herald-News*, 21 December 1977; *San Jose Mercury-News*, 6 January 1978; *Los Angeles Herald-Examiner*, 6 January 1978; *Burbank Daily Review*, 2 February 1978; *San Diego Union*, 17 January, 22 January, and 31 October 1978 (hereinafter cited as *SDU*); *Los Angeles Times*, 25 January 1978 and 8 February 1978 (hereinafter cited as *LAT*).

8. *Palm Springs Desert Sun*, 31 January 1978.

9. *LAT*, 21 March 1983, IV-5; Cotton, interview; and James Cassie, interview by author, 13 January 1994, Sacramento, California, tape recording.

10. Christopher Flavin, "California's Nuclear Halt: A Moratorium That Has Paid Its Way," *New York Times*, 31 July 1983. Large generating facilities are almost completely absent from current construction plans. See George A. Perrault, "Downsizing Generation: Utility Plans for the 1990s," *Public Utilities Fortnightly* 126 (27 September 1990): 15–18.

11. Cassie, interview.

12. Undated memo, Huey Johnson personal papers, San Francisco, copy in possession of author.

13. Elizabeth Nichols, "U.S. Nuclear Power and the Success of the American Anti-Nuclear Movement," *Berkeley Journal of Sociology* 32 (1987): 184; James M. Jasper, *Nuclear Politics: Energy and the State in the United States, Sweden, and France* (Princeton: Princeton University Press, 1990), 207. These authors rightly stress the importance of poor economics, declining demand, and bad management in the cancellation of most nuclear plant orders. Theirs is the mistake of seizing on particular events and forcing them into a theoretical structure without understanding the historical context. For a study that recognizes the importance of nuclear opposition to the Sundesert case, see Christian Joppke, *Mobilizing against Nuclear Energy: A Comparison of Germany and the United States* (Berkeley: University of California Press, 1993), 69.

14. Robert Batinovich, interview by author, 4 January 1994, San Mateo, tape recording.

15. For the most recent formulation of state-centered theory see Theda Skocpol, *Protecting Soldiers and Mothers: The Political Origins of Social Policy in the United States Social Policy* (Cambridge: Harvard University Press, 1992), 41. See also Peter V. Evans, Dietrich Rueschemeyer, and Theda Skocpol, *Bringing the State Back In* (Cambridge: Cambridge University Press, 1985).

16. Government capacity was a key component that allowed Jerry Brown to oppose nuclear power. See Evans, Rueschemeyer, and Skocpol, *Bringing the State Back In*; Jasper, *Nuclear Politics*; and Joppke, *Mobilizing against Nuclear Energy*.

17. Legislators had sought to expand and encourage public participation in the Energy Commission in passing the Warren-Alquist Act. See California Energy Resources Conservation and Development Commission, *Public Participation in the California Energy Resources Conservation and Development Commission: The Role of the Administrative Advisor, and the Funding of Public Participants* (Sacramento: The Commission, September 1975); and Michael R. Eaton, "Nuclear Safety and Public Policy: One View," [1977?], Sierra Club California Legislative Office records, Bancroft Library, University of California, Berkeley, carton 4.

18. Later appointed to the Energy Commission, Moretti would become a pronuclear champion. Richard Maullin, interview by author, 16 and 23 January 1994, telephone tape recording.

19. For details of the 1974 governor's race, see Robert Pack, *Jerry Brown: The Philosopher-Prince* (New York: Stein and Day, 1978), chap. 4; and Roger Rapoport, *California Dreaming: The Political Odyssey of Pat and Jerry Brown* (Berkeley: Nolo Press, 1982), chap. 9.

20. Maullin, interview; and Pack *Jerry Brown*, chap. 4.

21. Pack, *Jerry Brown*, 72–73; Maullin, interview; Emilio Varanini, inter-

view by author, 2 July 1992 and 12 December 1993, Sacramento, tape recording; Seymour Goldstone, interview by author, 5 January 1993, Sacramento, tape recording. Maullin argues today that he was more independent of Brown than observers of the time perceived.

22. Jennifer Jennings, "Another Energy Crisis—A Malfunctioning Commission," *California Journal* 7 (March 1976): 91–93; and Maullin, interview.

23. Ronald Doctor, interview by author, 13 December 1993, telephone tape recording; James Harding, interview by author, 1 January 1994, El Cerrito, tape recording; John Zierold, interview by author, 23 June 1992, telephone tape recording; and Goldstone, Maullin, Varanini, interviews.

24. Varanini, interview; and Jennings, "Another Energy Crisis," 91–93.

25. Jasper, *Nuclear Politics*, 107–19.

26. Jasper, *Nuclear Politics*, chap. 7; and Neil de Marchi, "Energy Policy under Nixon: Mainly Putting Out Fires," in *Energy Policy in Perspective: Today's Problems, Yesterday's Solutions,* ed. Crawford D. Goodwin (Washington: Brookings Institution, 1981).

27. Maullin, interview, and Joel T. Kelly, interview by author, 13 January 1992, Sacramento, tape recording.

28. Goldstone and Kelly, interviews.

29. Maullin, interview.

30. Kelly and Goldstone, interviews.

31. Ron Doctor, letter to the author, 8 May 1995; and Goldstone, Kelly, Doctor, Varanini, Harding, Maullin, interviews.

32. Maullin and Doctor, interviews

33. Ron Doctor to the author, 8 May 1995.

34. The early forecast was completed in a rush, staffer Tom Kelly recalled, and did not hold up well to utility criticisms. Kelly, Varanini, and Doctor, interviews; and Doctor, letter to the author, 8 May 1995.

35. Ron Doctor and Gene Varanini believed the staffer was eliminated because of the forecast controversy. Others including Richard Maullin, Seymour Goldstone, and Thomas Kelly argue that there were other performance problems with the forecasting chief. See interviews with Doctor, Varanini, Maullin, Kelly, and Goldstone.

36. Edwin A. Koupal, Jr., to Edmund G. Brown, Jr., 21 November 1975, Brown papers, carton c-3–5; and Ed Salzman, "State's Report Card: A in water, F in Smog Control," *California Journal* 6 (December 1975): 427–29.

37. Jennings, "Another Energy Crisis," 91.

38. Varanini, interview. Environmentalists were particularly gratified by the trend within the commission toward "regulatory independence and technical competence." Eaton, "Nuclear Safety and Public Policy: One View."

39. Goldstone, Kelly, Maullin, and Varanini, interviews. Varanini credits himself for envisioning the eventual structure of the Warren-Alquist legislation that specified the missions of the Energy Commission. As indicated by Charles Warren at the time of the bill's passage, however, he understood very well that the commission had the power to undercut nuclear development. Charles Warren to Henry W. Kendall, 16 May 1973, Union of Concerned Scientists Archives,

Institute Archives and Special Collections, Massachusetts Institute of Technology, Cambridge, MA, carton 33 (hereinafter cited as UCS Archives).

40.   State-centered theory is useful in arguing this point. It is not sufficient to look upon government agencies as merely reflecting the demands of certain interest groups. The state has a degree of independence to pursue its own goals. The legislative intent of the Warren-Alquist Act in creating the Energy Commission established a certain trajectory that no band of commissioners could ignore. Evans, Rueschemeyer, and Skocpol, *Bringing the State Back In*, 1–37.

41.   Doctor to the author, 8 May 1995. Cogeneration is the production of electricity from the waste heat of industrial processes.

42.   Utilities had revised their peak demand forecasts downward from between 6 and 7 percent growth to about 5. Over the seventies, utilities would constantly revise their forecast downward under pressure from the California Energy Commission, who criticized the utilities for not taking conservation seriously enough in their estimates. Nationally, utilities showed even more reluctance to scale back forecasts, and usually reduced their forecasts by a percentage point. California, Resources Agency, *Energy Dilemma: California's 20-Year Power Plant Siting Plan* (Sacramento: Department of Water Resources, June 1973), 25; and California Energy Resources Conservation and Development Commission, *California Energy Trends and Choices,* vol. 2: *Electricity Forecasting and Planning* (Sacramento: The Commission, 1977); Arturo Gandara, *Electric Utility Decision-making and the Nuclear Option* (Santa Monica: Rand Corporation, 1977), 34; and *Energy User Reports* 231 (12 January 1978): 22–23.

43.   When simple trend analysis did not work, many utilities resorted to macroeconometric forecasting, which looked at a few variables such as household income, electricity pricing, and future economic growth. The turbulent growth patterns of the seventies made these models no more accurate than trend analysis. Analysts concluded that more detailed structural models that looked at each appliance in the average home were necessary. This "end-use" modeling was the pioneering approach of the California Energy Commission. See Lyna L. Wiggins, "Forecasting Demand for Electric Energy: Trends and Future Directions," Ph.D. diss., University of California, Berkeley, 1981, chap. 3 (quote, 42).

44.   The Energy Commissioin had begun its forecasting with an econometric approach. When this modeling did not work well, the commission started to use an "end-use" approach. Doctor had used this modeling in his Rand report and helped push the commission toward this technique. What Doctor lacked in political acumen he compensated for by his expertise.

45.   Ronald Doctor to the author, 8 May 1995; Goldstone, Kelly, and Doctor, interviews; California Energy Commission, *California Energy Trends and Choices;* and Wiggins, "Forecasting Demand." By the early eighties, end-use forecasting had gained wide currency. See John C. Sawhill and Lester P. Silverman, "Do Utilities Have Strategic Options? Ask the Customer," *Public Utilities Fortnightly* 111 (31 March 1983): 13–17.

46.   Craig R. Johnson, "Why Electric Power Growth Will Not Resume," *Public Utilities Fortnightly* 111 (14 April 1983): 19–22.

47.   California Energy Resources Conservation and Development Commission, *Staff Proposed Electricity Forecasting and Planning Report* (Sacramento: The Commission, October 1976), vol. 2, I-1–15; and Energy Commission, *California Energy Trends and Choices*, vol. 2.

48.   Goldstone and Cotton, interviews; and Wiggins, 43–46.

49.   Doctor to the author, 8 May 1995.

50.   Maullin, interview; Dan Walters, "Brown and Labor: Marriage on the Rocks," *California Journal* 8 (July 1977): 227–28; Paul Priolo, press release, 6 April 1978, Sierra Club records, Bancroft Library, University of California, Berkeley, carton 228.

51.   Rapoport, *California Dreaming*, 60.

52.   The term "New Age" evokes a number of images. More recently, it has been a term of derision for those involved in the human potential movement. In 1977, New Age had a broader meaning referring to an effort to create a movement comprising environmentalists, feminists, advocates of appropriate technology, the human potential movement, and spiritualists. It is this more encompassing definition that is used here. See Mark Satin, *New Age Politics: Healing Self and Society* (New York: Delta Books, 1979 [1978]).

53.   Maullin, interview; and Rapoport, *California Dreaming*, 153.

54.   Quoted in Rapoport, *California Dreaming*, 153, 160; and Maullin, interview.

55.   Stewart Brand, "Lessons," in *Stepping Stones: Appropriate Technology and Beyond*, ed. Lane de Moll and Gigi Coe (New York: Schocken Books, 1978), 11. This faith that America's troubles would bring a revolution in attitudes infuses most of the New Age literature and some environmental groups. In addition to *Stepping Stones*, see issues of *Co-Evolution Quarterly*, the Friends of the Earth's publication *Not Man Apart*, and Hugh Nash, ed., *Progress As If Survival Mattered: A Handbook for a Conserver Society* (San Francisco: Friends of the Earth, 1977).

56.   The groundbreaking work for this philosophy was Amory Lovins, "Energy Strategy: The Road Not Taken?" *Foreign Affairs* 55 (October 1976): 65–96. See also Lovins, *Soft Energy Paths: Towards a Durable Peace* (San Francisco: Friends of the Earth International, 1977).

57.   Rapoport, *California Dreaming*, 177; Ronald D. Doctor to Edmund G. Brown, 7 September 1977, Brown papers, carton F-38–10; and Hal Rubin, "Woodchips and Windmills," *California Journal* 9 (June 1978): 187–89.

58.   Cassie, interview.

59.   Eaton and Zierold, interviews.

60.   Ron Roach, "Senator Frankenstein," *California Journal* 9 (June 1978): 191.

61.   The utility industry was so confident of a waste disposal solution that they did not fight hard for the exemption of the San Joaquin Nuclear Project or Sundesert from the 1976 legislation. Varanini and Maullin, interviews; and P[?] to Gray [Davis], 17 May 1976, Brown papers, carton c-2–1.

62.   The Sierra Club recognized that it now had a working antinuclear majority on the Energy Commission and hoped to bring the nuclear debate to a successful close by 1978. John Zierold to Bob Rutemoeller and others, 17 November 1976, Sierra Club California Legislative Office records, carton 1.

63.   Lawrence O'Donnell, "New Legislation and the California Experience,"

28 March 1977, Sierra Club California Legislative Office records, carton 4. O'Donnell surmised that a 3–2 majority was now opposed to Sundesert,

64.   California Energy Commission, *California Energy Trends and Choices*, vol. 1.

65.   O'Donnell, "New Legislation and the California Experience." The Carter administration had recruited a number of environmentalists, including Charles Warren. See Jasper, *Nuclear Politics*, 188–92.

66.   *Nucleonics Week* 18 (15 September 1977): 11.

67.   Zierold and Doctor, interviews.

68.   "Utilities: Weak Point in the Energy Future," *Business Week* (20 January 1975): 46–54; John L. Campbell, *Collapse of an Industry: Nuclear Power and the Contradictions of U.S. Policy* (Ithaca: Cornell University Press, 1988), chap. 6; and Edison Electric Institute, *Economic Growth in the Future: The Growth Debate in National and Global Perspective* (New York: McGraw-Hill, 1976), 2, 287–306.

69.   *SDU*, 10 June 1976, 1; and Robert Batinovich, interview by author, 4 January 1994, San Mateo, tape recording. SDG&E sales were expected to grow by nearly 6 percent annually through 1985. Energy Commission, *California Energy Trends and Choices*, vol. 2, 54, 147.

70.   Energy Commission, *California Energy Trends and Choices*, vol. 1: *Toward a California Energy Strategy: Policy Overview* (Sacramento: The Commission, 1977), 135–38. This is exactly what happened to other utilities that continued with construction projects. The financial implications for these utilities were disastrous. For example, the small-sized Public Service of New Hampshire was the lead utility on the Seabrook nuclear project and eventually filed for chapter 11 protection. It is impossible to know what would have happened to SDG&E had it obtained financing, but the most probable scenario would have been a plant cancellation after hundreds of millions invested in plant equipment and site preparation. Considering their precarious financial position in the seventies, SDG&E's likely fate would have been a Southern California Edison takeover. For examples of utilities that did not stop construction soon enough, see Henry F. Bedford, *Seabrook Station: Citizen Politics and Nuclear Power* (Amherst: University of Massachusetts Press, 1990); and Joseph P. Tomain, *Nuclear Power Transformation* (Bloomington: Indiana University Press, 1987).

71.   Maullin, interview.

72.   Southern California Edison's interest in SDG&E culminated in a foiled takeover in the early nineties. See Anthony Perry, "Power Plays: Can San Diego Stop the Edison Invasion?" *California Journal* 21 (February 1990): 119–21; and Perry, "PUC Pulls Plug on Edison Power Play," *California Journal* 22 (August 1991): 359–61.

73.   Batinovich, Cotton, Cassie, and Devore, interviews.

74.   In the case of the San Joaquin Nuclear Project, this drain system was not yet built and would have required farmers to build and finance part of the system themselves. Sundesert could simply have tapped into the Palo Verde outfall drain where 33,300 acre-feet of wastewater were available.

75.   Bookman-Edmonston Engineering, Inc., *Special Environmental Assessment of the Water Supply Phase for the Sundesert Nuclear Project* (Glendale: Bookman-Edmonston Engineering, 1974).

76. The extensive efforts made by SDG&E are well documented. See San Diego Gas and Electric Corporation Desert Nuclear Project in Blythe, 1974–75 files, California State Library, Sacramento, 3 vol. (hereinafter cited as Desert Project files). See also Cassie, interview. SDG&E's success with the Mexican American community highlights the difficulty that environmentalists had in recruiting minority groups. SDG&E representatives found that the Mexican American Political Association was more concerned with winning commitments for power plant jobs and improved funding for their schools than safety. Economic arguments had a telling effect among less affluent groups. See G. A. Bishop to W. A. Zitlau and others, 27 February 1974, Desert Project files.

77. G. A. Bishop to W. A. Zitalu and others, 4 March 1974, Desert Project files. Opposition consisted of a few individuals. There were only small organized groups opposed to Sundesert and not on the scale of those fighting the San Joaquin Nuclear Project in Kern County. *Daily Enterprise,* 14 March 1975, C5. See also Desert Project files.

78. *SDU,* 29 September 1976, 1; and Energy Commission *California Energy Trends and Choices,* vol. 1, 50–56.

79. Energy Commission, "Preliminary Report," 14 April 1976, I-21–26; *SDU,* 12 June 1976, 4, 16 July 1976, 14 December 1976, B1: and 15 December 1976, B1. An influential critique of nuclear economics and reliability had come out in 1976. See Charles Komanoff, *Power Plant Performance: Nuclear and Coal Capacity Factors and Economics* (New York: Council on Economic Priorities, 1976).

80. This form of financing was as unpopular for ratepayers as it was popular in utility circles. It was indicative of the rate revolt that was stirring that Missouri voters passed a referendum in 1976 that prohibited CWIP financing. States including California were acting to prevent such financing.

81. *SDU,* 10 December 1976, B6, and 12 July 1977, B4. Denial of rate requests hurt the utilities' construction plans in two ways. It reduced their income that could be used for construction. It also hindered their ability to raise capital through bonds or stock issues, since these offerings depended on a healthy balance sheet. SDG&E's Moody's bond rating had eroded to BBB, the lowest of "investment grade" ratings. *SDU,* 27 April 1977, B4, 22 July 1977, A15, and 5 October 1977, B4.

82. SDG&E senior vice president Robert L. Meyer explained, "If the Energy Commission finds Sundesert is consistent with additional need requirements, there should be no basis for assuming the PUC would be unresponsive to SDG&E's financial needs during construction." *SDU,* 22 July 1977, A15.

83. *SDU,* 10 February 1977, 1.

84. *SDU* 12 March 1977, B1.

85. *SDU,* 16 April 1977, B1; California, Energy Resources Conservation and Development Commission, *Preliminary Report on the San Diego Gas and Electric Company's Notice of Intention to Seek Certification for the Sundesert Nuclear Project,* 14 April 1977, I-9. The commission believed that oil was clearly not competitive. Coal appeared a feasible alternative but was still an economic risk owing to the difficulties of shipping fuel great distances. *Preliminary Report,* I-36–40.

86. Of the three bills passed in 1976, only the waste disposal bill had any

real significance. The feasibility study of placing nuclear reactors underground had no real influence since there was no more new construction in California. The requirement for spent fuel reprocessing technology was rendered moot by the federal government's determination that this technology was not necessary for the adequate functioning of the nuclear fuel cycle.

87.   *SDU*, 19 August 1977, A1.

88.   *SDU*, 11 August 1977, B12.

89.   *SDU*, 26 April 1977, B4, 29 April 1977, B14, 30 November 1977, B6, and 13 November 1977, A20.

90.   "Sundesert Nuclear Project (Blythe)," Sierra Club records, carton 217.

91.   In its preliminary report, the Energy Commission accepted SDG&E's estimate of need but noted, "The staff did, however, emphasize that [none of the demand forecasts] explicitly considers the impacts of various conservation measures upon demand . . . and thus that the company's projected need for additional capacity during that period may well be eroded as a consequence of a more comprehensive analysis of forecasted demand. In the absence of such analysis, however, the staff accepted the company's estimate." Energy Commission, *Preliminary Report*, I-9.

92.   Eaton, Maullin, and Varanini, interviews.

93.   Varanini told McCarthey that with the new language he did not believe SDG&E could win approval. Telephone conversation with Gene Varanini by author, 12 April 1994, notes of conservation.

94.   Eaton, Devore, and Maullin interviews; and *SDU* 21 October 1977 B4.

95.   *SDU* 27 August 1977 A17.

96.   The other owners of the project included the Los Angeles Department of Water and Power and a number of smaller municipal utilities in Southern California.

97.   Energy Commission, "Final Report," appendix C; Energy Commission, "Final Decision," 21 December 1977, California Energy Commission, Sundesert Nuclear Project, docket 76-NOI-2 Sacramento; Ronald D. Doctor to commissioners, 21 December 1977, Brown papers, carton A-13–7; and *SDU*, 22 December 1977 A10.

98.   Energy Commission, *Status of Nuclear Fuel Reprocessing Spent Fuel Storage and High-Level Waste Disposal: Draft Report* (Sacramento: The Commission, 11 January 1978), 117–220.

99.   Energy Commission, *Status of Nuclear Fuel Reprocessing*, 24. Emphasis in the original. The study was, to say the least, prescient. As the report noted, the problem was political as well as technical. Of the thirteen states designated as appropriate for the siting of a waste repository, four already had laws on their books restricting disposal or shipment of waste into the state. The report further concluded that public opposition would be a critical factor even if the repository was located on federal lands. See Energy Commission, *Status of Nuclear Fuel Reprocessing*, 184–85.

100.   "1985 Deadline for Waste Site Won't Be Met, DOE Study Confirms," *Energy User Reports* 240 (16 March 1978): 5–7.

101.   *SDU*, 17 January 1978, B6.

102. *SDU,* 12 January 1978, A9.

103. *Sacramento Bee,* 25 January 1978; and Cassie, interview.

104. Energy Commission, *Report to the Legislature: AB 1852—Alternatives to a Sundesert Nuclear Project: Final Report,* California Energy Commission, docket 77-NL-1 (February 1978), xviii.

105. Ron Knecht and Bob Logan to Jim Walker, Mark Urban, and Les White, 9 December 1977, Brown papers, carton C-3-7.

106. Energy Commission, *Report to the Legislature: AB 1852,* vol. 1, 51–79.

107. *Sacramento Bee,* 25 January 1978.

108. *SDU,* 13 January 1978, A1.

109. Hal Rubin, "Resources Chief Johnson—Global Dreamer, Land-Bank Zealot," *California Journal* 9 (March 1978): 80; and Huey Johhson, interview by author, 22 December 1993, San Francisco, tape recording.

110. Larry Liebert, "The S. F. Zen Center—Brown's Recruitment Depot," *California Journal* 9 (January 1978): 7.

111. Johnson, interview.

112. "Huey Johnson," *Whole Earth Review* 61 (Winter 1988): 64.

113. Sierra Club lobbyist John Zierwold believed that more was accomplished for the environment under Ronald Reagan than under Jerry Brown and Huey Johnson. This he attributes in part to Johnson's inability to work with the legislature. John H. Zierold, "Environmental Lobbyist in California's Capital, 1965–1984," interview by Ann Lage, 1984, Bancroft Library, University of California, Berkeley, 154, 156.

114. David E. Pesonen to Huey Johnson, Governor Brown, 25 October 1977, Brown papers, carton A-13-7.

115. "Possible Administration Policy on Sundesert: Development of Alternatives to Sundesert," 20 December 1977, Brown papers, carton A-13-7.

116. "Possible Administration Policy on Sundesert," [December 1977], Brown papers, carton A-13-7; and "California Energy Development Program: Overview," 23 December 1977, Huey Johnson personal papers, copy in possession of the author.

117. California, Department of Conservation, press release, [29 December 1977], Huey Johnson papers.

118. Tom Quinn to Richard Maullin, 22 December 1977, in Energy Commission, *Report to Legislature: AB 1852,* supporting document 24.

119. Ron Robie to Gray Davis, 24 November 1976, Brown papers, carton A-13-7; and Ronald B. Robie, "The State Department of Water Resources, 1975–1983," interview by Malca Chall, 1989, Bancroft Library, University of California, Berkeley, 28.

120. Jim Harding noted that the antinuclear movement pushed the idea of coal, in part, as a way of stalling both nuclear and coal. Harding for one was confident that if such proposals could stall nuclear construction a few more years, the economics of nuclear would eventually catch up with it. This was exactly the strategy Michael McCloskey proposed in 1974 to the Sierra Club (see chapter 3). See also Harding, interview; Robie, "State Department of Water Resources," 29; California, Resources Agency, press release, 2 March 1978, Brown

papers, carton F-31–10; and Ronald B. Robie to Huey D. Johnson, 8 February 1978, Brown papers, carton C-2–3.

121.　Nancy Berrand, "The Energy Conflict over the Ages Old Fuel: Coal," *California Journal* 10 (March 1979): 91–95; and California Energy Commission, *Energy Futures for California: Two Scenarios, 1978–2000* (Sacramento: The Commission, September 1980), chaps. 9 and 12.

122.　The Brown administration conspiracy theory was best articulated in Otto Kreisher, "The Sundesert Issue: Nuclear Safety or Brown Politics?" *California Journal* 9 (March 1978): 84. The *San Diego Union* devoted a phenomenal amount of printed space to the Sundesert episode, including an article that purported to prove that there was an "orchestrated campaign" by Brown to stop the plant. *SDU*, 22 January 1978, C3. SDG&E offered its own version in SDG&E, *California Energy Commission's Reversals Regarding Alternatives to the Sundesert Nuclear Project, June 1976–February 1978* (March 1978), California State Library, Sacramento.

123.　Maullin, interview; and conversation by the author with Edmund G. Brown, Jr., San Francisco.

124.　*Sacramento Bee*, 14 April 1978.

125.　Pete Wilson and other to Edmund G. Brown, Jr., 30 January 1978, Brown papers, carton A-13–7; Tom Bradley to Brown, 16 January 1978 and 7 February 1978, carton C-3–7.

126.　Ron Roach, "Senator Frankenstein," *California Journal* 9 (June 1978): 190.

127.　*SDU*, 27 March 1978, A1.

128.　Wilson Clark to Governor Brown, Dick Silberman, 4 April 1978, Brown papers, carton A-8–2; and Community Energy Action Network, *Newsletter*, 1 March 1978, Friends of the Earth records, Bancroft Library, University of California, Berkeley, carton 41.

129.　Some environmentalists were pleasantly surprised by Brown's "inordinately tough stand" when the governor had a history of "rarely taking such firm positions." Ron Rudolph to Jim Harding, 14 March 1978, Friends of the Earth records, carton 41.

130.　*SDU*, 5 February 1978, B1.

131.　*SDU*, 12 February 1978, C4.

132.　*Sacramento Bee*, 14 April 1978.

133.　*Wall Street Journal*, 28 February 1978, 14. On the PUC's efforts to overhaul electric pricing policy, see Douglas D. Anderson, *Regulatory Politics and Electric Utilities: A Case Study in Political Economy* (Boston: Auburn House, 1981), 135–65.

134.　*LAT*, 30 March 1978, 1, 9 April 1978, VI-1, and 3 May 1978, 31; and Batinovich, interview.

135.　Nichols, "U.S. Nuclear Power," 184; and Jasper, *Nuclear Politics*, 207.

136.　*SDU*, 12 April 1978, 15 April 1978, 1, 3 May 1978, 1; 8 June 1979, 3; *LAT*, 30 March 1978, 1, 7 April 1978, II-8, 9 April 1978, VI-1, 11 April 1978, 1, and 24 March 1983, IV-1; and Cassie, interview.

137.　New Hampshire was embroiled in its own nuclear controversy at Seabrook Station. *SDU* 29 March 1978, A4; and Paul Priolo, press release, 6 April 1978, Sierra Club records, carton 228.

138.   *LAT,* 8 April 1978, 20, and 15 April 1978, 28.

139.   *LAT,* 12 May 1978, 28. Younger was sure enough that energy would be an important political issue that he enlisted an advisory council of scientists including Edward Teller. The council recommended that conservation and nuclear power be the underpinnings of a state environmental policy. The council further charged that unnamed politicians were using fear in an unjustified attempt to feed public anxieties. Evelle Younger, "The Attorney General's Advisory Council on Energy and the Future of California," May 1978, Huey Johnson papers.

140.   *SDU,* 15 April 1978, A7.

141.   Roach, "Senator Frankenstein," 191; Bruce E. Jones, "The Politics of Regulation: Individual Rights v. Public Good," *California Journal* 10 (July 1979): 250; and California Council for Environmental and Economic Balance, *Environment and the Economy Newsletter* (August 1978): 1.

142.   By 1977, the number of bills passed by states challenging federal nuclear authority had mushroomed. See J. R. Wargo, "States Passing Nuclear Laws with Unprecedented Frequency," *Nuclear Industry* 24 (June 1977): 24–7.

143.   Richard Maullin to Marcus Rowden, 27 January 1977, Nuclear Regulatory Commission, docket 50–582 (Sundesert, Units 1 & 2), microfiche. See also Maullin to Rowden, 6 April 1977; Ben C. Rusche to Maullin, 11 March 1977; and Edson G. Case to Maullin, 19 May 1977. The commission also fought federal legislation aimed at restricting state power to regulate reactors. *Sacramento Bee,* 23 August 1977.

144.   The gravity of Maullin's actions was not lost on the nuclear industry. See O'Donnell, "New Legislation and the California Experience."

145.   *LAT,* 26 April 1978, 3; *SDU* 26 April 1978; *Sacramento Bee,* 21 February 1978. Younger refused to allow public inspection of the initial drafts of the attorney general's opinion on nuclear bills. Suits later forced his office to divulge these documents. They showed that all five of Younger's deputies believed the bills were constitutional. Only Younger disagreed. See Laurence H. Tribe, "California Declines the Nuclear Gamble: Is Such a State Choice Preempted?" *Ecology Law Quarterly* 7 (1979): 684, note 23.

146.   Environmentalists had always seen this issue of citizen rights as part of their fight against nuclear power. See Eaton, "Nuclear Safety and Public Policy: One View."

Chapter 6. Stick It in L.A.! Community Control and Nuclear Power in the Central Valley

1.   Jim Neufeld, interview by author, 2 August 1993, Wasco, California, tape recording.

2.   Neufeld, interview.

3.   In 1977, Vermonth and New Hampshire towns approved a nonbinding nuclear construction and transportation ban. In 1970, citizens in Eugene, Oregon, voted for a four-year *delay* of a proposed nuclear plant. Bruce Resenthal, "New England Townspeople Ban Nuclear," *Critical Mass Journal* 3 (April 1977):

1, 12; and Daniel Pope, "'We Can Wait. We Should Wait.' Eugene's Nuclear Power Controversy, 1968–1970," *Pacific Historical Review* 59 (August 1990): 349–73.

   4.   Joan Didion, *Slouching towards Bethlehem* (New York: Pocket Books, 1981), 173.

   5.   Robert McDuff to the author, 29 April 1996; *Bakersfield Californian,* 11 January 1996 (hereinafter cited as *BC*); Joseph Fontaine, interview by author, 21 August 1993, Tehachapi, California, tape recording; *Los Angeles Times,* 12 July 1994 A1 and 17 July 1994, B1 (hereinafter cited as *LAT,*); Gerald Haslam, *The Other California: The Great Central Valley in Life and Letters* (Reno: University of Nevada Press, 1994), 184; and Stephen Johnson, ed., *The Great Central Valley: California's Heartland* (Berkeley: University of California Press, 1993), 136, 165, 178. Cruel satire of Kern County, depicting it as a center for fascism and ignorance, survived long after the Dust Bowl migrations. Native sons of Kern have helped the image along. See Larry Welz and Larry Sutherland, *Bakersfield Kountry Komics* (Berkeley: Last Gasp, 1973).

   6.   *LAT,* 12 July 1994, A1, and 17 July 1994 B1; Fontaine interview.

   7.   *LAT,* 12 July 1994, A1. The author informally polled a class at San Francisco State University to write down any words they associated with the word "Bakersfield." The results from 58 students: (1) rural stereotypes (i.e., farmers, hicks, redneck, Okies, white trash), 71% (2) hot, dry, flat, ugly, 53% (3) boring, isolated, 31% and (4) conservative, 17%.

   8.   Maureen McCloud, "The Kern Brand of Politics—Conservative, Populist, Humorless," *California Journal* 9 (July 1978): 231–32; *BC,* 24 November 1974; Jack Pandol, interview by author, 4 August 1993, Delano, tape recording; and Haslam, *Other California,* 64. This superiority extends even to smog. One editor in Bakersfield argued that Kern County smog was somehow more wholesome than Los Angeles'. *BC,* 24 November 1974.

   9.   Trice Harvey, interview by author, 17 August 1993, Sacramento, tape recording.

   10.   The best works on Los Angeles' contentious relationship with its neighbors are Mike Davis, *City of Quartz: Excavating the Future in Los Angeles* (New York: Vintage, 1992), and John Walton, *Western Times and Water Wars: State, Culture, and Rebellion in California* (Berkeley: University of California Press, 1992).

   11.   Norris Hundley, Jr., *The Great Thirst: Californians and Water, 1770s–1990s* (Berkeley: University of California Press, 1992), 291–92, 303.

   12.   Pandol, interview. Such fears were justified since the state gave preference to cities over agriculture in ultimate rights to water. Hundley, *Great Thirst,* 303.

   13.   Harvey, interview.

   14.   The following discussion of Kern's political culture and its populist links is drawn from James Nelson Gregory, *American Exodus: The Dust Bowl Migration and Okie Culture in California* (New York: Oxford University Press, 1989), chap. 8; and Michael Kazin, *The Populist Persuasion: An American History* (New York: Basic Books, 1995). See also Jonathan Reider, "The Rise of the Silent Majority," in *The Rise and Fall of the New Deal Order, 1930–1980,* ed. Steve Fraser and Gary Gerstle (Princeton: Princeton University Press, 1989): 243–68; Alan Craw-

ford, *Thunder on the Right: The "New Right" and the Politics of Resentment* (New York: Pantheon Books, 1980), chap. 3 and 12; William A. Rusher, *The Rise of the Right* (New York: William Morrow, 1984); and Kevin P. Phillips, *Post-Conservative America: People, Politics, and Ideology in a Time of Crisis* (New York: Vintage books, 1983), chap. 3 and 9.

15.   Kevin Phillips had first argued that the New Right was a significant break with eastern establishment conservatism. Jerome Himmelstein has countered that the New Right's populism was simply a facade for the old version repackaged in new rhetoric. I agree with Michael Kazin's critique of Himmelstein that rhetoric can bring about significant changes when it speaks to deeply held resentments and mobilizes new constituencies. See Jerome L. Himmelstein, *To the Right: The Transformation of American Conservatism* (Berkeley: University of California Press, 1990), 92–93; and Michael Kazin, "The Grass-Roots Right: New Histories of U.S. Conservatism in the Twentieth Century," *American Historical Review* 97 (February 1992): 148.

16.   Kazin, *Populist Persuasion*, 4–5; 221–44. On the role of race in conservative populism, see Jonathan Reider, *Canarsie: The Jews and Italians of Brooklyn against Liberalism* (Cambridge: Harvard University Press, 1985); and Thomas B. Edsall with Mary D. Edsall, *Chain Reaction: The Impact of Race, Rights, and Taxes on American Politics* (New York: Norton, 1991).

17.   Kazin, *Populist Persuasion*, 229–42; and Fontaine, interview.

18.   Barry M. Goldwater, *Goldwater* (New York: Doubleday, 1988), 116.

19.   Howard Lamar claimed the West's unique region and resistance to the federal government made it more regionally conscious than at any time since the Populists. It was becoming a "regional villain," creating national disunity. Howard R. Lamar, "Persistent Frontier: The West in the Twentieth Century," *Western Historical Quarterly* 4 (January 1973): 6, 20. See also Michael McGerr, "Is There a Twentieth-Century West?," in *Under an Open Sky: Rethinking America's Western Past*, ed. William Cronon, George Miles, and Jay Gitlin (New York: W. W. Norton, 1992), 250–52.

20.   Gregory, *American Exodus*, 190, 218–21, and 242–46.

21.   James N. Gregory, "Dust Bowl Legacies: The Okie Impact on California, 1939–1989," *California History* 68 (Fall, 1989): 84–85.

22.   Michael W. Donley et al., *Atlas of California* (Culver City, CA: Pacific Book Center, 1979): 56–57.

23.   McCloud, "Kern Brand of Politics," 232.

24.   Haslam, *Other California*, 184; *LAT* 9 August 1992, B3, and 27 April 1995, A1.

25.   James Payne, interview by author, 20 January 1997, notes; Kazin, *Populist Persuasion*, 12–16; and Alan Brinkley, "Roots," *New Republic*, 27 July 1993, 44.

26.   Quoted in Gregory, *American Exodus*, 243–44.

27.   Carey McWilliams, *Factories in the Field* (Boston: Little, Brown, 1940), 262; Gregory, *American Exodus*, 220–21 and 242–44; Walter Goldschmidt, *As You Sow* (New York: Harcourt Brace, 1947), 22; and Haslam, *Other California*, 4–5.

28.   Jim Neufeld, statement to the Farm Bureau, 1 March 1978, Jim Neufeld papers, Wasco, emphasis added. Agribusiness had adapted the agrarian image for its own purposes in political lobbying and policy debate. Karen J. Bradley,

"Agrarian Ideology and Agricultural Policy: California Grangers and the Post-World War II Farm Policy Debate," *Agricultural History* 69 (Spring 1995): 240–56; Lowell McKirgan, "Taking America's Pulse," *U.S. News & World Report*, 28 May 1979, 27; and Hundley, *Great Thirst*, 291.

29. Gregory, *American Exodus*, 170; and Payne, interview, 20 January 1997. On localistic rhetoric, see Matthew glass, "The Rhetoric of Religious Localism: Mormon and Western Shoshone Opposition to the MX," in *The Atomic West*, ed. John Findlay and Bruce Hevly (Seattle: University of Washington Press, forthcoming).

30. "Initiative Makes a Big Comeback as Groups Seek to Bypass Legislature," *California Journal* 3 (August 1972): 229–30; and David D. Schmidt, *Citizen Lawmakers: The Ballot Initiative Revolution* (Philadelphia: Temple University Press, 1989).

31. For a history that discusses the rise of irrigation districts see Donald J. Pisani, *From the Family Farm to Agribusiness: The Irrigation Crusade in California and the West, 1850–1931* (Berkeley: University of California Press, 1984).

32. Water districts allowed local agriculture a large degree of autonomy. Arthur Maass and Raymond L. Anderson, . . .*And the Desert Shall Rejoice: Conflict, Growth, and Justice in Arid Environments* (Cambridge: MIT Press, 1978); and Donald J. Pisani, "The Irrigation District and the Federal Relationship: Neglected Aspects of Water History," in *The Twentieth Century West: Historical Interpretations*, ed. Gerald D. Nash and Richard W. Etulain (Albuquerque: University of New Mexico Press, 1989): 257–98.

33. Oildale rejected a 1972 antipollution, antinuclear initiative by a 7 to 1 margin, while in the farm communities of Shafter, Taft, and Wasco the initiative garnered only about 15 percent. By comparison, in China Lake and Ridgecrest, two military and scientific communities near the China Lake Naval Weapons Research Center, the initiative gained 34 and 27 percent respectively. A coastal protection bill later that year picked up only 26 percent in Oildale and about 30 percent in those farm towns. China Lake passed the measure with 64 percent while Ridgecrest nearly did so with 46 percent. See 1972 Primary and General Election Results, Kern County Elections Department, Bakersfield; Fontaine, interview; Joel Kotkin, "New Foes of Nuclear Power: The Farmers," *Outside* (May 1978), clipping, Neufeld papers. Agriculture was a strident environmental opponent and very pronuclear. Lettie M. Wenner and Manfred W. Wenner, "Nuclear Policy and Public Participation," *American Behavior Scientist* 22 (Nov./Dec. 1978): 301; Samuel P. Hays, *Beauty, Health, and Permanence: Environmental Politics in the United States, 1955–1985* (Cambridge: Cambridge University Press, 1987), 288–97; and Donley, *Atlas of California*, 56–57.

34. *LAT*, 10 June 1994, A1, and 19 June 1994, A3.

35. As historian Samuel Hays demonstrated in his study of the modern environmental movement, suburban expansion, greater disposable wealth, education, and the rise of service industries encouraged particular elements of society to value physical and spiritual amenities whose monetary value was unclear, such as greater personal freedom and health, a protected ecosystem, and a pleasing environment that was scenic and free from pollution. These values gained popularity especially among young, well-educated white Americans

who did not share their parents' concern with economic growth and techno-logical advancement. When searching for solutions to the harmful effects of modern society such as pollution, these new environmentalists argued for a re-turn to simpler lifestyles, local amenities, and community power. Hays, *Beauty, Health, and Permanence*, 1–39, 490, 527–43; and Ronald Inglehart, *The Silent Rev-olution: Changing Values and Political Styles among Western Publics* (Princeton: Princeton University Press, 1977).

36.   While public support for nuclear power fluctuated before the 1979 Three Mile Island accident, support for local power plants began to decline with the spate of 1976 antinuclear initiatives and fell below opposition in 1978. William L. Rankin, Stanley M. Nealey, and Barbara D. Melber, "Overview of National At-titudes toward Nuclear Energy: A Longitudinal Analysis," in *Public Reaction to Nuclear Power: Are There Critical Masses?*, ed. William R. Fruendenburg and Eu-gene A. Rosa (Boulder: Westview Press, 1984), 52–55; and "California: One Down, Many to Go," *Nuclear Industry* 23 (June 1976): 32.

37.   Left-wing activists made a far less successful attempt to use populist rhetoric to unite a disparate coalition of minorities, poor, and middle-class whites. Championed by Ralph Nader and Tom Hayden's Campaign for Eco-nomic Democracy, left-wing activism did share with conservative populism a distaste for the power elite and large institutions, and worshiped community co-operation. The left diverged in its emphasis on economic democracy, class an-tagonisms, and cultural diversity. Compare the two versions in Tom Hayden, *The American Future: New Visions beyond Old Frontiers* (Boston: South End Press, 1980); Harry C. Boyte, *The Backyard Revolution: Understanding the New Citizen Movement* (Philadelphia: Temple University Press, 1982); Boyte and Frank Riess-man, eds., *The New Populism: The Politics of Empowerment* (Philadelphia: Temple University Press, 1986); Richard A. Viguerie, *The New Right: We're Ready to Lead* (Falls Church, VA: Viguerie Company, 1981); Robert W. Whitaker, ed., *The New Right Papers* (New York: St. Martin's Press, 982); and Kazin, *Populist Persua-sion*, 275.

38.   Industry and political observers attributed the vote to the unique ri-valry between Kern and Los Angeles. "LADWP Ends Lead Role in San Joaquin Venture," *Nuclear Industry* 25 (April 1978): 19; and McCloud, "Kern Brand of Pol-itics," 232.

39.   *San Francisco Chronicle*, 20 January 1973, 1 (hereinafter cited as *SFC*); *BC*, 3 June 1975, 13; Robert Phillips, "San Joaquin Nuclear Project: A California Power Resource for the 1980s," presentation to the Public Information Forum, Elizabeth Apfelberg papers, Mandeville Department of Special Collections, University of California, San Diego, box 2. State-sponsored studies indicated that it was not the Coastal Commission but seismic and population densities that restricted all but about fifty miles of California's thousand miles of coast from nuclear construction. California, Resources Agency, *Energy Dilemma: Cal-ifornia's 20-Year Power Plant Siting Plan* (Sacramento: State of California, June 1973); and Martin Goldsmith, *Siting Nuclear Power Plants in California: The Near-Term Alternatives* (Pasadena: Environmental Quality Laboratory, July 1973, 1.

40.   *SFC*, 20 January 1973, 1.

41. John Walton, *Western Times and Water Wars*, 244.

42. Donald Worster, *Rivers of Empire: Water, Aridity, and the Growth of the American West* (New York: Pantheon Books, 1985), 319–23; California Department of Water Resources. "Speech of John R. Teerink: The Potential for Waste Water Reclamation in California," presented to Pacific Southwest Inter-Agency Committee, Water Resources Center Archives, University of California, Berkeley, 6 March 1969; and John R. Teerink to Harold Sipe, 27 June 1972, United States Atomic Energy Commission/Nuclear Regulatory Commission, docket 50–398 (Mendocino Power Plants Units 1 and 2), microfiche.

43. William Dunlap to William R. Gianelli, 24 November 1971, John R. Teerink to Harold Sipe, 27 June 1972, William R. Johnson to John R. Teerink, 27 July 1972, AEC/NRC docket 50–398; California Department of Water Resources, "Speech of John R. Teerink, Water and Energy Relationship in California," presented to the Advisory Council of the University of California, Water Resources Center Archives, University of California, Berkeley, 17 January 1972; and Department of Water Resources, San Joaquin District, *Potential Use of Agricultural Water for Powerplant Cooling* (Sacramento: State of California, September 1972).

44. *LAT*, 16 March 1973; "Power from the Desert," *Aqueduct News* 40 (March 1973): 1, 11; and *Fresno Bee*, 11 October 1972 and 21 December 1972.

45. *LAT*, 5 April 1972, 2, and 22 December 1972, 2; *Fresno Bee*, 11 October 1972, D10. In the Tulare case, it was estimated that opposition in the general public was near 90 percent and there was substantial resistance from the county board of supervisors. Many of the issues that would emerge in Kern, water use, ground fogging, questionable tax benefits, and wastewater benefit, had already been brought out in Tulare. See *LAT*, 2 August 1972, 1, and *Porterville CA Recorder*, 9 November 1971, 1.

46. A. Giambusso to L. A. Shea, 30 November 1973, Nuclear Regulatory Commission Project No. 499 (San Joaquin Nuclear Project), microfiche (hereinafter cited as Project 499).

47. *BC*, 10 July and 11 July 1973.

48. *San Jose Mercury-News*, 8 December 1973; City Council of Wasco, Resolution 551, 15 July 1974, Neufeld papers; *LAT*, 9 September 1974; *BC*, 3 December 1973; and *Fresno Bee*, 11 December 1973, E7.

49. Harvey, interview, and Kotkin, "New Foes of Nuclear Power." Compare to John Steinbeck, *The Grapes of Wrath* (New York: Viking Press, 1939), 45.

50. For the Owens Valley controversy, see William L. Kahrl, *Water and Power: The Conflict over Los Angeles' Water Supply in Owens Valley* (Berkeley: University of California Press, 1982).

51. The references to the Owen Valley by plant opponents are numerous. See assorted campaign literature in Neufeld papers; James Payne, interview by author, 19 September 1993, Wasco, tape recording; Florence H. Page to chairman of the AEC, 17 June 1974, Project 499; *Stockton Record*, 7 May 1975; *BC*, 20 and 27 July 1976; and Pandol and Neufeld, interviews.

52. This fear of Kern's enslavement to Los Angeles waste was evident in a majority of the interviews done for this article. See especially Neufeld, Harvey, and Payne, interviews. Groundwater was the traditional source for Wasco agri-

culture until the arrival of California Water Project. Department of Water Resources, *Report on Proposed Semitropic Water Storage District: Kern County* (June 1958), 8–14.

53. Neufeld and Fontaine, interviews.

54. Neufeld, interview.

55. Florence Page to chairman of AEC, 17 June 1974, Project 499; *BC*, 1 November 1977; *Stockton Record*, 7 May 1975; George Ballis to Jim Neufeld, 14 September 1974, Neufeld papers; Neufeld, interview; and *Wasco News*, 13–19 October 1976. LADWP arrogance was noted by nearly every opponent interviewed by the author.

56. Jim Neufeld, Elo Fabbri, Ordell Portwood to Semi-Tropic Area Ranchers, 12 July 1974, Neufeld papers; and *Wasco News*, 31 July 1974.

57. Speeches by Jim Neufeld, 10 June 1975, May, 27 July, and 14 October 1976; Jim Neufeld to Jack Pickett, 25 March 1977; and speech by Elo Fabbri, 27 July 1976, Neufeld papers.

58. Brian Balogh, *Chain Reaction: Expert Debate and Public Participation in American Commercial Nuclear Power, 1945–1975* (Cambridge: Cambridge University Press, 1991), 265–85.

59. George Hogerg, *Pluralism by Design: Environmental Policy and the American Regulatory State* (New York: Praeger, 1992); and David Vogel, "The 'New' Social Regulation in Historical and Comparative Perspective," in *Regulation in Perspective: Historical Essays*, ed. Thomas K. McCraw (Cambridge: Harvard University Press, 1981). On the democratization of power plant siting regulation, see Dennis W. Ducsik, ed., *Public Involvement in Energy Facility Planning: The Electric Utility Experience* (Boulder: Westview Press, 1986).

60. Typical of the nation at large, Kern enjoyed its greatest job growth in service sector jobs. In the seventies, employment rose 48 percent, but service sector jobs rose 63 percent. In professional employment the increases were more dramatic as health, education, and other professional services jumped by 81, 87, and 116 percent, respectively. United States Department of Commerce, Bureau of the Census, *1970 Census of the Population, General Social and Economic Characteristics*, part 6, California table 123, 1053–57; Bureau of the Census, *1980 Census of the Population, General Social and Economic Characteristics* part 6, California table 178, 1169–74; and McCloud, "Kern Brand of Politics," 231.

61. Frederic and Joy Lane, interview by author, 4 August 1993, Bakersfield, tape recording; Fontaine, interview; *Fresno Bee*, 18 February 1974; and *BC*, 22 March 1974. On Fontaine's views about nuclear power, see Joseph Fontaine and Phillip Berry, "Nuclear Safety Initiative," *Sierra Club Bulletin* 61 (March 1976): 21–22. The Kern environmental team was part of a statewide campaign including the Sierra Club Legal Defense Fund and the California Attorney General to expand the role of the EIR process. A critical ruling occurred in 1972 in the case of *Friends of Mammoth v. Board of Supervisors of Mono County* that required government agencies such as LADWP and private firms to provide EIRs for their projects. Robert Andrews, Jr., "Aftermammoth: Friends of Mammoth and the Amended California Environmental Quality Act," *Ecology Law Quarterly* 3 (1973): 349–89.

62.   Joy Lane to Art Gafke, 6 July 1974, Joseph Fontaine personal papers, Tehachapi, CA (hereinafter cited as Fontaine papers); and Joy Lane to Don May, 22 March 1975, Friends of the Earth records, Bancroft Library, University of California, Berkeley, carton 41. Other groups who were not environmentalists but had antinuclear motives were the League of Women Voters, the American Association of University women, and the Kern Comprehensive Health Planning Association. Joy Lane to Joyce [?], 20 July 1973, Fontaine papers; Frederic A. Lane to Kern County Board of Supervisors, 19 October 1973, and Lane to secretary of the commission, 18 January 1974, San Joaquin Nuclear Project files, Bakersfield Public Library, Local History Room (hereinafter cited as SJNP project files).

63.   Joy Lane, testimony before the Board of Supervisors of the County Kern, 15 April 1974, Project 499, and *BC*, 16 April 1974. The Board of Supervisors had little sympathy for Lane's antidevelopment warnings. But Lane repeatedly played on the public fear that the county might lose authority over the plant's fate to force supervisors to protect local control. See Joy Lane, testimony before the Kern County Board of Supervisors, 13 July 1976; and Joy Lane to Brent Rushforth and Tony Rossman, 24 June 1976, Fontaine papers.

64.   *Wasco News*, 1 May 1974.

65.   Fontaine, interview.

66.   Walton, *Western Times*, 244; *BC*, 11 April and 26 September 1974, and 15 January 1975; and *LAT*, 9 September 1974, II-1; and 26 September 1974, 3, 3 October 1974, II–4.

67.   Stuart Pyle, testimony before the Capital Improvements Subcomittee of the Board of Water and Power Commissioners on the Draft Environmental Impact Report for the San Joaquin Nuclear Project, in Los Angeles Department of Water and Power, *San Joaquin Nuclear Project Draft Environmental Impact Report—Revised* (hereinafter cited as *Draft EIR Hearings*), 31 May 1975, S.1–11; Floyd S. Cooley to Honorable Board of Supervisors County of Kern, 23 January 1975, SJNP project files, file Water Sources for Cooling; Fred Simon to Board of Commissioners, 9 June 1975, SJNP project files, file Los Angeles Department of Water and Power; and *BC*, 24 May, 4 and 10 June, and 15 September 1974.

68.   *BC*, 5 and 14 November, 17, 18, and 20 December 1974, and 15 January 1975.

69.   Thomas Wellock, "The Battle for Bodega Bay: The Sierra Club and Nuclear Power, 1958–1964," *California History* 71 (Summer 1992): 192–211. The lack of local oversight was common to most states in the sixties and early seventies. When a plant was canceled it was due to federal opposition. See Henry Bedford, *Seabrook Station: Citizen Politics and Nuclear Power* (Amherst: University of Massachusetts Press, 1990), 8; and J. Samuel Walker, *Containing the Atom: Nuclear Regulation in a Changing Environment, 1963–1971* (Berkeley: University of California Press, 1992), 57–112.

70.   Seymour Martin Lipset and William Schneider have made the most convincing argument that "Vietnam, Watergate, the energy crisis, recession, and hyperinflation demonstrated . . . that our institutions generally, and the federal government in particular, had failed to perform." Lipset and Schneider, *Confidence Gap: Business, Labor, and Government in the Public Mind* (Baltimore: Johns Hopkins University Press, 1987), 436; Daniel Yankelovich, *New Rules:*

Searching for Self Fulfillment 183; and Spencer Weart, *Nuclear Fear: A History of Images* (Cambridge: Harvard University Press, 1988), 349.

71. Balogh, *Chain Reaction*, 221–301.

72. Neufeld and Payne, 19 September 1993, interviews. In the early seventies, resistance from agricultural interests to EPA regulation of pesticides had been fierce. See Hays, *Beauty, Health, and Permanence*, 175, 189–93, 294–96.

73. *BC*, 16 July and 22 August 1975, p. 8; Fontaine, interview; and Haslam, *Other California*, 186. For employment statistics on Kern County, see the 1972–76 editions of Roger Carey, *California County Fact Book* (Sacramento, 1972–76).

74. Harry Samarin and others to gentlemen, 31 January 1975, Neufeld papers; Larry Levine, interview by author, 24 June 1992, telephone recording; and *BC*, 20 August 1976. The 1976 initiative raised public awareness of nuclear dangers to nearly 95 percent in the state. "California: One Down, Many to Go," *Nuclear Industry* 23 (June 1976): 8.

75. By 1978, polling showed that those who opposed the Wasco nuclear plant did so for safety reasons. Of the 36 percent who opposed the plant, 25 percent rejected nuclear power in all cases. The other 11 percent expressed concern about water issues or resented Los Angeles' receiving the plant's benefits while Kern County accepted the risks. *BC*, 25 January and 5 March 1978. See also the testimony in the *Draft EIR Hearings* of Pauline Larwood, 10 June 1975, S.1–47; Sandra Larson, 10 and 16 June 1975, S.1–53, 76; Barbara Huff, 10 June 1975, S.1–51; Barbara Patrick, 16 June 1975, S.1–76; C. H. Freeman, 16 June 1975, S.1–81; Carol Davis, 16 June 1975, S.1–82; and Patricia Weil, 16 June 1975, S.1–86.

76. The towns near Wasco such as Delano, Shafter, and McFarland, and white blue-collar towns such as Oildale, revealed heavy majorities against a coastal protection initiative in 1972. The antinuclear initiative, however, fared well in the same precincts with majorities or close defeats. See General Election—Kern County—7 November 1972, and Kern County Primary Election 8 June 1976, Kern County Elections Department, Bakersfield.

77. All voting data for this chapter were compiled from the 1980 block level census data for Kern County. Wealth was measured by averaging estimated property value for all the blocks in a precinct. Levels of education were aggregated only at the census tract level. Since Kern County made no attempt to draw its precincts to conform to the tracts, a firm correlation of education and voting patterns was not possible. However, education and property values were a very close match at the tract level, and wealth was a good estimate of education. For this analysis, a white precinct was defined as one with a nonwhite population of less than 20 percent. Using regression analysis, the correlation for white precincts in 1972 was .513, significant at the 5 percent level for eighteen precincts. The 1976 correlation was .597, significant at the 1 percent level for twenty-one precincts. See Census Bureau, *1980 Census of Population and Housing, Block statistics*, Bakersfield, California, Standard Metropolitan Statistical Area, (Washington, 1982) Table 2, p. 2–62. Kern County precinct maps are located at the California State Archives, Sacramento, CA.

78. Bob Jones testimony, [1976], SJNP project files, Kern Energy Education Program; *BC*, 8 June 1975; Neufeld to Jack Pickett, 21 March 1977, Neufeld pa-

pers; and George Nickel, interview by author, 4 August 1993, Bakersfield, tape recording.

79.   Robert Carter, interview by author, 1 August 1993, telephone tape recording.

80.   Carter, interview; Pauline Larwood, interview by author, 5 August 1993, Bakersfield, tape recording. In early meetings, business interests resisted working with labor organizations. Handwritten meeting notes, 22 and 29 May 1975, George Nickel personal papers, Bakersfield (hereinafter cited as Nickel papers).

81.   Nickel, interview; *BC*, 8 June 1975; meeting notes, 7 May 1975, George W. Nickel to Fred Mielke, 16 May 1977, and Ed Urner to Fred Mielke, 2 March 1977, Nickel to Mielke, 6 September 1977; and Bud Johnson to Nickel, 23 August 1977, Nickel papers.

82.   Robert Carter testimony, *Draft EIR Hearings*, 9 June 1975, S.1–19; *BC*, 16 July and 22 August 1975, 8.

83.   Neufeld, interview; and Pauline Larwood to Sam Tyson, 24 March 1977, Agricultural Protection Council files held by James Payne, Wasco, folder Board Correspondence Outgoing (hereinafter cited as Payne files). A study of the types of local activism promoted by left-wing populists is Boyte, *Backyard Revolution*.

84.   McCloud, "Kern Brand of Politics," 232.

85.   Thomas Schroeter, interview by author, 3 August 1993, Bakersfield , tape recording; "Meeting," 15 September 1976, Neufeld papers; Neufeld and Larwood, interviews.

86.   Neufeld, interview; and *BC*, 26 September 1976.

87.   Schroeter, Neufeld, interviews: "Meeting," 15 September 1976, Neufeld papers.

88.   *Californian*, 6 October 1976; Pauline Larwood, testimony before the Kern County Water Agency, 18 November 1976, Payne files; United States Nuclear Regulatory Commission, hearings, 9 December 1976, docket 50–275 (Diablo Canyon), 1741–42; and campaign paraphernalia in Neufeld papers.

89.   Pandol and Carter, interviews; and Camille Gavin and Kathy Leverett, *Kern's Movers and Shakers* (Bakersfield: Kern View Foundation, 1987), 29.

90.   Pandol, interview.

91.   Pandol, interview. On the community value of water, see Peter Iverson, "The Cultural Politics of Water in Arizona," in *Politics in the Postwar American West*, ed. Richard Lowitt (Norman: University of Oklahoma Press, 1995), 35.

92.   *BC*, 28 July 1976, and Agricultural Protection Council, meeting minutes, 19 April 1977, Payne files.

93.   Pandol, interview, and *BC*, 8 January 1976, 1.

94.   Walton, *Western Times*, 256–57; Michael Storper and Richard Walker, "Surplus and Subsidy in the State Water Project: Water Use and Cost Allocation by the Metropolitan Water District and Kern County Water Agency" (October 1982), Water Resources Center Archives, University of California, Berkeley; and Agricultural Protection Council, "Dependency of Kern on Surplus Water," Payne files.

95.   Opponents ran ads with a drawing of a fool asking: "Are we the fools

L.A. takes us for?" *BC*, 20 July 1976, 28 July, 28 August 1977; and Neufeld, interview.

96. Neufeld, interview, and *BC*, 1 August 1976.

97. This tradition of grievances also served Owens Valley well in its battles with Los Angeles in the seventies. See Walton, *Western Times*, chap. 7.

98. *Wasco News*, 9–15 November 1977.

99. Agricultural Protection Council, meeting minutes, 7 October 1976, Payne files, folder Agenda and Minutes, and Dave Bryant, testimony before the Kern County Water Agency, 18 November 1976, Payne files, folder SJAPC Public Statements on 16th Draft of Letter of Intent between KCWA and LA.

100. *BC*, 12 September, 15 October 1976; Current Planning Division EIR Section to files, 23 August 1976, SJNP project files, file Water Sources for Cooling; Kern County Water Agency, *Preliminary Plan for Agricultural Wastewater Drainage Project* (September 1976), Water Resources Center Archives, University of California, Berkeley, 54; and Neufeld, interview. A new study had thrown the feasibility and cost of the drain system in doubt, and it was far better to return to coastal siting. Bookman-Edmonston Engineering, Inc., *The Impact of Power Plant Siting on California's Water Resources* (Association of California Water Agencies, July 1976).

101. State Water Resources Control Board, *Water Quality Control Policy on the Use and Disposal of Inland Waters Used for Powerplant Cooling* (Sacramento, June 1975), 4; *BC*, 19 January 1975, 12 September and 27 December 1976; Gerald H. Kamprath to Louis H. Winnard, 20 December 1976, SJNP project files, file Water Sources for Cooling; and Harvey, interview.

102. City of Wasco, Resolution 76–658, 6 December 1976, City of Shafter, Resolution 527, 26 July 1976, Neufeld papers; Neufeld, interview; and handwritten KEEP meeting notes, 12 June 1975, Nickel papers.

103. Water Resources Control Board, *Water Quality Control Policy*, 4; *BC*, 19 January 1975, 12 September and 27 December 1976; and Ronald B. Robie to Claire T. Dedrick, 14 September 1976, Edmund G. Brown, Jr. papers, University of Southern California, Los Angeles, caton E-33–3 (hereinafter cited as Brown papers).

104. This was not a conflict between small and larger farmers. The original Wasco far, group was composed of agribusinessmen with holdings averaging less than nine hundred acres each. This is not a small holding, but it was not enough to make an individual prominent. There were many exceptions, including two opposition leaders who owned huge operations. *Wasco News*, 31 July 1974; Diana Dooley to Gray Davis, Lucie Gikovich, and Peggy Johnson, 25 October 1977, Brown papers, carton F-37–4; and Joy Lane to Fredric P. Sutherland, 11 June 1975, Fontaine papers.

105. *Farm News*, 26 October 1976; *BC*, 15 October 1976; and Neufeld, interview.

106. Gene Tackett, interview by author, 3 August 1993, Bakersfield, tape recording; Neufeld, interview; *Wasco News*, 13–19 October 1976; and Dan Morgan, *Rising in the West: The True Story of an "Okie" Family from the Great Depression through the Reagan Years* (New York: Alfred A. Knopf,1992), 240–53.

107. Tackett and Carter, interviews; and Morgan, *Rising in the West*, 252–53.

108. San Joaquin Agricultural Protection Council, "Executive Board Meeting," 17 November 1976, Neufeld papers; Larwood, interview; and *BC*, 25 January 1978.

109. *BC*, 23 February 1977, and "Resolution," 15 February 1977, Neufeld papers.

110. Harvey, interview, and *BC*, 21 December 1977.

111. *BC*, 17 and 25 January 1978; Larwood, Neufeld, and Schroeter, interviews; "Critical Mass No Longer Encourages Initiative," *Nuclear Industry* 24 (9 June 1977): 26; and KEEP, meeting minutes, 19 October 1976, Nickel papers.

112. Robert Benedict, et al., "The Voters and Attitudes toward Nuclear Power: A Comparative Study of 'Nuclear Moratorium' Initiatives," *Western Political Quarterly* 33 (1980): 23; Schmidt, *Citizen Lawmakers*, 73–77; and Andrew Szasz, *EcoPopulism: Toxic Waste and the Movement for Environmental Justice* (Minneapolis: University of Minnesota Press, 1994), 72.

113. Schmidt, *Citizen Lawmakers*, 73 and *St. Louis Post-Dispatch*, 1 April and 3,4 November 1976.

114. Opponents compiled an economic analysis of the project based on unrealistic assumptions. They assumed, for example, the *LADWP*, a government entity, would have no other partners in the project and would not provide any taxes to the county. The job losses they claimed did not differentiate between seasonal, low-paying agricultural jobs and the much better paying construction and operations jobs the plant would have. See San Joaquin Agricultural Protection Council, "An In-Depth Study of the Impact on Kern County of Siting the Proposed San Joaquin Nuclear Project Near Wasco," Public Citizen Inc. files, Washington D.C., folder Kern County Nuclear Initiative.

115. Neufeld speech, n.d. (emphasis added), and "Keep L.A.'s Nuclear Plant out of Kern County," pamphlet, Neufeld papers; *BC*, 1 November 1977; and Kern Citizens for No on 3, "Bulletin 2," and "Radio Spots," Public Citizen files, folder Kern County Nuclear Initiative.

116. Neufeld, interview; and Kern Citizens for No on 3, *Kern County Independence*, 24 February 1978, Neufeld papers.

117. For canvassing comments, see canvassing reports in Payne files. Oildale's stereotype persists. See *LAT*, 9 August 1992, B3.

118. *BC*, 2, 3, and 6 March 1978, and compaign literature in Neufeld papers.

119. Kern County for Yes on Proposition 3, *Kern County Voters Guide*, [1978], Neufeld papers.

120. *BC*, 23 February 1977 and 8 March 1978.

121. *LAT*, 14 March 1978, III-1; and *BC*, 7–15 March 1978.

122. The town of China Lake, the scientific community in the eastern Sierra had been strongly proenvironmental in the past, but on the SJNP they lagged behind the general county vote with about 60 percent of the vote. Consolidated Special Election—7 March 1978, Elections Department Kern County, Bakersfield; and *BC*, 24 February 1978.

123. For all fifty-six precincts, the correlation was a negative .457, significant at the 1 percent level. Excluding the non-Valley towns, fifty-one precincts gave a negative correlation of .645, significant at the 1 percent level.

124.   The correlation for whites was a negative .157, but not significant. The correlation for people of Spanish origin was better at .240, but was not significant. Despite a reputation for hostility to environmental issues, studies show that blacks support environmental spending more than whites. See Emmet Jones and Lewis F. Carter, "Concern for the Environment among Black Americans: An Assessment of Common Assumptions," *Social Science Quarterly* 75 (September 1994): 560–79.

125.   Maurice R. Stein, *The Eclipse of Community: An Interpretation of American Studies* (Princeton: Princeton University Press, 1960), 107–8; Arthur Vidich and Joseph Bensman, *Small Town in Mass Society: Class, Power, and Religion in a Rural Community* (Princeton: Princeton University Press, 1958). On the survival of community, see Raymond Williams, *The Country and the City* (London: Hogarth Press,1958), 104; and Walton, *Western Times*, 6.

126.   *BC*, 24 November 1974.

127.   As Pauline Larwood noted, the campaign had a substantial number of activists who came to Kern County to help. Her first rule was that they get a haircut. Larwood, interview.

128.   An exception was Agricultural Protection Council leader Pauline Larwood, who dates her own political awakening to the power plant controversy. Larwood later won a seat on the Kern County Board of Supervisors.

129.   There is little evidence that plant supporters or opponents sought the public backing of Mexican Americans, nor was there coverage of the issue in the United Farm Workers publication *El Malcriado*. McCloud, "Kern Brand of Politics," 232.

130.   This paradox of modern community between its supporting communal and individual interests has been noted by Claude S. Fisher, "Ambivalent Communities: How Americans Understand Their Localities," in *America at Century's End*, ed. Alan Wolfe (Berkeley: University of California Press, 1991), 89.

131.   Just like the Kern controversy, many revolts had economic motives, but as with the Sagebrush Rebellion or the Proposition 13 tax revolt, the public target was oppressive government. Richard White, *Its Your Misfortune and None of My Own: A New History of the American West* (Norman: University of Oklahoma Press, 1991), 567, and Kazin, "Grass-Roots Right," 148.

132.   Szasz, *EcoPopulism*, 82; Walton, *Western Times*, 287–339; Matthew Glass, *Citizens against the MX: Public Languages in the Nuclear Age* (Urbana: University of Illinois Press, 1993); Kazin, *Populist Persuasion*, 247, 251, 259; Davis, *City of Quartz*; Reider, *Canarsie*, 203–32; and Charles Piller, *The Fail-Safe Society: Community Defiance and the End of American Technological Optimism* (New York: Basic Books, 1991).

133.   Phillips, *Post-Conservative America*, 74–75.

134.   On the factionalization of recent politics and policy, see Balogh, *Chain Reaction*, 302–26; Robert A. Dahl, *The New American Political (Dis)order: An Essay* (Berkeley: Institute for Governmental Studies, 1994); and Richard A. Harris and Sidney A. Milkis, eds., *Remaking American Politics* (Boulder: Westview Press, 1989). Important works on the reassertion of community power are John Walton, *Western Times*, and Fisher, "Ambivalent Communities," 87–88.

135.   APC, meeting minutes, 13 January 1977, Payne files; *BC*, 15 March 1978.

136.   The Kern vote echoed a poll done in 1978 that found that New York residents opposed nuclear power plants sited near them by a 2 to 1 margin. This came at a time when a majority, but declining proportion, of Americans favored nuclear power in general. Jerry Brown's administration believed that such results supported its own antinuclear position. Wilson Clark to Governor Brown, Dick Silberman, 4 April 1978, Brown papers, carton A-8-2.

137.   Kotkin, "New Foes of Nuclear Power"; Anna Gyorgy and friends, *No Nukes: Everyone's Guide to Nuclear Power* (Boston: South End Press, 1979), 391–458; and Kitty Tucker, "Farmers Oppose Nuclear Plan," *Critical Mass Journal* 3 (December 1977): 1, 13. Nor were diverse coalitions restricted to nuclear technology. See Piller, *Fail-Safe Society*, and Glass, "Rhetoric of Religious Localism."

138.   Kotkin, "New Foes of Nuclear Power."

Conclusion: California Goes National

1.   James Cook, "Nuclear Follies," *Forbes*, 11 February 1985, 1, 82.

2.   James Jasper, *Nuclear Politics: Energy and the State in the United States, Sweden, and France* (Princeton: Princeton University Press, 1990); and John L. Campbell, *Collapse of an Industry: Nuclear Power and the Contradictions of U.S. Policy* (Ithaca: Cornell University Press, 1988).

3.   Congress, Senate, Committee on Environment and Public Works, *Nuclear Waste Management: Hearings before the Subcommittee on Nuclear Regulation*, 95th Cong., 2d Sess., 22 March 1978, 139.

4.   The scope of federal preemption had been only vaguely settled by the time of the legal challenge to the 1976 nuclear bills. Proposition 15 had been promoted because antinuclear activists recognized that earlier court rulings had been relatively narrow in asserting the primacy of the federal government in the regulation of radioactive effluents. See *Northern States Power Co. v. Minnesota*, 447 F.2d 1143 (8th Cir. 1971).

5.   See *Pacific Legal Foundation v. State Energy Resources, Conservation, and Development Commission*, 472 F. Supp. 191 (S.D. Cal. 1979); and *Pacific Gas and Electric Co. v. State Energy Resources Conservation and Development Commission*, 489 F. Supp. 699 (E.D. Cal. 1980).

6.   Laurence H. Tribe, "California Declines the Nuclear Gamble: Is Such a State Choice Preempted?" *Ecology Law Quarterly* 7 (1979): 722.

7.   J. R. Wargo, "States Passing Nuclear Laws with Unprecedented Frequency," *Nuclear Industry* 24 (June 1977): 27.

8.   For Tribe's legal argument, see Tribe, "California Declines the Nuclear Gamble," 679–729.

9.   Kim A. Griffith, "Ninth Circuit Upholds Nuclear Power Moratorium Provision," *Natural Resources Journal* 22 (July 1982): 689–98. See ruling, *Pacific Legal Foundation v. State Energy Resources Conservation & Development Commission*, 659 F.2d 903 (9th Cir. 1981).

10.   This is not to argue that the economic justifications for the nuclear bills

were invalid, but they were not the key reason the legislation was crafted by Charles Warren's committee.

11.   *Pacific Gas & Electric Co. v. State Energy Resources Conservation and Development Commission*, 103 S. Ct. 1713 (1983).

12.   See Omer F. Brown and Edward M. Davis, "The Implications of the Supreme Court's California Nuclear Moratorium Decision," *Public Utilities Fortnightly* 111 (26 May 1983): 35–38.

13.   Joseph P. Tomain, *Nuclear Power Transformation* (Bloomington: Indiana University Press, 1987): 14–19.

14.   Tomain, *Nuclear Power Transformation*, 19.

15.   Quoted in Eric C. Woychik, "California's Nuclear Disposal Law Confronts the Nuclear Waste Management Dilemma: State Power to Regulate Reactors," *Environmental Law* 14 (1984): 365. California was ahead of other states in its desire to regulate the atom. But it would be wrong to conclude that only California was interested in challenging federal power. Amicus briefs were filed with the Supreme Court by thirty-two states in support of California's nuclear bill.

16.   Barbara Epstein, *Political Protest and Cultural Revolution: Nonviolent Direct Action in the 1970s and 1980s* (Berkeley: University of California Press, 1991), 125–56.

17.   Pete Wilson to David Roberti and others, 1 December 1993, copy in possession of the author.

18.   A revealing indication of just how much SDG&E accepted the Energy Commission's ideas was revealed by the company's new chairman, Thomas Page, in 1983. See "1983 Electric Utility Executives Form," *Public Utilities Fortnightly* 111 (9 June 1983): 80–123.

19.   Jim Harding, phone conservation with the author, 13 April 1994, personal notes; and *New York Times*, 11 April 1995, C1. Both Lovins' and the Energy Commission's projections for the feasibility of renewable energy sources relied on escalating oil prices. For example, the Energy Commission produced a report arguing for an energy approach favoring alternative, renewable energy sources. Its recommendation relied in part on an assumption that fuel prices would continue to increase through the eighties at a rate of 3 percent each year. This did not happen, and, as the commission recognized, any advantage of renewable alternatives disappeared with it. See California's Energy Commission, *Energy Futures for California: Two Scenarios, 1978–2000* (Sacramento: The Commission, September 1980), 524–49.

20.   Seymour Goldstone, interview by author, 5 January 1993, Sacramento, tape recording; and Phillip Greenberg, interview by author, 21 December 1993, San Francisco, tape recording.

21.   Conrad L. Kanagy, Craig R. Humphrey, and Glenn Firebaugh, "Surging Environmentalism: Changing Pubic Opinion or Changing Publics?" *Social Science Quarterly* 75 (December 1994): 804–19.

22.   Daniel Pope, "Anti-Nuclear Activism in the Northwest: WPPSS and Its Enemies," in *The Atomic West*, ed. John Findlay and Bruce Hevly (Seattle: University of Washington Press, forthcoming); Dick Russell, "Heartland Protests:

Fighting the Nuke-Waste Shell Game," *Nation* 21 November 1987, cover, 594–97; and *New York Times,* 26 February 1990, B1, 5.

23. By the beginning of the nineties, surveys routinely recorded over 60 percent of the public opposed to new construction. "Public Opposes New Reactors," *USA Today Magazine,* December 1991, 12; and Christian Joppke, *Mobilizing Against Nuclear Energy: A Comparison of Germany and the United States* (Berkeley: University of California Press, 1993), 142.

24. *Bakersfield Californian,* 14 February 1978, B1.

25. Washington International Energy Group, "New Poll of Utility Executives Shows Deep Pessimism for Nuclear Power," 5 February 1996, Internet press release, copy in possession of the author; and *New York Times,* 14 April 1992, 1, D25.

26. "Shutting Down Rancho Seco," *Time,* 19 June 1989, 36.

27. Joppke, *Mobilizing against Nuclear Energy,* 159.

28. For an interesting assessment of nuclear power's future, see the entire special issue of *Public Utilities Fortnightly* 126 (22 November 1990).

29. Hazel Mitchell, interview by author, 7 July 1991, Bodega Bay, tape recording.

Index

AB 1852, 194–97

AB 818, 129–31

Adams, Ansel: as member of Sierra Club Board of Directors, 85–87

agribusiness: and opposition to San Joaquin Nuclear Project, 221–22; and populism in Kern County, 212–13

Agricultural Protection Council, 228, 231–35, 241

Air Resources Board, 201

Alquist, Alfred, 144, 178, 196, 202, 205, 291*n44*

Anderson, Lieutenant Governor Glenn: opposes Bodega Bay Atomic Park, 51

Another Mother for Peace, 154–56

antigovernment sentiment: in Bakersfield, 240; in Kern County, 223–24

antinuclear movement, 4–12, 244; affects state energy policy, 177; decline of, 246; and Democratic Party, 9; and environmentalism, 9–10, 46–47; in Europe, 7; in local and state governments, 248; and the New Left, 21–22; and populism, 11–12; and public health, 46–47; and scientists, 24; and women, 47

Assembly Energy Resources and Land Use Committee, 202

Atomic Energy Act (1946), 4–5

Atomic Energy Act (1954), 4–5, 171, 245

Atomic Energy Commission, 4–5, 63, 151, 254*nn6,8*; and Bodega Bay Atomic Park, 22, 28–29, 51–52, 54, 56–58; and canceled Malibu nuclear plant, 66; and disposal of nuclear waste, 119–20; opposes Point Arena nuclear project, 133; public hearings on safety of Emergency Core Cooling System, 105; and nuclear power plant site selection, 120–21; and

proposed nuclear plant in Malibu, 64–65; and reactor safety concerns, 27, 120, 141–42; on thermal pollution, 89. *See also* Nuclear Regulatory Commission

Bakersfield: antigovernment sentiment in, 240; description of, 208–10

Bakersfield Californian: on San Joaquin Nuclear Project, 231–32

Ball, Richard, 139–40

Balogh, Brian, 7–8, 281*nn9, 10*

Batinovich, Robert, 176, 204

Bay Conservation Development Commission, 121

Berry, Phillip, 36, 37, 94–97, 130, 263*nn72, 74, 75, 79, 81*; as President of Sierra Club, 94–95

Bethe, Hans, 163, 293*n24*, 297*n88*

The Birds, 17–18, 249, 257*nn1–4*

Blues Over Bodega, 43

Blythe, local support for Sundesert nuclear project, 191

Bodega Bay, 55, 58, 176; description of, 249–50

Bodega Bay Atomic Park, 17–67, 223, 260*nn29–32*, 265*n124*; approved by California Public Utilities Commission, 42; opposed by residents, 27–28, 34–35, 42–43; opposed by United States Department of the Interior, 52–53; projected economic effectiveness, 261*n44*; promotion of, 30

Bodega Bay Chamber of Commerce: creation of, 28

Bodega Head: seismic hazards of, 54–56

Bolsa Island, 124; desalinization project, 125–28

Bradley, Harold, 41

325

Bradley, Tom, 175, 201–2
Brand, Stewart, 187
Bridenbaugh, Dale, 165–66
Briggs, John, 129–31
Brooks, Paul, 86
Brower, David, 74–75, 80, 86–90, 275nn76,
  78, 79, 82, 83, 85, 92; and Bodega Bay
  Atomic Park, 36–37, 41; on David
  Pesonen, 37, 151; on energy crisis, 110;
  as Executive Director of Sierra Club,
  31–33, 48; and Friends of the Earth,
  70–71, 92, 97, 111; on limits to growth,
  103; resigns from Sierra Club, 68–69,
  90–92; on thermal pollution and Diablo
  Canyon, 89
Brown Act: violated by Pacific Gas and
  Electric, 114–15; violated by Sonoma
  County Board of Supervisors, 26–27, 40
Brown, Governor Edmund "Pat," 33,
  186–87; on atomic energy, 119; opposes
  Bodega Bay Atomic Park, 51; opposes
  Proposition 15, 161
Brown, Governor Jerry, 12–13, 149, 165,
  167, 169, 173–76, 186–88, 199; advocates
  alternative energy sources, 187–88, 200;
  appointments to California Energy
  Commission, 180; opposes Sundesert
  nuclear project, 197–98, 202–3, 205; pro-
  poses coal plant, 200
Brown, Willie, 53
Bryant, Dave, 228–29, 232, 234–35
Burch, James, 158
Burton, John, 53
Burton, Phillip: opposes Bodega Bay
  Atomic Park, 51, 53

California Coastal Commission: creation
  of, 135
California Democratic Council: formation
  of, 50–52
California Department of Fish and Game:
  and disposal of nuclear waste, 119–20;
  and nuclear power plant site selection,
  120–21
California Department of Water Resources, 216, 232; proposes coal plant,
  200–201
California Energy Resources Conservation and Development Commission, 11,
  134, 164, 176–83, 189, 205–6, 223,

244–47; creation of, 144–46; development of energy policy, 200–201; encourages public to attend hearings, 182–83;
  forecasts energy consumption, 183–84,
  186; powers of, 116–17; recommends alternative energy sources, 323nn18, 19;
  and Sundesert nuclear project, 174,
  191–97, 202, 306n97
California Environmental Quality Act
  (1970), 134, 214, 220, 222
California Going, Going. . . , 121
California Public Interest Group, 235, 227;
  supports Proposition 15, 155
California Public Utilities Commission, 27,
  35, 129–30, 137–38, 204–5; approves
  Bodega Bay Atomic Park, 42; on energy
  demand estimates, 135; public opinion
  of, 193–94; public hearings on Bodega
  Bay Atomic Park, 30, 35–36; on reactor
  safety, 120; on Sundesert, 174, 176, 192
California Resources Agency, 106; and
  Nipomo Dunes, 78–80; nuclear power
  plant siting committee, 115, 123–25; nuclear power plant site selection policy,
  120–23, 283n34; purpose of, 122; sued
  by Sierra Club, 131–32
California State Division of Beaches and
  Parks, 25–26, 36, 40; and Bodega Bay
  Atomic Park, 18; proposed acquisition
  of Nipomo Dunes, 75
California State Legislature, 1960–1970:
  description of, 137–38; and Sundesert
  nuclear project, 203–4
California state government: and Bodega
  Bay Atomic Park, 23–24; citizen participation in, 60; energy policy and legislation, 129–34; environmental protection
  legislation, 133–34; and nonmaterialism, 11, 244–46; and nuclear power
  plant site selection 115–16, 120–25,
  128–32; regulation of nuclear industry,
  129–46; regulation of utility industry,
  116–24; resource policy and legislation,
  121–24
California Tomorrow, 121, 130
California's Electricity Quandary, 140
Californians for Nuclear Safeguards,
  157–58, 161, 164, 167
Carlin, Alan, 139, 288nn110, 113
Carr, James (Undersecretary of the